THE MAN WHO STAYED BEHIND

Sidney Rittenberg

and

Amanda Bennett

SIMON & SCHUSTER

New York   London   Toronto   Sydney   Tokyo   Singapore

SIMON & SCHUSTER
SIMON & SCHUSTER BUILDING
ROCKEFELLER CENTER
1230 AVENUE OF THE AMERICAS
NEW YORK, NEW YORK 10020

SIMON & SCHUSTER AND COLOPHON ARE REGISTERED TRADEMARKS
OF SIMON & SCHUSTER INC.
DESIGNED BY LEVAVI & LEVAVI
MANUFACTURED IN THE UNITED STATES OF AMERICA

1   3   5   7   9   10   8   6   4   2

LIBRARY OF CONGRESS CATALOGING-IN-PUBLICATION DATA
RITTENBERG, SIDNEY.
THE MAN WHO STAYED BEHIND / SIDNEY RITTENBERG AND
AMANDA BENNETT.
P.   CM.
INCLUDES INDEX.
1. RITTENBERG, SIDNEY.   2. COMMUNISTS—CHINA—HISTORY—
CIVIL WAR, 1945–1949—BIOGRAPHY.   3. CHINA—HISTORY—
CIVIL WAR, 1945–1949.   4. CHINA—HISTORY—1949–1976.
5. UNITED STATES—BIOGRAPHY.
I. BENNETT, AMANDA.   II. TITLE.
HX418.8.R58A3   1993
324.251'075'092273—DC20
[B]   93-6541
CIP
ISBN: 0-671-73595-0

for Yulin

Contents

Notes on Spelling and Pronunciation

WE HAVE USED the pinyin system of romanization, with only a few exceptions designed to help readers who are not generally familiar with Chinese names. Thus, for the most part, we use modern place names—such as Beijing and Wuhan—even though those places were known by different names at different points in their history. Similarly, we use the modern pinyin spelling for nearly every person referred to, including historical figures like Mao Zedong and Zhou Enlai. However, we retain the old spelling or names in cases where we felt the new name or spelling would be too confusing. Thus, we refer to the Kuomintang leader Chiang Kai-shek, his son Chiang Ching-kuo, to Sun Yat-sen, the city of Canton, Yenching University and the Yangtze and Yellow Rivers. We took some poetic licence in using a translation of the historical name Fresh Flower Village, rather than inflict the modern name, Xuanhuadian, on readers. For similar reasons, we also chose to continue to refer to the northern city of Kalgan, rather than using its modern name, Zhangjiakou.

As for pronunciation, there are a few letters used in pinyin that can trip up the unfamiliar reader. Unfortunately, many major characters in the book—including the Rittenberg children—have names that employ these letters. The closest English sound to that represented in pinyin by the letter X is "sh." And the closest

English sound represented by the letter *Q* is "ch." So the children's names would be roughly pronounced like this: Xiaoqin: Shee-ow-chin; Xiaodong: Shee-ow-dong; Xiaoxiang: Shee-ow-shee-ang; Xiaoming: Shee-ow-ming.

Other important names in the book that use these letters include Mao's wife, Jiang Qing: Jee-ang Ching; my good friend in Yanan, Qian Xing: Chee-en Shing; my political contact Xu Maijin: Shee-oo My-jin; the Xinhua News Agency: Shin-hwa; and the top leader Deng Xiaoping: Dung Shee-ow-ping.

Other letters that often give trouble include the dipthong "zh," which is pronounced like a very hard *J*. Thus, the closest equivalent for Zhou Enlai would be Joe En-lie. The letter *Z* by itself is pronounced "dz," so Mao Zedong would be roughly rendered as Mao Dzi-dong.

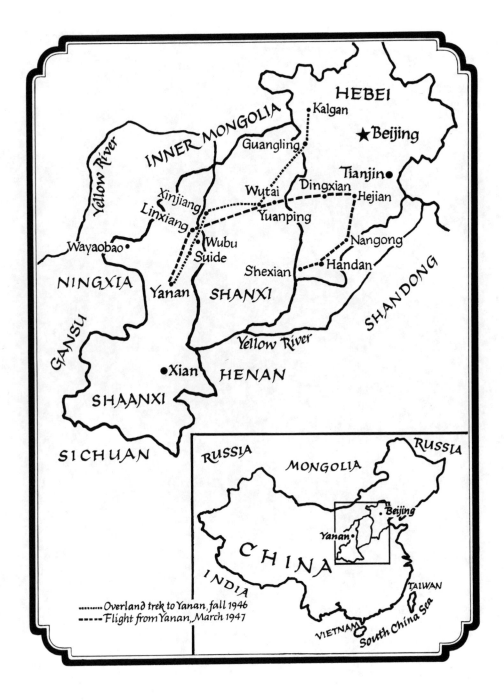

.... Overland trek to Yanan, fall 1946
------ Flight from Yanan, March 1947

Introduction

I WROTE THIS BOOK because I had to.

It was a promise I made to myself when I was in prison for the second time. If I get out, I told myself, I want to tell the true story of how it all happened. How an idealistic boy from Charleston, South Carolina, was caught on fire by the revolutionaries of China. How I gave everything I had to them, fervently believing that in their revolutionary dreams we would all find the salvation, not just of China, but eventually of the world. How I followed these dreams through hardship, and even long imprisonments. And how ultimately these dreams led me—and them—astray.

My story is the story of how I, and people like me, walked the Communist Road in the hope of creating a new and better world. And how for years we succeeded, sometimes beyond even our own expectations, in bringing hope and change to the people who needed it most. But at the same time, I want to paint a clear picture of the evils that ensued. I saw them. I lived with them. In some cases—to my shame and chagrin today—I participated in them.

◆

Today I believe that the means we chose to achieve our utopian end bore the seeds of destruction from the start. The original sin of our program was its premise that repression would be necessary against "a tiny handful of class enemies" to create a perfect democracy. And that bright promise lulled otherwise good people into cooperating with this repression. Thus my story is the story of a man who loved, "not wisely, but too well."

I have made this story as true as I know how to make it. I have concealed nothing, recast nothing, whitewashed nothing. All the events I recount are as I remember experiencing them. I have tried to strip away the benefit of hindsight to show myself the way I was, the way I thought, at the time.

This book is the product of thousands of hours of interviews, conversations, and correspondence between my coauthor and me. Without her, it would never have been written.

I told her at the start, "Your job is to drag the real story out of me," and it's a good thing I meant it because that's exactly what she did. I needed integrity, understanding, talent, and a bulldog insistence on truth—and I got them in spades. Together we drew on over a thousand draft pages I have written at various times over the past thirteen years, including one manuscript written in 1979, a little more than a year after I left prison the second time, when my memory of those events was the clearest.

My recollections were strengthened by my lifetime habit—one encouraged by the Communists—of scrupulous notetaking. Every evening, I would write down the day's events to ponder. Some of those notes survive, mainly from the Great Leap Forward in 1958 and 1959. Although others were destroyed or lost, the discipline of the daily writing greatly sharpened my powers of recall. I have also, of course, had the benefit of sixteen years in solitary confinement, with the leisure it offered for rumination.

For other matters I consulted public documents. There are many references to me, and to events in which I participated, in the Chinese press. During the Cultural Revolution, my speeches and press conferences were printed in Red Guard newspapers, which are available at Harvard's Fairbank Center.

I also consulted extensively with Chinese friends, here and in China, who have known me over the years stretching back to Yanan. I wanted both to help jog my memory, and to compare my version of events with theirs. During the three years writing this book, I traveled to China sixteen times, and spent hundreds of hours conversing with over fifty people.

In the end, however, this is a product of my own memory, my own story, my own life.

KEY NAMES

CHEN BODA: One of Mao Zedong's political secretaries and writers of political theory

CUI XIAOLIANG: Chinese Radio announcer. A close friend and aide in the Cultural Revolution

DENG XIAOPING: Communist leader under Mao; became author of China's economic reforms

DING YILAN: A leader at the Broadcast Administration and a close friend of both Sidney and Yulin

JIANG QING: Mao's wife; a leader of the Cultural Revolution

KANG SHENG: Mao's security chief and head ideologue

KANG SHUJI: Reporter at the Broadcast Administration, head of the committee that included Sidney and Li Zhuan; took power at the Broadcast Administration during the Cultural Revolution

LI GUOHUA: Underground worker in Kunming; friend

LI JUAN: Chinese Radio announcer; friend and ally in Cultural Revolution

LI XIANNIAN: Communist general; later president of the People's Republic

LIAO CHENGZHI: Head of Communist media; a leader in foreign relations

LIN BIAO: After the fall of Liu Shaoqi, Mao's chosen successor; died following an abortive coup during the Cultural Revolution

LIU SHAOQI: Formerly president of the People's Republic. Mao's chosen successor, overthrown and died in the Cultural Revolution

MAO ZEDONG: Chinese Communist Party leader

MEI YI: Director of State Broadcasting Administration

PENG DI: Friend from Yanan days, senior writer and reporter for New China News Agency

QIAN XING: Friend from Yanan days; later senior New China News Agency editor; Peng Di's wife

SHI ZHE: Senior Chinese security police official

SOONG QINGLING (MADAME SUN YAT-SEN): Vice chairman of the People's Republic

WANG GUANGMEI: Acquaintance from Yanan days; later wife of Liu Shaoqi

WANG LI: Media chief during early Cultural Revolution

WANG ZHEN: Outstanding Communist general; later, hard-liner as vice president of the People's Republic; friend

WEI LIN: Sidney's ex-wife; English language radio announcer

WEN JIZE: Vice director at the Broadcasting Administration; overthrown as rightist; later leader of Academy of Social Sciences; friend

XU MAIJIN: Communist functionary in Shanghai; later leader in cultural affairs

YU GUANGYUAN: New China News Agency writer; friend; leading Chinese economist

ZHANG HUA: A party leader at the Broadcast Administration

ZHOU ENLAI: Longtime premier, foreign minister, Communist Party vice chairman

SIDNEY RITTENBERG'S FAMILY

LI DUNBAI: Sidney Rittenberg
WANG YULIN: Sidney's wife
LI XIAOQIN: (later, Jenny) daughter, born March 4, 1957
LI XIAODONG: (later, Toni) daughter, born June 3, 1958
LI XIAOXIANG: (later, Sunny) daughter, born December 1, 1960
LI XIAOMING: (later, Sidney, Jr.) son, born February 15, 1966

CHAPTER ONE

The Death of Wood Fairy

I never meant to stay in China.

I never even meant to go to China. I wasn't enamored of the mysterious East. I dreamed of going to France, to England, even to the Soviet Union, but no one in the 1940s went to China for fun. Nor did I have a missionary spirit. True, I was a reformer, a revolutionary, almost a zealot for the social causes of the day. But China wasn't one of them. I never dreamed, as so many Americans did, of saving China. In 1942, when I was drafted into the army in the early days of World War II, I wasn't eager to travel ten thousand miles away. I was twenty-one years old, and preoccupied with the social problems of my own country.

Indeed, I began studying Chinese mainly as a means to an end. Very soon after I was drafted, the army tested me, plucked me out of the mud of soldiering, and shipped me off to study Japanese. I was aghast. When the Japanese lost the war, as I was sure they would, fluency in Japanese could only mean a long tour abroad with an American occupation government. So I talked my way into a Chinese course instead, figuring I could have a bit of adventure and a fast trip home once the war ended.

I spent thirty-five years in China and when people ask me now why I didn't leave after my tour of duty was up, or even later after many dreams proved false, many friends had turned on me, and my long years in solitary confinement had nearly broken my health, it's sometimes hard to know. But when I try to answer that question honestly, I nearly always think of Wood Fairy.

Which is strange, for I never even met her. She had died some months before I even arrived in China. But of all the soldiers, students, newsboys, hookers, ministers, mandarins, spies, cooks, and drivers I met in that first confused year of my stay in China, it is to a dead twelve-year-old girl, Li Muxian—Wood Fairy Li, the daughter of the rickshaw puller—that my thoughts keep returning. It was, if not for her, at least partly because of her that I stayed.

Shortly after I arrived in China, I was assigned as a Chinese language specialist in the judge advocate's office in Kunming, in southwestern China. During the war Kunming was an entry point for soldiers flown in over the Hump of the Himalayas from India to China. The place overflowed with GIs. There was a thriving black market in American medicine, Spam, cigarettes, gas, and clothing. Alcohol was plentiful and there was little to do in the evening but drink. So it wasn't surprising that the judge advocate's office was investigating claims for damages against the U.S. Army. Five of us were assigned there, all classmates from language school. My job was to verify the claims. I would drive my jeep though the streets of the town, find the plaintiffs, interview them, and translate all the information onto U.S. government forms.

The file of Li Ruishan the rickshaw puller was the first one I was handed. After reading through the documents, I drove off in my jeep to find him. His street wasn't hard to locate. It was a tiny twisting hairpin of an alley just off one of the main thoroughfares of Kunming, the Road to the Opening of the East. It was lined with mud-brick houses, crowded with people gargling, hawking wares, drying hair, washing clothes, peeling vegetables, and tending children.

Once in the alley, it wasn't hard to find Li's house either. When I drove through in my U.S. Army jeep, everyone was expecting me. Many of Li's neighbors and relatives had been out on the street that morning a few months earlier when an army truck had come barreling through, crushing to death the rickshaw puller's only child. They had seen the accident and knew that Li's wife, Wood Fairy's mother, was catatonic with shock and grief. They knew that Li had pressed a claim against the U.S. government.

Plaintiffs would never come to our offices themselves to present their claims. The distance was daunting. Our barracks was several miles outside town, in an encampment run by the Kuomintang army of Chiang Kai-shek, surrounded by a high wall and guarded by soldiers. But the main problem was that most people in Kunming in those days were illiterate. Rather than presenting their claims to us, they first went to their street chief, who was in charge of a dozen families. The street chief would then pass the claim to the block chief, who handled a dozen street chiefs. Together, they would compose the claim in flowing brush strokes on rice paper, and pass it up through the county government and on to us. At each level, the Chinese bureaucracy would exact its price in "squeeze" from the hapless claimant.

By the time I was handed Wood Fairy's case, the deposition of the driver who had killed her had already been taken. The air force sergeant had said in his statement that the night before the accident he had borrowed a six-by-six army truck to drive to the Streets of Paris nightclub in town. He picked up one of the skinny, half-starved dancing girls there and woke up the next morning to find himself AWOL with a splitting headache. He downed a couple of shots of whiskey for his hangover and took off for the base.

About halfway home, he made a sharp right turn into an alley that led to a road parallel to the base. He saw a little girl playing shuttlecock in the doorway of her mud house. Later, he told the provost marshal that he thought it would be fun to scare her. "I said to myself I'm going to see how close I can get to that little slopey girl, and goddamn if I didn't run her over, so I figured I've got to get the hell out of here," he said in his deposition. So he quickly headed the truck back to the base.

Now I was back in that same little alley and soon I saw rickshaw puller Li arrive, a crowd of neighbors accompanying him. He was a little taller than I, perhaps five foot eight, and looked to be in his mid-forties, so I guessed he was in his early thirties. In a twelve-hour day of trundling passengers, a rickshaw puller in Kunming during the war typically earned no more than enough for a bowl or two of rice for himself and his family. A bony man with a drooping mustache and bare feet, Li was worn out.

"Our life is nothing," he said, speaking very quietly and directly, in a Yunnan accent thick with consonants. "It is nothing but eating bitterness. She was all we had. We were hoping that she would have something better."

He was talking about a monumental injustice, but his speech was nearly expressionless. He hadn't seen the accident, but his wife had watched her daughter crushed to death by a driver who didn't stop. Li took me to their little room and pulled back the bamboo screen. His wife was sitting silent and motionless, staring at the wall. She never spoke again after the accident, and died a few months later.

Back at the office, I wrote up the report, recommending the highest possible compensation. I had warned Li that it wouldn't be much, but as it turned out, it was worse than I thought. A few weeks later, the assistant claims officer made his recommendation: $26 U.S. I thought there had been a mistake and took the matter up with him. I pointed out that in another recent case, we had paid a merchant $150 in compensation for his pony, which had been killed by another American army truck. "A horse comes with a price tag and a receipt," said the assistant claims officer. "A person doesn't come with a price tag. The only way you can figure their value is by finding out what they added to the family income, and what it costs to bury them. In this case, it was a little child who earned no income, and a pine coffin for a child costs only half as much as an adult coffin. Also, the rules are that you pay less compensation to those in lower income brackets. My original judgment stands."

I returned to that narrow alley, and when I handed Li the envelope containing the $26 I tried to apologize for the unjust treatment of his case. He took the envelope, bowed and walked away. But that afternoon, just before five, he appeared at my desk, having walked the many miles to the barracks and negotiated his way past the guards. This time he carried his own envelope, one pasted together out of scrap, which he handed to me. I found six dollars inside.

"What is this for?" I asked.

"To thank you for your help."

"Did you give money to the block chief too?" I asked.

"Yes," he replied.

"And to the street chief?"

"Yes."

I suddenly understood. In his mind, I had become one of the many forces that buffeted his life. Even after such a disastrous wrong had been done to him, Li still felt compelled to split his compensation with each official who had in any way contributed to his receiving the money—including a member of the foreign army that killed his daughter. Chinese officialdom lived on such squeeze and made life hard for those who tried to evade it. To Li, it made sense to try to placate even those who had persecuted him.

"I cannot take this," I explained to him, handing back the envelope. "It is against regulations, and it would be very wrong anyway because what you received was much too little." I thought I saw the beginnings of a faint smile flickering across his face at the words "gui ding"—regulations. He knew all about regulations, I supposed. At any rate, he bowed, thanked me, and then turned and left the office.

I never saw him again.

But later, even after things went bad, I often thought of Li, and of his little daughter. I think that I chose the road I did and stuck to it as long as I did because, like so many others I came to know, I genuinely believed it was the only way I could help change the miserable lives of people like Li Ruishan and his daughter, Wood Fairy.

For when the time came to choose, I had a bellyful of the misery I had seen.

◆

It was dawn on September 16, 1945, when we flew over the Hump into China, a planeload of soldiers sitting bolt upright in the back of a military transport. We had left at midnight from India the night before, flying scared into the darkness over the highest terrain in the world. We were strapped into parachutes we knew would be useless if we had to bail out over the Himalayas.

By the time we arrived in China, most of the American GIs stationed there were desperate to leave and return home. The Japanese had surrendered just one month earlier, and the occupying armies were slowly pulling out. The war in the Pacific was finally over. But those of us on the plane were just as eager to arrive as the others were to leave.

One of the reasons was India. We had spent five dreadful months sweltering in Camp Kancharrapara, about thirty miles from Calcutta, waiting to be sent to China. The bugs, the dirt, the heat, and the enforced idleness made India a hell for us. We all fell ill with dysentery and I was once sick enough to be hospitalized. So when we circled over Kunming that August morning, just as the sun was rising, we thought we had never seen anything so beautiful. Off in the distance, I could see the western hills rimming a red earth basin. At the foot of the hills, the ancient walled city of Kunming sat snug against a large lake. Around the city, the land shattered into a crazy-quilt of tiny patchwork squares and pie slices. Everything was lush and green and the air was balmy. After India, Kunming felt and looked like a paradise.

Another reason we were eager to arrive in China was simply that people here spoke Chinese. Back in those days there were few Westerners fluent in Mandarin Chinese, mostly missionaries, a handful of scholars, and some diplomats. In learning to speak Chinese, my classmates and I on that plane felt we had joined an elite corps.

Under the army tutelage, we had spent a year at Stanford University. We had drilled, recited, listened to recordings, pored over flashcards, and drawn characters in the air with our fingers until the strokes and tones blended together unrecognizably. Now we could speak Chinese, and we wanted to get to the place where we could try out our new skill.

Of all of us, I was the most eager. I had begun studying Chinese from the most banal of motivations, but the beauty of the language and a fascination with the people who spoke it had captured me almost in spite of myself. As a boy attending prep school in Charleston, I headed the class in French and Latin; in college at Chapel Hill, North Carolina, I excelled in German. But nothing had ever excited me the way Chinese did.

For me studying Chinese had been like going through Alice's little door into an enchanted garden. In Chinese, with its writing based on pictures, a word not only means what it means, it is what it means. The word "beauty" meant beauty, of course. But not just beauty. It meant to be beautiful, to beautify, to think about beauty. The word itself was beauty. A word in Chinese could jump around in any direction like a queen on a chessboard, as no alphabetized language could ever do. There were no declensions or ablative absolutes to hold it down.

The sounds too were like nothing I had ever heard. In spoken Chinese, a difference in pitch makes a different word with a different meaning, like a series of chimes. Night after night, I sat with my tutor in the basement of a building in San Francisco's Chinatown, shouting syllables at him as I tried to learn to ring those chimes.

"Chi," he would say.

"Chee."

"No, Chi."

"Chyi."

"That's better. Chi."

"Chi."

And so on into the night.

By the time we arrived in China I, of all my classmates, was the only one considered fluent in the language. I wanted to make the most of my time here. When the military truck that had met us at the airstrip dropped us off at our barracks, I looked around for the first characters I could read. From a sign across the road, I carefully spelled out three words: "Hei Tu Xiang"—Black Earth Village.

◆

Black Earth Village wasn't a very impressive place for the China Theater headquarters of the U.S. Army Signal Corps. Nor was our new home itself a very impressive complex. Since we were technically guests of Chiang Kai-shek's Kuomintang army, our quarters were called hostels; our signal corps occupied Hostel No. 8. But it was clearly a military compound, wooden two-story barracks surrounded by a long tan wall. Behind the compound, Black Earth Village sat on a little lane curving off from the dusty main road. I didn't want to waste any time before exploring my new surroundings. After a tedious lecture on hygiene and safety, Baker and Levy, my buddies from language class, and I clattered our way down the barrack stairs to make friends with the Chinese.

The village was just one street of tiny wooden stores crammed together side by side. There was a shop selling pastries, moon cakes, crinkly sugar biscuits, and sweet fried pancakes. There was a store selling nuts, dates, chestnuts, jujubes, and walnuts. A fruit store sold pomegranates and wonderful big golden pears; from a cloth store, big bolts of fabric poured out onto the sidewalk. At the end of the street was a blacksmith and the bean curd seller. Except for the six-by-six army trucks that turned off the main road into our compound, the only vehicles were rickshaws and pony carts.

The first people we saw were two soldiers, the Kuomintang guards stationed at the gate of our compound.

"Ni hao," I greeted them.

"Ni hao," they answered together.

We introduced ourselves. "Women shi Meiguo bing." We're American soldiers here to help you fight the Japanese.

"Megui hou," they said in their strange accents. We like Americans.

We began to talk and it was not at all like the Stanford language labs. Baker and Levy quickly lost the drift. Even I found it hard to figure out what they were saying. I had to piece together meaning from the context, for their accents were so difficult to follow, a soft, half-lisping Hunan dialect. All I could do was try to figure out the changes they made in standard Mandarin sounds, like swapping their Ds for Ts and Ls for Ns. Where were they from, I asked? Hunan, they said, but pronounced it "Fulan."

They told us that they belonged to the Fifth Division. We had already heard of that famous crack KMT division that had trained under the legendary General "Vinegar Joe" Stilwell in Burma. Did they get enough to eat? Yes, they said, they had plenty to eat. They looked it too; they were chubby-faced youngsters with red cheeks.

It was nearly time for a change of shift, and when their relief came, the two young guards invited my buddies and me to visit their company headquarters. We climbed a hill behind our compound to an ancient slate-colored building with a roof of tiles and a gargoyle or two poking their heads from the corners. It looked like either an old temple or an old school. Outside the building was a flat piece of land that looked like a village square.

I never made it inside their company quarters. I was shocked to a halt by what I saw outside in the square: instruments of torture that looked as if they had come from a book on medieval dungeons. There was a wooden board, like stocks, with holes for the head and arms. There was also a head-and-arm board that looked like it was meant to be carried, a kind of whole-body handcuffs. There was a railing with thongs attached just high enough to be above the reach of outstretched arms; if tied by the fingers or thumbs, a person would have to dance on tiptoes. There was also a two-part bench they called a "lao hu deng," a tiger bench, clearly meant to be used as a rack to stretch, and perhaps break, a body. Everything was old, but it was in good repair—obviously currently in use.

What were these things used for? I asked the two young guards. They both grinned.

"They're for soldiers who are bad," one of them said, using a coy word that means "naughty."

"Or for the lao bai xing, if they are bad," the other chimed in, referring to the common people of the village.

They were laughing, but it wasn't a joke. Baker and Levy and I looked at one another and then at these fresh-faced young boys. They couldn't have been more than eighteen, and I wondered if they weren't perhaps more like fourteen.

Why did you join the army, we asked?

They laughed again. "Mei banfa," they answered together. We had no choice.

◆

Everywhere else in the world, the war was ending. In China it was just beginning.

The surrender of the Japanese had put an end to the bombings and the air raids, and freed the people from the terror of invaders who had raped and bayoneted their way through Shanghai and Nanjing. But the defeat of the common enemy had removed the only thing that had held China together. The Japanese gone, the Chinese turned to fighting each other. During the Japanese occupation the Nationalist and Communist parties had cooperated only fitfully, often in name only. But scarcely had the surrender been tendered than the tenuous cooperation fractured. Far off, in northern and central China, Chiang Kai-shek's Nationalist government, which ruled the country, and Mao Zedong's Communist forces, which controlled large chunks of China, were racing to accept the surrender of Japanese troops, and to take over their weapons. The two sides were battling not just for the prestige of receiving the surrender, but for the future right—and ability—to claim its party as the legitimate government of China.

In Kunming, the motley uniforms of the troops that swarmed the streets mirrored the deep divisions that were about to plunge China into a fierce and bitter civil war. The Nationalists were easy to identify in their handsome, tailored slate-blue muslin uniforms, or khaki woolen jackets for dress. These were Chiang Kai-shek's own troops, and their very presence here was a testament to the rot that was eating at China from the inside. These crack troops, which were supposed to have been used to repel the Japanese, were being kept here in Kunming, fresh and far from the battle lines, so they could be used after the war to wipe out the Communists. Like our young guides at the compound, they were all sweet-faced boys from Hunan who, in contrast to the rest of the population, looked extremely well fed.

As for the troops of the warlords—the petty tyrants who held sway over local fiefdoms all over China—they were a ragtag lot, dressed every which way, bearing the unmistakable signs of wartime hunger.

In Kunming I soon saw that there was no law, nothing to protect ordinary people from their own government. On one of my first days out driving through the city, our jeep was halted by a

procession of men shuffling along with their ankles roped together.

"Who are they?" I asked the young lad who accompanied me.

"New soldiers," he said. He told me the army swept down on
nearby villages and just grabbed whomever they wanted and
carted them off.

"But there are only two guards and dozens of these country
boys," I protested. "Why don't they just escape?"

He shrugged. "Soldiers wear tiger skins," he said, meaning best
not to fool with them.

Nor were young men of the villages the only ones vulnerable.
Soon after we arrived, the KMT commander supervising our base
casually mentioned that he could get us all the women we wanted.
For one U.S. dollar, he said, we will guarantee you a virgin. Startled, we asked where he would get them? From the villages, he
explained. No one dared resist, he said. Soldiers wear tiger skins.
Over and over we were to hear that phrase. Even when serious
crimes had been committed, there were often no hearings, no
trials, no punishment. There was no law—only power.

One day, in downtown Kunming where my jeep was parked, I
saw two policemen, German Lugers at their sides, tying up a
ragged man and a little boy right beside my vehicle. "What's going
on?" I asked.

"We caught them hanging around your jeep," one of the policemen replied. "We are sure they intended to steal something from
it, except we caught them first."

"Oh," I said, wondering how they knew what their prisoners
intended. "And what are you going to do with them?"

"We will take them to the execution grounds and shoot them,"
said the other policeman, making fast the little boy's ropes. He
could not have been more than eight or nine years old.

What could I do? I was pretty sure the policemen wouldn't be
impressed by talk of rules of evidence and habeas corpus. "I'll tell
you what," I said. "I have an idea. You caught them near an
American jeep, so we should have a chance to handle them. Why
don't you tie them up very securely and put them in the back. I'll
take them to American MP headquarters. When the MPs get hold
of them, they'll wish they had stayed with you."

The two policemen looked at each other and chuckled. Then
they tightened the ropes and heaved the man and the boy into the
back of my jeep. I got in quickly and raced out of the lot and
down the street, afraid that the policemen might have second

thoughts and chase after me. Meanwhile, I was calling out to my two passengers in the back seat, "Don't worry, I'm going to let you go as soon as we get to a safe spot."

I turned several corners, swerving through the busy streets, heading for the outskirts of town. When we reached the fringes of a large park I pulled over, got out and cut the ropes loose with my knife. It seemed that they had either not heard me call out or had not believed me. They stood there, looking at me with the glazed eyes of the despairing.

"It's okay," I said. "I'm setting you free."

The man and the boy both stared.

Again I said, "You're free. You can go."

Slowly, a light of recognition appeared in the man's eyes. He fell to his knees. "Jiu ming en ren," he wailed, pulling the boy down beside him. "Jiu ming en ren." You are our benefactor who has saved us from death. The two touched their heads to the dirt before me.

I felt sick.

In a sudden rush of shame and emotion, I reached in my pocket, pulled out all the dollars I found there and gave half to the man, half to the boy. "Get out of here. Get out of here quickly," I said, "or the police may follow and seize you again."

I jumped into the jeep, and drove away as fast as I could.

Regardless of the people's fear of the KMT, and of the police, it was clearly the Communists, not the KMT, who had captured their imagination. Chief Cook Wang proved that to me.

Shortly after I had arrived in Kunming, Wang spotted me in the mess hall, shoveling Spam and bully beef onto my plate along with the other GIs, and chattering away in Chinese to the waiters on the chow line. A very well fed man himself, he waddled over and pulled me aside. "You don't want to eat this slop," he whispered. "You are a friend of China. You can speak Chinese. Wait until dinner is over and come back with us."

After the GI mess had been cleared away, I went back to the kitchen where the cooks were all pitching in to make their own meal, their long chopping tables covered with food. That night we ate sweet-and-sour pork, crispy-skin chicken, fried eggplant, and long thin beans. I reveled in exotic fare like Over-the-Bridge noodles, rice noodles in a scalding hot soup.

After that I sneaked back to the kitchen to eat as often as I could. And over the din of banging pots and a lot of good-natured shouting and slurping, the cooks talked about their lives in Kunming before the war. They told me about the Hanliu, the secret associations of artisans that stuck up for each other, and of the violent, bloody wars between gangs—the Red Gang, the Green Gang—that reminded me of the warfare between rival Mafia gangs.

Chief Cook Wang was a born storyteller, and the local folklore was rich and varied. As an evening wore on, they would smoke the Camels I bought from the PX and listen as he spun his tales. One of his favorites was about the hero Zhu Mao. All the cooks knew of him and loved to hear stories about him. While Zhu Mao had never been to Kunming, they said, he had traveled nearly everywhere else and his deeds were well known all over China. He was a tall, powerful man, so fearsome that no army could stand up to him and no fortress could keep him out. Bullets and spears couldn't hurt him. He could enter the thick of the fiercest battle and emerge unscathed. What's more, he was much beloved. He used his power in the service of the poor, righting wrongs and ending injustices.

I was puzzled. The cooks were using the word "Mao" as a given name, but it wasn't really a given name. It was more of a surname and a common one at that—certainly no name for such a hero. I asked Chef Wang about it and he simply shrugged. They were good stories, and he was ignorant of such literary questions as a name's meaning. One evening, however, as Chef Wang was telling another story about how the fearless Zhu Mao had swept through an area with his men, breaking into rich landlords' stores of grain and handing it out to poor peasants, I suddenly realized who this hero Zhu Mao was.

My mind flashed back to my classes at Stanford. "Maaah-Ow," one teacher would say, trying to teach us the diphthongs. "Mao, as in Mao Ze-dong." Then, "Zh . . . Zh . . . Zh . . . Zhu . . . Zhu . . . Zhu . . . as in Zhu De," referring to the Communists' famous commander-in-chief. In between lessons, my teachers talked to us about the Communists' Long March in the years before the war. To consolidate their hold on power, the Nationalists were determined to destroy the Communists, driving them further and further into the remote provinces of the north. As the Communists made their frantic flight from the Kuomintang pursuing them, they left behind huge posters telling of their progress and laying out their programs for social reform. Each one would be stamped with the names of the two top Communist leaders: Zhu Mao. So stories must have spread from village to village, and in these cooks' minds

—and perhaps, I thought, in the minds of peasants and common people all over China—these two men had blended into one superhero, a kind of latter-day Robin Hood.

◆

As I drove around Kunming in my little jeep, I often stopped to talk to shopkeepers and booksellers. One bookseller gave me my name—Li Dunbai. It was the name of a famous Chinese poet, Li Bai, separated by "Dun," which is the character for uprightness. It was supposed to sound like Rittenberg. But, the bookseller explained, it also sounded like a real Chinese name.

I also regularly bought the newspapers hawked by the newsboys who thronged around Righteousness Road. I plowed through each paper carefully, picking out the different political lines. There was the *Gong Yi Bao,* the pro-KMT Catholic paper. There was the *Yunnan Ribao,* the personal newspaper of the governor of Yunnan. The army general staff had a paper called the *Sao Dong,* which meant the "Mopping Up Daily"—a reference to the army's campaign against the Communists.

The Communists too had a newspaper, the *Xinhua Ribao,* the *New China Daily,* which was published clandestinely. I often bought a copy, although I could read only little snatches of it. Unlike the other papers, which were printed on newsprint, the *New China Daily* was printed in dim ink on a thin, tissuelike paper. The newsboys generally didn't hawk the Communist paper, but kept copies stashed at the bottom of their bags. They had to be discreet. Despite the official protection of the provincial governor, Communists in Kunming operated under a de facto death threat. More than once I had seen men marched through the street, their hands tied behind their backs, lugging their own stakes to the execution grounds where they would be shot. The signs on their backs identified them as Communists.

I visited Righteousness Road so often that soon the newsboys came to wait for me. When I pulled up to the street corner where I usually bought my papers, they would swarm around, a pack of dirty, barefoot pint-sized ragamuffins, and someone would drag a copy of the Communist paper from the bottom of his sack.

Since my schedule was my own, and my life was lonely, I came to spend more and more time laughing and hanging around these little creatures. They were tough to understand, since they spoke with such a thick brogue, but one of the elder ones designated himself an unofficial interpreter. Whenever one said something I didn't understand, he would repeat it at the top of his lungs, as if volume would help.

One day when I got ready to leave, sensing that something was wrong, I pulled open the glove compartment of the jeep and saw that my big GI flashlight was gone. One of the little newsboys had filched it while we were talking. So I closed the glove compartment and made my face grave. "We're all friends here," I said. "We talk together. We play together. We don't have any problems with each other. Friends don't steal each other's flashlights."

There was a great wriggling and squirming in the group and I could see pushing and shoving until suddenly a crestfallen fellow emerged. He stood before me hanging his head, while the others harangued him. Finally his hand went under his raggedy clothes and out came my flashlight. I picked him up and hugged him and everyone laughed.

I must have made some impression on these newsboys, or else someone had been watching me all along. For the very next time I pulled up to Righteousness Road to buy my papers the ringleader leaned against the jeep and whispered in my ear. "You like reading the Communist paper. Would you like to meet the people who put it out?"

I nodded and the boy jumped into my jeep. I swung away from the curb, and as he shouted directions we threaded our way through the center of Kunming. We stopped in a busy commercial section downtown on Zhengyi Street. He jumped down and pointed to a tiny wineshop, motioning me in. Together, we walked past rows of dusty bottles and a dimly lit sales counter, heading for the back of the shop. There, behind the store, was another hidden office. The little newsboy rapped on the door and then vanished, leaving me at the portal alone.

I was only a little nervous. I knew that as an American, and a soldier at that, I wasn't in any real danger. I feared more for my unknown, newfound friends. For all I knew KMT spies were watching me.

The door swung open. Two men stood up. They didn't seem surprised to see me.

They told me their names, but nothing more about themselves. One, a tall, handsome, angular man who wore glasses and looked like a matinee idol, was Cheng Baideng. The other had the appearance and the style of a professional underground worker, harassed, with the look of having slept in his clothes. He chainsmoked. He told me his name was Li Guohua, and he was obviously the man in charge. He had an air of authority about him, despite the fact that he was only a little shrimp of a man with a Melanesian-type face, a flat nose and jaw like the bottom of a teacup. His face was creased and withered and he had a gold tooth. He spoke in low tones with a very thick Cantonese accent.

From their guarded expressions, I got the impression that this was a place where these two men met, but didn't talk. Mr. Cheng suggested we meet later elsewhere. I didn't know any good meeting places, so one of them suggested a local café. We shook hands and parted. Although I was somewhat puzzled by our meeting, I was eager to see them again. I felt a kind of kinship with these strange and exotic Chinese Communists. Before I was drafted, I had been a Communist myself.

I was the only son of a well-to-do family. My father was a prominent Charleston lawyer, and my mother the daughter of a Russian immigrant. I had joined the American Communist Party in 1940 while I was in college, partly because the Communists seemed to be the only group taking a strong antiwar stance, and I was filled with a bitter rage at the speed with which America seemed to be hurtling itself into war. More than that, however, it was the Communists, with their strong posture on free speech and ethnic equality in America, and their roots in the American labor movement, who seemed to offer a hope of righting the injustices I saw all around me.

The two years I spent in the party opened my eyes to a whole new world. I organized steel workers and coal miners. I was arrested and interrogated by Red Squads in Birmingham. I held classes on political economy for cotton mill workers in Roanoke Rapids, North Carolina. I saw men and women who willingly lived in poverty to help other people out of their own poverty. And I saw people die for their cause. I felt that in the left-wing labor movement I had at last found a force for good, multitudes of organized, dead-serious men and women who shared my vision but who were determined where I was faltering, clear-eyed where I felt confused.

Still, unlike some other American party members of the 1920s and 1930s who set out for the Soviet Union seeking the perfect socialist state, I never thought of joining a revolution in another country. There was so much to do at home! At any rate, once in the army, I had to give up my party membership. The party didn't want to be accused of infiltrating the military.

Even though I was no longer a party member, I hadn't given up my ideals. I still wanted to work for a new society. And leaving the party behind had left a big hole in my life. I felt empty and adrift in China, a passive observer of everything around me, and not the active force for change I wanted to be. I hadn't gone looking for the Chinese Communists, but I was glad to make contact, although I wasn't sure where it might lead. Perhaps I could help them. Perhaps they could help me.

Mr. Cheng, Mr. Li, and I met for dinner at an open-air restaurant, where they told me their stories. Cheng was a writer, a translator of Steinbeck and Faulkner, and had worked with John Fairbank, the eminent Asian scholar. Now he was on the run, caught in Kunming by the war and the occupation. Li was involved with the newspaper, which, he said, was in a precarious position.

They seemed to be cultivating Americans, but not toadying as the KMT was. My buddies and I had been hounded by slick KMT officers, who pressed favors on us, trying to "make friends." We had resisted the blandishments of the KMT, but I eagerly welcomed the Communists' attentions. Li offered to get me some news bulletins from party headquarters in Yanan, deep in the mountains of northwest China, to let me in on what was happening in the areas liberated by the Communists. After that first meeting, I didn't see much of Cheng. But Li and I continued to meet regularly, and a kind of attachment grew between us. He began gradually to fill me in on the situation in China as the Communists saw it, and to tell me about the Communist organization that was so different from the organization I had known in the United States. I had been unaware of the underground network that existed here, where each party member knew only one other member so that no one person could betray the whole organization.

Through Li, I began to meet other Chinese Communists. One evening, he took me to the Qiao family's house. Mr. Qiao, it turned out, was the man who ran the wineshop that hid the backroom meeting place. Their home was pleasant and comfortable, the home of a well-to-do, but not wealthy family. And I saw that, even under siege, the Communists could have fun. We played Western music and danced; Li drank and joked around.

They told me tales of Yanan, the remote mountain village where Mao Zedong made his headquarters. To me, Yanan had just been a name from the news—like Pearl Harbor or Washington or Berlin. But that night, Yanan came alive for me as a real place, where real people lived and worked. In Yanan, Li said, there were regular Saturday night dances. Everyone attended, from the lowest worker to Chairman Mao himself.

Mrs. Qiao chimed in to say that she had lived in Yanan, where her daughter had attended nursery school. Women had an equal position in Yanan, Mrs. Qiao said. That impressed me. "You should go to Yanan," she urged. "We need help from foreign friends."

The others agreed. Partly they were teasing me, and partly just being sociable. But partly they were serious, and suddenly the thought filled me with excitement. Maybe it would be possible. Maybe when I got out of the army, I could go to the liberated areas, and see the Communists in action. Maybe I could go to Yanan and even meet Chairman Mao himself.

Gradually, I began doing little favors for the Communists. As a GI I could move easily around the city, free from the scrutiny of soldiers and police. Several times I helped underground workers escape. Once I drove an old man to the edge of town. Another time it was a young teacher who had been heavily involved in the student movement. He was being hunted everywhere; all entrances and exits to the city were being watched and all cars were being searched. The soldiers, however, wouldn't dare search an American military vehicle.

At the appointed hour, a very pleasant looking young man, maybe about twenty-five or twenty-six years old and dressed in a long student's gown, climbed into my jeep. Just as Li had instructed, I drove him out of town, along the road that led past our barracks and down to a school set back from the road where he was received by a man named Wu. I returned to the barracks feeling quite pleased with myself.

Li Guohua and I often met to go to the theater. I enjoyed chatting with him and felt that I was getting involved in Chinese cultural life. Our theater dates weren't foolproof, however. Because of the KMT spies, we still had to use great caution, and sometimes we had some close calls.

One night we were on our way to see *Family,* a famous play by Ba Jin, a modern Chinese novelist and playwright, about the fate of the third son of an aristocratic family who becomes an anarchist. The auditorium where it was produced was at the top of a very steep hill. My little underpowered jeep was chugging up the narrow road when, from the bottom of the hill, I heard someone shouting my name.

"Meesuh-tuh Li! Meesuh-tuh Li!" I looked behind me and saw

one of the KMT agents who had been courting me and my army friends puffing up the hill on foot, shouting after me. I was terrified that he would recognize Li Guohua. Pretending not to hear him, I gunned the jeep up the hill. Its tiny engine could barely make the grade, much less gather any speed. Even on foot, the agent was gaining on us. I kept hoping that he would tire, but he appeared bent on pursuit. "Meesuh-tuh Li! Meesuh-tuh Li!" I kept hearing behind me. Finally, with a lunge, the jeep reached the crest of the hill and sailed over the top into the anonymity of the parking lot where crowds were arriving for the performance. Li Guohua looked rattled. When I told him who had been pursuing us, he paled.

We bought our tickets and were walking into the theater when suddenly Li sat down on a long bench in the rear. Then he stretched out and his whole body began shaking violently. I was frightened.

"I'll get a doctor," I said, turning away.

He reached out his shaking hand. "No. No. No," he pleaded. "I'm fine." But he was still trembling uncontrollably and I sat beside him and watched in horror as he lay there drenched in sweat. Other people entered the theater, but they didn't pay any attention to us.

After about five minutes Li sat up. He was dripping and pale, but the convulsions had subsided.

"What's the matter?" I asked. "What happened?"

"Electrical torture," he said.

As we walked toward our seats, Li explained in a low voice that he had been arrested, imprisoned, and tortured by the KMT, and that he hadn't been the same since. I wondered: Was he terrified at the thought of being arrested again? Had he suffered neurological damage? I didn't know, but I asked him what the doctors had said. "It's nothing a doctor can help," he replied and then turned the conversation to an interpretation of the play.

About that same time, events began to unfold just as I had predicted they would. With the war over, the American forces were leaving Kunming and our offices were being closed. In late November 1945, orders were posted moving our whole company back to India to await our return to the United States for demobilization.

I didn't want to go. I was enthralled with my newfound friends, excited by what I was learning about the Communists. In the back of my mind was the tantalizing prospect that my friends had not been joking that night at the dance party, and that there might be some real chance that I could visit Yanan. I still wasn't thinking very far into the future. All I knew was that I appeared to be on the edge of an adventure, and I didn't want to leave before I had tasted it.

I went to my colonel and asked to be allowed to stay in Kunming. "We'll still have to wait months in India to get our discharges," I argued. "I've just started to learn the ropes here and the work I do is needed by the army. Why not let me stay for a while?" He was unmoved.

That evening, I was walking home through the headquarters compound when I noticed a light in the commanding general's office. I had never spoken to him, but General Henry Aurand had a reputation for being a Stilwell man and open to reason. I badly wanted to stay, so I decided to give it a try. I knocked on his office door and, once inside, I saluted, identified myself, and said that I had a personal problem I would like to discuss.

"Is it all right if my chief of staff hears it too, or shall I ask him to leave?" General Aurand said, waving one arm in the direction of the colonel sitting at one end of his desk.

Somehow I knew instantly that I had won.

"He is welcome to hear, sir," I answered, and I made my case as succinctly as I could.

The general's answer was that of a man used to dealing with problems briskly and efficiently. "Just tear up any orders you may receive except for those transferring you to army headquarters in Shanghai," he said. "You needn't speak to anyone about it. Just go about your business, and if anyone asks you, just send them to me."

I had no idea what might happen when I got to Shanghai, but I needed to prepare, and quickly. I passed a message to Li through the wineshop where we had met. When he contacted me, I explained that I would soon be leaving Kunming for Shanghai. He told me he would write a letter for me to carry to one of his friends there, who, in turn, could introduce me to someone who would be a friend to me in Shanghai.

If I still wanted to go to the liberated areas, Li said, this person could perhaps help me. We arranged to meet the next night on the same street corner.

We met as scheduled and he took me to his home, an ordinary low, stone Chinese courtyard house with one long and one short room. The atmosphere was tense. His wife began to offer me advice about Shanghai. "Shut your mouth," Li hissed. I sat down by his side near a table that was used as a writing desk. There were three letters on it. Names and addresses were written on each, and the envelopes were sealed. Li began to speak to me in whispers but, as an added precaution, every time he got to an important word, he wrote it. "When you get to Shanghai, you must go to . . ." and he scribbled a place name. "When you get there, ask for . . ." another scribble. "When you meet him, call him by the name . . ." scribble, scribble, scribble.

The only problem was that Li took it for granted that I could read running script, the kind of elegant cursive educated Chinese use when they are in a hurry. I was too pigheaded and proud to tell him that I couldn't read a word of what he had written. So as I was leaving, I palmed the paper. I didn't dare show the addresses to anyone, so over the next several days, I showed one character at a time to several different people in several different places. Finally, painfully, I pieced together Li's directions.

I would have been careful anyway, but Li's parting salute disturbed me. As we shook hands to say goodbye, his face became grave. "I have done everything I can to help you," he said. "And I have only one thing to ask of you in return. Never again under any circumstances tell anyone you saw me. Never again mention my name."

The Famine

Within a few weeks, I was assigned to Shanghai and hitched a ride on army transports for the sixteen-hundred-mile journey east. The judge advocate and his claims office were in a large building on Fuzhou Road, just across from the compound that housed the U.S. Army headquarters for China. I moved into the navy YMCA building, which had been turned into an army hostel.

On my second morning at the YMCA, I got up early so I was the first to open the front door. I stepped outside and stumbled. A frozen corpse lay stretched out on the threshold. It was a Chinese man, perhaps in his early forties, wearing layers of thin cotton clothes. He had wrapped himself in a tattered rush mat when he lay down to go to sleep. It had not been enough to protect him from that cold November night.

Nearly every day from then on I saw a corpse in Shanghai, sometimes sprawled out on the sidewalk, sometimes lying curled in a bundle with a mat spread over it. Both passersby and police scurried by, ignoring the dead in their paths.

"Why?" I asked a local Chinese.

"Because," he answered, "if anyone touches it he may be required by the police to take the responsibility for burying it. When people have such a hard time keeping the living alive, no one wants to have to take care of a dead stranger."

Although officially my job in Shanghai, as in Kunming, was to investigate civil cases filed against the U.S. Army, in reality the office was being dismantled and I had little to do. I spent much of my time walking through the city, tortured by the desperate faces that surrounded me. The streets were so clogged with refugees that many alleys were impassable. There was no housing for the masses of people driven out of the countryside by the war, or by famine, or by recent violent floods. In street after street, people improvised shelters, using rush mats to form tunnels they called "the rolling dragon." The matting was often set on fire from the coal stoves they used for cooking and for warmth. And then the entire street, and its residents, would go up in flames.

Inflation raged. Every day the signs over the money changers' shops changed several times. The exchange rate was in thousands of Chinese guobi to the dollar when I arrived, and in hundreds of thousands of guobi to the dollar when I left. Anyone who was lucky enough to be working would get their pay daily and run to the nearest grain store as fast as possible to convert the cash to grain. The coolies and factory workers were demanding relief, teachers took to the streets to demand inflation subsidies. Some days even the main streets were barely passable because of demonstrators blocking the way.

I often walked down Bubbling Well Road and onto Nanjing Road at night. I could see in the massive old colonial stone buildings the skeleton of the financial trading center that had once dominated Asia with its great wealth. I often strolled past the fabulous Wing On department store, the French bakeries, and elegant restaurants that still swelled with foreigners spending hard currency, or with rich Chinese.

There were girls all up and down Nanjing Road. Phalanxes of girls. Columns and regiments of hungry, ragged girls who blocked my way insistently, grabbing at my sleeve. "Quickie, Joe?" "Quickie, Joe?" some of them pleaded. They looked frightful, skin pockmarked and sallow, eyes glassy from hunger. "Gentleman's massage?" They came at me in waves. "Yes, Yes, good, good." They wore half coats of cheap imitation fur over their slit Chinese gowns. They weren't alluring. They were desperate, and their numbers were awesome.

I felt very much alone. Just as I was leaving the United States, my wife, Violet, had filed for divorce. The final papers had been sent to me while I was in India. I had been really stuck on Violet, a pretty, hazel-eyed farmer's daughter, and we got married while I was organizing a campaign for the right to vote in Birmingham, Alabama. We had had fun together in our first summer in Chapel Hill, working with union members and taking piano lessons together from a friend. But the next summer she fell in love with somebody else. So when she asked for a divorce a year later, I wasn't exactly surprised, but still, it hurt. Surrounded by millions of people in one of the most crowded cities on earth, I was lonely. I wanted companionship. I wanted affection. I wanted love.

I had fooled around a few times in Kunming, necking a bit with some of the jeep girls who hung around the junctions looking for rides or GI handouts. But I couldn't bring myself to do more with these lost souls who would sell themselves for a can of rations or a blanket. In Shanghai, I felt even less like taking advantage of the horror of their lives. A couple of times I went to Ciro's, a big long dance hall. You paid admission and danced as much as you liked. The girls made their money by taking guys home.

Several times I sat and talked with one of the dancing girls. She had an English name—like Cindy. She and I drank orange juice for a couple of bucks a glass and, after a while, she wanted me to leave with her. She was a nice young girl, but I just couldn't bring myself to go to bed with her. So I bought her more drinks and talked to her about her life. She was from Changzhou in Jiangsu Province, she told me. She had seven brothers and sisters and her father had sold her to one of the buyers who traveled out from Shanghai looking for young girls for the brothels in the city. At first she was terrified and cried all the time. She wanted to run away. But even if she could escape, she had no way of getting back to Jiangsu and no other means of earning a living.

Cindy wasn't angry at her parents, she told me. By selling her, they had earned enough money to keep the littler ones alive for a while longer. She had been in Shanghai nearly a year. Every so often she ran into a mean guy, who would beat her and make her suffer. But mostly the GIs had been kind to her. So now, she said, she was getting used to it.

◆

As soon as I could, I set out to deliver Li Guohua's letters of introduction to the Shanghai Communists. The characters I had so painfully deciphered instructed me to seek out a man who would direct me to another man. He, in turn, would direct me to the third, to whom I would deliver the principal letter.

My first contact worked at the *Lian Mei Wan Bao,* a Chinese language paper backed by the U.S. Information Service. My introduction simply said he worked there, but I didn't know whether he was an office boy, a janitor, or what. It turned out he was the editor, dressed in very proper Western attire, and obviously a big shot. But behind the cover of a U.S. government job, he was secretly a Communist. He shshhed me quickly when I showed him the little envelope with the note in it, and led me out onto the staircase. "You can find your contact at this address," he said, scrawling something on a piece of paper. And with that, he bid a hasty good night, turned and was gone.

I slowly translated his directions one character at a time and they finally led me one morning to the shop where I found Jiang Zhenzhong. I was shocked. It was a big money changer's shop on Sichuan Road, where fat-necked sleepy-eyed gentlemen in long gowns sat at desks with abacuses, changing gold bars and U.S. dollars for Chinese guobi. These shops were sleazy places and, it turned out, Mr. Jiang Zhenzhong was a sleazy character, a huge, blubbery old rake in an expensive blue silk gown, a typical Shanghai playboy, a fat merchant. I imagined he was rolling in money and spent his free time and cash on gambling and women. I wondered what I was doing there. Nonetheless, I gave him his letter and showed him the one for my last contact, a man named Xu Maijin.

"Come back here on Thursday," he said—two days away. "Mr. Xu will be here then."

I arrived at the scheduled time and, as soon as I walked in, Xu Maijin emerged from an inner door. He was dressed in a very neat three-piece serge suit with an overcoat and hat. Wearing glasses, he looked as if he might be the dean of a school. I tried to speak, but he waved his hand and the expression on his face clearly said, "Don't talk now."

We rode in a bicycle rickshaw to Joffe's, a famous Western-style restaurant, and I gave him his letter.

"Yes, yes, yes," he said, scanning it. "Li Guohua and I were in prison together." Then he gave me a warning. "Shanghai is a very complicated place. If anyone asks what you are doing with me, say I am Mr. Yang, and that I am your Chinese teacher."

Over coffee and cream puffs at Joffe's we sounded each other out. Xu didn't want money, but he wasn't above accepting some favors. We planned future meetings, which from then on took place either over meals or at the opera, which he justified by saying that it would give me an opportunity to perfect my Chinese. But it soon emerged that he was a man who passionately loved the opera. Xu could hear a passage in Kunqu, the most elaborate and famous forerunner of Peking opera, and hum all the versions from other operas. So our meetings were a good way of assuring himself a steady supply of tickets. He would pick the performance, buy the tickets, and I would repay him.

For me, I would rather have been beaten than to sit through Peking opera. I couldn't make it out as music, much less recognize any melody. And I couldn't understand why to make a little tiny point it took all that howling and stomping. The singers would go on and on for an hour or more, and Xu Maijin would lean over and say, "She loves him." For those Chinese who themselves could not follow the stylized language, written characters were flashed alongside the stage as subtitles. The whole thing was too literary and too cryptic for me. Still, there were parts of the experience I enjoyed. Hot towel vendors stood up on the balconies and flung their wares down at customers in the audience with deadly accuracy, and then snagged from midair the bills and change the buyers tossed up at them. And as we became regulars, I began to notice other regulars in the theater, especially an attractive young woman who twice had the seat adjacent to ours. But she never paid much attention to either me or Xu.

For his part, Xu kept me supplied with the New China News Agency newscasts from Yanan, and briefed me on the Communist views of events. The union demonstrations, for example, I learned were all organized by the party, using the company unions as a shell. So the throngs in the street were actually demonstrations of the hold the Communists had in Shanghai.

The Communists had a special strength in Shanghai. When the Japanese announced their surrender, the Communists' New Fourth Army was encircling the city, while the Nationalists were much further away. The New Fourth Army immediately sent in its propagandists, and citywide preparations to welcome the "heroic liberators" had already begun. But the plans were thwarted by the truce agreement negotiated between the Communists and Nationalists at Chongqing that ordered all troops on both sides to freeze in their present positions. Everywhere, you could still hear deep grumbling and disappointment at that turn of events.

Still, being a Communist, especially in the deep underground, was hazardous even in Shanghai. Xu told me a bit about how the underground worked. It was an organization unto itself, kept completely separate from the rest of the Communist organization. Xu told me that an underground worker who discovered that he or she was being watched by the KMT was supposed to disappear the very day the surveillance was discovered.

Some of the favors Xu asked of me seemed bizarre, but they were never unreasonable. He had a good friend, the well-known Chinese writer Xia Yan, who was addicted to Camel cigarettes. That was no problem, since I didn't smoke and I had access to almost unlimited supplies. Then he asked for a copy of the *Radio Amateur's Handbook* for the son of Lu Xun, the most distinguished left-wing author. That wasn't difficult either. And then he told me of another friend, an old comrade, who was very poor, had too many children, and needed condoms. That was definitely no problem. I just went over to the army prophylactic station and grabbed huge handfuls.

◆

Not long after we met, Xu Maijin said he wanted to introduce me to a friend, a woman who had just suffered a great tragedy. Her husband, Li Xiaoshi, had been a member of the Communist negotiating team working with Zhou Enlai in Chongqing and had recently been murdered when his car was machine-gunned by assassins who had apparently mistaken him for Zhou. She was terribly unhappy, and Xu suggested bringing an American friend around to cheer her up. Later I suspected that he was also probably looking to get another opinion about me before proceeding any further. Because as it turned out, his friend was quite an important person.

Her name was Liao Mengxing, and she was the elder sister of Liao Chengzhi, a high-ranking member of the Communist Party Central Committee. She went by the name Cynthia and, in Western fashion, had adopted her husband's surname, Li. She lived upstairs in an apartment in the old French concession with her daughter, Nunu, who was about twelve. Xu Maijin took me there for dinner one evening. I told her about my past, about my role in the student movement at Chapel Hill, about my life as an organizer. I must have passed the test, for at the end of the evening she invited me back, and suggested that she might introduce me to someone else. Cynthia Li, I soon learned, was secretary to

Madame Sun Yat-sen, widow of the great revolutionary hero, recognized by both Communists and Nationalists as the founder of modern China.

The night I dined with Madame Sun there was no talk of politics or of organizing. Mostly we discussed the work of another one of the dinner guests, Tao Xingzhi, a noted educator who was trying to break out of the traditional mode of rote instruction and set up a new system of schools.

Shortly after that dinner, I learned that Tao Xingzhi, too, had been assassinated, shot down in public, apparently by the secret police.

When orders finally came through for my honorable discharge, it was Madame Sun who found a way for me to stay in China. I had already decided that I didn't want to go home. There was really nothing to go home to, I had realized. Everything that we had achieved as party organizers had been destroyed during the war, and I was feeling increasingly discouraged about the wisdom of going back to that line of work in postwar America. Nor were there strong family ties pulling me home. Violet had divorced me and we had had no children. My father had died before I left the States, and my mother and I were not close. I was angry with her. After my divorce she had written to me suggesting that I name her as the beneficiary of my GI life insurance policy, instead of my wife. My mother's love of money and fine things had made my father's life miserable, I thought, and I wasn't about to let it destroy mine as well.

Besides, I was beginning to feel dirty and corrupted, the kind of corruption that comes from living side by side with misery and evil and not doing anything about it. I had drifted far away from my ideals and I wanted to get closer to these idealistic Chinese Communists. My friends in Kunming had fired up my imagination, and Cynthia Li was doing everything she could to stoke the blaze. "Don't go home," she urged. "Stay here. Stay here with us. You can help the party. Stay here and go to Yanan."

There was another idea lurking in my head, that I might find more than one kind of romance in China. Cynthia seemed to understand that too. "You should find a nice Chinese girl here," she said. "You could join our party." It seemed as good an idea as any to me.

The only way the army would discharge me in China was if I could come up with a legitimate job. So it was that Cynthia Li gave me a note in Madame Sun's name, written to an offi-

cial of the United Nations Relief and Rehabilitation Administration. UNRRA was a politically neutral organization that was
providing help for victims of the war and of the famine, a fine,
honorable job as far as I was concerned. "This is the American
friend I spoke to you about," the note read. "Please find a job for
him."

◆

The job I got was called "observer."

It was the responsibility of UNRRA to bring in grain, flour, and
other food for famine sufferers. But China being what it was, there
was chicanery afoot even in this area. The UN officials suspected
that great amounts of the relief supplies were being sold on the
black market by corrupt KMT officials. They also suspected that
the famine reports were doctored. No one doubted there was a
famine, of course. The refugees pouring into Shanghai gave ample
proof of the hunger gripping the country. But UNRRA suspected
that black marketeers were manipulating the reports, and even the
stores of grain themselves, in order to wring more money and grain
out of donors.

My first assignment was to travel into the regions of the KMT-
controlled Hunan Province where famine was said to be the worst.
I was to report on the extent of the problem and monitor the
distribution of relief grain to make sure that it was getting to the
people it was intended for.

One cold February day, I boarded a U.S. Navy tank carrier that
was heading up the Yangtze River toward Wuhan, en route to
Hunan with a cargo of relief flour. With me were two colleagues,
a former government information officer, and another young man
just out of service in naval intelligence. The Yangtze was strikingly
like the Mississippi, moving with the same broad sweep, the same
big lazy bends, the same coy curlicues. As we steamed upriver the
river folk drifted past, crammed onto their fishing junks and sam-
pans, the tiny boats where they lived from birth to burial. They
were almost like India's Untouchables, forbidden to spend the
night ashore, prohibited from marrying onshore people. They tied
their children to the masts on a tether so they would not fall
overboard, and subsisted on the fish, shrimp, and rats that they
could afford to eat rather than sell.

I stood by the old Chinese river pilot to talk with him as he sent
his signals to the steersman and the engine room, or took over the
wheel himself. He had spent forty years on that river. He knew

every rill and eddy, every rock and shoal. What did he think would happen now that the war was over, I asked.

He looked at me and smiled indulgently. "Nothing," he said. "Officials will change but taxes will still be collected, and whoever is in power will still have to get me to pilot their ships for them."

The trip up the river from Shanghai took a day and a night. It was early morning when we finally tied up at the port of Wuchang. We were ferried across the river to Hankou where we put up at the Jiang An Hotel, an old riverside inn. My traveling companions busied themselves immediately, but not with UN work. They had brought bags full of the thumb-sized slabs of gold which served as stable currency in the face of skyrocketing inflation. The war had disrupted communications between cities so that the price of a gold bar might differ by five to ten U.S. dollars from one town to the next. Fortunes were made every day by privileged people who could travel. Trading their gold bars for dollars kept my two companions fully occupied that first day, which was just as well for me. I didn't want any interference from them. What's more, since neither of them spoke much Chinese, if they had paid any attention to their work, I would have had to double as their interpreter.

To report accurately on the situation, my priority was to seek out some help from local people. Without it, I could easily be hoodwinked by corrupt officials. Before I left Shanghai, I had asked Xu Maijin to give me letters of introduction to the Communist delegation. And that night, while my colleagues were occupied, I went to seek out General Wang Zhen at the Deming Hotel where the Communists were quartered. Hankou, one of the three cities collectively known as Wuhan, had been part of the old German sphere of influence and the Deming had obviously been a grand German hotel. It was all gone to seed, its wooden staircases splintered, its furniture worn, and its carpets threadbare. I was lucky enough to find the general in his room. He read the letter introducing me as an American friend and enveloped me in a big bear hug.

Wang Zhen was a remarkable-looking man. His eyes were unusually expressive and set into a long, angular face from which a row of white upper teeth jutted out like a jackrabbit's. Known among the Communist leaders as Wang the Bandit, he had a reputation for great courage and ferocity in leading his troops into combat. He had a keen wit and biting humor as well as a fiery Hunan temper.

Over dinner General Wang filled me with tales of the military situation in China. It wasn't good. He told me that all the Communist forces south of the Yangtze had withdrawn north of the river under the truce agreement negotiated between Mao Zedong and Chiang Kai-shek, with the help of General George C. Marshall, the special representative of President Harry Truman. He scarcely attempted to disguise his distrust and disapproval of the agreement. "We lost vast areas south of the river, for which our comrades fought and died," he said. "We gave the peasants there back to the landlords so they could suck their blood again. We lived up to the agreement. We withdrew every man we had across the river. But what has Chiang Kai-shek done? Nothing but pursue and attack us on every hand."

I told General Wang of my mission for UNRRA, and asked his help. It would be too dangerous to introduce me to anyone in Hunan, he said. But he would help. He would send his aide with me. "This is Comrade Mao," he said, pointing to a tall young man standing in the doorway. "He's from Hunan, and he's a cousin of Chairman Mao's." The young soldier blushed at this. "He will take the train down one day after you, traveling in disguise. He will find you, and he can help you gather the data you need."

I could hardly believe my ears. Now I would show them at UNRRA what kind of work I could turn out, what kind of report I could come back with. I shook hands with the young man and thanked the general profusely.

The next morning my two companions and I were ferried back across the river to Wuchang, where we boarded the strangest-looking railroad train I had ever seen, made of captured Japanese trucks fitted with railroad wheels and running on narrow-gauge tracks. We put-putted west and south all day with our load of grain. And that night, we put in at the county seat of Linxiang, where we were bedded down at a local inn. It was a compound of adobe-and-brick buildings, all one-storied, with pounded earthen floors. Each tiny room had a cot with a cotton quilt for cover and a cotton quilted mat to sleep on. The hotel maid, a chubby young girl, came to each room and poured hot water into a basin so that we could wash. A thermos of boiled water was placed beside the basin so that we had our own supply of water for drinking. We were served a meal in our rooms: thick, hot noodles in chicken soup, some pickled turnips and turnip greens, a tiny fried fish, and piping-hot green tea.

The next leg of our journey was by regular railway, but a strange thing had happened. Our cargo of flour had disappeared during the night. "It's on another train," said the conductor. "Don't worry about it. It'll get there before you do."

So off we went toward Changsha, the capital of Hunan Province. But before we had even arrived at the next station, the brakes screeched and our train slid to a stop. We waited a few minutes, listening to the shouting and excitement up ahead. Then I got down and walked to the front of the train. There I found two armed Nationalist MPs binding two other soldiers with baling wire. The two men were wailing and protesting, but no one paid them any attention. By the side of the track, capsized, was an old-fashioned pump-handled railroad handcar.

I walked over and asked the MP sergeant what was going on. "They disrupted communications," he said. "That is an offense punishable by death."

"Just what did they do?" I asked.

The MP sergeant shrugged. "These men are stationed a short way down the track from here. They say their company commander ordered them to use the railroad handcar to go to Linxiang and bring him back some cigarettes. Before they could get to Linxiang, they met us."

"So what are you going to do with them?" I asked.

"We're going to shoot them," the sergeant said, obviously feeling that he was wasting time answering foolish questions from a foreign nincompoop.

I remembered the old man and the boy in the parking lot in Kunming. But this time there was nothing I could do, except protest. "But don't they get a trial?" I asked, deeply shocked.

"The regulations say that a summary death sentence may be passed and executed on anyone who disrupts communications lines," the sergeant told me.

Those regulations were clearly intended to cope with the Communists' disruptions of the rail and highway lines that were funneling KMT troops to front-line positions for the coming civil war. "But they were only following orders from their commander," I protested.

The sergeant turned away impatiently and joined his men, who were pushing and dragging the two unfortunate soldiers toward a ridge. They disappeared behind a clump of trees. We heard a crackling volley of rifle fire, and back came the ghastly little procession. The two victims were left where they fell.

We continued our journey without further interruption and we arrived in Changsha in early evening, just in time to have dinner with an American who had lived in China for years. He gave himself the most pious airs of anyone I had ever met. It made me fidgety to sit down and eat with him. He opened the meal at the long common table with the saying of grace; he called for a halt in midmeal for another prayer of thanks; he concluded the meal with another long prayer. Throughout the meal, he groaned most piteously about the sins of man and the hard road to redemption. I could barely eat for the pall he cast over the whole meal.

After dinner, he introduced us to a couple who worked for him. They were Westernized Chinese, Christians. If I had met them on a train, I could have guessed from their decorum, their well-scrubbed appearance, and their Western-style clothes that they had grown up in missionary schools. The husband, whose name was Ivan, was a quiet, pudgy man with a receding hairline. His wife, Sophie, was a tiny ball of fire who talked with a husky, cigarette voice, even though she didn't smoke. We chatted briefly about the office and their work, and I turned in early.

Around midnight, I was awakened by a soft tapping at my door. It was Sophie and Ivan. They slipped into my room and closed the door quietly behind them. "I wanted to talk to you, but not in front of the others," Sophie said. "General Wang sent a message to tell you that your friend will not be able to join you here, because the trains are being carefully scrutinized and it would be dangerous."

But in Sophie and Ivan, General Wang had indeed sent me help, even though his aide had not been able to come. They were full of information, details, names, records, and a map of the black market transport routes. They filled me in on what was happening to the relief flour being rushed to the starving refugees.

Just as with our shipment, the grain was being unloaded from the train near Yueyang, where it went into the depots of the KMT army logistical department. That department was headed by a leading member of the pro-Japanese faction of the KMT who was very powerful in Chiang Kai-shek's camp. Then, it was being shipped by truck across Hunan to Guangdong Province. Sophie and Ivan sketched out the roads. Then the grain was taken to the port of Zhanjiang where it was reloaded onto ships for Hong Kong and Southeast Asia. Once in those refugee-jammed seaports, it was sold at fabulous postwar inflation prices, and sometimes bought back by the same Western relief agencies that had donated it in the first place.

I was shocked and angry, but also exultant. I was going to blow up this entire operation. Just before dawn I went to bed, feeling that my mission had been nearly accomplished.

◆

A few days later, my two companions and I set out southward by jeep. An old Protestant missionary had drawn us a suggested itinerary, which would take us to the city of Hengyang, at the foot of the sacred Buddhist Mount Heng, thence to Qiyang, and finally to Lingling. Along this route, he explained, we would see one of the worst famine districts.

We drove up the dusty road and quickly realized that we were indeed driving into the famine. Bordering either side of the road in thin columns were the refugees, fathers and mothers with babies in their arms, pulling older children along behind them. Elderly peasant women with tiny bound feet hobbled along step after painful step. There were corpses too, lying by the side of the road where they had fallen. It was a horrifying sight.

Following the missionary's instructions, we were heading south, out of Changsha toward Hengyang. The refugees were trudging north. I don't know where they were going, or what they expected to find. Maybe they were heading toward Changsha, hoping that there would be grain or work in the city. At any rate, we never saw anyone heading south.

My companions were wisecracking but it was clear that they were upset. We could barely tell which way to look for the horror of what was before us. Mercifully, most of the refugees ignored us, trudging along like so many faceless ghosts. We tried to separate ourselves from the misery around us, partly to keep our own sanity, and partly because there was nothing we could do.

We drove on in complete silence. Once we got south of Hengyang, things got even worse. The corpses were so numerous that for the rest of the day they were almost never out of our sight. Most of them were very old people, or babies and small children. The road was thick with refugees, who silently parted to let us drive through. There were people with ox carts piled high with their own belongings, or pushing their household goods before them in barrows. I wondered how they went on, carrying such loads with no food in their bellies. The men strained under shoulder poles, the women under the weight of the babies strapped to their backs. I don't know how many people there were—thousands, hundreds of thousands—but they came on and on as if they would never stop.

We reached Qiyang in the afternoon, turning off the highway to thread our way through thousands of refugees into the town square. There they were filling the town, swarming like hornets, barely like human beings. They were desperate and, unlike the others along the road, they were angry. These hollow-eyed people stared straight at us, looking holes through us, surrounding our jeep. They didn't beg for money. They demanded food.

"Yao mi," the shout went up. "Yao mi." We want rice. Give us rice. The crowd took up the cry and surged forward against our jeep. They thrust their bowls up into our faces, the tallest and strongest pushing ahead. "We want rice," they roared together. "We want rice." There was a leper in the crowd who had lost both his arms up to the elbow. Clutching a bowl between his stumps, he held it out toward us.

Behind me in the jeep I heard another scream, closer to me, and in English. The naval officer had suddenly lost control and began to shriek. "Let's get out of here. I can't stand any more of this!" As the crowds pressed forward, he began to cry. "I want to go back to Shanghai. Let me go." He stood up and tried to jump out of the jeep.

The people were pressing so tightly against the jeep that we could barely move. But the driver kept his head and we inched forward. Meanwhile, a passenger I had picked up during one of the ferry rides along our route climbed onto the hood of the jeep. He was a young KMT officer who had told me he secretly sympathized with the Communists. I had asked him to accompany us, and now he was doing yeoman's duty pleading with the crowd to let us past.

We finally made it out of the town and back onto the highway. Once we were safely out of the crowd, the young KMT officer jumped down to scout the area, looking for signs of grain and hoarding. It didn't take long. Within a few minutes he returned, having discovered a full granary within a hundred yards of the starving crowds.

"Why?" I asked.

"They are waiting for prices to go higher before they sell," he replied.

The naval officer was finished as far as this mission went. He was pale and trembling, lying in the back of the jeep and muttering. He tried to get a grip on himself, but there was nothing he could do as long as we were surrounded by refugees and corpses. That evening when we arrived at Lingling, at the southern tip of Hunan, he was still jumpy and upset. He couldn't be calmed. So from the monastery where we were to stay we telephoned back to Changsha to have a jeep sent out to fetch him.

The monastery was run by monks from Austria and sisters from Luxembourg. Supper with them was a bizarre experience. After driving all day between the dead and the living dead, we sat down that night to a hearty meal. There was good red meat, poultry, port wine, and plenty of milk. Most striking in that region of supposedly scarce grain was the thick fragrant homemade bread covered with jam.

The table conversation, too, was curious. Few of the mission's people spoke much English, so the abbot and I conversed in Chinese. His Chinese was excellent. He promised to introduce us the next day to a local philanthropist, General Ou Guan, who was also prefect of this district of southern Hunan. This fine gentleman, the abbot promised me, could give us some insight into the local famine and relief picture.

The next morning, after a similarly hearty breakfast, I asked the abbot how they managed to get such wonderful white bread, way out from nowhere and in terrible famine conditions. "Come, I will show you," the old man said, and he led me downstairs to what looked like a barn door, which he opened.

There, in the dark, windowless room, just under the refectory where we had stuffed ourselves, was a double treadmill, each kept in motion by a little Chinese girl. They were ten or eleven years old, and they were there in the darkness, grinding the flour to bake the mission's bread. Two more girls crouched by the side of the large room, evidently ready to relieve the others when they were too tired to go on. The peasant families, the abbot explained, owed debts to the church, which owned their land, and were satisfying them through the loan of their daughters.

Later that morning, my KMT officer friend give me a shocking report of what he had found out by talking with the townsfolk and their servants. There was plenty of grain all over the region. Cui himself had noted the locations of several full granaries, which we planned to visit in person. The main culprit, the local people had told Cui, was this same General Ou Guan, who was not a benevolent philanthropist as the abbot had averred, but rather a combination of prefect, warlord, and bandit. One of the biggest grain hoarders and profiteers in the region, he seized the relief grain and sold it. Notorious for his callousness in the face of mass suffering, as well as for his cunning, he would ostentatiously give away small portions of his grain and make a great fuss of distributing UNRRA relief flour, to cover for himself.

After breakfast, we paid a call on the general at the prefectural yamen, which was the seat of local government for several counties. We were ushered in with much ceremony to the great man, who proved to be a rotund old codger in an antiquated uniform sporting a wide diagonal sash. As he got to his feet to welcome us, a gout-swollen foot brought a grimace to his face.

The crowds of hangers-on that surrounded the old general began murmuring their praises. "Such a good man," said one old gentleman in a long silk padded gown, wagging his beard. "He gives away everything that comes his way."

"A true living Buddha," said a diminutive man with a wiry mustache and a pointed beard.

Ou Guan himself waved his upraised right hand back and forth in a gesture of self-deprecation. "The common people are suffering," he said, "and the officials who are father and mother to them are grieved at heart because there is so little we can do to help them. We are all hoping and praying that our Great Friend, America, will bestow its favor upon us and send us more food for our people."

We left as quickly as possible and went on to our next meeting, which my KMT friend had arranged. It was at a boys' high school, whose students were mostly children of the gentry. They had more stories than we could have imagined about where the grain was stored and who was profiteering off the famine. What struck me as remarkable was not that they knew so much, because after all it was going on in their own families. It was that they were telling us what they knew.

For more than two millennia, China's Confucian code of education has taught that a dutiful son should lie to protect his father when necessary, just as an obedient vassal should lie for his lord. Now something was breaking through that stern code of ethics. What was it? The students answered this question themselves. "When the Japanese were here," said one, "we longed for the Nationalist government to return. Now we would rather have the Japanese."

"They were foreigners," another chimed in. "These people are supposed to be Chinese, but their own countrymen mean nothing to them. I hate them."

I had seen and heard enough. The following morning my companion and I drove to Changsha and caught a plane back to Shanghai.

CHAPTER THREE

The New Fourth Army

My next assignment, less than a month later, would take me to the areas controlled by the Communists. The UN relief organization was supposed to distribute grain impartially to both the Nationalists and the Communists. I had seen how the KMT handled the famine in areas it controlled; this time my job would be to see how the Communists did it. I was ordered to report to the provincial UNRRA office in Wuhan, and from there to proceed north of the city into the Dabie Mountains. There, I would find the area occupied by the New Fourth Army under the famous guerrilla leader Li Xiannian.

I was delighted with my assignment. At last I would be able to see the Communists in action, in their own territory. But I quickly discovered that, from my boss's point of view, my mission was twofold. It had long been rumored that UNRRA was being used, not just for humanitarian purposes, but for spying. Given the intelligence backgrounds of my partners on my last journey, I had all along suspected the rumors were true. My suspicions were confirmed when the chief observer briefing me on my assignment suddenly adopted a casual, almost diffident style.

He was a recently retired colonel from army intelligence, and, leaning back in his swivel chair with both thumbs hooked in the sides of his vest, he looked as if he had been sent from Central

Casting. If I happened to find out anything about a mutual defense treaty between the Chinese and the Soviets, he said nonchalantly, he would be happy to hear about it. The same went for anything about factional problems among the Communists.

With a gulp, I said that I would do what I could. I parked my conscience behind the word "could." I didn't want to turn him down outright, because I was afraid he would send someone else in my place. But I didn't have the slightest intention of spying for him, or for anyone.

A few days later, I was on another U.S. Navy LST, headed up the Yangtze again. At Wuhan, I met the UN observer I was to replace, a young French engineer who had been in the area for about a month. He was a well-organized, serious sort who gave me a detailed report of his experiences. The Chinese Communists were hardworking, he said, dedicated to their people, free of corruption, very friendly. They wanted peace more than anything else, and welcomed anything the American government could do to prevent civil war—although they were skeptical about our true intentions. "I envy you your first experience up there," he concluded. "It is indeed another world."

"Why don't you stay longer then?" I asked.

"I wouldn't dare," was his surprising reply.

"Why not?"

"Because if you stay there too long, they will make you into a Communist. You cannot resist them."

The area the Communists occupied in among the Dabie Mountains had for centuries played a vital role in Chinese history and politics. Anyone who would control China had first to gain control of the Central Plains, the region that ran from the Dabie Mountains to the Yellow River, and from the Grand Canal to the central Asian escarpment around Xian. These mountains overlooked the trunk rail lines from Beijing to Canton and Shanghai, and all of the principal overland roads, trails, and shipping lanes along the main rivers of central China.

Li Xiannian's Fifth Division of the Communist New Fourth Army sat right in the middle of this strategic area. But the reason wasn't strategic. The Communists had been trapped there by the cease-fire order that General Marshall had negotiated between the Communists and the Nationalists after the Japanese surrender. Li Xiannian had been on the road with sixty thousand men, including ten thousand who were old, sick, or wounded, when the cease-fire was signed. They were heading for the relative safety of the Communists' main forces in Jiangsu. But according to the terms of the agreement no one could move without permission of the cease-fire authorities. Mao had ordered Li Xiannian to obey those orders for the sake of the negotiations. So there Li and his troops sat while the Nationalists drew the noose in tighter and tighter.

Our procession of jeeps carrying in relief goods was the first such delivery since the Communists had become trapped in that area. The Nationalist troops surrounding the Communist forces had tried to prevent relief supplies from reaching their adversaries; but General Marshall, who was trying to negotiate an overall political agreement between the two sides, put his foot down. If grain didn't reach the Communists, he hinted, it might be cut off from the Nationalists as well.

Although we were carrying only a pitifully small load of grain, our party had an almost festive air about it. We knew how hard it had been to get even this pittance into the liberated area. My driver was a middle-aged Wuhan White Russian, who told me he loved to drive to the Communist area. "They treat me so well there. They take care of my vehicle, they get someone to wash and wipe it clean for me, they play cards with me at night. When I go there, I'm somebody."

We wound our way through the twists and turns of Hubei Province, heading for the foothills of the mountains. After about four hours, we crossed a creek, bouncing over the stepping stones laid down for foot travelers. The driver turned to me and said, "At the top of the next ridge, you will see the New Fourth Army scouts." We swept up the incline and there they were near the peak. Two young boys in blue-gray homespun uniforms, each with a clumsy 3.8 Japanese rifle slung over his shoulder. They seemed hardly any higher than the rifles. They wore shoes made of tree bark fibers, and caps with limp cloth peaks. I waved at them vigorously and they waved back.

Suddenly I felt proud and happy for them. I felt sure these young boys weren't like the swaggering soldiers of Kunming or Shanghai, or like the callous troops I had seen on my last trip to the famine area. These weren't petty tyrants who would kill their fellows over a pack of cigarettes. This was a people's army, and these were peasant boys armed to fight their own battle for their own futures and their own families.

While under encirclement, Li Xiannian's Fifth Division had set up its headquarters at Xuanhuadian, whose ancient name had been Xianhuadian, Fresh Flower Village, a town with one cobblestoned street just wide enough for four to walk abreast, and a maze of alleys crisscrossing it. A reception party was waiting for us.

"We are having a meeting to commemorate the April Eighth Martyrs," the official greeter told me. "You're going to sit on the platform." I guessed he was referring to some Communist leaders who had been killed a few days earlier in a plane crash. We crossed a small river on a long one-plank bridge, and arrived at a flat arena on the other bank where a wooden platform had been built. About a dozen figures clad in blue-gray uniforms were on the platform, and thousands of soldiers and civilians were gathered in the arena before them.

The memorial addresses were already in progress. As the speeches extolling the bravery and heroism of the dead comrades rolled on, my eyes swept over my fellow dignitaries on the platform. I was trying to identify the famous guerrilla general Li Xiannian, who was the commander of all these troops. I narrowed the choices down to a few, based on their military bearing, their air of authority, and the character and intellect I saw reflected in their faces.

All my choices were wrong. When Li Xiannian rose to speak, I recognized him as one I had immediately skipped over. He was a thin, tired-looking, carelessly dressed man with a look that was both quizzical and bored. I knew that Li Xiannian had begun life as a carpenter's apprentice and then ran off to join the Chinese Red Army when it came to his village. But I had not expected to see someone whose appearance reminded me quite so much of the gaunt plainness of Abraham Lincoln.

I soon discovered that here in the liberated areas there were none of the luxuries or excesses that had so repelled me on my last trip. As soon as I settled into my quarters, a dilapidated old schoolhouse that had been converted into a hostel, my interpreter led me around to meet with the senior Communist leaders. I was introduced to Li Xiannian in his quarters, which were nearly as simple as mine: he lived in a one-story adobe-and-stone house on the main village street. A cloth hanging in the entryway took the place of a door. Inside was a sitting room, which had a few straight-backed chairs against the wall.

General Wang Zhen, who had helped me with my earlier mission, was back at his job as deputy commander to Li Xiannian and commander of his own troops fighting the Nationalists. When we met, he threw his arms around me like a brother and invited me back to his headquarters. His adjutant was waiting with his supper —a large bowl of steamed rice, tea in a pewter cup, and a little saucer with a tiny bit of chicken and chopped red chili pepper.

Pointing at the chicken and chilies, Wang grinned and said, "This is really graft. My troops are always buying chicken and fish for me from the peasants. I keep telling them not to, but they don't listen. We are not like the mercenary KMT army. Our men are all volunteers, and they are fighting for themselves. We think and feel together. The peasants in this area are very poor," General Wang continued. "And this is a year of famine. We cannot increase the burdens they carry on their backs. Our troops are living on two meals a day, both of them nothing but porridge. I am a member of the Central Committee, and the leadership takes care of me so that I get enough nourishment to be able to lead. I don't accept it unless it is absolutely necessary."

I couldn't help comparing General Wang to the abbot in Ling-ling who had served me an elegant meal with red wine and soft white bread baked with flour ground by young girls walking on a treadmill. "How can your troops march and fight on nothing but thin porridge?" I asked.

"The Chinese Revolution is full of hardship and suffering," Wang replied. "We have been through more repression and betrayal than any revolutionary movement in the world. Our spirit is, 'Others rush forward when we fall in the ranks,' and we are not afraid to die for our ideals."

He spoke without flair or bombast. This man is no harebrained fanatic, I thought. He is a soldier dedicated to his cause, ready to die at any minute for what he believes in. The thought made me proud.

When he had finished eating, we walked out into the night air again and strolled along by the riverside. General Wang was in a mellow, reflective mood. "When I first applied for admission to the Communist Youth League in Hunan," he told me, "they wouldn't take me because they said I was antiforeign. They told me that it was only foreign capitalists and landlords who were our enemies. Working people all over the world are our friends. I couldn't understand it, though, because I hated those men and their dogs so much and I didn't understand politics."

"Which men and which dogs?" I asked.

"When I was around ten years old, I worked as a servant to a British railway boss in Hunan. I had to empty the chamber pot for him and his snobbish wife every day, sweep up and clean for them, wash their clothes, and help the cooks. They had a little pet dog that they treated much better than any Chinese. I really hated that dog. One day, when things were so bad that I couldn't stand the oppression and humiliation anymore, I killed the dog, ran off, and joined the Red Army. But at that time, I did not understand Communism and internationalism. I was really antiforeign."

We walked on in silence for a moment. Then suddenly he grabbed me by the hand. "You see," he said, "now I have learned. Now I have a friend who is a foreigner, an American—but not an American imperialist. Me, a Chinese peasant, I have my own American friend. Isn't that something?"

Nowhere I looked could I find any evidence of corruption. In fact, the first grain distribution I observed seemed a model of fairness and democracy.

I made my own way to the grain distribution area on foot, setting out at dawn accompanied only by an interpreter who had once worked at the Ford Motor Company in Detroit. We marched nearly all day, heading for Dingyuandian, across the northern border into Henan Province. It was some of the poorest country I had seen in China, much poorer than the lush rice paddy country the Nationalists held. Yet this was the only part of China I had been in where I saw no corpses. Not only no corpses, but no prostitutes. I didn't even see any beggars. Once in Fresh Flower Village an old woman came up to me with an alms bowl and my interpreter quickly ushered her away. "This is no way to handle your problem," he said, nonetheless fishing in his pocket for a bit of change. "Go to the border region government and ask for relief. We will help you."

My interpreter and I arrived in Dingyuandian late in the afternoon. The village was little more than a cluster of mud-brick huts, interspersed with some two-story stone buildings arranged around a cobblestoned main lane. The next morning, village officials led us to the town square, on one side of the main lane, where a temple to the local deities had been erected. The temple was on a raised platform, and the shrine had a roof nearly six feet high, with flying eaves and gargoyles.

The villagers were already assembling for the grain distribution. The village head, a rail-thin peasant who looked around thirty-five, called the meeting to order and introduced a young student, a girl who had come from a Communist organization in Wuhan for cadre training with the New Fourth Army, and who was to take charge of the distribution. She rose to speak. There were about fifty tons of grain to be distributed among the families of the area, she said, and then she declared the rules: The grain was to be distributed according to need. Each family would describe its own situation and make a request. Then family and friends would discuss it and a list would be drawn up of allotments, which would be posted in the village square. Anyone found guilty of graft, corruption, nepotism, favoritism, or black marketeering in connection with the relief goods, she warned sternly, would be "severely punished without fail."

Then the meeting began, and pandemonium broke loose. Everybody started to talk at once. Some shouted louder than others. I could hear their voices rising over the din. But despite the chaos, the job was getting done. The meeting ran until almost sundown, and the next morning the flour was delivered to the recipients' doors by students who carried it on their backs. It was the only relief flour I ever saw actually reaching hungry people in China. There was no sign of corruption, and from the way the cadres were scrimping to lighten the burden of the people, I felt certain that there was none. My job done, my interpreter and I trekked back to Fresh Flower Village that afternoon to find the whole town in an uproar. People couldn't wait to tell me the news: Zhou Enlai himself was coming!

At war's end, the Nationalists held the cities but the northern and western countryside belonged to the Communists. They were hulking in the mountains and prairies. They held sway in between the railroad lines and the trunk highways of north and central China in vast areas on both sides of the Great Wall, from the ocean to the great northwest, from the Soviet border to the Yangtze River. While the Nationalists staked their future on massive American aid, Mao Zedong and his Communists were battling for Chinese public opinion, and the goodwill of the peasants, workers, and small merchants.

The Americans had placed themselves uncertainly in the middle. The truce team led by General Marshall was trying both to support Chiang Kai-shek and to lead the two sides to a peaceful political settlement. The Americans hoped that a coalition government could be formed under the KMT, and civil war could be averted.

The situation in Fresh Flower Village was critical. With the growing danger of all-out hostilities there, it had become the focal point for the whole country. Despite the cease-fire, the Communists had no intention of waiting to be wiped out crammed into this tiny rural area, surrounded on all sides by increasing numbers of enemy forces. The KMT, for its part, didn't want them there either, where they could threaten Wuhan and even the approaches to the capital at Nanjing. Still, they had no intention of letting the Communists break through to rejoin their headquarters forces and regroup for further resistance. But if an all-out battle began in this strategic region, it would engulf the entire nation.

So as part of the Marshall mission, a special truce delegation had been formed to meet in Fresh Flower Village to try to find a peaceful solution. The first meetings were about to begin, headed by General Henry Byroade, General Marshall's aide. The KMT side was represented by General Wang Tianming, deputy commander of one of Generalissimo Chiang Kai-shek's field headquarters.

As vice chairman of the Chinese Communist Party's Revolutionary Military Commission, Zhou Enlai outranked them both. Still, I was told excitedly, he had decided to come in person to meet with his comrades here, and to show his concern for the hardships they were enduring.

Everyone went to the outskirts of the village at twilight to meet Zhou Enlai. As luck would have it, I wasn't there when he arrived. I was in the latrine. I had returned to my quarters for a moment and had stopped off at a public urinal on my way back. In the brief time I was gone, the entire party had arrived, been greeted, and had dispersed. I was still in the public toilet, buttoning up and preparing to leave when in strode an American brigadier general.

"You must be General Byroade," I said.

"That's right," he said, shaking hands crisply. "And what are you doing here?"

"I'm an UNRRA relief observer," I answered, showing him my UN credentials. "I'm also the only American anywhere around these parts."

He nodded his head sympathetically. He seemed to be encouraging me to continue, so I did. "I certainly would appreciate it if you could tell me what's going to happen in this area," I said. "I'm here with all these relief supplies, and I don't know whether to get ready to leave in a hurry, or to bring in more supplies, or what."

The general's jaw seemed to set. "I can tell you what's going to happen," he said. "These people are going to be wiped out. I have just come back from Manchuria. The Reds outnumber the government forces ten to one up there. The government can't win. But here the government has the upper hand and we're going to let them wipe the Communists out."

With that, he walked away and left me standing there in shock. Was this whole exercise a hoax? Had this American general been sent not to negotiate peace, but to lull the Communists into a false sense of security? It seemed hard to believe, but given what I had just heard from Marshall's chief aide, that's how it appeared to me.

I was horrified. Our government was deceiving the American people, I thought. I felt they were being treacherous to both Americans and Chinese. This wasn't American policy. It didn't represent the will of the American people. On the contrary, it was a duplicity being carried out behind their backs. Worse, I began to see my own role in a new light. Suppose Marshall's insistence that relief flour be sent to Fresh Flower Village was yet another piece in the conspiracy, a plot to lull the New Fourth Army out of its usual vigilance and allow enough time for the KMT to strike. I felt gullible, and manipulated.

I saw this as a war between the oppressors of the half-starved workers, beggars, and prostitutes in Shanghai on one side, and the clean-living revolutionaries of Fresh Flower Village on the other. How could my government, which pretended to be a neutral force, range itself squarely on the side of the evildoers? How could it cash in on its reputation for fairness and democracy by deceiving the Chinese Communists? It seemed contemptible to me. And I felt I had a special duty as a decent American to take a stand.

There in the latrine in Fresh Flower Village, I came to a kind of turning point all my own. I made up my mind that the only way I could help the Chinese people, and even the American people— who I believed would countenance no such duplicity if they knew of it—was to tell General Li Xiannian himself about the American government's intentions. Thus forewarned, he could protect himself against this treachery.

When darkness fell, I was escorted to the first meeting of the negotiating team in the Cao family ancestral temple, the biggest building in the village. In earlier times, the windowless building festooned with gargoyles had been used to hold the clan meetings of the Cao family. At the very front of the hall, three or four tables had been pushed together to form one long rostrum. Behind that sat the speakers. Before them were a half dozen tiny saucers filled with bean oil and lighted with a twisted cotton wick. Those flick-

THE NEW FOURTH ARMY 63

ering flames gave the only light in the darkened hall. I sat far in the back.

The Communists were seated at the left of the rostrum: the political commissar, Zheng Weisan, and the commanding general, Li Xiannian, together with General Wang Zhen. Byroade and the Nationalist representative, Wang Tianming, sat further to the right. In the center sat a handsome figure in the uniform of a KMT general. With a shock, I realized that it was the legendary Zhou Enlai. For purposes of the negotiations both sides wore KMT national uniforms. Even in the dark, I could see the shadow of a beard, too deeply entrenched to be threatened by a razor. This feature, unusual in a Chinese, had earned Zhou the nickname "Hu Gong," the bearded one.

First Li Xiannian spoke, stressing the dedication of the Chinese Communist Party to a peaceful political solution to China's disputes. KMT General Wang Tianming, for his part, was all indignation. He was a tall, balding, owlish-looking man with a long oval face and large bland eyes that looked out from behind a pair of scholarly old-fashioned spectacles. "Why, who on earth could it be that has a conspiracy to encircle and destroy the New Fourth Army troops?" he asked. "Certainly not the Nationalist army! The New Fourth Army are our own Chinese brothers. We fought the Japanese together and together we will work out solutions to our problems."

General Byroade sounded quite different in public from the grim-faced man who had spoken to me barely an hour earlier in the public latrine. The United States was here to help the two sides seek a political solution to their conflict and prevent civil war, he said.

But it was Zhou Enlai who held the meeting entranced with the simplicity of his speech. He was not just a member of the truce team, he told the audience. He was their comrade. As such, he shared their cares and suffering, and he vowed not to rest until they were safely out of the encirclement and the danger of attack.

The meeting over, I wended my way with the others toward the single-plank bridge leading across the river to our hostel. There, I ran into a small party carrying lanterns. It was Zhou Enlai, being escorted back to his quarters by General Li Xiannian. Li immediately came forward and introduced me to Zhou. "This is our American friend, Li Dunbai."

Zhou shook hands with a tight but unaffected grasp. Still gripping my hand, he said, "I saw you at the meeting. You applauded much more loudly when I spoke than when anyone else spoke. That is unwise. They will notice your reactions, and it will not be easy for you to work when you go back to the KMT areas. You should be more prudent."

I was dumbfounded. First, at being greeted so informally by this world figure I was meeting for the first time. And second by his perception. How on earth could he have seen me in that dark hall, and what made him pay that much note to one stray American? I asked him.

"It's our job to take care of our international friends," he answered. Although he was in his late forties, he looked young and dashing in his starched uniform. We walked along the path to the hostel together, picking our way carefully over the one-planked bridge in dim lantern light.

"I would like to be more useful," I told him. "I have offered to help in the work here, but they won't let me stay with them because they may have to break out of the encirclement and they don't want to take me with them."

Zhou suggested I call on him in Nanjing.

As we walked along, I passed on to General Li what I had heard from General Byroade. I told him everything Byroade had said, along with my interpretation. Li listened in silence. I had no idea what he was thinking.

After Zhou Enlai left, the meetings of the truce team didn't go well. The American representative was a colonel from General Marshall's Nanjing headquarters. Large-framed and raw-boned, the colonel was a straitlaced army man, honest, but with little experience in China. The KMT representative was Colonel Chen Qian, commander of the public safety headquarters. The Chinese Communist representative had not yet arrived, so my old friend General Wang Zhen filled in for him.

Even before any negotiations could begin, the meeting broke down in bickering. Each side claimed the other side's interpreter was a spy. Their argument proved fateful for me. The American colonel wouldn't stand for a lot of nonsense. He had brought no interpreter, and he himself spoke no Chinese. But he did have a solution. "Okay, okay," he said. "We can't spend all day just on interpreters. Here's what we are going to do. We have a neutral person here, a representative of the United Nations. He knows Chinese and I'm going to ask him to act as interpreter for all three sides while you two are straightening out your own interpreter problems."

His motion carried, for lack of an alternative, and I was invited to join the meeting. I accepted with trepidation. My Chinese at that point was conversational, but limited, and I had to struggle to understand the Hubei and Hunan accents around me. But I couldn't help being excited at the thought of being part of the truce talks.

The first meeting was pure comic opera. I sat with the three representatives and the two disqualified interpreters to monitor my translation. The American colonel opened the proceedings. The area around Fresh Flower Village was to be stabilized, he said. Waving a sheaf of papers, he declared that the truce team had received numerous complaints of violations, and he intended to investigate them one by one.

Colonel Chen took the floor for the Nationalists and thanked the American government for its good offices toward peace. "Unfortunately," he said, quoting an ancient Chinese phrase, "peace is being violated by those who fear nothing but the absence of chaos. The Nationalist government has thus far been extremely patient, not returning fire when fired on, and giving up ground wherever necessary to maintain the peace." He then went on to read a series of specific complaints. New Fourth Army snipers had fired on peaceful government troops at such-and-such a time and place; Fifth Division forces had attacked a certain hill, and the government lines had fallen back voluntarily to yield the hill . . .

Suddenly a gnarled hand crashed down on the little table clattering the cups and the teapot. "Malagebi!" roared General Wang. The phrase roughly translates as "Rape your mother." I chose "Son of a bitch" instead.

"I cannot bear to sit here and listen to any more of this 'lan yan' from the KMT representative," General Wang thundered in the thickest of Hunan dialects, more pronounced than ever when he was agitated.

"What's 'lan yan'?" I whispered to him in desperation. I wasn't anxious to advertise the limitations of my Chinese.

"Just say, 'hu shuo,' " General Wang replied directly to me with a calm and courtesy that belied his histrionics.

"I cannot sit here and listen to . . . this . . . this nonsense," I translated. "Lan yan," it appeared, was simply a more archaic term for the same thing. My exercise in linguistics proved futile because before anyone could say any more, General Wang pushed the table over and stalked out of the room, thus abruptly adjourning the meeting. Of course we had to report the incident to Li Xiannian. The American colonel was not going to stand for such disruptions in his business. I accompanied the colonel to Li's headquarters to act as his interpreter.

General Li listened to the colonel's report and smiled, a bit sadly, I thought. "Anyway," he said, "our representative, Colonel Ren Shishun, arrives tomorrow, so the team can continue its work. Colonel Ren has a very cool head; you should have no problem working with him."

This problem settled, General Li began to muse out loud a bit. "I hope with all my heart that the truce talks will succeed," he told the American. "Our people have suffered through war after war, ever since the First Opium War in 1839. The warlords all but destroyed our country with their constant battle until the Japanese took advantage of our inner weakness and division to trample over the richest parts of China. Now, at last, we have won the war, together with our allies, and we have a chance at peace to bury our dead, heal our wounds, and set to work rebuilding our country. Please understand that we want to be friends with the United States. We are Chinese Communists; we have our differences with our Soviet comrades, and we do not wish to be friends of theirs alone."

I deeply believed what General Li was saying. And despite my misgivings about General Byroade, I couldn't help feeling proud of this American colonel, who took his mission seriously and, I felt, was as in the dark as any about the hidden agenda he was abetting.

As for myself, for the first time in years I was feeling a clear sense of purpose. I was at a turning point of history, a meeting at which each side could express its most profound feelings and intentions and I was a player. It wasn't just a matter of translating their words, I thought. It was more. I could be a good, clear line of communication across which these people with vastly different backgrounds and cultures could talk to each other. I could help them understand, not just the letters and the words, but the flavor, the nuances, the emotions encased in them. I could help them bypass roadblocks, move away obstacles, and open the way to understanding and cooperation. I saw that I could excel in that, and I knew at last what I wanted to do.

I hadn't forgotten my original plan to go on to Yanan, to meet Chairman Mao and the Chinese Communist leadership. But here I was at a place where history was being made. The negotiations on both sides needed the work that I could do; they had no one else who could help them. Every time I got a chance, I asked if I could stay. Every time, they turned me down.

Eventually, my UNRRA work completed, I returned discouraged to Shanghai. Still, I was hoping that I could continue working with the United Nations until an opportunity to get to Yanan presented itself. I wrote my report to UNRRA and handed it in, stressing the contrast between my first tour of Hunan and the second mission into the New Fourth Army area. As far as relief work was concerned, the difference was like night and day.

A few days later, one of the vice directors of UNRRA invited me to his hotel room for a talk. He was friendly and effusive, mentioning friends we had in common and praising my investigations. They liked my work, he said, and found the two reports I had handed in thorough and complete. "We notice you like working in the Communist areas," he said. I nodded, and he continued. As a reward for my good work, I was going to be promoted—two grades at one leap. And, he added, I was to be sent into Manchuria, where the Communists were the strongest. He was sure I would be pleased.

I was. Very. But not for long.

There were, however, a couple of favors they would like to ask, he said with studied nonchalance. They were just little things, so he was sure it wouldn't be a problem for me.

First they wanted me to change my Hunan report. Nothing significant, he said, but just enough to make it more "diplomatic." For one thing, he wanted me to delete evidence I had uncovered that an American official had raped his Chinese secretary. And second, there was the matter of my pay. I had never drawn down my per diem from UNRRA, and the officials there wondered why.

I was earning around $600 a month, a whacking good salary for a young single American in China. In addition, the job offered free housing, food, transportation, and supplies. The per diem for field workers was $16—enough to feed scores of Chinese families. At that time when corpses were jamming the streets and roads, I had no intention of taking money that could better be used to feed the Chinese, and I told him so.

"That's what we thought," he said indulgently. "We admire your idealism, but we want to call your attention to the fact that this makes things difficult for the others. When the auditors come from New York, they want to know why some people get along without their per diem. So we'd like to ask you to collect yours."

I got up and walked out of the room, leaving the door open.

It appeared to be the end of my China adventure. I was frustrated and unhappy. The Communists didn't want me in Fresh Flower Village. And despite my friends' encouragement, Yanan seemed completely inaccessible. Now my bosses had proved more interested in collecting information about the Communists and protecting their salaries than in doing their work fairly and justly. I was discouraged and wanted to leave. But when I went to say goodbye to Xu Maijin, Cynthia Li, and Madame Sun Yat-sen, they urged me not to go right away. "At least say goodbye to Zhou Enlai before you leave for America," Cynthia and Madame Sun argued.

I didn't need much more encouragement to call on the charismatic Zhou one more time. After all, when we met in Fresh Flower Village, had he not asked me to do so? So the following Sunday I took a flight to Nanjing and made my way to the New Plum Garden Village where the Communist villa was located in a pretty little enclave of brick-and-stucco homes surrounded by modest grounds and gardens. It was nearly nine in the morning when I knocked on the door. Zhang Wenjin, Zhou's young secretary, opened it. I had met him in Fresh Flower Village and liked him immediately.

"I've come to say goodbye to Zhou Enlai," I said as we shook hands warmly.

Zhang smiled. "He isn't up yet."

"What time did he go to bed last night?" I asked.

"Around five. His usual hour."

"And when does he get up?"

"At nine."

"You mean he only gets four hours sleep a night?"

"Sometimes less. He has too much to do, too much on his mind. But come back at nine. I'm sure he'd like to have breakfast with you."

"But you can't let him overdo it like that. You should make him go to bed earlier."

Zhang met my suggestion with an indulgent smile. "No one can make him do anything," he said. "He has everything on his shoulders here. Everything. He is conscientious, and he must take care of many different things at one time."

I left and wandered around until after nine. When I returned, Zhang was beaming. "Come in," he said. "They're just sitting down to breakfast."

He ushered me into the dining room where Zhou was eating

breakfast with his wife, Deng Yingchao, and a number of party officials. Deng Yingchao handed me a beautiful little red apple. "This was grown in one of our liberated areas in Shandong," she said.

They cleared a place for me next to Zhou and I joined in the breakfast. Politely, I recalled our last meeting, remarked on his health, and expressed my concern about his overwork. He brushed aside my remarks. "I know how to steal leisure from business," he said.

I told him I was leaving China but he would have none of it. "You should go to Yanan before you go home," he said. "You should meet Chairman Mao and talk with him. You should see our old liberated areas where we've had time to do some construction. Fresh Flower Village was only a temporary situation. Then you'll have more to talk about and write about when you go back to America."

Zhou suggested a way I could get to Yanan, by tagging along with Mildred Price, a representative of a New York–based relief organization. She was due to leave shortly.

I reminded Zhou that I was interested in much more than just a visit to Yanan. I wanted to become a part of their work. "I could help with the English language program, for instance," I said.

"Time enough to discuss that when you get there," Zhou replied, and then turned his attention to other matters.

◆

It was four long months before I got to Yanan.

As Zhou Enlai had suggested, I teamed up with Mildred Price and became a field representative for United China Relief. Together, we made our way up to Beijing intending to fly from there into Yanan on the U.S. Army military transport. The army ran a weekly shuttle to all the places where truce talks were being held. Any American with a good reason—and relief work was reason enough—could hitch a ride for no charge. There was no other realistic way in. The civil war was intensifying and the vast territory between Beijing and Yanan was laced with battle lines.

We applied for our seats on the transport, but only Mildred was accepted. I was told privately that the American Truce Commissioner, Walter Robinson, had himself overruled my using the plane. I appealed to him personally, but to no avail. Because I was traveling at Zhou Enlai's suggestion, Mildred and I sought out General Ye Jianying, the Communist armies' chief of staff and chief party representative in Beijing. In an unusual move, the general himself went to Robinson's office. He too was turned down. It was the first time an American citizen had been refused a seat on the Yanan shuttle, and no one could tell me why. I felt my hopes finally were dashed. That night Mildred and I dined with General Ye in the garden of his villa. To salve my disappointment, he offered me a plan. Rather then going to Yanan, I should go to Kalgan, a Communist-held city on the Inner Mongolian border. There, he promised, I would be treated as a honored guest.

Kalgan was to the north and slightly to the west of Beijing, at a pass in the Great Wall. When the Japanese surrendered, the Communist Eighth Route Army had snatched Kalgan out of Japanese hands and made it their north China capital. It was the only city the Communists held outside of Manchuria. The area was used as a training ground for cadres, and as communications and supply center for people traveling between Manchuria and Yanan.

I traveled to Kalgan and discovered it wasn't at all like the Communists' temporary encampment under siege in Fresh Flower Village. This was a city, and a fairly good-sized one at that. Briskly, I set about seeing everything there was to see. I visited a tobacco plant, a university, and a hospital. I reviewed the publications the Communists put out for women and for young people. I told the tobacco workers how lucky they were to be working in their own plant for their own benefit. I told the students how lucky they were to be living under a real people's government. I told the artists how lucky they were to have the freedom to pursue their own art.

As I had hoped, at the end of a week, the Communists asked me to stay and work in Kalgan. Wary of depending too much on Moscow, they saw America as their preferred source of postwar aid. General Nie Rongzhen, the area commander, told me that Mao wanted loans from America to rebuild the country after the Communists won the war. They were setting up an English language radio station to take their case directly to the American people. They had no native speaker of English who could correct the grammar and style and help out with the broadcasts. I got the job.

I moved into a house once occupied by a Japanese family and settled into a life of translating and correcting scripts and training broadcasters. I made friends and attended study sessions. I roamed the countryside. I was happy to be working in Kalgan alongside my new Communist comrades, but I never stopped thinking about my plan to get into Yanan.

Ironically, it was the KMT, and not the Communists, who got me there.

One evening in September, the famous one-armed General Cai Shufan, a former coal miner who was chief of the army political department in Kalgan, came to see me in great agitation. The KMT had broken through Communist lines to the north in Zhangbei, he said, and were pressing their attacks toward Kalgan. He asked me to meet immediately with General Nie Rongzhen, the supreme commander and political commissar of the whole area.

I found General Nie sitting at his desk, with two sets of field telephones attached to the wall at his side and a huge porcelain-enamel teacup in front of him, from which he gulped down strong tea. I didn't have to be told that he was suffering from severe influenza. His red face and swollen nose attested to that.

"You must leave right away for Yanan," he said. "We want you to resume your voice broadcast work there. We must discontinue it here. The enemy is already using his American planes to bomb our radio station. I will write you a pass that will take you through our lines to Yanan and get you any help you may need along the way. Good luck!"

So I set off at last for Yanan.

For a month and a half I traveled, through Hebei Province, through Shanxi, Shaanxi, Suiyuan, and Chahar. For most of the way I went on foot, covering fifteen miles a day through the mountainous terrain, a mule cart carrying radio and printing equipment clattering along behind me. Sometimes I went by mule, horse, or in a captured Japanese army truck.

On the road, I ate Shanxi noodles steeped in soup and strong vinegar. I slept on a kang, the brick oven-bed of north and west China. I passed through Yuxian County, where the coal was so pure it could be lit like a candle. As I crossed a mountain ridge straddled by the Great Wall, local peasants pointed with pride to the spot where the famous General Lin Biao had defeated the Japanese and had been wounded. I visited a university where the president's chief claim to fame was that he had once been criticized by the great author Lu Xun.

Sometimes I had only a single companion. At other times we joined forces for a few days with groups making similar pilgrimages. I shared a captured Japanese army truck with the literary critic Zhou Yang; with Han Xu, a big-city youth; with Little Zhao, the son of General Zhao Shoushan, who was a secretly pro-Communist commander of the KMT Northwest Army; and with C. Y. W. Meng, a distinguished economist and newspaper man. At one point I traveled alongside Judge Chen Jingkun and his family. Chen had been Mao's high school teacher. He had risen to the head of Beijing's Superior Court, but had become disgusted with KMT corruption. One day he took his entire family for an outing in Beijing's western hills and disappeared.

It was a sobering journey, cutting as it did through territory that was under heavy attack by the Nationalists. But along the way, I felt myself drawn more and more into this strange and wonderful country that was undergoing such a radical transformation. On the final leg of our journey, we were given horses by the renowned General He Long for the ride to the Yellow River crossing, which would take us into Shaanxi Province and then into Yanan. When we arrived at a troop hostel that night, I discovered that the bag I had tied to my saddle had dropped off. Inside the tiny blue satchel were my toothbrush, some tooth powder, some soap—and my U.S. passport. The commander at the hostel sent men out combing the roadway, but I never found it again. I had accidentally shed the last of my belongings—and my last official tie to the outside world.

Two nights later, on October 19, 1946, we arrived in Yanan. It was a Saturday night. As I had been told what seemed like eons ago in Kunming, everyone was heading for the weekly dance. It was held in a stone building, long and low. I could hear a string bass, a couple of fiddles, and maybe a saxophone and a clarinet tooting away inside. The dim lights from the windows seemed blazing in the absolute darkness surrounding us. Someone pushed open the door and I peeped inside. There directly across the room from the door I saw a life-sized portrait of Chairman Mao Zedong. I recognized immediately the wide forehead and brow, and the tiny, almost feminine mouth. Framed by the doorway against the whitewashed walls the leonine head looked stern, almost baleful.

The tableau lasted for only a split second. For as I gazed, the band struck up a foxtrot and the portrait came to life, turned, gestured to his partner and began gliding across the dance floor.

In Mao's Caves

I felt a strange exultation.

Everything around me seemed clean and pure. The people. Their clothes. The building. The music. Even the fierce winds and bleak landscape of Yanan seemed unsullied to me. I was in a place far from the naked greed and corruption I had already seen too much of.

But as I watched Mao Zedong circle the room with his tiny dancing partner, I felt that here in Yanan was something even more. Yanan was not just a place where people were trying to live virtuous lives. It was the crucible in which the New China would be forged, and with it, the new world.

It was to Yanan that Mao Zedong had fled the Nationalists in the mid-1930s, leading his troops on the Long March. It was in Yanan that Mao had formed his famous Eighth Route Army. It was from Yanan that he had directed the military counteroffensive that had helped rid the country of the Japanese. It was in Yanan that he was struggling for survival in a bitter war with the Nationalists.

And it was here, in this wasteland perched on the edge of China's great northwestern grasslands, in a place once overrun by Mongols and Huns, that a band of dedicated and loyal intellectuals, students, scholars, artists, and economists were gathered to plan a new economy, a new literature, a new government, a new society. Here they had founded their arts academy, their newspapers and radio stations, their schools. As an observer for the United Nations in Fresh Flower Village, I had admired these Chinese Communists. In Kalgan, I had assisted them. But here in Yanan, I hoped I could do more. I hoped I could become one of them.

I stepped over the threshold onto the dance floor.

When Mao Zedong saw me, he stopped dancing and stood expectantly in the center of the long, low room. Following his gaze, everyone fell silent, and I was led across the floor for the formal introduction.

Mao took my hand in his. His grasp was firm, but he didn't really shake hands. There was no pumping, no spontaneous movement. He smiled faintly and bent slightly toward me. "We are happy to welcome an American comrade here to take part in our work."

The band struck up "Turkey in the Straw." Mao noted my startled expression. "Some American comrades taught us that song," he said with amusement. He led me over to the row of chairs that ringed the dance floor and we sat down.

"During the war with Japan, there were people who laughed at us," Mao said. "All we have is millet and old-fashioned rifles, they said, and that was true. But we used millet and old-fashioned rifles to defeat the Japanese. You'll find life very bare and simple in Yanan."

"That's fine with me."

"Your Chinese is very good. I have been trying to learn English for quite a while, but it is very hard for me."

"If I can be of any help in your studies, I'd be glad to try."

I could scarcely believe my good fortune. This was the Mao Zedong I had been reading about in the daily press, the Mao whose words I had studied in Stanford. I respected his vision for China and admired his philosophical brilliance. And here I was, twenty-five years old, bedraggled and tired from my five-hundred-mile walk, sitting and chatting with Mao Zedong as an equal. Only chatting wasn't exactly the right word. Mao had a way of focusing his gaze squarely on whoever was speaking, shutting out the rest of the room. The attention was intense and flattering.

One by one, other senior party leaders began entering the hall. A large-framed, chubby man, clearly much older than Mao, appeared and stood just inside the doorway removing his army great-coat. "Ah, Commander-in-Chief Zhu De is here," exclaimed Mao, slowly getting to his feet to greet the general, ostentatiously show-ing me his respect for his elder, but distinctly junior, colleague.

Zhu De sat down on my right side, so that I was between him and Mao. His face was weathered and deeply lined, and the smile that flashed frequently across his face had been etched in by age so that its lines were visible even when he was not smiling. While Mao was an eerie replica of his own political portraits, Zhu looked considerably older than his. Yet he seemed earthy and full of fun. "Have you had lice yet?" he politely inquired of me. "You can't be a real revolutionary unless you've had lice." He chortled. It was clearly one of his favorite jokes.

Zhu De was soon whirled away from me by a partner. He had a remarkably merry step and was obviously happy on the dance floor. Zhu De's wife, Kang Keching, leaned toward me. "He's a real activist at dancing," she said good-naturedly. "He never misses a number if he can help it."

"You know," I told her, "when I was in Kunming, there was a man who used to tell me stories about the marvelous exploits of Zhu Mao, as if he was one great man, not two."

She laughed. "You should come and visit us. We are organizing the women to spin, knit, and to do washing for the sick and wounded. You should see how eager and skillful the women of Yanan are. They're not content to sit around at home and do nothing but cook and tend the baby."

The band forged its way through the rest of its American rep-ertory, songs like "Red River Valley," "Swanee River," "My Old Kentucky Home," "Old Black Joe," "You Are My Sunshine," and a few Chinese revolutionary airs like the "March of the New Democratic Youth" and "Song of the Guerrillas."

The hall buzzed with activity as the soldiers, strategists, nurses, doctors, editors, translators, commanders, political officers, and theoreticians—everyone swirled around the floor together, the most senior officials dancing about with the most junior clerks. Suddenly, there was a commotion at the door and in swept a woman in an army greatcoat. She might have been pretty but for her scowl. "That's Jiang Qing, Mao's wife," someone at my side whispered. The word he used was "lover," the usual Communist term for spouse. "She's a tough one," my neighbor continued. "You don't ever want to cross her."

I stared at the slender young woman. She appeared to be in her early thirties, more than twenty years younger than Mao. "She doesn't look tough," I said.

"People often make that mistake," my neighbor said with a knowing grin. "She's only the Chairman's personal secretary. But anyone who wants to get in to see him has to go through her."

I was curious to meet her, so when the band began its next number, I introduced myself and asked her to dance. She was courteous and made me feel welcome. She was quiet, almost retiring, and I was hard pressed to see any toughness. In fact, she seemed preoccupied with her own frailty. "I am not in very strong health," she volunteered as we danced. "I have a weak stomach." A few minutes later, she complained about shortness of breath. "I get heart palpitations," she said, briefly disengaging her hand from mine, to lay it across her chest. Then she told me about her experimental movie group and invited me to visit them at my leisure, to see some of their work.

I spent the night in a nearby guest house. The next morning, Mao himself dropped me off at my new home. Mao and his old teacher, Xu Teli, picked me up in one of Yanan's two jeeps that they were using to drive to a meeting. Their route took them along the river, right past the path that led to the place where I would live and work.

The village of Yanan scarcely existed anymore since the Japanese had bombed it so viciously a few years back. The real life in Yanan took place in caves carved into the mountainsides. At every curve in the canyon, there was a little hamlet made up entirely of these caves. They honeycombed the canyons, joined by narrow rock ledges that formed paths from level to level. A stranger could walk right under a whole townful of people and not be aware of their existence above his head.

Elder Xu sat in the front seat of the jeep, and Mao and I sat in the back. It was a tiny vehicle, and to fit into the back seat Mao had to sit with his knees hunkered up and pressed against his stomach. But somehow he managed to keep his air of rustic majesty.

We rode on like this for some time, as Mao expounded on one of his favorite themes. "The imperialists and the reactionaries are only frightful if you are afraid of them," he said, twisting around toward me as if he was addressing a whole hallful of people. "If you are not afraid, why then they are not frightful at all. They can cause a lot of trouble, but their inner impotence belies their omnipotent appearance. The real strength lies with the people. The people are the source of all historical progress."

While I was flattered to be singled out for Mao's attention, I couldn't help contrasting him with Zhou Enlai. When I was with Zhou, I felt I was with a real friend, a comrade. With Mao, I felt I was sitting next to history. With Zhou I felt warmth, with Mao, awe.

The jeep stopped at the path leading up to Green Ridge Mountain. A guide was waiting for me and together we climbed up the path that led to a maze of caves.

Housed in these caves were the mouthpieces of the Chinese Communist Party, speaking to China and to the world, among them the *Emancipation Daily News,* the Central Committee's official organ, and Radio Yanan, which had been sending out transmissions in both Chinese and English in Morse code. There was also the feeder news wire for all these organs, the New China News Agency. There was even a great printing press hidden in a huge stone cavern at the foot of the mountain, believed invulnerable even to atom bombs.

Together, all these institutions were called Emancipation House. In the main cave, I was greeted by the acting director, Yu Guangsheng, a former New York Central Railway worker who was temporarily in charge while the real director, Liao Chengzhi, was recovering from a stint in Chiang Kai-shek's prison. Yu welcomed me with a warm handshake and amazingly good colloquial American English. My job, he explained, would be to act as adviser to the English-language broadcast section at the news agency. As soon as the twenty-minute daily voicecasts from Kalgan had been halted by the bombing, trial broadcasts had begun here in Yanan. And although the operation had plenty of skilled translators and interpreters, there were no native speakers of English to oversee it. "We need someone to train our people, to polish their English and to give them all kinds of help and advice," Yu told me.

It was exactly the kind of job I had been hoping for. Here in Yanan, at the center of the Communist operations, I could look ahead to the future. If the Communists won, I imagined a historic role for myself acting as liaison between their government and the American government. The thought thrilled me.

After welcoming me, Yu handed me to C. T. Sim, who was to be my boss. He was a Singaporean who seemed quite British, a little cold and aloof, very proud and a strict disciplinarian. His

English was excellent, and he was working as a stringer for an American news wire. His second-in-command was an affable returnee from Indonesia named Chen Long, "Old Dragon," who was a bit on the stolid side, but warm and friendly to all. The other mainline members of the group were a couple from Beijing's Yenching University, Peng Di and his wife, Qian Xing.

I retired early that night to look over my new home. It was a cave, just like the one that housed our offices, dug about eight yards deep and about five yards wide into the mountainside. Inside was a bed made from a wooden door, placed on two saw-horses that stood against the back wall of the cave. In this back wall was a door leading into another series of caves deeper in the mountain that served as air raid shelters. Altogether they formed a circular cave corridor that ran all around the mountain, with exits high and low on all four sides.

There was a door at the left side of the front of the cave, and a paper-and-lattice window to the right of the door. When there was light outside, it came dully through the paper into the cave. At night, most of the cave dwellers used a little butter dish to burn a small twisted cotton wick lying in a bit of bean oil for fuel. It gave a tiny, eerie glow that served to help you find things in the cave at night, and that was about all. I was more fortunate. Like the more senior leaders, I was given a small kerosene lantern, by which I could see to read and write at night.

Yanan's loess caves were famous all over China for being warm in the winter and cool in the summer. Nonetheless, it was winter and my cave was cold. Outside the door I found a sack of charcoal sticks, which were to be burned for heat in a tiny brazier just before going to bed.

That night, lying in bed in my cave, I could hear off in the distance the soulful howling of the wolves. Then I heard something else, a rhythmic tinkling sound—ka-ching, ka-ching, ka-ching—as if a percussionist in some great, far-off orchestra was playing the bells. The sound was clear, yet seemed distant, rising and falling, half hidden in the wind.

I walked out onto the ledge in front of my cave and looked into the darkness. There in the distance along the dry riverbed I saw a row of yellowish lanterns, not swinging as they would if they were being carried by a procession of men, but bobbing gently up and down in midair without any visible means of support. "Luo tuo," said a voice beside me on the ledge—camels. It was my neighbor, a thin Hunanese man with a stringy goatee. "Camels are the only thing in the world that make that jingle-jangle sound and show that kind of serpent light at night," he said. Behind us in the dark, his wife was rocking their baby to sleep in her arms.

"Where are they from?" I asked.

"From the Mongolian grassland, or from the Hui people, the Muslims of Ningxia where the great salt wells are. Our salt comes from there on the camel caravans. The drivers take back cloth, needles, and flour for the herdsmen."

I watched the lights float through the valley below. Then I returned to my cave for the night. What a strange and wonderful place this was, I thought. And I felt a great sense of peace and contentment as I heard those camel bells down below, tinkling away slowly into the night until sleep enveloped me.

◆

The next morning and every morning thereafter I was awakened by another sound from far off down the mountain.

"Ehhhh, da dou-jiang leeeeeehhh."

The cry echoed through the hills.

My little orderly was already up and about, pouring out the morning washing water and fanning up the flame in the charcoal brazier. I pulled on my cotton padded suit, splashed my face and hands, and walked out on the ledge in front of my cave.

The voice rang out again. "Ehhhh, da dou-jiang leeeeeehhh." Come get your bean milk, oohhh . . .

It was the bean milk man, wending his way up the mountain. I could see him standing on a flat landing about halfway up, a peasant man with a white towel wrapped around his head, carrying a shoulder pole with a deep bucket on either end. His cry was a signal, and people came pouring out of their caves, threading their way down the steep slope, carrying every imaginable variety of container—washbasins, cups, mugs, glasses, bowls, gourds. Everyone was entitled to one cup or bowl of bean milk every morning. It was as nourishing as whole milk, slightly bitter, but wonderful with the fried dough twists we ate at breakfast.

The sun rose behind our mountain and I could see the morning light reflected on the hills before me, bouncing off Yanan's famous Pagoda Mountain, on whose higher slopes stood a multistory Buddhist pagoda. People took turns trotting down the mountain, filling their cups with hot bean milk for their friends and family. For one long companionable moment, we stood on the ledges, drinking our bean milk and watching the rising sun.

Then we went off to work.

Like the early Christians our lives were circumscribed by our caves, our catacombs. I walked down from my cave to the next ledge of caves that ran around our side of the mountain and over to the left where the work caves were. Our English language section office cave was right next door to the section that translated foreign wire service stories into Chinese for the leaders to read, and the international news section.

The routine seldom varied. I got there around seven-thirty, said hello to everybody, and sat down at my writing table to read the scripts written from the New China News Agency, dispatches printed in fuzzy ink on primitive homemade paper that was plastered up on the wall to dry before it was used.

The room was like a museum of ancient typewriter models. One editor had an old Underwood like the one my father used at home to type the editorials he continued to write long after he had given up his journalistic career to become a lawyer. Another had a Royal, and yet another a funny-looking Remington, a kind that I had never seen before. I had a slick little Swiss Hermes that I had brought with me from Kalgan.

C. T. Sim divided up the important stories for the group to translate, assigning them to Chen Long, the deputy section chief, Peng Di, Qian Xing, and Zheng Defang. Less important stories were given to section members like Deng Guang, whose English was less good. Hu Xiaowei, the secretary in the section, had a big Royal over which her fat little fingers flew as she typed up the corrected scripts into final form.

After each editor finished his translation, I polished the draft, made a few changes here and there, and perhaps raised a few pointers about the possible political impact of the story and what I thought was needed to improve it. All the stories carried a political message. The Chinese Communist Party wanted peace, national unity, democracy; it had negotiated patiently to spare the people more fighting after all the decades of warfare; it had called for a democratic coalition government. The KMT, on the other hand, had used the negotiations to buy time until the American air force could move KMT troops into place, and then had attacked, breaking the peace and continuing its one-party dictatorship.

The stories spoke of the threat of the atomic bomb and exhorted Third World countries to rise up and oppose American imperialism. Others covered activities in the areas under Communist control. They were success stories about peasants dividing up landlords' farms and going overnight from paupers to free farmers. Or about businessmen who were flourishing in the Communist-held towns after KMT monopolists had put them out of business in the areas they controlled. Or about villagers electing their leaders in the guerrilla bases or land-happy farmers sending their sons to join the Liberation Army so that the local landlords could never fight their way back and strip the farmers of their newly acquired land.

No matter what the content, in form most of the stories were hard, metallic propaganda. But to me they represented the truth. We were chronicling the most ancient and populous country in the world undergoing a sea change from an absolutist regime under which idle landlords lived by exploiting half-starved peasants to a nation of freeholder farmers. These farmers would be the foundation for a thriving economy and a democratic political system, as they had been in Europe and America. But more than that, the Communists were not going blindly forward to polarize society into rich and poor as the West had done. They were going to set up a socialist society, in which cooperation and mutual aid were the cornerstones, not private profit and greed.

I was intensely proud of my role in this revolution. It was one that could only be played by someone like me, an American and a Marxist, who knew the Chinese language and agreed wholeheartedly with the beliefs and goals of the Chinese Communists. No matter what job I was given, it made me swell with pride to think that this new gospel of liberation was getting to the outside world through my hands, that my labor was going into its making.

The colonel who was in charge of the American army liaison mission in Yanan soon after we met let it be known that he considered me un-American, a traitor. In fact, I felt like a real patriot. I felt I was acting in accord with the best American traditions that had become perverted back home. The propaganda I was polishing did not attack the America of the Constitution and the Bill of Rights, or the interests of the average American. I had nothing but contempt for those who I felt were going against those interests to serve their own greed and ambition. I was merely continuing the fight I had waged in Alabama and the Carolinas against the Big Mules, the fascists, the imperialists, the economic royalists, as FDR had called them. I was convinced that what I was doing would save the Wood Fairies of the future from foreign armies. But it would also help people everywhere throw off oppression and pave the way for a truly democratic America.

Whatever the story, I worked like mad on it. Not a misplaced modifier, not a faulty tense could escape my relentless pencil. I became a fierce guardian of grammar, number, tense, the use of articles, the use of the comma, the choice of words. I wanted everything to be clear and correct. It never was, of course. What went out was a queer mixture of Chinese and English. Many times the translations I was polishing were just too odd to patch up properly.

Our voicecasts from Yanan would carry only as far as Nanjing and Beijing. Our audience therefore was the foreign press there, and our hope was that reporters would pick up our news items and opinions and use them in their stories. Our Morse code transmissions, however, reached all over the world. And in our work every day, we acted as if the whole world was listening.

Every day at noon we carried our finished translations up the mountain to the director's caves to be cleared for broadcast. Then I held training sessions after lunch for my colleagues, discussing the most common errors they made in order to improve their translations. I used texts they were familiar with and enjoyed reading, like Edgar Snow's *Red Star Over China,* the book that had been so widely circulated in China, and had brought so many of them here to Yanan.

We also had access to a wide variety of other material. I often wondered if James Reston and the other reporters and commentators in London and Washington and New York knew how assiduously our little band of journalists, many of them trained in missionary schools, were poring over their writings by the light of bean oil flames. We got dispatches from the American wire services by Morse code. We read *The New York Times* regularly, *The Wall Street Journal, The Christian Science Monitor, The Washington Post,* and *The Baltimore Sun.* Even in the remote caves of Yanan, we were in touch with America and the rest of the world.

I had been working in Yanan for a month when Zhou Enlai returned. It was November 1946, when he flew back on the American air force shuttle. Everyone went to the airport to welcome him, including Chairman Mao. At the foot of the staircase descending from the plane, Mao grasped Zhou's hands. "Vice chairman, you have been working hard," he said. Zhou passed down the line, greeting us all. "I am glad to see you again, old friend," he murmured to me as he passed.

Everyone was happy to see Zhou back. He was only the number three man in the party after Mao and Liu Shaoqi, but he was clearly the most popular of the leaders. Still, his return had a momentous and ominous import. Although the Communist forces had just scored a series of military victories in the north and northeast, they were in retreat from their key cities and territories everywhere else. Fresh Flower Village had fallen. Kalgan had fallen. Linyi, the New Fourth Army headquarters in Shandong, was under heavy siege. There were even rumors that Yanan itself would have to be abandoned. Zhou Enlai was returning to Yanan with his delegation and with the Beijing and other local delegations because the truce talks with the Nationalists had completely broken down. With full-scale civil war erupting all over China, the Communists were recalling all their publicly known delegation members to Yanan and to relative safety.

Behind Zhou, a steady stream of people was descending from the plane. I looked up in surprise at the sight of a Shanghai merchant, dressed in a flowing blue silk gown, with a Western-style felt hat on his head. Then I looked again. It wasn't a merchant at all, but a young general I had known in Fresh Flower Village—he had thrown a tea kettle at a KMT general's head—in disguise. Then came an even bigger surprise. Next down the airplane steps came Xu Maijin himself, my original contact with the Communists in Shanghai. And he wasn't alone. He was accompanied by an attractive woman of about twenty-five or so. She looked familiar to me, but it wasn't until a few days later, when I ran into her in the dining hall, that I recognized her. She was the woman who had occasionally sat next to us at the opera in Shanghai. My mind flashed back to all those errands that Xu had asked me to run, including one for GI-issue condoms for the cadre who didn't want any more children. Suddenly I was pretty sure I knew who that old cadre was.

But the biggest surprise was yet to come. Another Shanghai merchant emerged from the plane. It was Jiang Zhenzhong, the fat, lazy capitalist who ran the money changer's shop in Shanghai where I had met Xu Maijin. I was chagrined. This was the man I had dismissed as a typical corrupt Shanghai merchant. Instead, he was one of the party's most loyal operatives, living in disguise. So much for my ability to penetrate party secrets, I thought ruefully.

We worked long hours in Yanan. We plodded and ran from cave to cave attending meetings. Still, my new life was far from tedious. It was full of friends and fun.

Against the front wall of each cave, just below the window, there were small wooden tables and chairs for work, study, or card playing. Many nights I sat with my new friends, swapping our life stories in the eerie flickering of the bean lamps or of my kerosene lantern. Two of my workmates, Qian Xing and her husband, Peng Di, quickly became my best friends. We spent many a long night nursing a bit of chicken brewing in a tin can over our charcoal braziers, or making home-style dumplings with some precious wheat flour that their friends had brought in from the outside.

Peng Di was a dour lad from Jiangxi who had shown great heroism during the Japanese bombing of Hunan where he was in school. He had little patience for the kind of intellectual inquiry and discussion that his wife indulged in. He talked about his commitment to action and change, and of his hatred of the KMT. On one of our long dark nights huddled in the cave, he told me that as a high school boy he had raced from one building to the next, rescuing people from the burning rubble caused by the Japanese bombing. He hated the Japanese, but he also hated the Nationalists who had plunged their own people into a conflagration in the provincial capital at Changsha in what they called a scorched-earth policy to stop the Japanese. Peng Di had vowed to work to drive both the Japanese and the Nationalists from his country.

Qian Xing was the daughter of some Beijing Brahmins and had attended a missionary finishing school for young ladies. She spoke the kind of Beijing Mandarin that rippled out like pearls, and had a highly developed taste for poetry, literature, and classical music.

Sometimes another friend, Yu Guangyuan, would drop by the cave to regale us with stories of his trips into Shanxi, and of his conversations with the courtly, turbaned peasants of the area. When Little Yu talked, his bushy eyebrows went up and down like the carriage on an old typewriter. His voice would rise in pitch as he described what he had seen, and he would jump up and begin pacing back and forth in the little cave, carried away by excitement.

One Sunday, my friends decided to give me a treat, and they took me across the Yanan River—"Yanan Waters," the local people called it—to a wooden shack restaurant that boasted the only offering of fried noodles in the area. We stuffed ourselves and trudged back home in the winter darkness, singing the "Song of the Guerrillas."

On Friday nights we all watched American films together at the U.S. Army mission. The army shuttle plane brought in the movies for the American soldiers and staff who were still acting as liaison between Washington and the Chinese Communists. The Communists provided the Americans office and living quarters in the center of Yanan. The Americans, in turn, would share films and other treats with the Chinese from time to time. Before I arrived, the movies had been translated by an army translator. But the first time I attended the movie a party official pulled me aside and asked me to take over. "We're missing the American flavor of the films," he complained.

It was clear the Chinese enjoyed the films tremendously. Even the most senior leaders—Mao, Zhou, and Zhu De as well as the border region military commanders, Wang Weizhou and Wang Shitai—would come whenever they could. We watched Laurel and Hardy films, and Nelson Eddy and Jeanette MacDonald, and they plied me with questions about American life. "Does everyone in America have a car?" they asked after seeing so many of them in the films.

I was fascinated by their interest and obvious admiration for almost everything American on the screen. I could see they regarded us as free and prosperous, in sharp contrast to the official party statements about America, and also in contrast to their strange lack of interest in the Soviet Union, the society that supposedly they looked up to. They greeted the films with riotous laughter and shouted commentary. "He's undergoing ideological struggle," they shouted at the screen when a character couldn't make up his mind.

They teased and ribbed me, and poked fun at me, just like one of their own. One Laurel and Hardy film featured the two chasing an escaped pig, knocking down everything in their path. I used the expression for pig I had learned in Kunming—lao zhu, meaning old pig. The room broke into hysterical laughter. Lao zhu was a homonym for "Old Zhu," the familiar way of addressing anyone named Zhu. And there were several people named Zhu in the room. "Lao Zhu, you've escaped," they shouted at Zhu De. "Look at what he's calling you!" they hollered at Zhu Zhicheng, our

mountain's party secretary. As for me, they tormented me end-
lessly about my error. "But that's the way they say it in Kunming,"
I protested, embarrassed, but pleased at the teasing.

My position in Yanan was unique.

From the beginning it had been decided that I would eat, not
with the members of my section, but with much higher level officials. That meant not only a better grade of diet for me, but access
to top secret information. For in Yanan, much day-to-day information was exchanged over meals.

Three levels of food were served at mealtimes. "Big kitchen"
food, which almost everyone ate, usually consisted of one large
pot of vegetables and coarse grain like corn or millet. Every other
day there would be some pork fat in the vegetable dish, and on
the days in between, one meal with big steamed wheat buns. Such
food represented a major rise in Yanan's living standards from
earlier days, largely because of the Communists' success in farming
the nearby areas.

"Middle kitchen" food was given to department heads, and
included a finer grain and a little more meat every week. The "little
kitchen" food was reserved for the most senior leaders, those who
were required to work long hours and make major decisions. That
was the food I shared. We ate meat every day, although there was
sometimes not enough to go around. We often had eggs too, and
soup every day. Central Committee members, invalids, or any of
the many people certified with tuberculosis were allotted a cup of
milk a day in addition to their regular diet.

Every day at mealtimes we would stop work and gather around
the square wooden table in the little dining room, poking with our
chopsticks at the dishes brought in by the cooks. There was no
formality or courtesy about these meals. If there were eight pieces
of chicken and seven diners, the race went to the speediest. We
didn't sit, we stood; the reach was better.

There was a steady stream of conversation and banter, spoken
in all sorts of regional accents, but with an undertone common to
Yanan. Even decades later, I could recognize people who had
been in Yanan by the expressions they used. Sometimes it was just
a matter of picking up the local patois. To say "talking nonsense,"
for example, we would always accuse the speaker of "strumming
a crazy lute." Someone who wrote a story that was not based on
fact was "ke li kong," which was the Chinese transliteration of the
name of a character in a Russian play who did just that.

For me, eating in the little dining room meant rubbing shoulders with the leaders of the Chinese Communist Party. One day Mei Yi showed up for dinner. I recognized him immediately. He was the spokesman for Zhou Enlai's Nanjing delegation, and it was Mei Yi's name that filled the papers during those days of negotiations. I looked at him curiously. A homely man, he was tall for a Chinese, nearly six feet, with a long face and thin eyebrows that gave his face the plucked appearance of a Chinese opera singer. He was from the Chaozhou area of Guangdong Province and spoke with a heavy southern accent that even his decades in the north couldn't shake.

Eating in the little dining room also meant having a pipeline to direct, inside information. During one evening meal, I got a full description of how Chairman Mao was fighting this war, and how the Communists expected to win. Shi Ximin had just come back from hearing a five- or six-hour report from the armed forces' deputy chief of staff for operations, Li Tao. He was standing, holding his bowl and eating as he talked. The rest of us were also slurping away, our caps on against the cold.

"Although to us in the gullies the situation looks bad, actually it is very good," Shi began. Another hallmark of Yanan language was its formal, political character. Many of the most senior officials had begun life as uneducated peasants. Whatever education they had acquired from the party, they took readily to the literary sound of propaganda. Shi's speech was no exception and people grunted and listened carefully as he ticked off data about Chiang Kai-shek's troops: how many were his dependable elite troops, and how many were simply miscellaneous local warlord troops who would desert if they weren't paid or fed properly. All through his discussion, Shi referred to Generalissimo Chiang as "General Di-saster," a pun on his title.

It was obvious from the figures that Chiang's forces still completely outnumbered the Communists. The Nationalists were much better armed too, with Japanese and American equipment. "We don't have tanks or planes or anything but light artillery," Shi continued relentlessly. "What's more, they have about two-thirds to three-quarters of the territory. We have only one-third to one-fourth. And they have all the big cities. The only big city we have is Harbin," a city in the far northeastern corner of China. To me the view from the gullies looked dismal indeed.

"But," Shi went on, "our strategy is the same old strategy that the People's Army used against the Japanese. It is to concentrate overwhelming forces and destroy the enemy piece by piece. When he comes after us, we retreat. When we attack him, we do so only when we outnumber him by four or six to one. And we attack only when his forces are tired, demoralized, and hungry. If they are tightly encircled and then treated right, they will come over to us." That way, Shi explained, we would be knocking out the enemy's armies, and at the same time building ours, taking possession of his modern weapons. His forces are diminishing, and ours are increasing.

Someone snickered appreciatively. "That's General Disaster's job: to act as our chief of transportation," he said. There was a standing joke in Yanan that the Americans didn't realize how well they were supplying the Communists with arms. They supplied Chiang, who in turn inadvertently supplied the Communists.

"Since July, we have been knocking out KMT brigades each month right on schedule," Shi Ximin concluded. When we get to one hundred brigades destroyed, there will be a turning point in the war. And then we will go over to the big counteroffensive for a decisive victory." The others around the table nodded pensively and continued their meal.

◆

For quite some time, I had heard that Anna Louise Strong would be coming to Yanan soon. I had met her at Stanford where I was studying Chinese when she came to lecture our army classes. U.S. China policy, she told us, should take into account the growing forces of democratic revolution in China, and should encourage the Chinese revolutionaries to seek friendship with America, instead of falling exclusively into the Soviet orbit.

I had liked Anna Louise Strong and had looked up to her ever since our first meeting. So when she finally arrived in Yanan on the military shuttle, I was glad to see her again. She was a very feisty woman, over sixty years old, and stiff-jointed already. As a renowned left-wing journalist, she had done several important interviews with the Communist leaders, including a long definitive one with Mao himself, which had been printed all over the world. I had seen her last in Kalgan, where she was brimful of plans. Mao Zedong had given her permission to write a comprehensive biography. She also planned to write the definitive history of the Communist Revolution. She had asked me to collaborate on both books and I agreed.

Strong had a long history of working closely with the Chinese Communists, and the Chinese loved and respected her. Still, her hair-trigger temper and salty tongue unnerved them. What's more, she spoke no Chinese. So Liao Chengzhi assigned me to help her and watch over her for part of every day. "This is your job," he said with a vigorous chuckle. "Take half of your work time off every day to spend with Anna Louise and keep her happy. Help her find things to write about, read to her, translate for her— anything, but keep her quiet."

While Strong clacked away at her portable typewriter, I told her of my overland trek to Yanan, giving her plenty of material for the stories she was filing with the *National Guardian,* the *St. Louis Post Dispatch,* the *Boston Globe,* and the *San Francisco Chronicle.* We translated several pieces of Chinese literature together, with me handling the Chinese and her polishing the English. And we interviewed several of the senior leaders, including Zhu De, on the military situation.

Then we were given a much more important task.

One evening after supper, Liao Chengzhi's orderly came running into my cave. "Old fatty wants to see you right away," he said, and I recognized the affectionate nickname for Liao. I went to his cave and Liao was excited. Vice Chairman Zhou Enlai wanted me to go to his home cave right away.

When I arrived, Zhou's adjutant led me into what turned out to be a two-room cave. The main room faced the door and a bedroom branched off just past the entryway. At the far end of the main room, facing the door, sat Zhou Enlai, on the left side of a small table, facing Anna Louise Strong.

The furniture was only slightly more elaborate than that in my cave. There was another little wooden desk to the right of the door where Deng Yingchao, Zhou's wife, sat. Folded over the end of the bed, which was visible through the doorway, were the same plain white homespun cotton quilts that everyone used.

When I walked in, Zhou got up and extended his hand. "We want you to interpret, but we decided not to wait since you are late," he said. "I've been answering Comrade Strong's questions about the world situation and about China. You can be my living dictionary and supply me with the English terms when I can't think of them."

Deng Yingchao offered me tea and some chocolates from a box on her desk. Then she returned to her desk, to her writing, and Zhou and Strong returned to their interview. As I sat there and listened, I found he was speaking English very competently. His English was broken, but his logic was sound. The brilliance of his intellect enabled him to select simple English words and phrases that expressed his concepts with force and clarity.

Occasionally, Zhou stopped and asked me for a word.

"Wu duan means?" he said, turning to me quizzically.

"Arbitrary," I replied.

"Coup d'état?" he asked.

"Coup d'état," I replied, and he laughed.

Zhou talked to Strong of the perfidy of the KMT authorities who talked peace while using negotiations to buy time to launch all-out civil war. He was sharply critical of the American government. While he respected and admired General Marshall personally, he said, he felt President Truman had doomed the talks from the start by favoring Chiang Kai-shek, and letting Chiang know that.

As Zhou fished for the right phrases in English and formulated his views on the political situation, he kept up a running fire of advice and discussion with his wife, who was writing a letter to an international women's group, and with their adopted daughter, Sun Weishi, who was walking back and forth in the cave with her head thrown back, interrupting with questions about a play she was directing in the local experimental theater. To all of their questions, Zhou gave thoughtful, detailed answers, without seeming to break the flow of his interview with Strong.

But the climax of the interview was still to come. Zhou picked up a small pamphlet printed on discolored newsprint, and asked me to translate the title.

"*A Decision on a Number of Issues Concerning the Party's History,*" I read. "A top secret document, adopted by the political bureau of the Central Committee."

"Even most of the comrades in our own party are not aware of the existence of this document," Zhou said. "It is known to members of the Central Committee alone."

Zhou knew that Strong would be in Yanan only a short while. He wanted me to translate the document into English for her, so that she could carry it with her to Europe and hand it personally to the first secretaries of the Communist parties of the Soviet satellite countries—Poland, East Germany, Czechoslovakia, Hungary, Bulgaria, Romania, and Albania.

Zhou summed up the message of the document briefly. Based on past painful experience, the document said, the Chinese Communist Party recommended that the revolutionaries of each country must make and carry out their own policies. They must not allow themselves to be given orders by any foreign body. Otherwise, the document warned, the revolution would fail.

Such a message from China was dynamite. It was calling on the captive states of Europe to throw off their reliance on the Soviet Union and follow their own judgment in their countries' affairs.

The next day we set up a little translation office next door to the office Anna Louise Strong had been provided. We maintained a strict veil of secrecy over our work. And in the course of our translation, I found our precautions well taken. Beyond the information Zhou Enlai had already conveyed, the document also contained an analysis, naming names, of every incorrect line that had ever cropped up in the Chinese Communist Party since its inception. Hardly anyone escaped criticism, except for Mao himself and Liu Shaoqi. Even Zhou Enlai and other famous figures were criticized for strategies that had nearly destroyed the revolutionary movement.

I was thrilled with my assignment. It was positive proof that I was indeed trusted and that I was being admitted into the inner circle of Communist leadership. But I had not yet been allowed to become a member of the party.

From my very first days in Kalgan I had asked to join the party. It was clear that everything good that was happening in China came from the party. The party had taught the soldiers to farm, and to coax out of the hostile earth the crops that supported us. The party had taught the peasants to spin and knit. The party was sending teams of earnest young men and women into villages to teach basic sanitation and public health. In Chinese villages, the first lesson was usually about why and how to brush your teeth. On my march between Kalgan and Yanan, I could easily tell the party had been there first if the peasants knew about cleaning their teeth.

In Kalgan, party officials had put me off, so when I arrived in Yanan I repeated my request to join. Many weeks went by without comment. Then suddenly one day Liao Chengzhi told me that my request was being considered and scrawled a letter of introduction to An Ziwen, the vice minister for the party's central organization department.

The next day I showed up at An Ziwen's cave. He was a tall, intently serious north Shaanxi cadre. There were two hurdles that needed to be passed to join the Communist Party, he explained. First an exhaustive background check had to be made. The party immediately rejected unpopular people, or those with legal problems, or whose lives included disreputable marital or sexual affairs, or people whose political background looked suspicious. The party was constantly under attack in those days, and officials wanted to eliminate the possibility of spies infiltrating.

For Chinese applicants, I knew, that background check was as elaborate as an FBI clearance. The party would send people back to the applicant's hometown to confirm that they had attended the schools and done the things they said they had done. I had written the standard autobiography, but there was no way of verifying my claims. I presumed that party officials had asked Anna Louise Strong to vouch for my story.

The other hurdle was the applicant's political attitude. They wanted only truly dedicated Communists. And for that, they relied on gathering their impressions of me and my work, and finally on a personal interview. An Ziwen looked at me squarely in the eye and said, "What is your reason for wanting to join the Communist Party of China?"

"I am not a very good Communist," I said. "I want to learn to be one, and I can't do that unless I join the party."

He started a bit, surprised by my answer. I even felt that he was probably displeased by it, as if it was not the right answer. But I wasn't sure what was.

I was concerned. But then An added, "Our comrades have turned in many good reports about your enthusiasm and your energy. We are impressed."

Each applicant for membership was required to have two guarantors. I offered generals Li Xiannian and Wang Zhen, saying that they probably knew me better than any other members of the Central Committee and should be able to vouch for me.

Then An told me something surprising. As a foreigner, I would be required to pass one more hurdle. "There is a special rule of the Chinese Communist Party Central Committee on the admission of foreign comrades," he said. "It is a rule that is not written down anywhere and is kept secret, but it exists nevertheless. The rule is that a foreigner can only become a party member by direct approval of the five members of the Central Committee Secretariat." That meant Mao Zedong, Liu Shaoqi, Zhou Enlai, Ren Bishi, and Zhu De. "I shall have to submit your application to them for approval, and you should know the answer in a week or two."

That concerned me too, since it was very unusual for a foreigner to be admitted to the Chinese Communist Party. I knew of only one American who had been admitted, George Hatem—now known as Ma Haide—whom I had met in Beijing at the delegation office. When he went to the Communist areas of China he gave up his American citizenship and joined the Chinese Communist Party. But he wasn't very political, or very involved in party life.

I fretted and worried for more than a week until, finally, Liao told me that everything was fine. The secretariat had unanimously approved my application and I was now a member of the party. There was no probation period for me, as there was for most new Chinese members, but I was not to be generally known as a party member at this point. Liao explained that a small portion of my monthly stipend was payable to the party as dues. And that was that.

As a foreigner, my role in the party would be limited. I could only take part in meetings in my own department. But being a party member meant so much more to me than meetings. It meant being a part of a movement, a cause, a revolution—almost a religion. When Ding Tuo, my contact in the party, gave me a list of my fellow party members, I found to my astonishment that nearly everyone in our propaganda organization belonged. Those who didn't usually had some major failing in their background or character.

And it was clear that they all took their party membership very seriously. I talked long into the night with Peng Di and Qian Xing about their own reasons for joining. Qian's attraction was pure, ascetic, almost that of the early Christians to their religion. "When we came here," she told me one night, "we gave everything we had to the Revolution. We gave ourselves to the Revolution. We had to remold ourselves, to get rid of our subjectivism, selfishness, vulgar interest, anything and everything that interfered with our devotion to the cause. We put aside our personal problems and ambition, and we just became a part of the Revolution."

It was an utterly joyous self-abnegation and clearly every party member was expected to achieve it. We called it revolutionary optimism. I was happy that we were all pulling together to free the wretched and hungry of the earth, and this joy overrode any worries or personal problems that might occur in our everyday lives.

We were all bent on self-improvement. Every week in the office we had meetings in which we brought up complaints and criticisms. Mao demanded that party members learn the Confucian injunction to "be glad to have your faults pointed out," so a good comrade was supposed to listen to criticism cheerfully—and indeed to thank the speaker of it. Mao had worked out a little jingle to teach this principle:

Let everyone say what they think;
Get it all out;
Hold your critic blameless;
Control yourself as you listen;
If you have the fault—change it;
If you don't have it—guard against it.

Every night, a good party member spent fifteen minutes reflecting on the day's events, figuring out what he or she had done right and wrong. Experience, said Mao and Liu Shaoqi, was the basic teacher. Many of my friends carried little notebooks and religiously jotted down self-improving comments. Criticizing one's fellows, helping them mend their flaws, was a moral obligation for a party member.

I felt, as they did, that I was getting much more from the party than I gave up. For in return, as Qian Xing said, "We have the knowledge that we are pursuing the truth. We have the party. The party is like our mother. The party takes care of us. We don't have anything, but whatever there is, we know we'll get our fair share of it."

I knew what she had said was true. In prosperous America I had grown up anxious about prejudice, poverty, and hunger. Here in dirt-poor Yanan, I had virtually no wants. I was issued three suits of clothes a year, one in winter, two in summer. My medical care was free. My food was free. My monthly stipend went into my trunk and gathered dust. The party satisfied my every need.

◆

Even though the Chinese Communists weren't yet considered enemies in America, and indeed most Americans in China admired them greatly, there were a few who were openly hostile both to the Communists and to me.

One of them was the colonel in charge of the American liaison office. The Chinese had given the Americans office space in the guest house where they also housed their distinguished visitors. There were three American officers there, a colonel, a lieutenant colonel, and a major, and two or three sergeants. Because Anna Louise was staying in the guest house, I ran into the army people every day. They were all friendly to me except the colonel. He hated the Chinese Communists. He cursed them and made fun of them. He hated me for working with them to put out the *Masturbation Daily,* as he called the *Emancipation Daily.* And he refused to have me to Thanksgiving dinner, which almost caused an international incident and a court martial.

The colonel invited all the other Americans in Yanan, including the medical people who were stationed at a Friends' ambulance unit. I was the only exception, and when his men—who were good sorts and who liked me—protested, the colonel erupted. "I'm not going to invite that traitor," he roared.

That got the major, a hot-headed Texas oil man, mad. "He's not a traitor, he's a fine man," the major roared in turn, and knocked the colonel down.

In the end, the Chinese intervened. It was their guest house, and if the colonel was going to invite every other American, he would have to invite me, they said, or they would not attend either. He did so, but sullenly. So I went and ate canned turkey, mashed potatoes, and pumpkin pie. And I laughed with the major, who complained that his hand still hurt from the effort it cost him to get me an invitation to that dinner.

A few days later, I was walking down the mountain with Peng Di to attend a meeting with Zhou Enlai. We were on the road to army headquarters, when off in the distance a tall lanky figure emerged from the military building.

"There's Li Xiannian," Peng Di said.

I began to run. When Li spotted me, he began to run too, only it was more like a lope, his long, thin figure stretched out, and his arms and legs flapping. He looked very gray and worn, and his gait was almost comical. We ran into each other's arms and he gave me a big hug.

"I heard you were here, but I didn't know where," I said.

"I'm staying out near the hospital," he said. "I'm about to get married. Come to my wedding."

So I had guessed right about poor Shang Xiaoping, his first wife. I had run into her on the road between Kalgan and Yanan. At the time, she was married to Li Xiannian, but her sad expression, combined with the fact that she had no children, convinced me there were problems between them. When she arrived in Yanan, he had wasted no time in divorcing her.

I agreed to come to his wedding and we went on our separate ways. When I met him again, I was alone, and after shaking hands, he had a message for me. "By the way," he said. "I wanted to tell you that we appreciated the information you gave us." I knew immediately that he was talking about my conversation with General Byroade in Fresh Flower Village. "A lot of our comrades didn't believe it," Li continued. "They thought you got it wrong. But I believed it, and the facts proved you right. We appreciate that, and we won't forget it."

Then Li became jocular. "When we win this war, I am going to be mayor of Wuhan," he said. "Then you can come and live there, and I'll find you the prettiest girl there for a wife."

I was glad to hear that my information had helped, and sorry that it had proved so accurate. But I was hard-pressed to see how the Communists were going to win now. Every day, I heard that more territory had been ceded to the Nationalists.

I became even more concerned on one blustery day shortly afterward, when we all went out to the outskirts of Yanan to welcome General Wang Zhen's famous 359th Brigade. They had taken a roundabout route from Fresh Flower Village, marching west across Hubei to the southern part of Shaanxi. There they had tried to open up a new Communist-controlled area, but the unfriendly people, hard soil, and barren mountains had proved too tough even for them, and they were returning to Yanan to regroup.

Our welcoming party met them at Ten Mile Inn. I was horrified at what I saw. Like the soldiers at Valley Forge, these boys came straggling back barefoot from a thousand-mile trek. Many of them didn't have grass sandals to protect their feet from the November freeze and only about two out of five even had weapons, mostly old, beaten-up Japanese army rifles they had captured. I believed that the Communists were going to win, but if they did, it would have to be by moral force, popular appeal, and superior strategy and tactics—not military might.

And if they did win, I believed they were the people who would save China's poorest and most destitute. Under the Communists, the Wood Fairies of China would be safe. The Communists would redeem the pallid young prostitutes on Nanjing Road, and snatch the little girls from the treadmill where they ground the abbot's flour. They would keep young soldiers from being led away to die. I began to interpret events in the light of that belief, even ones that were hard to swallow, like the meeting held to denounce Zhang Yongtai.

Zhang Yongtai was a landlord, typical of the ones around Yanan. They were hardly rich, or even comfortable, by Western standards, and yet, among the starving, poverty-stricken peasants of China, these local landlords were like squires. They were the only ones who could read and write, and so had enormous power to interpret, and even to set, laws. The landlord was absolute master in his village. Peasants had to bow their heads in his presence, and step aside and let him pass when he came walking down the street. They had to send their wives to labor in his house, their children to work in his kitchen, their sons for unpaid labor in his fields.

Around Yanan, Mao had introduced a new phase of land reform. He had offered the local landlords a program of swapping their land for government bonds. Landlord Zhang Yongtai had been touted as a model of acceptance in the party press—but his fellow villagers wouldn't buy it. Led by the village party organization, they were holding what they called a struggle meeting with Zhang to pour out years of hatred.

When I arrived, the struggle meeting was just starting. Zhang came out into the middle of the threshing floor and bowed to the village elders, and the party land reform team members, who sat at a long table facing him. He also bowed to his audience, the assembled mass of the villagers gathered together facing the threshing floor.

Zhang spoke of how he had always abided by party policy and law and had never gotten into any trouble. He spoke briefly of his minor infractions. Then he ended with a noble offer. He had already packed his things and was leaving for the front lines of the battle early the next morning with his son. They were both volunteering for the Chinese People's Liberation Army to fight for the security and happiness of the peasants in the liberated areas.

During most of Zhang Yongtai's talk, the peasants had maintained their normal meeting time hubbub, allowing him to have his say. But when he got to the part about volunteering for the PLA, the crowd suddenly changed. A man jumped up and, with clenched fist, shouted, "The Liberation Army is the peasants' army. How could we allow a reactionary landlord to join! Zhang Yongtai is deliberately insulting us!"

A roar of response arose from the crowd. "Down with Zhang Yongtai! Totally overthrow Zhang Yongtai!" The meeting leader egged the villagers on. "Don't fear to speak out," he cried. And the other land reform team members began to lead the peasants in shouting slogans.

"Let those with anger vent their anger!"

"Let those who have been wronged tell their wrongs!"

"Bitter waters must be poured out!"

"Pour out your bitterness! Put down your burdens!"

"Revenge! Revenge! Down with the reactionary landlords!"

"Revenge!"

Suddenly a peasant woman with tiny bound feet and hair in a bun got up and picked her way to the threshing floor. She stood right in front of Zhang Yongtai. I could see him staring at her wide-eyed with fear, like a man who saw a ghost.

The woman held in her hand the hard sole of a cloth shoe, which she had been weaving. Slowly, with obvious difficulty, she began to talk, weeping as she spoke and wiping the tears away with her jacket sleeve. "My husband," she said, "was away at the market fair. I was alone in the house, putting away some salted vegetables. Zhang Yongtai came in without calling at the door. He put his hands on me, and said that now my old man was away this was his chance to be alone with me. I tried to keep him off, but I'm only a woman and he is strong. He dragged me into the back room and . . ."

The crowd leaped to its feet, howling. "Revenge! Revenge! Let those who have been wronged tell their wrongs! Bitter waters must be poured out! Revenge! Revenge!"

Zhang Yongtai took several steps backward from the weeping woman. But she followed him, the painful tiptoe walk of Chinese women with bound feet. She raised her hand, and with the hard, rough shoe bottom began to beat Zhang on his face and head. Blood ran down his scalp into his eyes. He fell down on his knees, but the beating continued. The woman sobbed and screamed words I couldn't make out, and went on beating.

"Revenge," the crowd screamed. "Revenge! Revenge!"

I felt sick. But I wrested myself from that feeling. This was revolution, after all. I knew the revolutionary theory. Unless the peasants arise and strike the landlords down with their own hands, they will never be able to throw off the weight of centuries of oppression and fear.

As much as I hated such violence, I told myself that shying away from it was a sign of my petit bourgeois background. I believed that only this kind of class war could eliminate all wars. If that was what it took to bring about peace on earth and goodwill to all the multitudes of downtrodden people in the world, I should not flinch from it.

High Autumn and Bracing Weather

When the brutal wind came whipping down from the Gobi Desert, the Chinese called it "high autumn and bracing weather." I called it cold. The wind pierced my padded jacket and howled around my cave at night. I still slept alone and I often thought of Wei Lin, the rosy-cheeked young announcer I had fallen in love with in Kalgan.

I had walked Wei Lin home from the broadcast station every evening, laughing and joking. I hadn't realized how fond of her I was becoming until she slammed the door on any prospect of romance. We couldn't become close, she said, because she was waiting for her fiancé, who was away in Prague. Honor forbade me from pressing my case further, and I soon left Kalgan, and her, far behind. But on the day of my departure for Yanan, I had some hint that she might not have been as reluctant as she seemed. On my bed were mittens she had knitted for me, and an affectionate little note. "I knit these muffins for you," she wrote, in English. "I'll always precious our friendship."

I hadn't seen her again after that, but the longer I was away from Wei Lin, the more I pined for her, daydreaming about being with her. And that's probably why I got in all the trouble I did.

It wasn't that I lacked for female company. Peng Di and Qian Xing had more or less adopted me and Hu Xiaowei, the secretary in the news office, and the four of us were so inseparable that people called us "the family." But poor Xiaowei, despite her good heart and kind nature, was fidgety, and frail. What she needed was mothering. Peng Di, Qian Xing, and I mothered her in abundance, but that didn't solve my problem.

People were always trying to fix me up with someone or other. Once George Hatem's wife, Su Fei, gave a dinner to introduce me to Wang Guangmei. Actually I had already met Wang Guangmei; she was the slender, athletic secretary who had shown me in to my meeting with Ye Jianying in Beijing. But an "introduction" in Yanan was not just for the purposes of introduction. It was a quiet announcement that friends and relations considered you a suitable match.

Wang Guangmei and I both treated the introduction dutifully. She accepted my invitation to have dinner with me, which in Yanan meant braving the winds to walk down to one of the frame cafés in the bombed-out village to eat twice-cooked pork. Over dinner, she told me about her experiences working on a land reform team in north Shaanxi, and I told her a bit about my work. Being a very proper young woman, she invited me back at the same time the following Saturday to the same restaurant, where we again dined on twice-cooked pork. I found her pleasant, companionable, and completely uninteresting as a possible marriage partner, and I was sure she shared my feelings exactly.

There was one woman in Yanan I did find attractive—very. She was Sun Weishi, Zhou Enlai's adopted daughter. We had met for the first time in her stepfather's cave, when Anna Louise and I were interviewing Zhou. I took to Sun Weishi at once. She had a sweet face, beautiful hair, and large eyes full of insight and humor. She was kind and quick-witted, with a good, sturdy physique, a sort of tomboy. I could have fallen in love with her in a minute. But something stopped me: my reverence for her stepfather, perhaps, or perhaps I also had an inner fear that no matter how Zhou regarded me professionally, he wouldn't consider me a proper match for his stepdaughter. But mainly, I was terrified that she would reject me. So I did my best to build up a conspicuously platonic relationship with her.

My troubles began when I met a woman whose intentions were clearly not platonic. She came to my cave alone one afternoon before supper, a very bold and forward move for a young Chinese woman, ostensibly to meet the American comrade who had joined the revolution. She had heard, she said, of the good life in America, and she so admired people who gave up their comfortable homes to throw in their lot with the Chinese people.

I had never seen her before and I didn't particularly like her. She was a tall woman with a long thin face, and she was wearing a red and green sweater that she had knitted herself. She suggested that we should get together often, and I could help her practice her English.

The next day, I asked someone in the English department about her. "Jail bait," he said. "She's shameless." It appeared that she had been married, but summarily divorced when her husband had returned early from a meeting and discovered her in bed with another man. I found this troubling, but at the same time a little exciting. I had been without a woman for such a long time—and here was one with a reputation who was practically throwing herself at me.

The next time I saw the woman, she was on her way to the radio station to announce the Chinese program. Would I like to walk to the sending station with her, she asked? Against my better judgment I didn't refuse, and along some of the remote path areas we did a fair amount of necking. She was looking for a lover, she said, or a husband—the word she used could mean either. That alarmed me. I told her I thought we were getting too close, and I thought we should stop seeing each other. She looked at me very gravely and we said goodbye.

About a week later, I came back late from a play. It was dark. It was quiet. And there she was at the door to my cave. I knew the moment I reached for her hand that I was making a big mistake. But at least, I thought, she was a party member and knew enough to be discreet. The next evening when I received a summons to the party secretary's cave I knew I had been wrong.

Zhu Zhicheng, the party secretary, was a big thick-set man. When I arrived at the door of the cave, I found him walking back and forth, clearly upset. "Motherfucker! Motherfucker!" he muttered, and then got right to the point. "Our comrade says you two have been in love for some time, and that now she is pregnant and wants to get married," he said.

I was astounded. She couldn't possibly be pregnant, I told Zhu. What she was saying just wasn't true.

"True or not, she can make a lot of trouble," he answered. "She is loose, and she has anarchistic tendencies, but basically her heart is with the Revolution. The party has decided the best thing is for you to marry her."

That wasn't possible, I explained. I was ready to make many sacrifices, but I wasn't about to marry this woman. I was sorry for what I had done, and sorry that it had caused any problems for the party. But I wasn't going to let a single night change the course of my life. Besides, I said, I just didn't love her.

Over the next few days, the problem escalated. The woman was adamant: she wanted a husband. I was equally adamant: I wouldn't marry her. Over and over, she appealed to the party, complaining and demanding that I be made to comply. And one by one, party members visited me to convince me to do my duty. My attitude perplexed them. I could tell from the look on their faces that they had clearly expected better of me.

Zhu Zhicheng repeated his claim that the woman was basically a good comrade, and that marrying her should cause me no pain. C. T. Sim, the dour Singaporean in charge of our news section, took me for a long walk to warn me that the party didn't take such sexual transgressions lightly. "We have found from experience that people who have this weakness are more likely to cave in under pressure from the enemy. It is a very serious problem." What's more, he wanted me to know that if the party decided to compel me to go along, I could be made the target of a struggle meeting, and he assured me I would find it terrifying. "People will shout at you and demand that you confess and repent, and you will not be able to explain or to reason with them," he told me.

My friends Qian Xing and Peng Di were particularly dismayed. "It's like a tiny piece has been chipped off from the pure marble of your character as a follower of Communism," said Qian Xing.

With a sort of quiet vexation, Peng Di added, "Couldn't you have just waited? You're bound to meet someone. How could you have been taken in by someone like her?"

Liao Chengzhi, our head man, was almost the only party leader who did not try to pressure me to marry the woman. That Saturday night, I went with him for our usual soak-and-scrub at the stone bathhouse. Sitting in the steamy tub, the former merchant seaman laughed sardonically at my plight. "Sucker," he said. "How could you be such a sucker? Don't you know the facts of life?"

For a time, my one night of illicit sex was a big problem for me. Part of the Communist Party's appeal to the peasants was its moral puritanism, a sharp contrast to the Nationalists, who kept concubines and caroused wherever they went. There were also many people, like Qian Xing, who firmly believed in moral rebirth through self-cultivation and the transformation of character. If people were dirty and exploitative in their relations with the op-posite sex, it was a basic flaw in their character.

But it was more than just the illicit sex, which wasn't, of course, unknown in Yanan. Within a few weeks of his return from Shang-hai, Xu Maijin had asked for a divorce from his wife, and the mother of his three children, to marry Fang Qiong, our mysterious theatergoing companion. Li Xiannian had been married almost immediately after divorcing the unhappy Shang Xiaoping, while Mao himself divorced his second wife—his first had been mur-dered by a local KMT warlord—to marry Jiang Qing.

The powerful unwritten rule, however, was that such affairs had to be discreet in order not to affront public morality. When the party refused a request for a divorce, you remained married. Xu Maijin's affair with Fang Qiong remained private until after they were married. My bad luck was that, for her own reasons, this woman had decided to make an issue of it. But once she had done that, I had compounded the problem by breaking an even more important rule. My bigger crime was that I had refused to follow the party's wishes. Had I obeyed the party on that first day and agreed to marry the woman, the problem would have vanished. But I had refused to do so, and had thus called into question not only my moral character, but my political character as well.

Fortunately, the woman dropped her case after a while and began circulating a story about using some mysterious means to get rid of the baby. Later, she approached me with a proposal that we remain friends and see a lot of each other, a proposal I had sense enough to turn down. Finally, the whole thing appeared to blow over. But not before virtually everyone in Yanan had heard of the incident, and had expressed an opinion about it. I couldn't eat a bite for several weeks afterward without someone making reference to my woes. "Well, foreign devil," someone would say, using the affectionate term with which they sometimes addressed me. "I'm learning something about foreign devils. I'd better watch my wife very carefully around you."

◆

For all my devotion to the Communists, I continued to clash with them over the need for the individual to subordinate his will to that of the party leaders. I had learned from Peng Di and Qian Xing that another woman in the English section had just given birth to a baby. The baby was in poor condition, the mother couldn't nurse, and because there was no milk for the baby, it was probably going to die. Hearing this, I took a Sunday hike out to the Quaker medical team. A young New Zealand doctor immediately gave me several large cans of milk powder and spent the better part of an hour copying out detailed instructions on how to mix the formula and exactly how much to feed the baby.

Feeling very pleased with myself, I took the milk powder back, and asked the people in the English section to pass it along to the woman, whom I hadn't met yet. "You'd better take the milk powder to Comrade Zhu Zhicheng," the party secretary, they all told me. "Let him handle it."

So I did, suspecting nothing. But when I told him what I had done, Zhu looked, not happy, but a little grave. "There are two ways of handling this problem," he began. "You made an individual effort to get milk for one particular comrade who happens to be in your section. I can simply send this milk to her. But the problem with that is that you don't know the whole picture in our organization. There are a number of families who are in worse trouble than she is and who need the milk more. Or you can give the milk to the party committee and let us distribute it according to need. Which way you decide to handle it is up to you. I will follow your wishes in the matter."

Regretting that I had brought Zhu the milk powder in the first place, I agreed that the most reasonable solution was to give it to the collective, which would then decide who needed it most and distribute it accordingly.

"Good," Zhu said. "Then that's the way we'll handle it. When you get to know us better, you will find that we do not stress private assistance to people in need. We put our emphasis on getting everyone to support the collective, which can handle cases of need better than any private individual."

I was hurt and upset. I had done what I thought was a good deed. But instead of being praised for my initiative, I was being criticized for a violation of collective morality. What was wrong with also encouraging individuals to do their best to assist other individuals? That seemed more productive than simply leaving all such endeavors to the collective.

Around New Year's, I clashed again with the party. I had worked many hours to translate a particularly long and important editorial on foreign policy that had appeared in the *Emancipation Daily*. I thought that the editorial was vital to the world's understanding of some important party policies, and I treated it accordingly. Then, soon afterward, I attended a conference with Zhou

Enlai, who happened to compliment the news agency on the swift and excellent translation and transmission of the New Year message. "Who did that translation?" he asked me.

"I did," I replied. "Others went over it and checked it after I did the initial translation."

"Congratulations," said Zhou.

I was very proud of myself, but when word of my exchange with Zhou got around, it generated a lot of bad feelings toward me in the English section. "Why did you take the credit for the translation when we all worked on it so hard?" asked C. T. Sim, the section chief. "We do not approve of individuals taking credit; the glory should go to the team, to the collective."

Again I felt wronged. I had given a truthful answer to Zhou's question and I felt that the party was encouraging a kind of jealous resentment whenever individual achievement was mentioned.

I thought back to a conversation I had had with Liu Shaoqi on my very first day in Yanan. Sitting on a carpenter's bench at the Saturday night dance, I had told him of my puzzlement at certain parts of his book, *How to Be a Good Communist.* "I read some of your work and I found it extremely interesting," I said. "But I've got some problems with it too. I have always thought that a good revolutionary adopts the cause as the only source of his personal joys and sorrows, and subordinates his own will to the needs of the movement. That way, he can find a stable, expansive, dependable source of happiness, forgetting his own problems and focusing on service to the great majority of people.

"But in your book," I continued, "you stress that when the interests of the revolution clash with personal interests, then the individual must be prepared to forfeit or forget about his personal interests and solve the contradictions in favor of the revolution. Since the interests of the individual are at one with those of the revolution, I don't see why you need to talk about resolving a contradiction that shouldn't exist in the first place."

Liu was a chain smoker. He sat with his right elbow propped up on the wrist of his left arm, letting his cigarette hand droop downward between puffs. The crotch of one knee was perched high upon the other. His thin face was scored by severely critical lines around his mouth that described an arc on each side as he blew the smoke toward the ceiling.

"The personal interests of the revolutionary are basically at one with the interests of the revolution," Liu agreed, taking a deep puff on his cigarette. "But basically doesn't mean absolutely.

There are times when he may have to give up his home, his work, his studies, his health, even his life, because the revolution requires him to do so. At such moments, he must have made up his mind fully in advance as to which choice he will make: to serve the people unstintingly, and to the best of his ability, or to cling to his own personal interests and let the people down, or even betray the revolution.

"In China the struggle is extremely cruel and complex," he went on. "It takes tireless effort and firmness to work with those who try to take the middle of the road, who both insist on pursuing their own personal interests before all else, and at the same time seek the satisfaction of associating themselves with the revolutionary cause. At some point they will find that a choice is thrust upon them and they stand the risk of being battered to pieces in the battle of the two camps."

◆

Despite my transgressions, I was making many friends in Yanan. And socially, I had become very much part of the inner circle. On New Year's Eve, 1946, all of Yanan turned out for a dance, and Anna Louise Strong and I were invited to a special predance party with the members of the Central Committee. Card tables were set up that evening in a simple but festive room. On the tables were plates with jujubes, walnuts, and two kinds of flaky pastries, one with sweet bean paste inside, another containing nuts and honey.

The card game we played was called five hundred points, and it was similar to gin rummy. Six of us sat down at one table: Mao Zedong, Liu Shaoqi, Zhu De, Zhou Enlai, Anna Louise, and me. It was the first time I had played cards with them, and if the party leaders were enthusiastic dancers, they were fierce card players. I was impressed by the terrific intensity with which they played.

You would have thought Zhu De was planning a military campaign the way he pored over his cards, muttering to himself. "Oh, I've had it now," he shouted when an unfavorable card was played. Then he would pick over his hand and slam his cards on the table when he had made his suit, crying out triumphantly, "Ha! I've trumped!"

Mao talked hardly at all. He looked carefully over his cards, and his movements were slow and graceful. He took the game very seriously. Afterward Anna Louise said, "Mao plays cards like a philosopher." I thought he was playing like a strategist, keeping his face blank, figuring the odds on what cards his opponents held. He studied the cards, then looked at the board, then looked at his cards again. He would pick up cards with a long-armed reach and, when he won, would silently lay his hand down in a neat arc.

Liu Shaoqi seemed thin and drawn, and kept clearing his throat nervously as he played. Zhou Enlai was a flashy player. His eyes darting all over the place, he would look first into one face and then into another. And then with a stage sigh, he would say, "Oh well, this is all I can do," and lay down his hand.

I didn't play nearly as well as they did. I didn't take the game seriously enough. But I enjoyed their play and the relaxed repartee. After each hand, Zhou gently ribbed the others. "That was a stupid play," he said. "You should have known that guy had the card you needed."

At one point when we were joined by Zhu De's wife, Kang Keching, he good-naturedly accused her of telegraphing her hand. "Oh, go on," she teased. "You're so drunk you don't even know what cards you're holding in your own hand."

The next morning all the members of the news department leadership piled into an old captured Japanese army truck to go to Chairman Mao's cave to wish him a Happy New Year. We drove to the place where he lived, called the Date Orchard. It was a cold day, but it was sunny, and we found him pacing back and forth in the sunshine outside the cave door. Jiang Qing was watching their daughter, Li Na, play with their nurse. A pretty little girl who looked five or six, Li Na was introduced to me in the traditional way, which meant that she addressed me as "Uncle" from then on. She was bouncing a small rubber ball and I rode her around piggyback. Meanwhile, orderlies were bustling about setting up chairs for a performance that the local people had arranged for the Chairman's New Year's festivities.

We all shook hands with Mao. "Happy New Year, Chairman," we said.

"Our custom is to celebrate New Year's with the common people," Mao explained to me, "so we have invited them to join us here." He strolled among them shaking hands and chatting. I got the feeling that, having been a country boy himself, Mao lived on very easy terms with his country neighbors. But just as at the first dance I attended in Yanan, I was struck by his cool, aristocratic stance—and his aloofness.

◆

Just after New Year's it became clear that we were soon going to have to leave Yanan.

In December, KMT general Hu Zongnan had begun moving his troops out of the Xian area, from points about 150 miles to the south. He was closing on Yanan, and the party ordered all dependents and nonessential personnel evacuated one day's march away, into the mountains. It was a shock to everyone in Yanan, who for years had felt secure in this remote hideaway. The crisis soon passed after the KMT made an unsuccessful military probe, intended as a test of strength. The families returned, but the old feeling of security did not.

I knew now that we would soon be abandoning Yanan to the Nationalists because Zhu De told me so himself, in an interview he conducted with me and Anna Louise. Chiang Kai-shek, Zhu told us, was planning a campaign that the Communists named the Dumbbell, because of its shape on the map. One end of the dumbbell was in Xuzhou, where four provinces meet along two of the principal rail lines, and between three of the four major rivers. Chiang was amassing huge forces there to attack eastward against New Fourth Army headquarters. The other concentration of troops was in Xian, at the other end of the rail line that formed the bar of the dumbbell. From there, Chiang planned to attack Yanan. He wanted the prestige of taking Yanan, which would improve his image and his chances of getting more aid from the United States.

But, said Zhu, the Communists were determined to shatter this dumbbell strategy and to make it the turning point in the whole war. First of all, they would retreat, not fight, using the ancient strategem of luring the enemy deep into their own chosen territory. "Yanan isn't really a capital," he said. "Still less is it a military or economic center. It means nothing to us. Let Chiang tell the world he has captured our headquarters. We will abandon it and let him do so. He doesn't know this territory, and he doesn't know the people. His armies won't be able to feed themselves, and he is bound to overextend himself, to scatter his forces and to lay himself open to guerrilla attacks.

"Our strategy, then," Zhu continued, "is to lure them in, deprive them of food and supplies, drag them around the countryside up and down mountains on wild goose chases until they are completely exhausted. Then we will attack them with our main forces, which have been resting, studying, and regrouping. The KMT soldiers are conscripts, who will be more than interested in land reform, and in getting even with their officers. When they become tired, we will destroy their units, taking over most of their men and all of their arms and supplies. We will then use them to destroy more of their own armies."

As confident as Zhu De sounded, however, the senior leaders were clearly anxious. As the weeks dragged on, the atmosphere became progressively more tense, and under the pressure of constant round-the-clock meetings, the leaders began looking more and more strained. One day I was visiting George Hatem in his two-room dwelling near the military headquarters where meetings were always being held. George was a special adviser to the Liberation Army office's foreign affairs department, and so shared their quarters. He lived in a stone house, built to mimic the security of the caves, but constructed in a traditional style around a central courtyard. He and Yang Shangkun, who was deputy director of the PLA office, shared a courtyard with the foreign affairs section's ambassador-trainee, Huang Hua. George's little boy played with Yang Shangkun's son.

I was just getting ready to say goodbye to George when, without warning, Mao Zedong appeared in the doorway, skipped polite introductions and simply strode right into the room. Rearranging two chairs, he slouched back in one and slung his feet out over the other. "I'm tired," he said. "I've had a whole morning of meetings and I've just come over to relax for a while."

He looked tired. His mouth drooped and he heaved a big sigh. He fished in his pocket for a packet of the strong local cigarettes he favored. Then he pulled off his jacket, a brown woolen knit with a rounded collar. George poured him some tea. Mao slurped it and lit a cigarette, chain-smoking them one after the other, lighting the next one from the last. His fingers browsed the curios on a side table. In Yanan, dinosaur bones uncovered by the local peasants were much prized; George had a fine specimen, and Mao picked it up and admired it. It was clear that he didn't want any serious talk; but it was also clear that he was very wound up.

George, a doctor, asked after Mao's health. "How have you been sleeping recently?" he asked.

"Badly," Mao said. "Very badly. Ever since I've come back from Chongqing I've felt very tense. I just can't relax."

Neither George or I knew exactly what he meant. But I suspected he was brooding over internal disputes about the wisdom of going ahead with an all-out civil war. One faction of the leadership believed that the United States would respond in force, including nuclear weapons, if the Communists were to offer armed resistance to the Nationalists. That, in turn, would lead to a third world war. The other argument—to which Mao subscribed—held that the United States would provide major help to the Nationalists but that the American government feared world war more than the Communists.

Lighting another cigarette, Mao idly picked up a *Saturday Evening Post* that was lying on George's table. He flipped through it, examining the insurance company ads, and the pictures of automobiles and fashionably dressed men and women. "Do you know Larry Rossinger?" he asked me, referring to an American China scholar who had recently visited Yanan. "I quarreled with him a few months ago. Rossinger said that the American ruling class is confident in their power, and think they can rule the roost. What do you think?"

I told him that wasn't the way I saw it at all. I thought there were different groups in America, and that the group represented by MacArthur, which was warlike and adventurous, wasn't in the majority. The predominant group, I argued, represented by Truman, Marshall, and people like Dean Acheson, was much more bent on conciliation.

Mao listened very intently, and again I felt a sense of wonder at having the attention of the great man. His focus was so intense that it tended to draw me out, to make me say more than perhaps I had intended.

"Most of my comrades don't agree," Mao said. "They don't agree with that estimate of the American ruling class. They agree with Rossinger. They think the U.S. leadership is cocky and bent on world conquest. I don't think they are confident. I think they lack confidence. I think that's why they are being so aggressive and belligerent."

We agreed, it appeared. But that didn't seem to make Mao warm up to me. His attention didn't seem to include affection or friendship. Seeking to make a little joke, I pointed to a picture in the magazine of a middle-aged executive type who was reaching out for some headache medicine. "Here's an American imperialist who looks worried," I said, thinking he would find amusing such a caricature of weakness in a member of the American ruling class.

Mao did not find it amusing. Instead, he trained a look on me that I interpreted to mean: how can you say something so flippant? Maybe he was just overwrought, but I couldn't help feeling that the reason for the disapproving glance was that—unlike Zhou

Enlai—Mao didn't really like me and didn't really trust me. I felt awkward, but just then Mao's adjutant poked his head through the door to summon him back to his meetings.

◆

On the first weekend in March, Anna Louise Strong left on the last American shuttle out of Yanan. Knowing that the battle was about to begin, the U.S. Army had pulled all its liaison officers out of Yanan and had warned the rest of us to leave too. I myself had received a formal letter from the chief of the liaison mission, the man who had wanted to exclude me from his Thanksgiving dinner, enjoining me to leave with the army group. The American government, the letter read, would not be responsible for my safety in Yanan. I hadn't relied on the American government for my safety before, so I ignored the letter.

On the afternoon of the very day that the last plane left, the first B-29 bombing of Yanan took place. The planes began coming over, wave after wave, while we were still eating breakfast. We couldn't walk outside, so we threaded our way to work through the network of air raid shelters inside the mountain. There, I found work proceeding as usual. Nobody mentioned or even seemed to notice the bombing, beyond a brief warning from C. T. Sim to be ready to move the typewriters into the air raid shelters if necessary.

Just as he finished speaking, the machine gun fire started. Liberation Army guards were firing from their dugouts on top of our mountain at the incoming bombers. Before we could pick up our typewriters and move toward the air raid shelters, we heard the rising whine of a falling bomb. There was a brief second of silence and then the blast, which blew out the wooden door and window frames of our cave. Earth crumbled from the ceiling. We fled for the shelters and crouched in the darkness waiting.

Then the freakish whine began again and I was suddenly seized with a feeling of doom. Raising my arm, I shouted, "Down with U.S. imperialism!" Immediately, there was an ear-splitting explosion, this time a direct hit on the mountain slope just above the roof of our cave. A section of the roof fell in, and our colleagues from the next cave came scurrying through the corridors of the shelter.

But something odd had taken place. When I raised my arms and shouted, all attention had turned to me. But rather than treating my act as a brave gesture of defiance, my colleagues seemed disapproving. One editor stooping next to me turned and said, "For us Chinese, the prospect of death holds no terrors. We are not afraid to die."

As the bomb hit and the earth shook and rained down on us, I marveled at his words. Didn't he see that my gesture was a sign of courage? I sensed in my heart what the answer was: he realized that I was terrified.

That afternoon, the evacuation of Yanan began. An advance party had been sent ahead to a location that had already been prepared a day's march away at a place called Tile Kiln Fortress. The rest of us were told that there would be no work the following day. We were to use the daylight hours to rest and get ready to move out. We would leave the next night under cover of darkness.

That night, I was almost paralyzed with fear. Again and again, as I tried to sleep, I heard the approaching roar of planes, the whine of falling bombs, and the ear-shattering roar of explosions. Over and over I started upright in my wooden bed. My mind seemed to turn in upon itself. I could see myself being burst open by the concussions or blown apart by the bombs. I had to escape.

Early the next morning, I announced that since I had not rested well, I was going out into the countryside to find a quiet place to nap. I walked and walked and walked, moving swiftly along the yellow loess roads, never stopping or looking back. I finally reached a high ridge from which Yanan and its surroundings were completely out of sight. I felt much better. Leaving the road, I climbed up a hillside to some pastureland and sat down on the edge of a gully where I knew I could hide if the bombers appeared again.

I tried taking a nap, but I was too tense. So taking out my notebook and pen, I wrote out "Ode to a Nightingale," one of my favorite poems. I found Keats's imagery soothing, and after a while, I dozed.

I awoke to find an old peasant man and a little boy standing over me. "Aren't you cold out here?" the old man asked, puckering his mouth up with concern.

"No," I answered sheepishly. "I'm warmly dressed. See?" I showed him the heavy woolen sweater I was wearing under my cotton padded suit and overcoat. Feeling that I owed them an explanation, I went on. "I was up all night working, and we have to march all night tonight, so I decided to find a quiet spot to get some sleep during the day."

The two of them said nothing, so I continued. "I am a foreign expert with the Xinhua News Agency on Mount Qing Liang in Yanan."

"Good!" the old man said, with a pleased expression. "So you're a friend. Where from?"

"America," I answered.

"Why don't you come down to our village," the old man said with a broad, genial smile. "We'll give you some tea and find you a place to rest that's quiet and comfortable. You've come a long way. You must be tired."

Only then did I realize that I had walked all the way to a village about fifteen miles from Yanan.

"You run down first and tell them to get some fresh water boiling for our friend here," the old man said to the boy, "so that it's ready for him when he gets there."

The boy was off down the hillside like a little goat, and we picked our way down after him. When we arrived at the village, the old man steered me toward a building with a large door, like a garage. He pulled open the door and said, "Go on in. It's warm inside."

I was greeted by a thunder of voices. "Hands up!" I looked around and saw a crowd of very determined young peasants, armed with every kind of weapon imaginable—rifles, red-tasseled Chinese spears, even hand grenades—all of them pointed at me.

They searched me and left the building, all except for two guards. Then a young man came in, who introduced himself as the district government leader. Who was I, he demanded to know. What was I doing in their village? I explained as well as I could and he listened carefully, thinking over what I was saying, but he was obviously not convinced.

Then he produced my notebook. "What were you writing up there in the hills?" I told him it was a poem and he asked me to read it, line by line, and explain to him what it meant. He clearly understood my embarrassed disquisitions on the meaning of an ode written a century and a half earlier, but he couldn't understand why I had come all the way from Yanan to their hill country to write these romantic musings on mortality.

Finally, the young district leader made his decision. After feeding me a bowl of steaming hot noodles, he would send me back to Yanan under armed guard. If I belonged to the news agency as I claimed, then I would be handed over to my unit, and the case would be closed. We started out and had walked for no more than ten minutes when we met the advance guard of our news agency unit coming in the opposite direction, from Yanan toward Tile Kiln Fortress. I had unwittingly taken our route for evacuation that morning, and our people were already pulling out.

Hu Xiaowei's fiancé, Zhao Disheng, was part of the advance party. He greeted me heartily and immediately signed the release paper that the two guards had brought with them. "I told you he was all right," one guard said to the other. "He didn't look like an enemy spy to me."

The agency truck soon caught up with us, with Liao Chengzhi and the other leaders in the back and Ah Pu, Liao's wife, and their baby daughter in the front seat with the driver. "Climb in," Liao told me curtly.

I was still terrified by the thought of being bombed again. I wanted to walk so that I could run for cover whenever there was an air raid, rather than riding in a sitting-duck truck. But Liao, for the very first time, was angry. "No, no, you get in this truck. I don't have the slightest bit of confidence in you anymore." I had rarely seen him angry, which made his fury more potent. Still, I could understand his rage. I had caused them a great deal of trouble at a time when they had trouble enough.

I got in the truck just as a KMT plane appeared in the sky and began making lazy circles directly above.

CHAPTER SIX

My Long March

Tile Kiln Fortress was about sixty miles from Yanan. It was a village of caves, like Yanan, that had been selected by our news organization as our rear base, with a print shop and a backup sending station. We arrived before daybreak, were assigned living quarters in the local caves, and immediately resumed work. Because we were so close to Yanan, I still expected to be bombed at any moment. I listened tensely for the telltale drone of approaching planes and contemplated my own imminent immolation.

But as I looked around at my comrades, I realized I was alone in my terror. Through all the bombings, the cave-ins, the hurried evacuation, the wails of the children and travails of the sick, I saw not one adult, man or woman, who seemed frightened. Not one. Everyone was calm, even diffident. It seemed almost beneath their dignity to discuss the air raids, let alone betray a fear of them. If anyone mentioned the bombing, it was only to poke fun at the KMT, to mock its marksmanship.

I wasn't alone in noticing this difference in our reactions. The next evening after supper, my old Shanghai friend, Xu Maijin, invited me to walk with him outside the village. We took a narrow winding path that followed a small stream. It was March, a thaw was just beginning, and I could hear the gurgling under the thin, melting ice. We stood and watched the jelly-red tints of the sky, dyed by the setting sun.

Then Xu spoke, gently. "What is your problem, Comrade Li Dunbai? Some of us think that you must suffer from a bad heart, and that's why you react in this way to air raids. Is it true?"

I shook my head. "No, there's nothing wrong with my heart, or anything else. It's just that right now I panic at the very thought of bombing. I've tried to overcome this fear in every way I know, but I haven't been able to. I don't know what to do."

Xu repeated the message that the old editor crouching in the cave had given me. Clearly it was something they wanted me to understand. "We Chinese Communists," he said, "have a different view of life and death. We hold with the old Confucian doctrine to 'Regard Death as a Returning.' We are not afraid to die. No true revolutionary should be afraid to die. Just think of the bad effect that your behavior has on the nonparty masses, who expect us to set an example and point the way forward. The comrades have asked me to talk with you and help you. I'm hoping you will be able to raise your consciousness and learn to control yourself."

But I hadn't the slightest interest in learning to control myself. All I wanted was to get away from the bombing, away from the danger. I wanted to claim the spots closest to escape routes, and to have the right to drop everything and run whenever I heard the drone of incoming planes. I resented the party's attitude. Instead of helping with my problem, party members were simply demanding that I fall into line and react as they did.

Xu was silent. He was disappointed in me, I knew, and puzzled. The gap between me and them grew deeper and plainer than ever. This was not Birmingham, Alabama, or High Point, North Carolina, and I was not the passionate, dedicated youth that I had been in 1940. Here, I was helping the Chinese with their cause, not fighting for my own people's rights. I was willing to endure a lot, but I wasn't ready to be blown away by a five-hundred-pound bomb. I still wanted the greatest good for the greatest number, but I couldn't bear the extent to which they were prepared to sacrifice individuals for it.

I cared about myself as an individual. I cared about my own self-preservation. I cared about the pursuit of happiness, not just for the masses, but for myself. And right there at that moment, after the sudden shock of my first bombing, that self-preservation took the form of a physical terror I could not control.

Still, in my heart I felt that my terror could not be justified, that they were right and I was wrong. Until I could overcome my selfishness, I could never really become one of them, never really share their struggle, never really make common cause with them as they forged their new world. Until I was ready to die for them, I could never really live as one of them. I felt a deep sense of weakness and guilt.

◆

For most of the next four months, our little band of revolutionaries was in flight. Chiang Kai-shek, with superior arms, manpower, money—mainly supplied by the American government—pursued the Communists, hoping to surround and annihilate us. In reality, it was the other way around. The crafty Mao, like the leaders of the American Colonial forces fighting the British, used his knowledge of the land, his close ties with the peasants, and his brilliant strategic mind to drag Chiang Kai-shek and his Nationalists into fights they couldn't win. We seemed to be fleeing the KMT, but in fact it was we who were leading them on, into the jaws of defeat.

This was a war full of satire and travesty, full of mocking lampoons and laughs-up-the-sleeve. For Mao Zedong, Commander-in-Chief Zhu De, and the bullet-headed General Peng Dehuai, leader of the armies around Yanan, were masters of trickery. Later, Zhu De explained it to me: "We have a job that few other commanders have faced," he said. "We not only have to command our own troops, we have to command our enemy's troops as well. We threaten a city, or feint a military movement, or spread disinformation in order to move KMT troops to exactly where we want them. When they enter our trap, we destroy them."

And just as if he was reading from Mao's script, Chiang Kai-shek obligingly played his role. To the KMT, Yanan seemed a great prize in terms of publicity and prestige. It was good for American newspaper headlines, and they in turn were good for persuading hesitant congressmen to throw more American money down the steadily widening rathole in Chiang Kai-shek's capital at Nanjing.

Militarily, however, Yanan was worse than worthless to the KMT. It sucked one of their crack army groups into a desolate, semidesert country where there were no rations, ammunition, or supplies to replenish their stocks, and where the people were bitterly hostile. Wherever Hu Zongnan's forces went, they found that the fields and granaries had been stripped bare. Everything useful that could not be taken away had been carefully buried or concealed. All people and animals were gone.

After Yanan fell, we kept on moving, packing up under cover of darkness, setting off further and further into the mountains. Mao Zedong was in another group nearby. When he moved, we moved. Sometimes we stopped in a hospitable village for a night or two. Sometimes we settled in for longer. Wherever we were, we hand cranked our generators and sent out a Morse code broadcast. But always we were listening for the whine of the KMT bombers, and waiting for the signal to move on.

Our path took us climbing through the steep mountains of Shanxi and down through valleys filled with orchards and wild-flowers, then across the Hebei plains. We passed through villages that had barely been touched by the centuries. In one village, an old woman who had never seen a foreigner insisted I was an idol, just stepped down from a niche in some temple. We crossed areas so primitive that a difference of a few miles—from a lush river-bank to an alkaline area beyond the reach of irrigation—meant the difference between prosperity and near-starvation.

We moved deeper and deeper into the mountains, while Mao Zedong remained near Yanan to play a sardonic cat-and-mouse game with his adversary. Mao deliberately telegraphed his moves, and he led Hu Zongnan a merry chase from the mountains to the treacherous gulches, from the salt wells to the desert, from one hard climb and endless trudge to the next. He made it a point never to be more than one day's march ahead of the KMT. He knew that Hu Zongnan would be Chiang's hero if he was able to capture Mao Zedong in person, and Mao played that card for all it was worth. At every encampment he would wait until his scouts brought him the news that the enemy was only an hour's march away before he would methodically put on his coat, mount his horse, and lead his little headquarters party off down the trail. At dusk, he would insist on being close enough so that KMT scouts could tell that he was within an easy day's march.

"Weren't you afraid of a sneak raid in the night?" I asked C. T. Sim, who had been in the party accompanying Mao.

"The KMT didn't dare stir outside at night," he replied. "It was unfamiliar terrain to them, and it was very complicated terrain at that. Our scouts and the local People's Militia were laying for them, and they knew it. Mao understood the mentality of the enemy commander and his subordinates."

Time and again, when the KMT troops were exhausted, low on

both food and ammunition, and sick of the whole campaign, Peng Dehuai selected the most vulnerable cul-de-sac, cut off the enemy forces inside the pocket he had chosen, and hurled against them overwhelmingly superior forces, well fed and well rested, in a battle of total annihilation.

Even as we marched, we were preparing for victory. A few days after we set out from Tile Kiln Fortress, we arrived at Suide, just three or four hours' march away from the Yellow River. Along the way, our caravan ran into old Judge Chen, Mao's former teacher. He was the man whose mule-drawn sedan chair I had walked beside on the road from Kalgan as he lectured and railed against the KMT. "What are you doing in Suide?" I asked.

"We're trying to rush the draft of the new Constitution to completion, to be ready for the founding of the People's Republic," said the venerable judge.

◆

Leaving Suide, we marched on. In our group were old people, young people, families, babies, invalids. Many were city-bred intellectuals, not toughened fighters. Still, we averaged twenty miles a day through rough, mountainous terrain.

The Communists were superb organizers. Our news contingent was divided up into several columns. One included the headquarters cadres, to which I belonged. Another was for wives, children, and invalids. Each column had its leading nucleus, and each sent out an advance party early in the morning to requisition caves and mud huts for our night quarters, food and water, and anything else we would need. Large numbers of troops guarded our flanks on either side, taking parallel routes to ours, to insure that KMT forces wouldn't discover our movements and launch sneak raids against us.

There were only two people, to my knowledge, who refused to follow the order of march, and who started off by themselves early each morning. One was an editor named Lin Hong. He appeared sick and disgusted at China's endless warfare and shocked at the evacuation of Yanan. Although a party member, he refused to obey discipline and set out by himself every morning.

The other was me. I set off together with my unit, but would soon stretch my legs and leave the others far behind. I felt that by doing so I was lessening my chances of running into an air raid from which I could not hide. At the first drone of aircraft, I dashed off to some secluded spot and hugged the ground, head ringing, exhausted, gasping for breath, with every last ounce of romance and adventure pounded out of me.

Once we were in camp for the night, however, I returned to my colleagues, helping out wherever I could. I paid especially close attention to my friends Peng Di and Qian Xing, both of whom had been diagnosed with active tuberculosis. At night, the three of us would be quartered in the same peasant's room on the same kang bed. We had a copper washbasin that became famous as a "three-use basin." At morning call, I got up first and emptied the basin—it was used as a chamber pot during the night because it was very cold outside. Then I washed out the basin with hot water and ashes taken from the fire under the kang. I used the clean basin to fetch water for washing our faces and hands, then I scrubbed it again with ashes and hot water and went off to the camp kitchen for a basinful of morning porridge, which we all ate together with three big spoons. I didn't really think about catching tuberculosis; it seemed far more remote than the bombing.

Climbing and descending through valley and mountain, we marched for days through the Taihang range, crossing Mount Wutai, a sacred peak of Buddhism. We passed through villages the KMT had occupied only a few months earlier. I was horrified at the poverty there, worse than anything I had ever seen before. I found an old woman living in a house bare of everything—furniture, clothing, food. Her son was an opium addict and had sold all their belongings to feed his habit, leaving her to starve with her grandchildren. I saw a young girl, maybe thirteen or fourteen, wandering naked through the hills behind the village, because her family had only one pair of pants. I saw an old man who every day climbed up to his family crypt dug out of the cliff's side, put on his shroud and sat in his open coffin, hoping that death would claim him and spare his family the expense of caring for him.

Finally, after we crossed over to the twin villages of East and West Dipper, the geography changed. We moved into a broad alluvial basin on the banks of the Hutuo river, one of the richest and most beautiful areas we had yet seen. This was the only place in north China where the peasants grew both rice and wheat along the riverbanks, using the fresh river water for irrigation. Beans and green vegetables were also plentiful and the area was famous for its success in developing pig farming. So we had plenty of food once again, and clean river water to bathe in every day along banks sweet with honeysuckle. To cap it all, there had been no air raids in this area and we seemed safe.

Shortly after we arrived, the village people invited us to see their annual drama festival. It was a stunning example of how brilliantly the party used local talent and traditions to bring the peasants under its wing. The story was told in Hebei Province's bang-zi idiom, an ancient operatic form sung in a soulful, soaring, wailing blues mode, accompanied by the traditional Chinese opera fiddles, by a bundle of pipes, and in particular by a wooden clacker from which the term "bang-zi" derives.

The first scenes showed the misery and suffering of the peasants under the KMT. Then came the Communist-led Eighth Route Army troops during the war with Japan. When the Communists entered the village, the local people were terrified and immediately took off to the hills to hide. But what did they spy? The soldiers were fetching water, sweeping out courtyards, feeding and protecting the chickens and pigs. When the householders realized that this army truly was a people's army, they returned to the village and sent for their wives, children, and neighbors. Rents were cut, wages raised, schools and nurseries opened for working mothers. Then came land reform. As the play unfolded, I could see land reform through the eyes of the peasants themselves—their exultation when their despotic masters were overthrown.

The singing and acting began at sunset and lasted until sunup the next day. When dawn broke and the last scene had ended, the farming people got up, stretched, and headed straight out to the fields, often without even going home first.

The play was not merely propaganda. It portrayed what had actually happened in this village, and I could feel what it meant to tens and hundreds of millions of dispossessed, despised, and ignored Chinese peasants to have a new type of organization send in ardent young city students to teach them new ideas and songs, to unify them, to give them the voice to express their hopes and needs, and to lead them in the struggle to attain them. The Communists had breathed new life into the walking dead of China's countryside and I didn't want to acknowledge the gulf that was forming between myself and the Chinese Communists. I yearned to be fully part of them.

◆

After several restful, relaxing weeks by the Hutuo River, we finally received word to move on again. Packing up our things and leaving the mountains, we crossed the southern fringes of the great Hebei plains in Japanese army trucks that the local people had converted to burn charcoal, as there was no other fuel. A train ride and a day-long march took us to our new—and semipermanent—home, a village deep in the southern end of the Taihang mountains, the great range that runs south to north from the Yellow River to the Great Wall, and that forms the natural boundary between Hebei Province to the east and Shanxi to the west.

Our new home was actually a cluster of three ancient hamlets whose names—Western Garrison, Eastern Garrison, and the Walled City—dated back more than two thousand years. Here in relatively isolated safety, we found out what it was like to live, not just with hunger, but with terrible, terrible thirst. The whole area suffered from drought.

A tiny stream ran down at times from the southern slopes of the mountains, but it was so thin a trickle that we were limited to one pan of water a day for drinking and washing. Able-bodied villagers walked miles each morning to carry back two crocks of water on their shoulder poles for their households. The lips of elderly villagers were cracked. The oxen were listless and seemed only to shrug their shoulders when they were beaten and urged to move out into the fields at a slightly greater than snail's pace. The yellow loess topsoil was brick-dry, ready to fly upward like a cloud of smoke the instant there was the slightest breeze.

I lived with a peasant family in an adobe hut lined with gray-blue mountain stones and covered with a homemade gray-tiled roof. We resumed radio transmission and quickly reorganized into our semipermanent news operations.

Although planes rarely flew over the area, air raid alarms were frequent and I never got over my terror. Whenever we received an air raid warning or heard the sound of an aircraft motor, I would shoot out of the room, sprint down the village street, and climb up the nearest mountainside to hide myself. It became such a familiar sight that I once heard a group of old peasants, squatting in the village street to eat their noonday meal and chat together, say, "There goes Old Li."

◆

Then Wei Lin arrived.

After such a long time of fantasizing about her, I could scarcely believe my eyes when I saw her there in the office. I had long ago recommended that she be transferred here to act as announcer. But I had never actually expected that my suggestions would be heeded.

Wei Lin was as pretty and vivacious as ever, with her severe student haircut, round face, and chubby cheeks. I was delighted to see her. Still, my feelings were tinged with sadness because I felt that she could never be mine, nor could I let myself do anything to attract her and make her break her vow to wait for her fiancé.

Every afternoon, I listened to her read her script, sitting in the flagstone-paved courtyard of the former squire's house where we had made our office. After work, we talked and laughed together, but guardedly. I seemed to see her frown, displeased, when there was too much mirth between us, and I would slam on the brakes immediately. At twilight, we joined in the evening storytelling, ribbing and roasting, hill climbing, stream wading, and singing with our comrades. But never once did we pair off and walk or talk as a couple.

It was hard to keep my feelings in check. One day at sunset, Qian Xing, Peng Di, Hu Xiaowei, and I were sitting on some big rocks near the pretty little stream, singing songs from the *One Hundred Best Songs* collection. We sang "In the Gloaming," and it made me sweetly sad when I thought of my love that could never be returned. Qian Xing observed what was going on in my face and gave a little whoop, "Da jia kuai bei chang." "Hey, everybody, stop singing, stop singing. It's making some people sad at heart," she called out with an impish look of half-real, half-mock concern. I blushed.

Finally, one morning about three weeks after Wei Lin arrived, she handed me a little note. I had been waiting for some sort of rebuff, and my heart dropped when I read the folded knot of paper that said we needed to talk. I was sure she was going to tell me that we had to keep more distance between us.

Sadly, I waited for her in my room after lunch that day as she had instructed me. When she entered, she went to the far end of the room and sat down on one of the chairs. I sat on the kang and waited.

"We have to talk," she began. "I can't bear the way things are going, and it isn't good for our work."

It was just as I feared. "What's the problem?" I asked.

She began to cry, great big tears running down her round cheeks. She put her hands to her eyes. "I never thought I could be in love with two people at the same time," she sobbed.

When we came out of that little room hand in hand, no one who saw us had any doubt about what had happened. "You clever devil," said Deng Guang, an old bachelor who worked in our office. "You're a real tactician. You advanced by retreating. You figured if you kept holding back, the tension would build up and in the end you would win." I had no such intentions. Still, once Wei Lin had changed her mind, things moved with astonishing speed.

◆

We were married in October of 1947.

As required, we had sought permission from the party organization. Zhu Zhicheng gave his permission, but I was startled when Wei Lin told me that Zhu had privately warned her away from me. "We all like this young American," he said. "It's not just you who like him. But you should realize that we don't know a thing about him except what he has told us himself. We don't suspect him, but we don't really know much about him." Zhu admonished her sternly not to tell me what he said, but he had not reckoned on the force of affection. She came and told me immediately. I put the matter aside, planning to consult with Zhu privately later. I was so happy, such minor matters didn't seem important to me at the time.

The wedding was a merry one. The gathering was in my house, which had been decorated by a corps of volunteers. Liao Chengzhi, a talented cartoonist, had drawn a huge picture of a bespectacled foreigner drooling at the sight of the buxom part of Wei Lin, with two lines of poetry inscribed at the top:

Why mope at the sky, Foreigner?
True love is bound to end in marriage.

Both Wei Lin and I had to talk about the course of our love and how it had led to marriage. What we said was very simple, but the listeners made up for it by adding lurid descriptions of my so-called tactics. It was hilarious and it lasted for hours, with one after another of our colleagues speaking, singing, or doing some sort of parlor trick. "We have only one night, you have a lifetime," they teased. "Don't be impatient."

But soon after the wedding, the goodwill toward us began to fade. Almost immediately, our conspicuous love and happiness began to evoke objections and protests. Even my friends Qian Xing and Hu Xiaowei complained that we neglected our friends and displayed our happiness so lavishly that it made the lonely-hearted, the single, and the suffering feel worse. Qian Xing reproached me once: "You've brought home a daughter-in-law and forgotten your mother."

My position among the Chinese Communists was becoming increasingly anomalous. On the one hand, as the only American working in the area and the only American party member, I had already become nearly a legend. All sorts of myths were concocted about my exploits, my appetite for hard work, and my devotion to the cause. I still had my close friends, in particular Peng Di and Qian Xing, and I was still one of the most popular fellows around. But on the other hand, it was clear that more and more these days I was a stranger at the party.

Back when we had first arrived at East/West Dipper by the Hutuo River, I had suddenly been moved from the senior leaders' Little Kitchen meals to the lower-ranking Middle Kitchen—plus a hefty supplement of meat, eggs, sugar, and fruit to make up the difference in nutriment between the two kitchens. I had been agitating for such a move for months. I thought eating with the real people would demonstrate my revolutionary consciousness. Instead, I found that it cut me off from the source of inside information I had enjoyed.

Later on I found myself isolated from news department meetings. Several times when C. T. Sim, the head man, and Chen Long, his deputy, were absent and I attended the daily strategy meeting in their stead, I noticed that the meeting leaders looked unhappy at my presence. Finally, Chen Long was notified outright that I was not to attend those meetings. I demanded to know why, since I was a party member. Why should I be discriminated against? I could not get a straight answer.

My own actions didn't help matters. I desperately wanted to be one of them, to be included. But I still couldn't accept the outright crushing of individual wills and desires that the party seemed to demand. I rebelled against the system that required all announcers to live in isolation at the sending station, in a village about two miles away. All married couples thus separated were allowed to sleep together just one night, on Saturday. In defiance, I began a regular evening trek to Wei Lin's new home, walking back in the morning in time for work.

Li Xianhou, the sending station's political instructor, called me in for a serious talk. Radio station security, he said, demanded that cadres, and especially a conspicuous foreigner, not be seen walking through the mountains. What's more, he admonished me, this was a matter of revolutionary discipline. If I violated the discipline that others had to observe, that would make them angry both at me and at the organization. I was unmoved. I explained to Liao Chengzhi that I had to train Wei Lin in the evenings. He said nothing, which I took for approval.

And so Wei Lin and I were happy for a while. We talked baby talk, we teased and joked and laughed. When Christmastime came, we were overjoyed to discover she was pregnant. A few weeks later, we were devastated when she miscarried and almost died.

My friends and colleagues greeted the news coolly. They held me responsible for not keeping away from Wei Lin when she was pregnant. I had caused the miscarriage through my lack of self-control and discipline, they decided. Meanwhile, Wei Lin started complaining to me that her friends were beginning to treat her more formally, like a stranger.

One evening I came home from the office after she had stretched out under the kang covers to sleep. When I entered the room, she propped herself up on her elbows and looked at me with a crazed set to her eyes—a wild, staring, anguished look. Then she began to cry.

"What is it, what's happened?" I asked, rushing over to comfort her.

"There's something very bad in me," she said in a low voice. "At times I want to kill you. Kill you!"

The only emotion I could sense in her was fear—fear of herself, not hatred for me. "Never mind, you're tired and tense," I said.

◆

Mao's strategy was so effective that by late spring of 1947, Chiang Kai-shek's dumbbell campaign had been smashed and he was no longer able to launch major offensives anywhere in China. The Communist armies had struck southward across the Yellow River, driven nearly to the Yangtze across from Chiang's capital at Nanjing, and freed the city of Shijiazhuang to be their own north China capital. The American government and most of the press discounted Communist claims of victory. But talking to the field commanders and translating and polishing the reports as they went out, I knew they were true. Sometimes I would work all day over the battle reports, and then get up in the middle of the night to handle late-breaking news. My role in making this historic information available to the outside world filled me with pride—whether anyone believed it or not.

Having smashed the KMT invaders of Yanan, Mao then led his small headquarters contingent across the Yellow River to northwest Shanxi Province for rest and reorganization. There he launched the Rectification Campaign of 1947. Rectification was the container for Mao's real magic. It was the way he imbued his key cadres with his own philosophy, his own way of looking at life, analyzing issues, working out and implementing solutions. Rectification was ideological surgery. Through rectification, the cadres could be brought into line with the party's policies—not just on the surface but completely. The aim of rectification was to produce cadres who had been ideologically transformed.

During rectifications at our headquarters everyone had to read a few theoretical pieces, hear a guidance address, and then each individual had to make a detailed self-examination of his or her life and career before a group. What were your successes? What were your failures? What were the factors in your character and consciousness that led to these successes and failures? What trials and crises have you been through, and how did you hold up under the stress? Other members of the group would then tear the self-examination apart, pointing out problems or shortcomings that were being hidden or skirted.

I had heard many a hard-bitten Communist Party veteran say that the party couldn't possibly fall under the control of enemy agents or spies. During rectification, everything hidden came to light, they said. Mao firmly believed that it was only possible to really know a person when that person had been observed under severe trials and testing. Otherwise, he argued, there was no way to determine what was wishful thinking or empty talk, and what was the person's real position, purpose, and character.

I knew by now that party tactics could be brutal. I had seen a great number of high-ranking cadres who had been badly traumatized by earlier rectification campaigns. Some had been branded as spies, locked in dark caves, relentlessly interrogated to see if, under pressure, they would confess. Zuo Moye, a bustling department head, had never really recovered from his grilling. He was a hypochondriac who suffered terribly from headaches and an inability to sleep. Jiang Qisheng, the editor of Xinhua's foreign news department, was worse. I was sharing a kang with him one night when he was suddenly stricken with a resurrection of the horrors he had undergone. He fell face down on the hard brick and began to moan and cry like a small child. Someone sent for his wife, Zheng Defang, who lay down beside him and held his head to her breast, soothing and comforting him with soft words, until he fell asleep.

I pitied these people, of course, but in some ways I looked down on them too. While my unwillingness to give up my rights as an individual made me an undisciplined party member, my early philosophical training left me enraptured with the role of rectification. It seemed to be the Hegelian dialectic in action, whereby an individual weeds out negative characteristics and rises to new heights of humanity. I thought the party had a right to demand self-examination and self-improvement from its members. And in a time of war, I thought the party also had a right to assiduously purge itself of spies and potential spies. If one was accused of being a spy—even wrongly—I felt a good comrade should bear with the trial stoically.

Also, I had seen much good come from rectification. I thought people came away from rectification with a better understanding of themselves and their shortcomings, and with a program for correcting them. C. T. Sim had very successfully passed his rectification, turning from a fussy, chattering little bureaucrat into a quiet, collected, kindly person who seemed to have a good grasp of party policy, and who carried with him a genuine concern both for his own staff and for the future of the human race.

The first self-examination in our section was made by the deputy chief, Chen Long, who told the group how he had joined the party in college. Then he gave an account of his political experience since he joined the Revolution. In his self-criticism, he focused on his weakness as a leader. He was hesitant and indecisive, a failing he attributed to his lack of study and to his father's influence. His father, Chen Long said, had tried to accommodate the Japanese invaders in Indonesia.

When he was done, we all gave him credit for a sincere effort, and then proceeded to tear a great deal of his self-examination apart. He had not gone deeply enough into some of his less successful experiences, he had not been brave enough in digging for the ideological roots of some of his weaknesses; he seemed at times to be trying to cover up more serious problems by hiding them behind some trivial flaws.

I was dying for the opportunity to make my own self-examination. I had two things in mind. I wanted to raise my own level of consciousness and try to purge some of the anxieties and fears that had caused me so many problems. But also, I secretly felt that, if given a chance, I could demonstrate what an interesting and praiseworthy career I had already had.

To my astonishment, everyone from Liao Chengzhi down was reluctant to let me undergo rectification. They made all sorts of excuses. I was too new. I would find it too strange and taxing. It was their tradition not to get into heavy criticism of foreign comrades. Finally, they compromised and let me make a brief self-examination. I talked about my fear of air raids and my weakness in relations with women. But when I finished, there was virtually no comment or criticism. People talked about how much progress I had made, about how good I had been at adjusting to their way of life, and how hard I had worked.

I felt good.

Later, I heard that Li Mei, a young woman who had come with Wei Lin, had also been told that it would not be necessary for her to make a self-examination if she didn't care to. The reason given was that she was not a party member. When she did make a brief, factual report, she received no criticism, only faint praise. But then I learned that she was under serious political suspicion. In mealtime conversations, I heard it explained that it was bad policy to get involved in criticism or self-criticism with people who were suspected of having a really major problem. If the problem wasn't a question of ideology, but of possible connections with the enemy, it was better to avoid tangling with them. Otherwise, you might only help them to camouflage their true nature more skillfully.

I never linked the two cases together, hers and mine.

◆

Finally, in late spring of 1948, the news came that we were to move again. Yanan had been recaptured and the KMT troops in the area had been wiped out. The last remaining KMT crack troops were tied down defending Beijing and Tianjin, the northeast, and the Shanghai/Nanjing area. Mao Zedong, Zhou Enlai, Liu Shaoqi, Zhu De, and the others had set up a new Central Committee headquarters in the Taihang Mountains west of Shijiazhuang, a large city about five hours from Beijing. We were heading back to the Hutuo River.

We moved to a cluster of hamlets around the village of Xibeipo, where Mao's headquarters was located, and the months we spent there were among the most idyllic I had yet known. The civil war was nearly over. There were still days in which the alarms wailed and I went bounding out into the hills or hid in a cave. But now even the danger of air raids seemed remote.

There in that tiny village I felt most strongly the feeling of belonging that I had all along wanted. It seemed that my transgressions had been forgiven and forgotten and I was one of them again.

We worked together every day, and after supper all of us went walking out of the village along the country roads, joining evening strollers from neighboring villages and other units of the news agency. No one seemed special, no one was too high or too low to mingle together.

The traditional Saturday night dances had resumed. I went to them frequently and began running into Mao Zedong once again. With victory so close at hand, senior party officials were coming and going for high-level meetings, planning to take Tianjin, Beijing, and Shanghai, and to begin to set up the new management of those cities and get their economies running.

One day I met Mao very early in the morning. The sun was rising and I had just gotten up and was going for a walk. We lived in a valley between two rows of mountains, with the beautiful bright clear river running in a narrow strip down the center. It was cold and misty, with the kind of overcast that would burn away before noon. The winter wheat had already sprouted, and the ground smelled rich and loamy, a combination of earth, water, and the night soil and ash mixture the peasants used for fertilizer.

As I walked along the narrow dirt trail, I could see a figure looming in the mist walking with slow, deliberate strides, his hands clasped behind his back. It was Mao, and about forty yards behind him was a guard with a sidearm, carrying his overcoat. Mao apparently didn't see me. He cut off across the fields, walking along one of the raised earth ridges that demarcated plots.

I walked up to the guard who was carrying Mao's overcoat. "Why don't you give that to him," I suggested. "It's cold out."

The guard laughed. "He won't put it on. It's no use. They make me carry it, but he won't use it. And he won't let me get close to him. He's afraid it will scare off the peasants."

Mao walked over to a group of peasants who were squatting down, puffing on their long, thin-stemmed pipes with the tiny bowls that have to be filled and lit after every four puffs. They looked up when they saw him coming, but nobody moved. He squatted down beside them. What an effort it must be, I thought, for him to hunch down like that at his age—he was about fifty-five or so—and with his stiff, lumbering build. But then I could see him talking, and I could hear some laughter. I knew that the peasants couldn't understand everything that he was saying in his thick Hunanese, and he couldn't understand all of what they were saying. Yet it struck me that he seemed quite at home with them, and they with him.

It seemed remarkable to me that Mao felt so safe here in the middle of war-torn China. Like all the party leaders, he was living in this village under a code name, Li Desheng. Zhou Enlai went by the name Hu Gong, the bearded one. Liu Shaoqi was known as Xiao Zhang—the schoolmaster; and as for Liao Chengzhi, we called him San Ling'er—or 302—which was his prisoner number from the Chongqing dungeons run by the KMT secret police along with U.S. naval intelligence. Everyone recognized Mao for who he really was. And yet the KMT had never been able to find him.

Just then Mao headed back for the trail. I waited until he arrived. "Good morning," I said.

"You're up early," he replied.

"I'm just taking a walk. You're up early too."

"Oh," he exclaimed. "I haven't even been to bed yet."

"Why not?" I asked, although I knew the answer.

"Da zhang mang." I'm busy with the war.

Later that morning, I recounted my visit with Mao to one of the war correspondents at the radio station. He told me Mao hadn't been to bed in two weeks. He had been in the map room plotting out strategy and issuing instructions for his troops.

◆

During 1948, I realized I had paid a price for my care of Peng Di and Qian Xing. I began to feel odd and found myself running a fever in the afternoon and evenings. Several doctors sought the cause in vain. It wasn't until Dr. Huang Shuze, who for years had cared for China's top leaders, examined me that he was able to hear what the others could not: signs of active tuberculosis in both of my lungs.

There was no specific medicine available for tuberculosis. What was I to do? Dr. Huang put it to me plainly. "This will test how much you have really absorbed from your stay in China," he said. "If your response is the typical Chinese revolutionary response, then you will not let it prey on your mind. You will take the precautions and the therapeutic measures that the doctor advises, and at the same time you will forget all about it and be perfectly confident that you will overcome it." I spent a month in the hospital, reading, sleeping, and taking walks. I read the Chinese classics, *Outlaws of the Marshes* and *The Tales of the Three Kingdoms.* Then one day as I was taking my evening stroll outside the village, I ran head-on into the hospital's political commissar. He looked excited. "What's going on?" I asked.

He told me that the party's central revolutionary military commission had just concluded a top-level conference. Plans had been laid for final victory in the war, which was now officially titled the War of Liberation. At that moment, the PLA was attacking two major KMT strongholds: Jinan, capital of Shandong Province, and Jinzhou, a city that controlled the corridor from Manchuria down to the passes in the Great Wall and southward to north China.

He outlined the strategy for this final campaign. He said that the People's Liberation Army was going to capture both Jinan and Jinzhou, and when that happened, Lin Biao's forces in the northeast were going to wipe out all the KMT main forces in Manchuria and liberate the whole of that area. He would then move his troops down through the Great Wall passes into north China, joining forces with the PLA in that region to liberate Beijing and Tianjin. Finally, northern, eastern, and central forces would then march southward toward the Yangtze River crossings, hoping to catch and destroy the remnants of Chiang's main armies north of the river and completely destroy them.

I was elated beyond words. At last I could see victory in sight.

When I recovered enough to return to the news agency, I lost no time in sharing the good tidings with my colleagues. It caused a sensation, although not the kind I expected. Everyone was dumbstruck at what they considered a very serious leak of military information. And many of the lower-ranking officials were clearly jealous that I had access to such secret information before anyone had relayed it to them. The party branch secretary criticized me and told me to make a self-criticism at the English section party group meeting. So, once again, I had overstepped the boundaries of acceptable behavior.

◆

Early in 1949, the party announced that it was going to settle problems that had been left over from the Rectification Campaign. One day I ran into Lu Ye, a war correspondent, dashing madly about the office, gulping water and whining to whoever would listen: "It's going to start again," he wailed. "They've asked me to write another autobiography." He was clearly terrified. He had been through a rectification before and had been faced with spy charges.

Shortly afterward, I was also asked to prepare a new autobiography. Ding Ming, my wispy-bearded Hunanese neighbor in Yanan who had also been a victim of spy charges, offered to help me. I recited details from my political past, he wrote them down and I signed it. Ding said the party only wanted to clarify some details in my background. Unlike Lu Ye, I wasn't afraid. I welcomed the scrutiny. After all, I thought, I had nothing to hide.

◆

A few days later, Chen Long, the number two man in the English section, dropped into my quarters for a chat before breakfast. He said that because I had been with them for quite a while now and had achieved a good deal in my work, the party had a better understanding of me than at the beginning. He encouraged me to keep moving forward and not to worry about anything. If I had any problems or questions, I was to take them up with him. I thanked him and said that everything was fine.

A few days later, I was in the English section office after hours, alone with old Han Tuofu, an eccentric research worker whose nerves had been wrecked under torture in a KMT prison. I considered him a kind of friend, and we often laughed and joked together. That night, however, he was in dead earnest. "I've been watching how you operate and you're very clever," he said. "You're always making personal friends among our comrades, giving them little gifts or helping them learn this or that. You think I don't see what you're really up to, but I see right through it. You'll find out one of these days."

What could he have meant? I chalked his words up to his eccentricity. Still, his remark about "our comrades" bothered me. Wasn't I his comrade too?

At breakfast about a week later, I got a sudden message: Come to Liao Chengzhi's quarters at once. When I arrived there, Liao was standing in the middle of the room with a piece of paper in his hand. "You're being sent off on a special assignment," he said. "They'll be here to pick you up in half an hour. Get your things ready quickly."

While I was gathering my wits, Liao showed me the paper,

which was signed by the party Central Committee's central organization department. It read: "A responsible comrade of the party Central Committee will pick up Comrade Li Dunbai and take him to a special mission in Beijing."

So I was going to enter Beijing ahead of everyone else in the news agency! I was thrilled. The party had been negotiating with the KMT for the surrender of Beijing, and peace and victory were close at hand. Obviously, I thought, this summons meant that I was being sent to help in talks between the Chinese Communists and the United States on establishing diplomatic relations between the new regime and my own government. I was at last to play the role that history had cut out for me and I was enraptured at the idea.

There was no time to say goodbye to Wei Lin, so I scrawled a hasty note to her, saying we would meet soon in Beijing. I rolled a change of clothes and some toilet articles into a little pack and went back to Liao's office to await my escort. As we were standing there chatting, Ding Ming rushed in with a foreign wire service cable in his hand. It was from the Soviet Tass news agency, and in his reedy, quavering voice, he read the cable out loud. "The notorious American State Department spy, Anna Louise Strong," had just been arrested in Moscow.

"Is that so?" exclaimed Liao Chengzhi, looking sideways at me. "Can that be possible?"

I was startled. The elderly Anna Louise Strong a spy? It seemed incredible, but I didn't have much time to think about it, for just then, a messenger came in to say that a jeep had arrived to pick me up along with Comrade Shi Zhe. I was pleased to hear that. Shi Zhe was an amiable elder cadre, the deputy chief of the urban work department of the party Central Committee, which had something to do with the party's security apparatus. He would be good company on the long journey to Beijing.

Heading toward the jeep, Liao Chengzhi showed the first real affection toward me since we had left Yanan. He put his arm around my shoulders as we walked along together and said, "Never mind, little foreign devil. Everything's going to come out all right in the end. Don't worry about it. Whatever happens, don't be like Liu Bei when he entered the city of Jingzhou."

What did that mean? I remembered the story of Liu Bei from my reading of *The Tales of the Three Kingdoms* after I got tuberculosis. But what had Liu Bei done after he entered the city? I racked my brains, but for the life of me I couldn't remember.

I appreciated Liao's warmth and support and climbed happily into the front seat of the jeep beside the driver. Shi Zhe got in the back beside a smiling young man. The driver started up the jeep and off we went along the banks of the Hutuo River, toward Beijing.

Our route followed the river, threading in and out along its curves and bends on the little pressed-earth car road. Peasants with gleaming white towels turbaned around their heads were carrying water home on shoulder poles, the long buckets swaying in measured cadence to their light steps. I was daydreaming pleasantly of my new role under a Communist people's government when the young man I had secretly christened "the Smiling Lieutenant" sitting next to Shi Zhe in the back seat suddenly let out a loud "Ai-yah!" and raised his hands in a gesture of chagrin. "I forgot the thermos bottle," he said. "It's a long, dry trip. We'd better go back and get it."

Shi Zhe looked at him with vexation written all over his stern face. "I suppose we'll have to," he said. Then, to the driver, "Turn around and take us back to Huishe village. We have to pick something up."

We retraced our entire route and then the jeep turned left to ford the Hutuo River, which was low in the winter season. The little car climbed up the opposite bank and made for Huishe. We pulled into the village street and stopped in front of a Chinese compound with a high adobe wall, much like other former landlords' residences in the area. "Why don't you just wait in the jeep," said Shi Zhe, climbing out together with the young lieutenant. "We won't be a minute."

I was glad to wait outside. I had on my full complement of outdoor winter clothes and I didn't want to peel them off just to go inside for a few minutes. I kept my seat and waited. After four or five minutes, the smiling young lieutenant emerged. "Comrade Shi Zhe says for you to come in and have a cup of tea," he said. "He's run into something that will hold him up for a few minutes, and you might as well be comfortable."

I got out of the jeep and followed him in through the gates of the compound. On the inside, it proved to be just what it looked like from the outside: the typical home of some local squire, a quadrangle of one-story buildings. One wing was to our left as we entered the gate, another to our right, and the main hall and master bedroom were directly in front of us at the rear of the compound.

The young lieutenant ushered me into the room to our left, where there was a small square table and a few wooden chairs. "Just take a seat," he said, still smiling, "and they'll bring you tea in a moment." With that he left the room.

I waited for about two minutes. Then I heard someone—or something—approaching over the flagstones of the courtyard outside. It was a steady tapping sound. Tap . . . tap . . . tap . . . tap. I waited, curiously, expecting to receive my tea. Then the door opened and a man entered, tapping a cane before him. He was of middle age and medium height, dressed in a somber woolen cadre suit. But what struck me most were his eyes. They were as big as cartwheels. And it wasn't just their size, it was their intensity. They were pained, embittered, staring, blazing, accusing eyes.

He began to speak in a low, rasping voice. "Li Dunbai, we have received orders from the Chinese Revolutionary Military Commission to arrest you. You have accepted instructions from U.S. imperialism to sabotage the Chinese Revolution."

The Year of Darkness

The earth shook under my feet and the room swam before my eyes. Something stabbed at my brain, a fleeting shock that left me reeling. Me? Under arrest? This couldn't be real. I stared at the man, unable to speak.

Suddenly the room was a flurry of action. A half dozen young guards swarmed over me, searching my clothes and my body. They took away my belongings. One of them even opened my mouth and poked around in my teeth. When the search was over, they handed me a pair of cotton undershorts, cotton cloth socks, and black cotton padded pants and a jacket. I put them on. Then they led me out into a room across the courtyard and left me there.

This room was smaller than the first, and the windows were completely boarded up so that no light could enter. Most of the room was filled with a big brick kang. The door was wooden with a peephole cut in the upper portion. One of the guards who had escorted me returned to hand me a brass washbasin and a tiny bit of towel. When he started to leave, I began to cry. Unexpectedly, the guard turned to comfort me. "There, there," he said. "What's the matter with you? Do you think there's any problem that the organization can't solve for you?"

With that he closed and padlocked the door, leaving me in total darkness.

It was January 21, 1949.

An hour later, I was escorted back to the larger room. I sat in a chair with the door on my left and the table near the wall in front of me. Shi Zhe and the smiling lieutenant were on the other side of the table. The young man wasn't smiling anymore.

Shi Zhe glared at me. "Li Dunbai!" he said. "There are two roads in front of you, and you must choose which one you will take.

"Road Number One: Confess your crimes, fully and completely. If you can pour it all out just like that, I promise you that nobody will ever know you were once here in this little room. Our aim is to take this dagger that the enemy has plotted to use against us, turn it around and use it against him. So if you make a clean breast of things, we will get right back into the jeep and go on to Beijing, where you will perform your glorious special mission against the enemy. Surely, if there is the slightest bit of sincerity in you, if you have any real consciousness and humanity, you will pick this road.

"Road Number Two: Try to conceal your crimes, try to keep covering yourself up and posing as a revolutionary, and refuse to tell the truth. If you pick this road—and as I say, it's up to you—then you will have to spend some time in this room, thinking up ways to deal with us. But in the end, you will talk anyway. I can guarantee you that. We have ways of making people talk, lots of ways. Please—no matter how you look down on us Chinese—please believe that we know our job. We know how to make anyone talk—anyone, not to mention someone like you.

"So take the second road if you want. But I assure you," Shi said, patting his chest and knees suggestively with both hands, "you will not be able to stand it. The party's policy is clear and simple. Lenience to those who confess, harshness to those who resist. Take your pick."

While he was talking, I had began to realize that my arrest must have something to do with Anna Louise Strong's arrest in Moscow, although I wasn't sure how they were connected.

I still couldn't believe what was happening to me. "This is all a mistake," I stammered. "I have nothing to do with imperialism or sabotage or spying."

CRASH! Shi Zhe slammed his fist down on the table. "Just keep lying and pretending and see where it gets you. What do you take us for, boobies? Do you think it's a simple matter for us to arrest a foreigner and bring him here? Would we have done it without ironclad evidence to prove our case?"

"There are always mistakes," I muttered. "I didn't mean—"

But Shi broke in again. "Never mind what you mean. I'm telling you that you will make a terrible mistake if you decide to try us out, to see how tough we are. After all," he said with a somewhat overdone sneer, "for you Americans there is nothing more precious than your own life, is there? Your life, your wine, your money, your women . . ."

His taunts helped me because they made me mad. "That's not true," I said. "Americans can be as heroic as anyone else when they feel they have cause to be. Look at Midway, look at Guadalcanal, look at all the heroes in the South where I come from . . ."

"Don't talk dialectics to me," Shi stormed, pacing back and forth with his hands thrust into his pockets. Then he repeated the word in what I supposed was Russianized German: "Dee-ah-lesh-tish."

I began to cry again. "It's like a terrible nightmare," I replied. "And now you're threatening to torture me." I deliberately latched on to his statement that they had "ways of making people talk" and I would not be able to stand it.

"I never said that," he replied. "We have made that mistake in the past, but we will not make it again. Even if some of us wanted to get a little rough sometimes, Chairman Mao wouldn't let us."

Then they delivered me back to my cell.

◆

I sat on the edge of the kang. I'll lie down, I thought. I'll try to rest my seething brain.

Rap, rap, rap! From the outside someone pounded on the door and a pair of eyes appeared at the peephole. "You are not allowed to sleep!" a voice said.

"I'm not sleeping," I protested.

"Just keep walking, and behave yourself, or else sit up straight on the edge of the kang. You can sleep at night, after Lights Out, but not in the daytime."

Just keep walking up and down in this tiny pitch-black room? How long could anyone stand that?

I began to pace.

The space between the kang and the wall was about three paces by four paces. Four steps forward. Turn. Four steps back. Back and forth, back and forth. Lines from an old poem came to my mind:

One eternity and six paces;
Two eternities and six paces.

How could they arrest me? How could they accuse me of being a spy? How could they keep me here in this dark room? How could they think such things of me? How could they hate and fear me? Hadn't I been completely open and honest with them? Hadn't they seen the love, the ardor that I felt and demonstrated toward them? It didn't seem human. The Chinese Revolution all of a sudden seemed a monstrous, totally impersonal engine of history, rejecting and despising all human love and trust.

But I wasn't an enemy of the Revolution. I passionately believed in it. I didn't hate the party. I loved the party, its aims, and its struggle to change the world. I didn't even hate the men here who were persecuting me, devoid as they might seem of human sympathy and emotion. They were prosecuting my case because they considered it in the interests of the much oppressed, long-wronged Chinese people. They had to purge themselves of enemies, I told myself. It was just that in my case they were wrong. I wasn't their enemy, I was their friend. The problem wasn't with the party or its methods. It just happened that I accidentally got caught in a snare set for someone else, like a sparrow caught in a wolf-trap.

It was all a big mistake, I told myself. But then a terrible thought occurred to me. If the fact that they wrongly charged me with such a horrible crime ever became known, it could harm the party. It could damage the image people had of the leaders I had come to love, of Mao Zedong and Zhou Enlai. It might even cause an international stir. I couldn't let such an accident be turned against the party and all it stood for. I had to work hard to stay whole and brave and sane, not just for my own sake, but for the sake of the Revolution.

It was clear to me that a mental breakdown was the main threat.

The image of all the mentally wounded I had known flashed in my mind, memories of those cut to the brain by the wrongs they had been done in the Yanan Rectification Campaign: the shivering Jiang Qisheng, the hypersensitive Zuo Moye, the frightened Lu Ye, the plaintive Ding Ming. Come what may, I would never permit myself to be wounded as my friends in Yanan had been. They had ended up with a gulf between themselves and the people they had tried to serve. They were embittered, they were hurt, they were traumatized.

I made up my mind. This dark little room would be a test for me and a proving ground for my philosophy—and philosophy would win. If I came through this ordeal, it would be with perfect understanding. I disdained being like those who had been wounded in spirit. I would be myself to the end and stand with the people, no matter what.

But for the time being, the only thing I could do was pace up and down. At lunchtime, a steamed wheat roll and a bowl of vegetables were pushed through the door. Suppertime came and went, a bowl of millet. Then a guard came and placed a little bean oil lamp in a wall niche just above and to the right of the door. It gave off an eerie orange glow, just enough to let me see the difference between the edge of the kang and the floor.

I paced and I paced, thoughts flooding my mind. What could I do? What could I do? Finally the guard called in to me that it was time to sleep. I stretched out on the hard, cold kang covered only with my overcoat, cotton padded clothing, and thin cotton quilt. As I gazed at the tiny bean oil lamp, my mind still circled round with the unfathomable riddles and unthinkable wrongs that had begun with a stop in a courtyard for a cup of tea. The bitterness of the cup I was given to drink instead was beyond anything I had ever drunk. The flavor stayed in my mouth.

◆

A rapping on the door awoke me the next morning. The keeper thrust a washbasin, a cup of water, and a toothbrush through the door, and then removed it when I had finished. Breakfast was a bowl of rice porridge and some salted vegetables.

I began walking back and forth again. Four paces. Turn. Four paces. Turn. I reviewed my situation. My health was not good. I was still suffering from tuberculosis in both lungs. I was desperately lonely. I who had flouted party discipline because I couldn't stand to be apart from my wife for a single night was now facing a separation from everyone that could go on, who knew for how long. What's more, I was still terrified of bombs, and here I was trapped in a place where I could not move an inch toward a shelter.

I had to do something positive. How could I convince these

highly trained, hard-boiled characters I was dealing with that I was not a spy?

Then I made a decision. I decided to fight my case by accepting their rules. I decided to believe in the party. I felt that as long as I told the truth about everything, the party would understand me and judge me fairly. By giving a clear and provable account of my positive side, and at the same time going out of my way to reveal to them anything that might cause the slightest bit of suspicion, I could show them that I had no intention of hiding anything.

I felt better with this strategy in mind. I began to piece my story together, and for two whole days I walked back and forth in that black room, thinking, planning, worrying, sorrowing.

After breakfast on day four, the door was unlocked again and the guard led me across the courtyard to the interrogation chamber. This time, it was the young lieutenant who was sitting alone behind the table, while the guard took up his position with his back to the closed door. His name was Xu, and for a moment his ingratiating smile returned. "What have you been thinking about during these days?" he asked, as if he were a schoolteacher talking to a student just back after the holidays.

"I've been planning to tell my story, just as you both said— factually, holding back nothing whatsoever."

"Don't be in such a hurry to talk," Xu remarked coldly. "Your first problem is to set your attitude straight. Without a change in your attitude, it will be impossible to state your crimes clearly and in full. Your attitude was very, very bad when we last tried to talk with you."

"The change is that I'm now ready to talk," I replied, "and I know what I need to say. But I don't understand what you mean by changing my attitude. Surely it wouldn't be a good attitude if I admitted charges that are not true."

Xu looked daggers at me. "Who is asking you to admit anything that isn't true?" he snapped. "Did I ask you to do that? Did Comrade Shi Zhe ask you to do that? I must warn you, we are being very polite to you, but you had better be careful what you say. Our patience is not without limits.

"In order to change your attitude," Xu went on, "you must study and understand the party's policy: lenience for those who confess, harshness for those who resist. So don't try to prepare to tell your story now. It's useless. Just study the party's policy and work on correcting your attitude. Do you understand?"

"I'll certainly be glad to study whatever you give me," I said.

"Just study those simple lines: lenience to those who confess, harshness to those who resist."

With that I was taken back to my dark room.

◆

That afternoon and night, I worked on cracking the policy code. Lenience for those who confess. But if I was innocent, then confessing meant stating my innocence and answering any questions they might have, didn't it? Surely they couldn't say I was resisting just because I didn't accept the charges they hurled against me. All I had to do was to stick to my guns. But on the other hand, they had set themselves up as the sole authority. Their attitude was if we say you're guilty, you're guilty and to deny it was to attack them, which was a bad attitude.

Could it be that this arrest wasn't real at all, but merely a test? Was this a form of rectification, a more rigorous and onerous test they put important new party members through to toughen their spirit, weed out their defects, and prepare them for more responsible tasks in the revolution? If that was the case, then they weren't thrusting me out at all, but rather embracing me more completely.

My mind leaped at that happy thought. But if it was not a test? They were thrusting me out and the terrible pain of their rejection surged through me. I wanted so much to be one of them. How could they not know that? How could they cast me out?

My mind began to swing back and forth in that dark little room between taking what they said at face value and searching for some hidden intention that would throw a more cheerful cast on what they were saying and doing. I became nearly frantic with my see-sawing thoughts, not knowing what was right, not knowing which instinct to trust. One moment, I felt the full weight of their rejection and their ominous threats. The next, I toyed with the idea that perhaps I was the fool and these comrades were hoping and praying that I would pass this test of loyalty, and go on to remold myself ideologically and enter the true inner circle of the party. Either way, I told myself, the only way out was to try to keep a cool head, be tough—polite, but firm—and stick it out.

One morning days later, I was led to the interrogation room to face Xu again. "You said you wanted to tell your story," he began. "We've decided to let you talk. But I must tell you at the start that we don't want any prettying up or window dressing. Give the facts exactly as they are, neither covering up nor exaggerating. Be careful to distinguish clearly between what you know is a fact, what you think is probably a fact, and what you may have heard or seen but are not really clear about. And keep in mind the party's policy: lenience for those who confess, harshness for those who resist."

I began with my family background: nonproletarian, of course, but not ruling class either. I told Xu what good men my father and grandfather had been, how they had worked in the interests of the underdog, how honored and respected they were in Charleston, and how our family revered honor and truthfulness. Then I talked about my education. I was rebellious toward the ROTC in prep school, and I joined the radical student movement at Chapel Hill, influenced by my mother's father, a Russian Jewish revolutionary. I joined the American Communist Party when I was only eighteen, working in the labor and civil rights movements in the South. In the army, I worked hard for the chance to learn Chinese and go to China, and once I arrived I began doing everything in my power to support the Chinese Revolution . . .

Xu listened politely, taking everything down, for parts of three days. He asked for, and I gave, a particularly detailed account of my activities after arriving in China. When I had finally finished, he told me to return to my cell and rest up a bit. He would have some questions to ask me a little later.

I went back with a much lighter heart. He had not challenged, or sneered at, or contradicted anything I had said, including the portrayal of myself as a sincere revolutionary. For the first time, I saw light at the end of the tunnel.

The next morning, I was taken to the interrogation room to confront Xu again. "You have talked very little about your social contacts," he said calmly. "You should give an account of your social contacts. Make up a list and we'll discuss it."

That was a good sign. I could easily do that. There was nothing suspicious in any of my contacts. I would even tell them everything I knew about Anna Louise Strong. If she was a spy, it was better that they know all about my relations with her, which were pretty limited at that. Still, I didn't believe she was a spy, and I didn't think they did either.

When I was taken back to the interrogation room the next morning, Xu opened with a question. "Well, what have you been thinking about since yesterday?"

"I have prepared some social contacts to talk about," I answered, "starting with Anna Louise Strong."

"Oh, very well," he said. "If you choose to start with her, go right ahead." He picked up his pen expectantly.

I began the story: how we met, who introduced us, where and when I had seen her afterward in the States, what we had talked about, how I happened to work with her in China.

Suddenly Xu threw his pen down and glared at me in disgust. "This is a complete waste of my time," he said. "Do you think I have nothing better to do than sit here and take down this gossip? Get back to your room and think carefully and honestly about what we have been telling you: lenience to those who confess, harshness for those who resist. And I warn you, if you keep going on like this, you will learn the meaning of harshness."

I was stunned. Just when I had thought I was winning some understanding from him, this sudden body blow.

Xu must have read my thoughts. "Just because I take down what you say and don't expose or rebuke you," he said sternly, "don't think I'm taken in for one minute by all the rubbish you are giving us. Your attitude is wholly dishonest—and you know how important attitude is in deciding your fate. You are staying away from all serious problems and giving us a lot of inconsequential nonsense. Do you think we are children, easily hoodwinked by someone like you?"

"It looks like you're determined not to give me a chance," I said, very downcast. "You're demanding that either I admit to being a spy, which I am not, or there's no way out. You've already drawn your conclusion and reached your verdict. You're just trying to get me to corroborate it."

"Shut up!" Xu roared at me, his thin face flushed and his cadaverous eyes full of hatred. "Who told you we've already drawn our conclusion? You're vilifying the Chinese people, and I warn you to think of what the consequences of this course of action can be for you. You know our policy—I recite it to you dozens of times a day. You'd better think it over and set your attitude to be a little more honest."

◆

It was three days before I faced Xu again. I was prepared. I recited a list of my most dubious-sounding contacts and activities. I had tried my best to join the OSS while I was a student at Stanford. I had a cousin who had done work for the FBI. I was shockingly weak in the face of the KMT bombers, which had damaged the party in the eyes of the masses. I had erred morally in my dealings with that woman in Yanan.

When I began to describe how the chief of the observer section at UNRRA had asked me to gather intelligence about the Communists in the liberated areas, I began to sense some interest from Xu. But he was very guarded, obviously not wanting to betray any feelings about what I was saying. When the session was over, he told me I would be given paper and pencil with which to write down the gist of what I had said.

I wrote that afternoon with a real sense of achievement and relief. At last, I had been able to come up with something that they would accept.

But when we met again, Xu picked up the pages I had written as if they were soiled and disagreeable. "Sometimes," he said, "we ask you to write down a bit of data when you may be skirting the edges of a problem without telling the real story, or when you may pretend to be discussing something important but are really hiding something else by discussing it. We do this simply to give you another chance to change your attitude and be honest. You have failed miserably, again, and have therefore forfeited the opportunity. We have decided to let you just sit and think over your attitude and the party's policy. Get back to your room!"

I was wretched. Again I had been given some hope, only to be cruelly rebuffed. I was doing my best to be a revolutionary, to bare my bosom to the party, to take a rigorous self-critical attitude. And they kept scorning me, accusing me of being dishonest.

This was not only a miserable nightmare, it was a crazy nightmare. Nothing made sense. The fear of aloneness and insanity began to grow and to prey on my mind. I felt a desperate longing for some sense, some logic, some human feeling and understanding. My brain was working overtime, running in the same narrow track between hope and despair, swinging back and forth, back and forth.

◆

Two weeks went by in silence and darkness, and a cunning little idea began to grow on me. If I made up a story in which I claimed to be a spy, but didn't implicate anyone else, perhaps I could win their lenience. I would be sent for labor reform at some far northern or western wilderness post. I would work there for years on end, winning the respect of my fellow inmates and my captors. Finally the day would come when I could reveal that my story had been faked. I would explain that I had done this to protect the party from disgrace and so I could prove I was loyal and dedicated.

Convinced I could carry it off, I went to the door and called out to the guard, "Report!"

"Hush! What is it?" came the reply.

"I've thought it all through, and I want to confess," I said.

Nothing happened that day, but the next morning after breakfast the door opened and a guard handed me three pieces of tablet paper and a pencil. "Write," he said. Then he gave me my glasses, which I had not seen since my first day in solitary. He left the door open so I could have a little light to see by.

I sat down and wrote a simple fable about coming to the Communist liberated areas with the mission of collecting intelligence. I was to find my own ways of sending it back to the United States, to a mythical friend of mine who had channels for getting it to the proper people. I handed my "confession" to the guard and waited to see what would happen next.

The next morning, I was taken to the interrogation room. I jumped when I saw both Xu and the man with the cane who had made the accusations against me. "The most outstanding quality of the petit bourgeoisie," said the man with the cane, "is that they disclose a little and hold back a little, disclose a little and hold back a little. Your problem can only be solved if you disclose the entire story, holding back nothing. Do you understand?"

"Yes, I understand," I replied, relieved at the mild tone of his voice. "The facts are all there in the deposition."

He shook his head. "Go back and think it over carefully," he said. "Carefully. It's time that you did something to settle your problem."

Several days later I was taken back to the interrogation room. This time both Xu and Shi Zhe, looking particularly grim, sat behind the table. "So you've decided to talk," Shi said.

"Yes," I replied. "I've understood the party's policy and I want to tell everything."

"Listen to me," Shi said. "Try to tell it all in one breath, including your connections, your contacts, how the arrangements are made for you to accomplish your mission, and where in your life you made the first misstep that led to your downfall. You didn't become an enemy agent overnight. Only when you make a clean breast of all of this can we begin to help you and finally bring you to salvation and a new life of service to the people."

I went cold. This place was affecting my powers of judgment! If I were a spy of course there would have to be contacts and channels for sending messages. How could I confess without naming names? But that was impossible. Anyone I named would be damaged. Even if I picked foreigners who were long since gone from China, if they were still alive and had friends and contacts in China, they all might suffer. Naming Chinese who had died wouldn't do either. Their relatives might be victimized by my false accusations.

I looked at Shi Zhe in utter dismay.

He looked back at me with a curious expression on his stern face. "So you are a secret agent?" he asked, curtly.

I nodded.

The strange expression vanished, replaced by a naked anger. "I've seen all sorts of agents," he stormed. "Some agents have their own kind of integrity. You're an agent with no integrity."

He looked at me again and I began to fall apart. "Is what you are saying really true?" he asked.

I burst out crying. I felt my heart would break. I shook my head and sobbed, "No, no it's all a pack of lies. I'm not a spy, I've never been one, I could never be one. I tried to make up a story so that I could win the party's confidence. I can't stand any more of this. You won't let me do anything but confess to something that I'm not guilty of, and I can't lie about it. I thought I could, but I can't. Now I don't know what to do."

Shi Zhe got up, clearly agitated, thrust his hands into his pants pockets, and began to pace up and down the room. "We may have to do this all over again," he said reflectively, stopping and looking at me with the kindly expression I had seen on his face at Yanan receptions. "I overestimated your level of consciousness. I thought you would understand what we were doing. Did we ask you to exaggerate or to make up stories? Didn't I tell you at the very beginning that it was a crime to hold anything back and it was also a crime to exaggerate. Didn't I tell you that?"

"Yes," I replied. "But you also hinted at torture if I didn't talk."

"We want you to tell your story truthfully here and to rectify your style, to remold yourself ideologically," Shi said. "This is good for you, it's in your own best interests. You should be able to pass this test. But you lack faith in the party."

My spirits instantly lifted. So my suspicion had been right—this was rectification. It was a test I was supposed to pass. Shi didn't really believe I was a spy, and he was shocked and angered when I had tried to confess. Everything was clearing up at least. "I'm sorry," I said. "I should have had more faith in the party."

"Never mind," said Shi Zhe. "Sometimes we can't help going in a roundabout way. We may have to take things a little slower. You have a problem, that's for certain. You are guilty of crimes. Your only way out is to tell the truth to the party. How can we clear you if you don't tell the truth? Now, go back and think things over."

So they were just testing me after all! They only wanted to help me transform myself, and I wanted that too. I felt happy and relaxed, and ready for their next move.

◆

The following morning, I was in good spirits and Xu was smiling again. "Comrade Shi Zhe criticized me for not helping you to understand better," he said. "From now on, whenever you need help, just let me know and we can talk. When it gets too much for you, I will help you remove the burdens."

I felt the sun come out. Human warmth and comfort were exactly what I needed.

"So what have you been thinking since yesterday?" Xu asked.

"I've been feeling bad about trying to deceive the party," I said. "How silly I was to actually think that the party suspected me of being a secret agent! How could such a thing be?"

Xu gave a half laugh and an indulgent grunt, as if he couldn't really decide how to respond.

Back in my cell, it now seemed quite clear that neither Xu nor Shi Zhe really thought I was a spy. It was a great relief to me. That night I slept well, and the next morning I crossed the little courtyard with a firm, if humble, tread. From now on, it would be a different Xu facing me. I would tell him my problems. He would listen whenever I needed him, and he would help me. But when Xu looked up from his papers and I met the full fury of his face, I knew that the earth had fallen out from under me again.

"Li Dunbai," he began. "You think you're very clever, don't you? You think that we're a bunch of yokels, easily taken in by a smart fellow like you. I must advise you that the disgusting performance you have put on for us during the past few days has completely failed. Nobody was taken in. You know the party's policy. You still have a limited time, limited, I repeat, to change your attitude and begin to confront your problem and to solve it. You had better think things over carefully. We are running out of patience.

I was taken back to my cell, sunk in despair.

◆

From then on, outside sights and sounds began to recede from me. Little things that I had awaited each day—like the bowl, cup, and spoon at mealtime, the sounds of sparrows, of dogs barking and roosters crowing, or the sound of music from some far-off radio—began to slip by unnoticed. My attention was drawn completely inward, focusing on my own anxiety, puzzlement, hurt, and my constant search for the answer to this nightmare of a riddle. A broken record sounded in my head, repeating the same questions, replaying the same lines from my interrogators. I was walking at a fast clip now, back and forth, back and forth in that room of darkness and silence.

I had never before feared harsh words or curses. I had faced down both during my days in the South as a labor organizer. But those were our enemies reviling me. These were my friends, people I dearly loved, admired, respected, and wanted to serve. It was their misunderstandings, denunciations, and threats that I found so cruel. The pain of their suspicion and rejection almost overwhelmed me.

After some days, a man I had never seen before came to my door and talked to me through the peephole. He had a heavy accent that I could not identify. "How is your health, Li Dunbai?" he asked in a gruff but kindly tone.

"Oh, I'm doing okay," I replied.

"You had better think things over very carefully," he said. "We have already liberated Beijing and we are preparing to cross the Yangtze and liberate the whole land of China. You are being more stubborn than Chiang Kai-shek. Can American imperialism be so lovable that you can't bear to turn your back on it? Or is it that you're more afraid of American imperialism than you are of us?"

Then as suddenly as he had appeared, the man was gone.

After several more days the keeper opened the door one morning, holding a cup of hot water and two large white pills. "You've been having a bit of the flu recently," he said. "Take this medicine."

"I haven't had the flu," I answered in surprise. "I'm fine."

"Take the medicine!"

With some trepidation, I swallowed the pills. After that I was given the pills three times every day.

A few nights later, I lay down on my right side and gazed at the bean oil lamp in the wall niche. As I drifted off to sleep, its flickering flame seemed to turn into a tiny little man, and then to a dancer. I slept for only a little while before pain suddenly jerked me awake. I shot bolt upright. My hand grasped my head. I had had a horrible nightmare. A little orange flame-man had been dancing in my brain, causing a terrible, violent pain in my head. I was breathing heavily and my pulse pounded. I was terrified. Of what? Of nothing. No, not of nothing. Of madness.

I couldn't sit still. I had to get up and walk. I had to. "Report!" I called out softly to the guard.

"What is it?"

"Please," I said, "I'm having a problem. Please let me walk for a while."

"What do you mean, walk?" he asked indignantly. "You get back on the kang and go to sleep at once!"

"But I can't. Something is terribly wrong. Please let me walk for a while, and then I'll go back to sleep."

"Get back on that kang and go to sleep," he repeated. "You'd better behave yourself, if you know what's good for you."

"Then please call Section Head Xu," I pleaded. "He promised to help me. Please tell him I need his help now."

I crawled back onto the kang. It felt as if there was an iron hoop clamped around my head. I was terrified, and still no sign of Xu. I had to get up. I had to walk. But as soon as my feet hit the floor, the guard shouted, "Get back there and lie down."

"I want to see Section Head Xu," I said.

"He's not coming. Get back up there!"

I could not stand it. "Section Head Xu! Section Head Xu!" I cried. I hoped he was sleeping somewhere inside the courtyard and would hear me. "Help me, I need help. Xu! Xuuu!"

Suddenly I heard the lock turn. Xu flung open the door and stood there in the light of the guard's flashlight, his long thin face contorted with rage. "Li Dunbai, what are you shrieking about?"

"I'm frightened and I'm very tense and I can't lie down or sleep."

"Lie down immediately and behave yourself. It is not permitted to create a disturbance in the middle of the night."

"But you promised to help me, remember? Don't you believe me? I really need help, right now."

"I'm not saying I don't believe you. I'm just warning you." He held up a brightly shining pair of steel handcuffs. "If you break discipline, we will use discipline to punish you."

That was a new and bitter hurt. Xu had promised help when I

needed it, but now he turned coldly away and left me to plunge down into a bottomless pit of suffering.

I forced myself to lie down until daybreak. But even in the morning light I was terrified. Nothing like this had ever happened to me before. What was in those drugs?

That morning Xu seemed amused. "What were you making all that fuss about last night?"

"I'm having a big problem with tension," I replied. "It may be some side effect of the medicine I've been taking."

"Side effect?" He seemed surprised.

Just then the guard gave me a little white steamed bun. "Here," he said. "You haven't been eating enough lately."

Was this food drugged too? I took a bite. Suddenly I was seized with faintness and keeled over sideways, passing out before I reached the floor.

The next thing I remember was three or four of the guards carrying me like a sack of potatoes. I was laughing hysterically and trying to shake them off. They were angry, and holding me tight. They dumped me on the kang in my cell and locked the door.

I had no idea how long I lay there, drifting back and forth between anguished, fitful nightmares and an almost equally anguishing semiconsciousness. I knew who I was and that I was not well. But that was all. There in the darkness the torment of my reality merged seamlessly with the torment of my dreams.

At times during those days I was lying on the floor wrapped in my overcoat. The guards tried to hold me down and one pressed the coat tightly over my mouth until I was suffocating. Then it seemed I was a child back on the operating table in a Charleston hospital having a wound sewed up, fighting off the ether cone, struggling to keep from having to inhale the acrid fumes.

Then Mao Zedong rose before me like a genie from a bottle. His large face glared mockingly. I was in agony. I had been castrated. I was naked and helpless, and he was gloating over me, relishing my pain. Then he became a threatening homosexual, looking at me with those weirdly effeminate eyes, trying to force himself on me, pressing in closer and closer. I wouldn't do it. I wouldn't let him do it. Then, in a heap near the door, I saw the tiny shrunken body of George Hatem. He had also been emasculated. He was lying in a pool of blood, groaning terribly. "Sid, Sid, you've got to do it, Sid . . . for my sake . . ." Every time I resisted them, they cut into George. I could hear his screams and the sound of the knife cutting into him. I couldn't help him. I would never do their will. I was disgusted, revolted. There were foul stenches in the air.

Then I saw the gorilla. It had the face of Zhu De, the old commander-in-chief. He had been forced into the body of a gorilla and he too was suffering, his kindly old face frozen into a gorilla leer, great fangs showing from between the thick lips, his head covered with spikes of hair. Then the gorilla became Mao. Mao was the gorilla. Mao was Satan, the evil genius, the cruel monster. When the name ran through my head, it seemed the most obscene, horrible word. Mao. Mao. Mao.

Then slowly the curtain lifted and I was lying on the floor alone. Near the door was my silk-lined fur overcoat. It had been torn to shreds, collar and silk lining ripped apart, sleeves torn off, a little heap of ravaged overcoat that had been the body of George Hatem, the gorilla, Mao, and Zhu De. I slept.

But the nightmares didn't stop. Once I became Fred Astaire dancing with Ginger Rogers, whirling, leaping from kang to floor and back again, with true grace and poise, exulting in the fulfillment at last of my lifelong yearning to lose myself in some perfect poetry or song. The music followed my every movement, and I danced, danced, danced until I fell on the kang exhausted and slept.

Then Wei Lin came to me and we locked our bodies together. I was lifted up and thrown down again by the sheer ecstatic force of our embrace, and I pitched violently about the kang, head over heels, before I crashed back to the floor and passed out.

But however terrible, my nightmares wouldn't let me give up. Outside the door stood my friend Peng Di, running, running. I could see his eager face. "Keep running," he cried. He was wearing the peaked cap that had gone with him through the march from Yanan to the Taihang Mountains. He looked frightened for me. "We're with you. You've got to win. We're all behind you. Qian Xing is behind you. Keep running. Win. Win."

Then outside the door another voice pleaded with me. It was Zhou Enlai's daughter, Sun Weishi, her arms swinging athletically, wearing the white blouse and gray trousers she had worn when I last saw her. She looked fresh and healthy, lovely and good. "Zhou Enlai wants you to win," she sang out. "Zhou is behind you. We want you to win. Keep going."

When my head cleared a bit, it was only long enough to see the real nightmare that was my existence. It was Xu. He was clear and solid, no phantasm. "Li Dunbai," he said with scorn. "Do you have any more foreign tricks to show us? Do you know any more foreign opera to sing?"

Comrade Xu was making fun of me! I stared at him in anguish.

"Do you know what your name is, Li Dunbai? Do you know who you are? Is your head clear now?"

I heard his cruel words, then I receded back into blackness.

Many weeks and months went by like that, and every day, three times a day, I was given two pills. When I was not trapped in the morass of my nightmares, I sat bleakly on the edge of the kang. I could hear the chattering magpies and the sounds of other birds and barking dogs. But whatever the sound, when it got to my ears it became sad, anguished, flat.

I was always dying or dead or waiting to die, but I did not want to die. I did not want to be sad, to hear only mournful sounds, to see only worried, sad, angry faces. I did not want that, but where was hope? Where had hope gone? They had taken even hope from me.

I drifted into dreams again. Summers on Sullivan's Island in South Carolina I used to play with a beautiful little neighbor girl named Hope. She had two sisters, Faith and Charity, and they vowed to be nuns and never marry. I could see Hope's long hair, freckles, and soft Irish eyes. She was calling me, calling me from far away. But from where?

Then Hope sent me a poem. Through my misty, half-clouded senses the words came rising up clearly.

> To suffer woes which Hope thinks infinite,
> To forgive wrongs darker than death or night;
>   To defy Power, which seems omnipotent;
> To love, and bear; to hope, till Hope creates
> From its own wreck the thing it contemplates;
>   Neither to change, nor falter, nor repent;
> This, like thy glory, Titan, is to be
> Good, great and joyous, beautiful and free;
> This is alone Life, Joy, Empire, and Victory.

Hope had come back! To defy power darker than death or night! To hope till Hope creates from its own wreck the thing it contemplates! There lay power, strength, beauty, and freedom. Nobody gives you freedom. You create your own future from the wreck of your present, and you are free. The answer was there ready-made. It did not have to be reasoned out. Hope found the solution, and Hope was the solution.

One day I was moved from my cell and the colors I saw when I came out of that darkened room were blazing and spectacular, like nothing I had ever seen before.

They put me in the back of an old Japanese army truck and stretched a big tarpaulin over the back so that I could see nothing and no one could see me. But through the crack between the edge of the tarpaulin and the truck railing, I saw warm, rolling fields that were a bright yellow like scrambled eggs, and blue sky that looked like the rims of Dutch teacups. Everything had a bright, Easter egg hue about it, wondrous, strange, but unreal, and I could not focus on anything. I could only gaze out in a sort of passive melancholy and wonder mildly what was happening to me now.

After several days' journey, I was taken to a little one-story house inside a courtyard with a high wall at the back and a long one-story brick building at the front. There was one usable room to the left of the front door. The central room was where the guards patrolled, and the room on the right had been bricked up. I was put in the room on the left. There were two windows, one at the front, another at the side; both had been boarded up and then plastered over with newspapers.

There a new set of nightmares began. I saw Wei Lin on the wall like a Madonna in a niche. She looked very beautiful, but very sad. Usually she was crying, and the thought of her nearly killed me. The guards were dirty, aggressive, and hostile. Like the Mao of my dream one of them kept trying to force himself on me when no one was around. I refused, and from then on he found little ways to get even with me.

They took me out in the courtyard for sun. I was too weak and too dazed to walk around. All I could do was lie in the pathway. One day there was an eclipse of the sun, and the guard took advantage of my dopiness and confusion to encourage me to stare at it wide-eyed. Increasingly accustomed to obedience, I complied. After that I found my eyes swollen and stuck together, things began to shimmer before me, and my vision grew considerably dimmer.

Three eternities went by in that room. I couldn't distinguish time. I drifted in and out of consciousness, and when I came to I would be doing wild, mad things. I was terribly hungry and several times I awoke to find myself eating mole crickets. Another time, I was eating the plaster off the walls, and it seemed to taste sweet. I could hear the guards' taunts through the miasma: "Are you really nuts? Let's see you eat shit. If you eat shit, we'll know it's true." And I woke up to find myself eating my own feces.

I knew I was sick. I knew this wasn't my real self, yet I couldn't get my real self back.

Once, when one of the guards opened the door and shouted at me harshly about something, I ran over and gave him a shove with both hands. A bunch of five or six of them came in and beat me, shouting, "What do you mean by striking our guard, eh? What do you mean by that?"

Every time I did something wild, the guards put me in hand-cuffs. They were ingenious little manacles, made so that when I resisted and tried to pull myself free, they gave a little "click" and tightened themselves around my wrists. I cried out and screamed and begged the guards to take them off, twisting and turning, trying to get some relief. That made them tighter and tighter still, until they were cutting into the flesh of both wrists. I passed out and woke up sometime later to find the handcuffs removed, and both wrists slashed and bleeding.

From time to time, the guards came to repaper the windows. Mostly the room was too dim and my eyesight too poor to read anything from those papers. But one day they used a different kind of paper. This one had a huge banner headline, printed in red. Even in the dimness of the bean oil lamp, I could read its message: the People's Republic of China had been established. In my depressed, hazy state, the news could only make me feel sadder. It had happened without me. The thing I had so hoped and worked for had taken place while I was buried alive. I didn't know how old the newspaper was. I had no idea how long ago Mao had won the war and the New China had come into being.

Shortly after that, however, the haze began to lift and the nightmares to recede. I was still wobbly, and the tension pressing on the front of my head, especially at night, still worried me badly. But I was definitely climbing out of the worst of it.

My main keeper began to fuss at me like a mother hen. "Work, work, do some work. Clean the floors, wash your clothes." The keepers brought me water, and indeed the task of keeping my room clean began to help me discipline my mind. Then suddenly one day, the door opened and in walked the warden of the prison. His name was Yao Lun, a lean, long-faced man with a quizzical look. "We now basically understand you," he said. "Don't worry about those questions we asked you before. It's all pretty clear."

Was he telling me I was no longer accused of being a spy? I could hardly believe my ears. My emotions were too dulled to take in the news completely.

"You know, however," Yao continued, "we still have to settle your case, and that is going to require a lot of work. In the meantime, you can't go out and work or study." Still, he said, while they were keeping me under arrest, they would bring me reading and writing materials, and allow me the light to read by.

I thanked Yao as profusely as I could with my dulled emotions, and he left. The boards were knocked off the windows immediately, and my little room was flooded with unbelievable light. The guards carried in a writing table like the one that had been in the interrogation room in my first prison. They brought in a stool and a stack of newspapers and the first thing I looked for was a date. They were issues from the spring of 1950.

I had been in darkness and alone for over a year.

CHAPTER EIGHT

Learning to Live

After that, everything was different.

Everything, that is, except the fact that I was a prisoner. I could read, I could write, I could go outside and sun myself. The guards had been changed. The tormenters had been replaced by a group of soldiers fresh from Manchuria and Lin Biao's command. They were friendly and actually willing to chat briefly with me. But I continued to be confined and had to seek the guards' permission to do anything. What's more, my case still wasn't closed. Although the party hinted it knew I wasn't a spy, I wasn't officially cleared of the charges.

None of that seemed important. What was important was that the terrifying danger of madness, or a return of the nightmares and the melancholy, seemed to be receding. Everything paled before that fact. I was so grateful for the respite from pain that the conditions attached to it seemed trivial. I almost felt that I couldn't have handled freedom at that time, even if it had been offered.

Indeed, I rebuffed a hint from the prison warden that I might be allowed to return home to the United States if I gave up any connection with China. The thought horrified me. In the first place, I wasn't sure I would survive such a move. I had no one, no job, no home—nothing to return to in America. The only people who might welcome me would be those opposed to China. In my present emotional state I knew I couldn't care for myself, work, make any decisions. When I caught sight of myself in the wash-basin water, I didn't like what I saw. My face was haggard, tense, and tight. It looked gaunt, anguished. Blue and red lights danced before my eyes and things seemed to shimmer. It had been so long since I had sustained any human conversation that even putting together more than a few sentences of coherent speech was hard for me. What would become of me if I returned to America?

But more important, I knew that if I left my name would never be cleared in China. I would leave as a spy, my departure would be taken as an admission of my guilt, and I would never be allowed to return. I would be separated forever from the people I loved as my own. I could never allow that to happen. No, I had to stay, recover my health, recover my mental powers, and wait until the party cleared me.

◆

The newspapers I was now allowed to read revealed to me a world that seemed far away and unreal. The erstwhile wartime allies were now squabbling. The United States seemed to have taken on the role of policeman and money changer for the world. China was unified and at peace with itself for the first time in more than a hundred years. The new Communist government was bent on sweeping away the inflation, corruption, and banditry of the old regime, organizing people into production to feed, clothe, and house themselves. Come summer, the Korean War broke out, and I spent long hours trying to puzzle out, from the twisted logic of political propaganda in the *People's Daily,* the real nature of the conflict.

I read the newspapers one by one, one each day. The keepers brought them to me in stacks, about two months old. When I had finished one batch, I wrote a note requesting more. The first book they brought me was volume one of the *Selected Works* of Mao Zedong. It was just off the presses. I tried to study it, but found that my wits were too scattered and my eyes too hazy to allow me much focus. So I began to try to discipline my mind, copying out characters and making notes of things that seemed important to me.

I wrote long letters to my wife and gave them to the guards. I wasn't convinced she would get them, but it felt good to write them nonetheless. As my mind cleared I began to be able to think of her as a person again, not as a fantasy or a goddess, or simply an intense emotion. I am studying, I wrote her. I am in good health. I love you. I hope you are well.

I knew there was a possibility that when I got out Wei Lin would be gone. I knew I had to guard myself, to be prepared. Still, I was lonely and I longed for her. I thought about her all the time and asked about her as often as I thought prudent. She's fine, the guards assured me. She's fine and she's waiting for you.

The guards were kind. They brought me snacks from their own quarters and told me about their girlfriends and their homes. They talked to me as a person, not as a prisoner. I didn't want to press my relationship with them, for fear of having their companionship abruptly withdrawn, but their small acts of kindness helped to heal me. My appetite improved. I began to sleep. I still had panic attacks, but they were fewer and milder than in the past, and I could talk myself through them.

I suspected that the drugs they had given me had pushed me into my nightmarish frenzy. But I also thought my mental confusion had been a kind of retreat from reality. When things had become too hard to bear, I had simply flipped a mental switch and gone elsewhere. I thought it was important, then, to try to reconnect myself to reality as much as possible.

But one thing I did not want to do. I didn't want to forget what I had been through. I didn't want the skin to heal over any splinters, leaving them to hurt without giving any sign of why they were hurting. I wanted my moods and memories controllable, open, operable, knowable. I tried to remember everything.

My biggest concern now was survival.

To survive I had to heal myself, and to heal myself I had to find a goal, something bigger than myself to focus on, something bigger than this tiny room, something bigger than my own situation, something to help me understand, to help ease this terrible pain.

I could not allow myself to be angry. Within me a battle boiled between rage and acceptance. Many days I awakened with my gorge rising. How could they do this to me? How could they do this to anyone? How could they keep someone locked away from humanity, someone who hadn't done anything, who hadn't been convicted of any crime? They were making me unfit for society, unfit for life.

I often asked the prison authorities: How long will I be in here? How long will this last? But whenever I mentioned time, whenever I said it's been a year, it's been over a year, how long will I be here, they brushed me off with seeming unconcern. We have comrades who have waited twenty years or more for their cases to be cleared, they said: what is a little time when we are fighting such powerful enemies all around us? I got lectures, but no answers. Fury threatened to consume me. Yet I knew I had to contain my rage or it would kill me. If I didn't take control, I would turn in on myself and become lost again in my own private world. I would become so absorbed in my own personal wrongs that I would never come out.

I briefly examined my religious faith. I found some comfort in Bible stories and old hymns, but I didn't believe in a personal God. The poetry of my childhood again came back to help me. I thought of the Leigh Hunt poem that my sister Elinor and Aunt Nell had read me, and I felt deep sympathy for Abou Ben Adhem, the subject of the poem. "Write me as one that loves his fellow men," he told the angel of the Lord.

It was the Communist Party that had come closest to helping me love my fellowmen the way I wanted to. And it was in the party that I had felt most loved and accepted. Ever since I was little, I had struggled to find acceptance. Growing up a Jew in South Carolina, I had never felt completely accepted, no matter how respected my father and grandfather were for their accomplishments. I remember being snubbed and shut out of places. When I had worked as a labor organizer in the South, I was really proud to be accepted as an equal by the workers, who didn't usually like college boys. And when the Chinese Communists accepted me as one of them, it made me more than proud.

I had to find a way past the terrible pain and anger at their rejection. The lines of another poem came back from my childhood. They had been waiting there all along, almost from the day I was arrested. It was a poem by Edwin Markham, another one my aunt and sister had read to me when I was sick.

> He drew a circle that shut me out—
> Heretic, rebel, a thing to flout.
> But Love and I had the wit to win:
> We drew a circle that took him in.

That's what I had to do. The Chinese Communists had cruelly thrust me out. Somehow, I had to draw a larger circle and take them back in with me again. I would love them back. I would make it impossible for them to reject me. I had to become more like them than they were. Whether or not they intended my imprisonment as a trial, a rectification, I would use it that way.

The first thing to do was to take stock of my life, and looking back over my past I could see how they might have suspected me. I had been halfhearted and wavering. I thought of how I had disappointed them with my self-indulgent affair in Yanan. I thought about my argument with Liu Shaoqi, and of how I had shut my mind when he spoke of the sacrifices that being a party member required. I thought about how I had argued that the Leninist dictatorship of the proletariat wasn't suited to Chinese conditions, and how the minority Muslim and Buddhist people of Tibet and Xinjiang should be able to vote on independence.

I thought especially about my fears of the bombings, my running away at the slightest danger. In Yanan, I realized I had just been playing at being a revolutionary, I had wanted the benefits of feeling at one with them, but I hadn't been willing to pay the price. I assumed that my arrest had something to do with Anna Louise Strong and whatever spy charges she had faced. But although I had insisted over and over that I was not a spy and that they had no reason to suspect me, I now realized that they did have a reason. I had not been a committed revolutionary. I had been a Communist in name only.

The Chinese people had taken me, an American, into their sacred revolutionary organization. But I had not fully appreciated what this meant and what obligations it imposed on me. I had been acting like one of the Sunshine Soldiers and Summer Patriots that Thomas Paine wrote about during the American Revolution. I was guilty, and this was my guilt—low consciousness, selfishness, lack of commitment, opportunism. From that vantage point, I saw their investigation of me as reasonable and my imprisonment as offering me a rare opportunity for self-training and transformation.

I understood. I forgave. I felt inspired and uplifted. I was now learning to be a moral person, a servant of the people. I had found a clear purpose. I would rid myself of the narrow selfishness that had kept me scared and running from bombs and danger. I would stop running. I would be like one of them. In Yanan, I had felt guilt at my weakness, but suppressed it. Here in prison, I could take that guilt and turn it into something that would make me a stronger, better party member, a stronger and better person.

Suddenly, I felt my head clear. I had the sensation of being one with the universe, of having lost all the little bitternesses and private wishes that kept me at odds with other people. I felt as if I stood at the pinnacle of the universe and was in tune with its universality as well as with all of its multifarious particularities. I was immersed in an ecstatic, exalted sensation that made me feel weightless and tingle from head to foot.

It seemed to me that this was the feel of intellectual emancipation, the consciousness of having set aside the dread of death and hardship that accompanies man and weighs him down from cradle to grave. I had thought it through and through. I would no longer be afraid. From now on, I would focus on my own shortcomings and make stern demands upon myself so that I could transform myself into a seasoned Marxist revolutionary in China. I must learn to live by dialectic logic and Communist ideals twenty-four hours a day. What more fulfilling life could I lead? What fears or hardships could touch me then?

I had to use my eyes to look beyond my own prison cell. I had to see what was going on in the world at large, even if the only way to do that was by reading the newspapers that had been brought to me. I had to understand Marxism thoroughly in order to be able to see and comprehend reality as it was. I had to open my ears to hear, not just what I wanted to hear, but my own errors. I had to learn to distinguish what was in the people's interest from what was harmful to them.

And so I saved my own life.

I found the tranquillity I sought, the strength to continue through the madness of prison. When I opened my mind to the truth, it was to the party's truth. I closed my mind to everything but that and would not allow it to waver. I gave myself over to the party wholly, completely, and fully. I silenced my inner voice of protest. I stamped down my rage and dulled my indignation at their treatment of me. I branded as selfishness my concern for myself as an individual and gave that up too. Whatever the party asked me to do, I would do—including sitting in this prison cheerfully and without complaint until they were ready to let me go.

I remembered a line from Dante: E 'n la sua volontade è nostra pace. Yes. And in His will is our peace.

◆

In the summer of 1951 I was moved from my small private house into the prison proper. It was an old building I had heard referred to as Prison Number Two. There was a central hub that radiated long corridors like spokes on a wheel. Each corridor was lined on both sides with prison cells, and each cell had a red wooden door and a large iron bolt, padlocked on the outside. At the far end of each corridor past the latrine there were big red doors that were always kept closed and locked.

My cell was unusually large, about five paces by eight paces. A door laid across low sawhorses served for a bed, and there were two windows, open only at the top with heavy wire netting on both sides. I had a chamber pot and an earthen urn for clean water. I was also given a large thermos for hot drinking water.

The move was a terrible blow. The guards I had come to depend on for a few words of conversation every day were gone, and I was now under the eye of regular prison guards. To make it worse, I was no longer permitted my ordinary clothing. Instead, I was given two suits of new black cotton pajamas, each with the Chinese character for "prisoner" sewn on the back. I was not chained, but frequently I could hear the sound of leg irons clanking in the corridor as other prisoners dragged themselves to the latrine or crossed the courtyard to the interrogation chamber.

I was subject to prison discipline. Every morning at six, the keeper rang a hand bell. By the time I was out of bed and dressed a keeper had opened the door quickly to pass me hot water for washing and brushing my teeth. About a half hour later, my breakfast arrived in a set of porcelain-enamel containers, stacked on a frame with a carrying handle. Usually I got rice porridge, pickled vegetables, and a steamed bread roll.

I also created a discipline for myself. Every day I did calisthenics that I had designed. Then I took a circular walk around the room, reversing direction every few minutes. After breakfast, I studied for two hours. Then I cleaned my cell with a small square of cloth, which the keepers gave me for that purpose. I was still trembling and faint, and had to force myself to think clearly through every step. First get the cloth. Then get the water. Then wet the cloth. In this slow, methodical way, I scrubbed the floor, then the window sills and frames, and then the plaster walls as high as I could reach. Sometimes the keepers brought me a mop and I did the floor again.

As my attention span lengthened, I began to study classical Chinese. I practiced writing in calligraphic style with a Chinese brush and ink slab. I taught myself to read Chinese sheet music on the numbered scale that was used to print songs in the newspaper, and I learned to sing soundlessly the popular propaganda songs that were being published. Also from the newspapers, I began to pick up some knowledge of industry and agriculture, the secrets of growing high-yield cotton and wheat and how to handle coal cutters and loaders.

Day after day, night after night, my life went on like this with scarcely any variation in routine. My only amusements were snatched in secret. My door had a little peephole about three and a half inches long and two inches high, covered on the outside by a little piece of cloth. The cloth was meant to keep me from seeing out, but sometimes when the guard lifted it to look at me, he let it drop unevenly and I could peek into the corridor. I had to be very careful, because some guards would suddenly double back and catch me peering out. But I often was able to get brief glimpses of the guards and other prisoners.

Such was life in the early days of the People's Republic that many of the things I read about in the newspaper were immediately reflected in my prison. Once I read of a crackdown on superstition and cultism. There was a cult, it appeared, that practiced a bizarre worship of a mythical figure, a kind of god of war. Their real crime, however, was organizing a band of fanatics to oppose the Communists. Shortly after I read that article, a large group of the priests of this cult appeared in the prison. I could hear their leader denouncing his own crimes, loudly proclaiming his devotion to the people's government, acknowledging his mistakes. At night these priests were locked in cells like mine. But in the daytime they sat in their opened doorways making matchboxes.

A few months later, I read of a big crackdown on brothels and the arrest of all the madams and pimps in Beijing. Soon afterward, I heard female voices in the corridors. Quite excited, I looked through the peephole to see women and girls sewing and washing clothes in the corridor. Some of them were quite pretty—or maybe they only seemed that way. It had been nearly two and a half years since I had even seen a woman.

◆

Late in 1952, I made friends with an enemy.

I had heard a soft tap-tapping on one wall of my cell for a long time before I realized someone was trying to communicate with me. I did not dare tap back. If I was caught passing messages, I might be punished very severely. They could take my books away. They could return me to darkness. The thought was almost unbearable. But more unbearable was this life without human company.

So I chanced it. I tapped back.

For a while I tapped randomly, just to signal that I was listening. Then after a time, always checking the corridor first to see the position of the guard, I tried tapping out a message in Morse code. I racked my brains to remember the system I had learned from Street & Smith, the pulp magazine detectives. Dot-dash, that was A. Long dash, that was L. I tapped out a few letters. A flurry of taps came rushing back. Whoever it was knew Morse code. Unfortunately, I could remember hardly any of it, so that method wasn't going to work. I tried to think of some other way of communicating.

A few days went by before I hit on the idea of tapping out the rhythms of popular songs. I had been reading in the papers that a very active campaign against counterrevolutionaries had just been launched, and that the Communists were rounding up KMT secret agents who had either not been able to leave China or had been planted by the KMT. I figured my neighbor might be a KMT agent. There was a very popular song in Nationalist café society called "How Can I Not Think of Her?" I tapped out the first few bars.

He responded with great enthusiasm, tapping out the entire melody.

Then I started on American popular songs, and he knew them too. I wanted to find out who he was so I tapped out the song "Who?" from a Tommy Dorsey record. "Who stole my heart away . . ." I tapped it over and over, emphasizing the word "Who."

Back came the KMT party anthem.

To let him know who I was, I tapped out "Qi Lai," the stirring Chinese Communist anthem, and was rewarded with a scrabbling sound on the other side of the wall that sounded like anger, or despair.

I knew what he meant. I tapped out "There's a Long, Long Trail A-Winding," the mournful World War I ballad. We're in here for a long haul, I was telling him. We tapped back and forth like this for four or five days before I decided it was too dangerous to continue.

◆

I became obsessed with studying. Only through study and learning, I felt, could I lift myself out of my own selfishness and guilt.

"Be pure!" "Be scientific!" "Be revolutionary!" Those were my three mottoes.

I started with Mao's essay "On Practice." In a class society, he wrote, all ideas come from a particular class. There are no ideas that don't bear the stamp of the social class of the individual who has them. That helped me understand some of the roots of my guilt. I had been born wrong, born into the wrong class. What's more, I was from an imperialist country. I was by my very being a weak link in the revolution and I had to be more—not less—committed than the others.

I had to study the behavior of real revolutionaries to find role models for myself. It was a natural thing for me to do. As a child shrinking from my mother's rages or from the taunts of bullies much bigger than I, I had easily lost myself in fairy tales, easily cast myself as the good knight, the triumphant defender of virtue.

Now my life depended on my doing that same thing. I read Nicholas Ostrovsky's early Soviet novel, *How the Steel Was Tempered.* It had been translated into Chinese by my friend Mei Yi. It was almost scripture for young revolutionaries around the world, and I had read it once before in Birmingham. This time I read it intently, trying to model myself on the young revolutionary hero, Pavel Korchagin, trying to force myself into the mold of a dedicated revolutionary who could look back over his life with no regrets about time and energy spent in wasteful, selfish pursuits. Korchagin had found happiness and meaning even after he became a paraplegic. Couldn't I do the same in my own trials?

I thought of the other heroes I had known and could model myself on: Joe Gelders, the white physics professor in Birmingham with the weak heart who had stood up against the Klan for black equality; Old Man Mason, the Roanoke Rapids mill hand who had declared he was a "natural-born Communist"; Homer Pike, the Quarry Workers Union organizer in North Carolina whose last words to me as he lay dying from the murderous assault of the owner's son were about taking care of the men in his local.

From the newspaper, I also picked up some Chinese role models. A Chinese soldier in Korea, a young boy named Qiu Shaoyun, had allowed himself to be burned to death by an American firebomb rather than rolling around to put out the fire and betraying his comrades' positions. I must become similarly dedicated, similarly unconcerned about my own life and problems.

At the same time, I was busy laying the intellectual groundwork for becoming a true believer in Marxism—and in Mao. From the mimeographed catalogue of prison library books I had chosen a book of Mao's uncirculated lectures on philosophy. The two essays that came out of these lectures, "On Practice" and "On Contradiction," were Mao's justification of his political differences with Stalin.

In the early 1930s, Stalin had arranged to have Mao replaced as the leader of the Chinese Communists with his own hand-picked men. The result, during the war with the Nationalists, had been the Communists' swift, complete military defeat and the flight across half of China that came to be known as the Long March.

After Mao resumed power during that march, he had begun a systematic analysis of military and political thinking. His conclusions—mainly that judgments can best be made by those closest and most familiar with the actual situation, and not by some leaders from afar—were hints of a serious rift to come between the Chinese and the Soviet Communists. Mao taught his cadres not to take orders from Moscow, and not to try to apply directly to China what they read in Marx and Lenin.

I saw in Mao's words a striking drive to seek truth, and to use that truth in the service of humanity. When I read his "On Protracted War," I became convinced the man was a genius. Mao wrote his analysis of the course of the Sino-Japanese war in 1938, before the first year of fighting was over. The war was to last for seven more years, and it followed Mao's scenario to an amazing degree.

I also saw in Mao's interpretation of the relative strengths of China and Japan the uncanny ability of a disciplined, rational mind and a predilection for collecting and studying hard facts. Japan had great military, economic, and political-organizational strengths, but lacked the manpower and material resources for a long war and stood morally accused before world opinion. China was weak but huge, and had more reasons to fight, a greater capability for enduring a long war, and strengthening international support. And I saw too how Mao had created and trained the kind of military, political, and economic organizations needed to fight and win the "people's war" that the KMT was unwilling and unable to fight.

I was especially struck by Mao's belief in man's ability to win the initiative in difficult circumstances. He can do it, said Mao, by setting himself a rational goal, analyzing both favorable and unfavorable factors in his environment, and then developing a rational plan for changing both it and himself in order to realize that goal.

Day after day I had lain on the floor of my cell afraid that I was dying, that every breath might be my last, or that I was already dead. Now, I would learn and use Mao's method of analyzing the basis of my problems and of working out a method, a strategy and tactics for attaining my objective. The study of "On Protracted War" made me an almost blind follower of Mao Zedong and his thought.

So came wisdom and ignorance, hand in hand, to play the fool with me.

◆

I marked the passage of time by events described in the newspaper. Early in 1953, banner headlines announced the death of Stalin. Later came the ascent to power of Nikita Khrushchev. Strangely enough, it never occurred to me that this was my ticket back to the outside world. It was only years later that Chinese officials confirmed to me that I had been arrested on orders from the Soviets, and in connection with Anna Louise Strong's arrest in Moscow at the same time. Stalin was apparently afraid that foreigners who grew too close to the Chinese leadership would dilute his influence and perhaps ultimately sway world opinion away from him and toward the Chinese. So he ordered us both arrested as spies. It was only after his death that these, and many other frame-ups, were revealed. But since I had never connected Stalin with my arrest I did not relate his death to any possibility of release. And indeed, release did not come quickly.

Through 1953 and 1954 I read and studied, all in Chinese. I read the classical economists Adam Smith and David Ricardo. I read all three volumes of Marx's *Das Kapital.* I embraced the classical exposition of labor as the creative interaction between man and nature through which man transforms nature for his own purpose, producing wealth in the process. I absorbed from *Das Kapital* the concept of the essence of man as represented by his essential activity, labor. I absorbed Marx's argument that genuinely human life could only begin after the bare essentials of food, shelter, and clothing were no longer a matter of desperate, competitive struggle. I learned from Marx that freedom requires the overcoming of alienation. Capitalist society has produced freedom and wealth such as the human race has never known. But at the same time it has caused the laborer to be separated from the fruits of his labor, and has produced a tendency for people to become dominated by the material products of their own labor.

I also accepted Marx's argument that all freedom is relative and realized that for me, in solitary confinement, understanding the reasons for my incarceration, wrong though it was, made it possible for me to enjoy a certain measure of freedom. I was able to utilize the party's belief in persuading even captured enemies of the justice of their cause to obtain the conditions under which I could lead a quiet life of study and progress.

When I read in the paper of some crimes that foreign missionaries had supposedly committed in Hebei Province, I wept copiously. How could I fault the Chinese for suspecting me when other foreigners did this kind of thing to them? Once when one of the prison authorities came to see me, I declared with great vehemence that I was intensely loyal to the Revolution and would never change. "No matter how long you keep me shut up here," I said. "If I die here and you do an autopsy on my heart, you will find every fiber to be pure red. I will cling to my convictions no matter what happens to me!"

The man grew very agitated, and reassured me at once. "The organization understands you perfectly at this point," he said. "We know you, so set your mind at ease on that score."

◆

It was about ten o'clock on April 4, 1955, when a keeper unlocked the door and walked into my cell. "Someone wants to talk with you," he said. "Come with me."

A doctor's visit, I thought. Or another questioning session. Or perhaps a change of cell. I followed him out of my cell, down the far end of the corridor, past the latrine, and through the big red doors that were never opened. There were two chairs placed face-to-face in a little hallway just beyond the doors, which were closed and locked again after we passed through. A man I had never seen before was sitting in the chair facing me. "Sit down," he said, motioning toward the other chair. It was the first time in six years I had sat on a real chair, one with a back on it.

The keeper remained standing behind me. "This is Bureau Chief Ling Yun," he said.

"Li Dunbai," Ling began, "we have spent a great deal of time and effort in investigating your case. We have found that you are a . . ." He hesitated a moment, as if trying to figure out whether to call me a comrade or a what. "A good person. You have been wrongfully charged and imprisoned. You have suffered a great wrong. On behalf of the central people's government and the ministry of public security, I apologize to you for this wrong."

I was stunned and burst out crying.

I was overjoyed to hear that justice was being done at last, but I could not bear to hear the word "apologize." I had had to make myself see things the way my captors saw them or my little world made no sense and was not acceptable. That was why I had taught myself so well, endured so much, hoping to protect them from disgrace. I wanted to be innocent, but I didn't want them to be guilty. "No, no," I insisted. "Don't apologize! It was right to investigate me, because the organization didn't know who I was and charges were brought against me."

Bureau Chief Ling looked at me with a slight frown and said, "You have your own viewpoint on what happened to you and your behavior has been good. We understand your feelings. But you were wronged. It was a mistake, and that is an objective fact. You are now free to leave here. Do you have any questions?"

"Only one question," I answered. "What about Wei Lin? What about my wife?"

Bureau Chief Ling faced me across the table. His matter-of-fact tone didn't change. "Wei Lin got a divorce and married again. She waited for three years, without really knowing what had become of you. Then she became ill and her friends advised her to remarry. Her husband works at the foreign ministry."

After all those years of waiting and wondering, the tortured dreams of her, the passionate longing to see her, his words should have come as a hammer blow. But they didn't. I didn't feel anything. My six years in solitary had so resigned me to losing everything that even the news that my wife was gone, married to another man, left me cold. My only reaction was one of detached bemusement. Why for so many years had they told me she was waiting? "Why hadn't they told me the truth?" I thought. But that brief moment of doubt passed.

"We trust you will know how to handle this problem emotionally," said Ling.

"Don't worry about it," I said. "I'm not the person I was when I came in. I've learned what's really important. Personal issues come second with me now."

Ling nodded approvingly. "Now let's go," he said. "We've found a place for you to stay for a few days, before we move you to some more permanent situation."

I turned to head back down the corridor toward my cell. "I need to get my dictionary and my papers," I said.

The head keeper put his hand on my arm to stop me. "We'll bring everything out to you," he said. "You don't want to go back in that place again."

The Brave New World

So my whole world changed again in the twinkling of an eye. I was a free man and my life lay ahead of me. But I was incapable of feeling the kind of wild exultation that would have been my normal reaction. I governed myself carefully; I was full of doubts and suspicions.

At times while in prison, I had worried that I would never be able to go out into the world and live a normal life again. I seemed to have become dependent on prison routine, on being instructed and taken care of, on having little communication with others and simple wants and emotions. Could I handle the complexities of normal life? After lunch at the apartment of one of the prison authorities, I decided to make at least a try at negotiating the outside world.

It was years after I had been moved in a truck to this prison before someone told me I was in Beijing. Now I finally had a chance to see the city that had surrounded me for so long. Rather solemnly I started out the gate, giving a sidelong glance at the three guards with rifles and bayonets. No one stopped me. I was wearing ordinary Chinese cadre's clothes that I had been given in exchange for my prison dress, a tunic over a plain white shirt and unpressed trousers. I walked to the outer gate, a tiny, unprepossessing door in an ordinary-looking wall. I passed through the gate and was out in the world again for the first time in six years.

On the street, I took a few steps and then looked back at the prison that had been my home. From the sidewalk, barely a stone's throw away, that great dungeon where so many of us had been buried was nearly invisible. All I could see was the distinctive-looking roofs of some of the prison corridors: red tile in a jagged formation with a raised vertical skylight under a high ridge running down the center to light the dark walkways inside.

I turned to look at the street lined with hucksters' stalls. It was called Dongguanxiang, the Eastern Official's Lane. There were vendors selling bean curd laid out in gleaming white squares. There were old women selling the strong thick black soybean broth that old Beijing residents were especially fond of. There were peddlers with children's toys, little paper lions that brought good luck. There were vendors of red dates and candied hawthorne fruit on sticks. There were hawkers of buttons, ribbons, and cloth. I passed them all and walked on until I came to a modest gate leading into the city proper.

I walked through this gate and had just come out on the other side when I froze suddenly. There ahead of me was a uniformed policeman. My heart pounded and my step faltered. I waited to see what would happen. He merely glanced at me, however, and turned back to directing traffic.

I kept on walking until I arrived at the Soviet exhibition building. I recognized the spires from pictures I had seen in newspapers. It had been presented to China by the Soviets as a monument to their economic aid. I saw a sign out front announcing an exhibit of artworks by modern Chinese masters. I wandered in and tried to focus on the pictures, but I couldn't. I looked around and saw a handsome man, lost in reverie before a painting. With a start I realized it was an old friend, the scholar Deng Tuo, who had been editor-in-chief of the news center in Kalgan.

I moved away quickly. I didn't know what to say to Deng Tuo. I didn't know what people knew about me, or what I was allowed to speak about. Fighting back panic, I retraced my steps to the safety of the prison grounds.

The next morning after breakfast, a prison department head came to escort me to the central organization department of the party to be given a job. That was just what I wanted. I was convinced that the way forward for me was work and study. If I lost myself in my work and improved my understanding through study, maybe I could find peace and happiness again. If I let myself be crushed by fear, then I would die. It was as simple as that.

We boarded a bus and got out in front of a large, gloomy gray building on Xidan North, a busy Beijing intersection. A steady stream of people flowed in and out, monotonously dressed in blue or gray, with only an occasional hint of red or yellow. Inside there were phalanxes of secretaries, dossier-keepers, extract clerks, field investigators, personal investigation and assignment cadres. To my senses, still unaccustomed to much activity, it all seemed very busy and confusing.

We walked up two flights of stairs and through several doors before we came to the right office. We opened the door and walked in. Suddenly, a large bear of a man rushed out from behind his desk, enveloped me in a big hug, lifted me off the ground, and began to weep on my shoulder. "We know all about it," the man said. "You were magnificent. Don't think about it anymore. It's all over now and it'll never happen again. Do you remember me?"

I recognized the man's ruddy peasant face with long bushy eyebrows, big eyes, and a high brow. "Han Jingcao," I said. "Of course I remember you." Han had been one of my friends in Kalgan, who worked in the news agency there. He parted his hair in the middle so that it rained down on both sides of his head, adding to his bearlike look. We had liked each other from the start.

Meanwhile, across the room, the department head accompanying me was standing with his mouth agape, plainly alarmed. I had friends in high places, and he looked as if he was toting up the damage I might be able to do him one day.

"Do I still have my party membership?" I asked Han Jingcao.

"Absolutely," he answered. "You're a full member in good standing of the Communist Party of China, and all your time in prison counts as time spent serving the party."

"What about work?"

"What would you like to do? We can find you a nice place to go take a long rest, or we can give you money enough to go back to America, or we can give you a job, or we can give you money to travel in China or abroad. The choice is yours, whatever you like."

"I would like to go back to doing exactly the same job with the same people," I said. "Right now."

"Things have changed," Han said. "The news agency and the

radio are two separate organizations. Someone from the propaganda ministry will come to discuss your choice of a new job."

After six years of being a nonperson, suddenly it seemed I was
a prize catch. Both the Broadcast Administration and Xinhua, the
New China News Agency that was China's main wire service, had
put in bids for my help. I knew why I was needed. It was hard to
find a foreigner fluent in both Chinese and English. And if that
foreigner was a party member as well, it meant that he could be
trusted with a job in their sensitive propaganda apparatus.

Over the next few days I was courted by the news agency's Ding
Tuo, who in Yanan had been in charge of handling my party
affairs, and by Mei Yi, another old friend from the news office in
Yanan, who now headed the Broadcast Administration. Ding Tuo
played on my former friendship. My old acquaintance Wu Lengxi
was the new director at Xinhua. My old friends Chen Long, Peng
Di, and Qian Xing were all at the news agency, he said. There was
no one I knew at the Broadcast Administration—no one, that is,
but Wei Lin. My ex-wife, it seemed, had moved on and was now
an announcer. Everyone treaded gingerly around that subject,
fearing I would become upset.

Mei Yi, when he arrived to talk to me, spoke to my sense of
duty. The Broadcast Administration was the cabinet-level body
that managed China's nationwide network of radio stations and
the international station called Radio Beijing. "You are more badly
needed to polish English scripts and train announcers and editors," he said. "The news agency has foreign comrades working
there already. Lu Dingyi himself has taken an interest in your case
and wants you to be happily settled." I remembered Lu Dingyi,
the dour propaganda chief I had met in Yanan. Now he was not
just minister of propaganda, but also a political bureau member
and a vice premier.

"The Broadcast Administration needs you most," an official
from the propaganda ministry told me. "But Minister Lu is afraid
you would be unhappy because your ex-wife works there."

I wasn't concerned, I told him. If she had decided to wait for
me, I would certainly have been there for her. I would never have
left her. But since she had decided to get on with her life, I had
no interest in standing in her way. I was sure we could work
together with no problems. It was decided that I would begin
work at the Broadcast Administration just after May Day.

◆

I spent the rest of the month of April living in the North China Hotel, a party hostel just outside the northern walls of the Imperial City. I practiced taking buses around the city by myself. I practiced talking to people, a sentence at a time. I fought off panic attacks that came on me suddenly. I was skittish and shy around uniformed people, whom I expected to begin issuing me orders at any moment. I was frequently hesitant lest I inadvertently break some rule. Later, the desk clerks at the hotel said I was the only guest they had ever had who had followed the rules about letting the front desk know where I was going when I left the hotel, and what time I would be back. I had spent six years asking permission to use the latrine. Such habits were hard to break.

I still couldn't escape the feeling that I was undergoing some sort of test. On the last day before I was to report to work, I was invited to join party dignitaries watching the May Day Parade from the reviewing stands in Tiananmen Square, in front of the Forbidden City. The parade was exactly as I had seen it reported in the newspaper for several years. For a short time I found it entertaining, but as it dragged on, I grew bored. There were marching contingents from the armed forces' schools, and government and party institutions. There were contingents representing industrial workers, along with groups of writers and artists, neighborhood committees, farmers, and even sanitation workers. Each group had sponsored elaborate floats and pageants to show their 1955 objectives, and what they had accomplished during the first part of the year.

After the parade, one of the deputy secretary-generals of Hebei Province gave me a lift back to the North China Hotel. In the car, he asked what I thought of the parade. I hesitated, searching for appropriately superlative terms. He filled in the gap. "Not much color to it, eh?" he said dryly. "Rather boring, wasn't it?"

Not at all, I protested. I had found it varied and exciting. I wondered whether he had guessed my true feelings and was leading me on. Was he gathering information that would go into my dossier as evidence of hostile thinking?

I had been freed from my outer cell. The inner cell that I had built myself was still intact, and strong.

◆

At eight-thirty A.M. on May 2, 1955, a car arrived at the North China Hotel to take me to Mei Yi's office at the Broadcast Administration, which was housed in a group of old buildings filling a long, narrow courtyard at Liubukou near Beijing's Xidan shopping center. I was escorted to the director's office where I was met by a serious young secretary with a pear-shaped face and a single thick pigtail of shiny black hair falling down to the middle of her back. She showed me into Mei Yi's office and remained behind for a moment.

"This is Comrade Wang Yulin," said Mei Yi, rising from his desk to greet me. "She is my confidential secretary." I shook hands briefly with the secretary. She looked competent, but awfully young for such an important job. She poured tea and left the room.

"No one knows where you've been except for the members of the leading party group and your own party branch," Mei Yi began. "For your sake we must not let the information out. When you fill out personnel papers, leave the autobiographical information blank. If anyone asks you about it, just refer them to me. Don't let anyone talk you into discussing your background. Just say it is confidential party information."

"But why?" I asked. "There's nothing secret about my background."

Mei Yi shook his head. "You don't know what these people are like," he said. "Your past history has been examined and you have been cleared. But if some people see that you came over with the American army and worked as an UNRRA observer, they will raise all sorts of questions and spread all kinds of stories behind your back. There is no reason for you to carry this handicap around with you, so just keep the story to yourself."

There was a long pause during which I pondered the meaning of his words. So it was over but it would never be really over, I thought.

Suddenly I heard an argument outside the director's door. There had been three people in the outer office when I came in: the secretary, Wang Yulin; a portly older woman; and a mousy young man with close-cropped hair. I could hear a strident voice that must have belonged to Comrade Wang. "Well," she said, "it seems to me you have to be pretty dumb not to know whether your own husband is an enemy spy or not!"

I pricked up my ears. They were talking about me.

Then I heard a male voice. "But you can't blame his wife. After all, she waited three years for him, and he didn't get out for six years."

"What would you do if your husband suddenly disappeared

and you had to wait for six years?" That voice must have been the older woman's.

Back came the voice that belonged to that pigtail. "Do? If I loved him, I would wait for him. Six years, ten years, twenty years —otherwise, what do you mean by love?"

Wang Yulin was taking an unusual position for a young Chinese woman. The proper party position was that if the party said your husband was a spy, then he was a spy. And normal party practice was that if you were separated from your spouse for three years without hearing from him, you could get a divorce automatically. True love didn't have much power in the Communist Party.

I listened for more, but the argument seemed to have tapered off. Mei Yi resumed speaking as if he had heard nothing. "The same thing applies to your party membership," he said. "Let it be known only by those who need to know. Let the others guess if they like, but don't tell them directly."

I said nothing, and he went on. "I hope we won't have any of that old trouble from you about living like an average Chinese." Like all high-ranking officials, he said, I would be assigned a superior grade of housing, would be given a better, more elaborate diet, and would have the use of a Broadcast Administration car and driver at all times.

I didn't argue.

"It is very important that you enjoy the full status and treatment of a foreign expert," Mei Yi said. "You have to establish the weight of your authority in the Foreign Broadcast Department. We do not have many party members in that department, and none whatsoever in the English Language Section. You will be the only one."

I was sure he could see the astonishment on my face at that piece of information.

"You will take part in some of the meetings of the leading party committee and will sit in on sessions of the editorial board," Mei Yi continued. "I am arranging with the central propaganda ministry for permission to have you attend high-level policy announcements and to read the classified Central Committee cables. Approval is only a matter of time, so please bear with me."

I nodded, slowly trying to absorb what he was saying. It seemed that things were going to be very different from the past. I was being taken into the inner circle of the party, treated like a tried and true party member for the first time. I had not even been

aware of the existence of classified cables from the Central Committee. Now, I was going to be privileged to read them.

"Remember that the other foreign comrades, including the Soviets, will not have any of this classified information that you will
have," Mei Yi cautioned. "Nor will our rank-and-file party members and lower-ranking cadres. You will soon see who has access
to what information. You must be careful not to take a liberalistic
attitude toward this information. You must keep it to yourself.
But you know all this, don't you?"

"Yes," I said. "Don't worry, I know how to handle it."

And that was the end of the conversation. As Mei Yi showed
me to the door of his office, he nodded toward his secretary.
"Comrade Wang Yulin will be available to help you get settled in.
You should call her whenever you need supplies or assistance."

I smiled at the secretary as I walked out. She had bright, candid
eyes and a stubborn set to her mouth. She was wearing a blue
cotton Chinese gown, slit modestly at both sides, white anklets,
and black cloth shoes. I liked her looks, but I didn't plan to put
her—or anyone else—to work on my personal needs.

The next day was Tuesday and I moved into the assigned living
quarters for Broadcast Administration officials. Like other more
senior officials, I had a sitting room, a bedroom with a double bed
and a new embroidered cotton quilt, a bathroom, and a big closet.
My quarters were on the Lane of the Fried Dough Twists just
north of the Imperial Palace grounds—and only a forty-five-
minute walk from the prison in which I had lived for six years.

My new office was in a long, dark, rectangular room in an old
building across from the western wall of the Imperial Palace
grounds. About a half hour after I arrived that Tuesday morning,
I was arranging my desk when Wang Yulin appeared with a notice
on a clipboard. "There's an editorial meeting at nine-thirty," she
said in a businesslike tone. "Check your name off here."

On the clipboard, I saw a printed list of those who attended
such meetings. The ones who had already been notified had written a single character by their names: "Zhi," meaning "I know
about it." I saw my name handwritten below the printed names,
and I wrote in my "Zhi" just like the others. I was as excited as
my dulled-down feelings would allow me to be. And I was nervous. I didn't know if I would conduct myself properly. After all,
I was shaky, my voice had not entirely recovered, and I was still
having terrifying panic attacks.

At nine-thirty, I walked to the conference room right across from Mei Yi's office. The subject of the meeting was agricultural cooperatives and an editor gave a short briefing. Chairman Mao emphasized that participation in the co-ops must be voluntary, the editor stressed. Poor peasants would probably join them first. The middle peasant, that is, farm families who only broke even in most years, shouldn't be pressured to join, but should only join when they saw they could earn a better income by doing so. The editor explained that Chairman Mao figured the whole process would take three to five years.

This briefing was important because all our reporting was based on party policy. Our broadcasts about farm co-ops should make all Chairman Mao's points, and should also impress listeners with the wisdom and the successes of the policy. None of us had any problem with that. We all saw radio and newspapers as vehicles for teaching the people about party policy.

I listened intently to the discussion, since I wanted to be especially clear on policy. At the same time, I couldn't help watching Wang Yulin as she walked in and out of the room bringing documents for Mei Yi and other leaders to sign. I was impressed by her self-assurance and the quiet confidence with which she approached even senior cadres. What a straight back, I thought to myself. And what beautiful hair, today braided in two long glossy tails.

I managed to speak up twice during the meeting. Once I commented that the voluntary nature of the co-ops should be especially stressed for foreign listeners since most foreigners believed that everything in socialist countries was done by coercion. The second time was to report that at the May Day Parade a few days earlier I had approached another dignitary on the stands, a young woman named Hao Jianxiu, who was being honored for her model work as a spinner in a factory. I had asked her to do an interview with the English group for broadcast abroad.

I expected praise for my initiative. Instead, I was met with dead silence. Nobody moved. Then, gently, Mei Yi explained to the group that since this was my first day at work I was not familiar with how things were done at Radio. Interviews were planned in advance, he said, and approved by the proper authorities. They couldn't be set up just on the whim of one person.

It was the same old problem: the individual versus the collective. I would have to watch myself, I realized.

◆

Sunday was our free day. That Saturday evening, I was waiting on the shuttle bus for the last of the passengers bound home to our compound when Wang Yulin poked her head through the door. "Li Dunbai," she said, "don't go out Sunday morning. I am coming over to help you straighten up your room."

And then she vanished.

The bus pulled out and the deputy bureau chiefs on board began teasing me mercilessly. "Now don't you dare go out, Li Dunbai," they sang out in falsetto tones. "You wait at home for me, understand?"

I didn't take their jibes too seriously. I suspected that Mei Yi, knowing I wouldn't ask her myself, had instructed Wang Yulin to take care of me. And indeed when she bounded in at about ten o'clock the next morning she was all business. She inspected my sitting room, bedroom, and closet, and she didn't like what she saw. She began to rearrange the furniture. Then she remade the double bed that I had made that morning. I still used the army style of bed making that I had learned in prison. She fluffed up the pillows and covered the bed with the embroidered cotton quilt. She took all my clothes out of the closet and refolded, restacked, and rehung everything.

By then, it was almost time for lunch. "Ma Yingquan and He Jiexin have invited us to go rowing with them at Shichahai Park," Wang Yulin said. "Would you like that?"

"Sure," I replied.

Ma was head of administration in the Broadcast Administration's logistics department and an old friend from the days in the country. He Jiexin was his wife and the woman in charge of the classified documents room. I remembered her as the skinny little girl-bride, sobbing on the day of her wedding to Ma, which I had attended in Western Garrison village in 1948. I had wondered how they had fared.

It seemed that big-city life agreed with He Jiexin. The portly woman who arrived at my quarters with Ma was a head taller and dignified. She had already had her second child, the couple explained. We all set out by bus for the park, the northernmost of the former Imperial parks in Beijing. We rented a boat and rowed pleasantly around the lake for a half hour or so, joking and laughing together. Then, suddenly, Ma rowed the boat close to the southern shore, jumped out, and held the bow for his wife to climb out too. Up the bank they clambered and made for the street, calling back as they went, "You two will have to get the boat back by yourselves. We have something to attend to."

Flabbergasted, both Wang Yulin and I realized we had been set up. Yulin's face was grim. "Gai si," she yelled at the departing Ma's back. Drop dead! Then she turned to me. Old Ma is always up to some mischief, she exclaimed. "I'll fix him good when I get hold of him."

"It doesn't matter," I said. "We'll just go on and have a good time by ourselves, that's all."

"I know, but he'll go back and spread stories about us going rowing together in the park."

"What do we care about stories?" I said with a shrug. I didn't care, but she did. At age twenty-two, she didn't want to risk her reputation of being indifferent to suitors. And in fact, from her easy, comradely manner, it was clear she felt under no threat at all from me. I was thirty-four, a foreigner, nearly blind in one eye, and balding. I must have seemed quite elderly to her. As for me, my feelings were still too shrouded to think about courting. I was simply glad to have found a nice new friend.

We rowed around and chatted for another half hour or so. Then we turned the boat in, left the park, and walked down the street to a point near my old home, the North China Hotel. There were some street vendors selling a local confection known as "frank-furters." They were really made from black beans and I found the bitter bean taste highly offensive. Nevertheless, when Wang Yulin bought one and gave it to me to eat, I grinned and bore it.

What a wonderful country, I thought to myself. How freely young people can use the well-kept parks and playgrounds with-out charge, enjoy a thousand different snacks from the street stalls, go to the movies or eat delicacies in little restaurants. I was pleased at the signs I saw all around me that showed I had been right to throw my lot in with the Communists, and to wait patiently through my time in prison to rejoin them.

We then took the bus to Xidan crossing, where we went to a little shop called Mandarin Duck Dumpling House. We ate pro-digious quantities of the half-beef, half-pork dumplings, named for the famous Chinese lovebirds that are supposed to pair off early and remain faithful to each other for life.

◆

There had been many changes in Beijing and in China as a whole while I had been in prison. The city was nothing like the

Beijing I had visited on my way to Kalgan, or the wartime Shanghai that had so troubled me. There was no visible police surveillance, no signs in the restaurants like the ones I had seen everywhere in Kunming and Shanghai warning people "Don't discuss affairs of state." There were no pickpockets, prostitutes, beggars, no corpses in the streets, no ragged people, no people starving because they couldn't get work or could only earn a bowl of rice a day for coolie labor. The garbage and offal were also gone. The streets were clean, street vendors were lined up in an orderly marketplace fashion, and there was an air of calm and confidence everywhere. Yes, Beijing was a very different place from the dirty, squalid town I had passed through in 1946.

The Communists were still busy consolidating their control of the country they had won just six years before. As I had seen from the May Day Parade, their hold on big industry had grown massively from the days before I went into prison. They now controlled the industrial production of the entire country, including the enormous Kailan mines at Tangshan that had once been run by the British. In top-level meetings at the Broadcast Administration, I learned that agricultural co-ops were also spreading throughout the countryside. And I could see for myself how the party was bringing small businessmen into the fold.

Walking around the city, I occasionally saw parades of Beijing's "capitalists" marching through the streets banging drums and cymbals, or with floats and banners celebrating their part in the gradual socialist transformation of their private businesses into government-owned enterprises. Once at a meeting I heard Mei Yi report a sardonic remark from Liu Shaoqi, the number two party man. The capitalists are dancing in the street by day and going home to cry on their wives' shoulders at night, he said. I felt sure that, although they might personally feel the loss of their businesses, the country as a whole would benefit and they too would benefit as human beings.

My old Yanan friendships had also changed. For one thing, we were no longer thrown together in the companionable poverty of the mountain caves. A rural-based revolution had become a city-based government. Chairman Mao was not just the leader of a hardy little band of revolutionaries in the hills, but chairman of the party that governed a country of over a half billion people. My gentle friend Zhou Enlai was premier and a world-class diplomatic celebrity. I read about his meetings with Nehru, Tito, Sihanouk,

Sukarno, traveling to the Bandung Conference, and attending the first Geneva Conference on the troubles in Vietnam.

My two party sponsors were now high-ranking government officials. General Wang Zhen was minister of state farms and the lanky General Li Xiannian was minister of finance. All top officials lived tucked away in a large compound called Zhongnanhai— South Central Sea—in an annex to the Imperial Palace grounds in the western part of the city. There were no more cozy little dances or chance meetings on dusty roads.

Even my more ordinary acquaintances had wound up in positions of power. Having been in Yanan, at the beginning, was enough to guarantee a distinguished career to almost everyone. My old friends Peng Di and Qian Xing were posted abroad for the New China News Agency. Jiang Zhenzhong, the Shanghai money changer on whose premises I had held the first secret meeting with Xu Maijin in 1945, and who later showed up with Zhou Enlai on the plane to Yanan, was in the Broadcast Administration as head of logistics.

Shortly after I arrived at the Broadcast Administration, I had my first meeting with my ex-wife. Everyone tried to prepare me for it. She had been sick, they said. She had had tuberculosis and major gynecological surgery. "She isn't the girl you used to know," Mei Yi warned. Still, our meeting was strained and sad. I could scarcely believe it was Wei Lin. When I had last seen her, she was a pretty, chubby, round-faced student, lively and full of fun. Now she looked old and drawn. The life and all the fun had gone out of her and something else bothered me. There was a new, hard set to her mouth and a cold look in her eyes. I felt that something dreadful had happened to Wei Lin while I was in prison, not just to her body, but to her spirit as well.

CHAPTER TEN

Redder than Red

From the time I was released from prison, everything I did was colored by one furious urge: to prove myself a loyal Communist. I emerged from those six years in solitary wanting nothing more than to show party authorities that I had changed. I wanted them to see that I was no longer a flawed and faltering weakling, but a true party stalwart. Partly I felt it was my responsibility as an American not to be a weak spot in the armor of the Chinese Revolution. Partly I feared a reprise of my imprisonment. If I was conspicuously Red, I secretly reasoned, I could ward off the possibility of future suspicions and attacks. Mei Yi's cautions not to reveal my background struck a chord that reverberated with my continuing panic attacks and light-headedness. I feared the scrutiny I felt sure would never end.

But my zeal stemmed mainly from my conviction. I saw a better world around me than the one I had left behind. I wanted to help make it better still. And I wanted to belong. My need to be accepted had not been stanched by my imprisonment, but rather intensified by it. To my astonishment and delight, they had taken me back as one of their own, trusted and honored in a way I had never been before. I was almost overwhelmed with gratitude and I wanted to prove that their trust wasn't misplaced. No more shrinking from danger or running away under fire. No more breaches of party discipline. From now on, I vowed, the party came first.

Such devotion wasn't hard to sustain. I found similar commitments all around me. The party was at its peak of prestige. Everything was "us," "our," "we," not "me," "mine," "I." Our policies. Our government. Our radio. Our People's Liberation Army. Our party.

Party members had political privileges, but membership wasn't about material gains. Party members paid less attention to their clothes and possessions. They were supposed to be above that. A woman who recut her standard cadre suit to make it more appealing would be criticized. Why do you want to stand out from the others? she would be asked. That was Communist, but it was also Confucian. All sorts of Confucian ideals were adopted by the Chinese Communist Party and painted red.

Membership in the party was very hard to obtain and required discipline and devotion. Party members were given the hardest jobs and were supposed to work the longest hours. They came back to work after dinner and on Sundays. Often on a Sunday afternoon, I could look around and see the newsroom at the Broadcast Administration filled with either party members or those trying to become members.

The party was a zealous, committed group, hard to get into and devastatingly disgraceful to be expelled from. I heard quite a number of college graduates say they didn't want to join because they couldn't take the discipline. For most people, however, their main ambition was to get into the party. All of us in the party were constantly approached by those who said they wanted to train themselves to be accepted as party members. People consciously and willingly put themselves through all sorts of trials to be accepted.

The party had established a political dictatorship, but to stabilize its power, the party tried to handle ordinary everyday affairs democratically, right down to the food we ate. Over the past two years, the government had begun buying farm staples directly from the peasants and distributing them through a coupon system. To make sure that every man, woman, and child in China had his or her fair share, staples like grain, oil, and cloth were issued each month. When people were married, they got an extra hundred feet of cloth for wedding quilts. When children were born, they got fifteen feet more. There were coupons for meat, a fixed amount each month at a low price, and then unlimited amounts at a higher price.

The system seemed close to the ideals that I had fought for back in the labor movement in the South. Work units decided through democratic discussion how much grain each person in the unit needed each month. It was called "Report Your Own Needs, for Public Deliberation"—Zi bao gong yi. Like the Communists' distribution of relief grain I had witnessed nearly a decade earlier as an UNRRA observer, it was done at a series of public meetings. One editor, for example, reported when it came her turn that she needed an average of twenty-six pounds of grain a month.

"But you're pregnant," a colleague said. "You will need more nourishment—twenty-six pounds isn't enough. You should take thirty." After some back-and-forthing, the group finally decided that she should get twenty-eight pounds a month, and this figure was reported upward for approval by the appropriate party committee.

When the party was putting together its policy on agricultural cooperation, the basic guidelines were set by the Central Committee and there were weeks of discussions held in every village so that each farmer and each farm family could have their say. Then, based on those discussions, the Central Committee formulated a new draft and sent it back for comment. Back and forth, back and forth the draft went, with the party, of course, making the final decision.

From the newspapers I read that this sort of democratic process was going on in every village, every office, every school, every mine and mill. Hundreds of millions of people were enjoying the benefits of the party's way of deriving its policies from the people, and then returning them to the people for implementation and revision in the course of practice.

So here I was, living in a land where the working people had been dirt underfoot, and where they were now masters. I could see Wood Fairy's father, Li Ruishan the rickshaw puller, well fed at last, sitting in on one of these discussions, solemnly smoking his water pipe and putting in a word here and there in his quiet way. The terrible injustices that had led me to stay in China were at last being rectified. I was proud to be a member of the Chinese Communist Party, the only American citizen to belong.

As all good party cadres did, I considered that my work went far beyond just doing my job. I taught nighttime classes in political economy, and coached people individually after class. We would discuss topics like "Why is the socialist economy superior to a capitalist economy?" But the party concerned itself not just with economic and professional matters, but with every aspect of a person's life. As good party members, we were expected to be political advisers, marriage counselors, psychiatrists, financial consultants, confessors. I spent hours talking to people about the problems they had with their mothers-in-law or finding nurses for their babies, or helping them transfer from one housing unit to another.

Nothing was too big or too small or too intimate to bring to the party member of your choice. When a young mother's baby died of a rare disease, she came to me frantic with grief and fear that the next child would die too. I counseled her and found medical information that would reassure her. When one man tried to choose between his sophisticated big-city girlfriend and his sweet, simple country fiancée, I spent hours laying out for him the principles of a good marriage. When a woman came to me, put out because she wasn't getting glamorous-enough assignments, I lectured her about devotion to duty.

◆

I had been working at the Broadcast Administration for less than a month when I discovered the party was even more diligent about its own membership. I was sitting at my desk reading through scripts for the evening broadcast when Wang Yulin came in with a summons to a high-level party meeting that evening. I dutifully inscribed my "Zhi" to show that I had been notified. And that evening, all party cadres from department heads on up assembled in the mess hall for a briefing. We bumped and jostled our way in, sitting ten to a side on benches before the greasy wood tables.

Wen Jize, a vice director in charge of international broadcasts, looked serious in his formal blue broadcloth suit. He read a statement with solemnity. A five-man committee including Mao, Liu Shaoqi, Deng Xiaoping, who was party general secretary, Luo Ruiqing, who was minister of public security, and Peng Zhen, who was mayor of Beijing, had come to an important decision. In the years since liberation, the statement read, the party had successfully cleaned out the most obvious of spies, KMT sympathizers, and secret agents. Now the time had come to look for the harder cases, the counterrevolutionaries who had burrowed deep into their organizations and were secretly waiting for a chance to strike back.

Everyone in the room knew that a notorious counterrevolutionary clique led by Hu Feng had recently been exposed. Hu Feng was a party member, but was also an outspoken critic of the party's tight control over artists, writers, and academics, which he said stifled them. A few weeks earlier, after sending a long critical letter to Mao, he had been charged with plotting to seize power under the cover of his cultural work.

Now the statement instructed each organization to draw lessons from this experience, and to check closely into the background of each suspicious person to expose hidden spies and saboteurs like the Hu Feng gang. The propaganda organizations, including the Broadcast Administration, were told to be especially vigilant, as they were sensitive targets for a hidden enemy.

I was already growing anxious. This document was summoning party officials to begin burrowing into people's backgrounds again. Mei Yi had specifically warned me to keep my background secret. What was going to happen to me? My muscles twitched but I tried hard to control myself. I didn't want my expression to give me away. I glanced around the room. Was anyone watching me?

Just as I had in prison, I felt, at least in part, I might have done something to feel guilty about. The *People's Daily,* the party's official newspaper, was already printing excerpts from Hu Feng's writings with comments by Mao himself. These excerpts, the paper said, proved that Hu and his cronies were counterrevolutionaries. But try as I might, I just couldn't see it. Hu Feng's writings were critical of Chairman Mao and his policies, but I could discern nothing more serious than that. Now the failure on my part to detect a counterrevolutionary danger seemed a sure sign of my low level of consciousness. I had to squash all doubts. "They must have evidence they're not publishing," I thought. "The party always tells the truth, no matter what you think. Just shut up and accept it."

As it turned out, I had nothing to fear from this investigation. Not only was my background not under scrutiny, but the task of scrutinizing others fell to me. Committees to handle the cases were set up at every division, in every department and subdepartment, at every level. And because there were no other party members in the English section at the Broadcast Administration, I was given the job of going through all the dossiers of my co-workers. That pretty well eased my mind. I figured if I were truly a target, the party would never put me in a position like that, with access to other people's confidential records. Still, I couldn't be too careful. I had the distinct feeling that being active in this campaign was a kind of protection against being wronged again myself, and I was determined to do a conscientious job of it.

We were looking for people with bad political histories, who, for example, had once joined the KMT's Three People's Principles Youth Corps when they were in college. We were looking for people whose parents had been big landlords or major pro-KMT capitalists, or whose friends included that sort, or who had contacts in Taiwan or abroad. We were looking for people who harbored counterrevolutionary thoughts or had been heard to utter counterrevolutionary slogans.

The list of intellectuals with suspect political backgrounds included most of the English section's key personnel, since they had all come from universities under the old regime and many had "complicated" connections. So the Broadcast Administration leadership and the security department made a preliminary scan and handed me two dossiers to review.

Everyone had a dossier. These plain manila folders were deceptively simple-looking. Inside were loose sheets of paper, handwritten or typed, and piles of material held together with straight pins. It wasn't hard to collect data for these dossiers. Every dutiful party member was supposed to watch his or her peers and colleagues, alert for signs of hostility to the party. If someone trained as a bookkeeper was unhappy about working as a laborer in a steel mill, it should be reported, so that the person could be counseled to be happy with his or her role in the Revolution. If someone was resentful about being passed over for a promotion, that too should be reported so that his attitude could be corrected.

Few considered such reporting wrong. It was part of our duty to the party, and to our friends who would benefit from the help. I regularly briefed the branch secretary about people in my section, and Mei Yi on the members of the foreign study groups I attended. I was sure these reports were included in their dossiers. Only certain high-ranking party members were authorized to go through these dossiers, or to authorize others to do so. People never saw their own files. But whatever was in a party member's dossier, it contained the key to his or her future—even to his or her life.

The two files I handled were those of staffers in the English section, both with bad family backgrounds. One had been in KMT air force intelligence and was suspected of still having intelligence ties. The other had been implicated by a political prisoner, who accused him of being part of a ring of counterrevolutionaries. Both also had work demerits, one for allowing the listeners' letters to pile up unanswered, and the other for a broadcasting blunder. When Klement Gottwald, the party chief of Czechoslovakia, died, the man had followed the broadcast message of condolence with a tape of peals of riotous laughter and horse laughs. At the time, he said it was a mistake. Still, there was a demerit in his files.

I spent a long time reading each dossier, walking up and down, drinking big mugs of strong black tea. I was pleased to be entrusted with such a task, and confident I could do a good job of it. After I had finished reading their files, I recommended that I talk privately with the two men, tell them the charges against them, and give them a chance to explain. In the end, both were cleared. The one in intelligence hadn't been in espionage. He had worked in some intelligence office, like a map room, but as far as the records showed, he had never been trained in any spy work, and there was no indication he was engaged in any undercover activities. As for the other, we decided the prisoner who had accused him of being a counterrevolutionary was lying to try to lighten his sentence.

Other cases, however, didn't go so smoothly. And anyone suspected of concealing antiparty sentiments or activities was scrutinized by bigger and bigger groups. One such case involved three young members of the English section. Cheng Hongkui was an announcer; Gu Yiting was his wife, a translator; and Wei Mengqi, also a translator, was a close friend and former schoolmate.

All three were from bad family backgrounds, and all from St. John's University in Shanghai. When reports of their conversations began to surface, things looked grim for them. Cheng had been heard to complain that the area around the Fragrant Hills was closed to hikers and picnickers when the air force set up an installation there. Once at an open-forum meeting Cheng had also said that it made him feel bad to see high-ranking party members drive by in their big limousines, curtains drawn against the prying public.

The three also admitted that one of their friends had once asked Cheng what would happen if, as an announcer, he tried to shout something like "Give Me Freedom" over the air. Cheng had answered that the monitor in his studio would immediately turn the mike off and probably call one of the guards who were at all entrances to the studio area. This was considered an admission that they had talked about sending reactionary messages over the Radio Beijing airwaves.

My role in this case was tangential. The three suspects had admitted liking English literature, a possible ideological problem. I was resident expert on the political quality of the literature they read, books by Arthur Koestler and Somerset Maugham. I had never read Koestler's *Darkness at Noon,* but I knew from reviews that it was an attack on the Soviet Union. I considered Somerset Maugham effete, so I readily agreed their taste in books was decadent. But their real crime seemed to be that while outwardly quiet and respectful, underneath they were arrogant and exclusive, with the kind of rich man's air that had been so common before the Revolution. Even during the investigations, they always seemed confident and above it all.

In fact, they seemed to laugh off the entire investigation—until the Broadcast Administration took legal action. The security department got a warrant and searched their rooms. Although none of the accused group was suspected of violence, the security people took this search very seriously. I saw three or four men set out and heard one of them say, "Better take a gun with you." They found nothing except for the Western literature everyone knew was there.

In the end, Cheng Hongkui was pronounced a member of a reactionary clique, and he and his wife and their new baby were sent with their friends to a labor camp in the cold wastelands of Manchuria. I never saw any of them again. Many people at the Broadcast Administration felt they had been sentenced to a rather romantic fate. A movie about an old army officer who went to Manchuria to hack a new paradise out of the frozen waste was popular at the time. No one had any real idea about what an exile to such a harsh life would be like. For me, I felt that good honest farm labor would do them good. Hadn't I been willing myself to undergo years of privation for the sake of the party? Well, they should be too.

◆

As for my new job, in many important ways I had significantly more power and authority than I did in Yanan. Because of my growing knowledge of party politics, I was increasingly able to judge a newscast, not just for its grammatical correctness, but for its political content as well. Everything was done according to party policy. We weren't reporting news. We were propagating policy.

I was one of the few who had access to real news, which came in secret, restricted-circulation documents. The lowest level was the Cankao Xiaoshi, or Reference News, which contained digests of foreign news—from *Le Monde* and *La Prensa* to *The New York Times* and *The Wall Street Journal*—that was considered safe for the average low-level cadre to read. The next higher level, Cankao Ziliao, or Reference Materials, came out twice a day, one thick magazine of forty pages or more, along with one thinner one, and was circulated among higher-ranking officials, like central department heads and provincial party secretaries, and to those of us in propaganda organizations. The more important, and possibly explosive, international news, like political attacks on China by foreign leaders and writers, went in there.

The real harsh truth about domestic and world events went in the Neibu Cankao, or the Internal Reference, a flimsy magazine about the size and thickness of the *Reader's Digest,* which was published by the ministry of propaganda and distributed selectively on a need-to-know basis. Even when the *People's Daily* burst with the news of good harvests and enthusiastic peasants, you could open the Neibu Cankao and read that there had been a crop failure or a flood in the area.

And then there were the secret cables that only selected high-ranking party officials were cleared to read. News of important decisions of provincial party committees, changes in central party policy, movements, criticisms, punishment, new alliances—all went onto tan-colored sheets the thickness of newsprint. They were called red letterhead documents, from their red headings, and could only be read in the documents room, another secret room similar to the one in which the dossiers were kept. Only people specially cleared were allowed in to read, and only certain documents at that.

There were four clearance levels, marked by the Chinese ordinals Jia, Yi, Bing, and Ding, the equivalent of A, B, C, and D. Only one person of all the seven thousand people who worked at the Broadcast Administration was cleared to read Level D dispatches, and that was Mei Yi. He was at a ministerial level, with the only people above him being the members of the Central Committee and the Politburo, among whom a selected few got reports of military and diplomatic intelligence.

Because of the sensitivity of the materials Mei Yi was cleared to read—which often included minutes of Central Committee meetings—they were delivered to him by classified motorcycle messenger. Such elite messengers were usually ex-army officers. The Broadcast Administration had its own elite messengers, who were cleared to ride directly between our offices and Zhongnanhai, where the senior leaders like Mao, Liu Shaoqi, Zhou Enlai, Zhu De, and Deng Xiaoping lived and worked.

Level A readers were party leaders from each subsection, like the head of the French section at the Broadcast Administration. These ratings were geared to administrative level, which, like ordinary civil service rankings, also determined pay and privileges. Level A clearances included Grade 17 or 18 cadres in a general numbering system that started at the bottom with Grade 22 and worked up. Level B, which was my level, included the heads of bigger departments, the lowest tier of high-ranking cadres. Level C included deputy bureau chiefs and higher. I would sometimes be given a particular Level C document, but I was generally limited to Level B and below.

I never asked to be allowed to go to the documents room. No one ever did. One day a call simply came to inform me that I had been cleared to go in. When I got there, the clerk on duty checked my level and presented me with the folder of documents that had been cleared for someone at my level to read. People's classification could change as they were promoted, and the classification of documents could change too as events shifted.

It was there in the documents room that I found the information essential for the correct handling of my job. In a message about a visit from a head of state like President Sukarno of Indonesia, there would be the issues which prompted his visit, what he was likely to ask for from China, and what China was likely to give him.

There were also instructions about the propaganda tone for reports of the visit: enthusiastic, neutral, cool. I always studied such documents carefully so that I would know how to handle broadcasts of the story, and how to coach reporters, for example, when they were sent to the China/Indonesia Friendship People's Commune in the outskirts of Beijing to interview an ordinary farm family on their deep, warm feelings of friendship for the Indonesian people.

◆

Caught up as I was in the party and in my work, I still hadn't forgotten Comrade Wang Yulin. She and I had fallen into the habit of getting together nearly every evening after work. Because her job as Mei Yi's confidential secretary kept her so busy, her day could end as late as mine, anywhere from nine to eleven at night. Then we would prowl the streets of Beijing looking for good things to eat. Sometimes we crossed Beijing's main thoroughfare, Changan Boulevard, to go to Saliwen's, a famous old snack house that, the story went, had been founded by a family named Sullivan long ago. Saliwen's served cold bowls of almond bean curd, made with the crushed kernels of apricots, frozen and congealed into soft cold gelatinous squares and served with haw jelly. That's what Yulin ordered for me, saying that it was like ice cream, something she had never tasted. For herself, she ordered her favorite: a bowl of red bean puree, also served cold.

Sometimes we went around the corner from the office to a place called the Kindness and Success Restaurant for hot rice porridge with chicken and tiny beef rolls crimped artistically around the edges. Occasionally Mei Yi joined us there, once joking that someone was sure to call the public security ministry to turn him in for meeting with a foreigner. Other times we walked the long block down to Xidan to eat Peking duck rolls. And sometimes we walked all the way down Changan Boulevard to the gate of the Imperial Palace, turned and walked back to Xidan crossing where the night snack bar of a Sichuan restaurant served bowls of flaming hot dan-dan noodles, which always made me cough and sneeze.

As Yulin and I walked, we talked, and I was impressed by her straightforwardness and her impeccable proletarian background. Her father was one of a long line of cabinetmakers and woodworkers who turned out beautiful carved Chinese furniture. She had been born near Beijing, but when she was four the Japanese invaded and the whole family fled to the mountains in neighboring Shanxi Province.

After that flight her family was almost destitute. When they fled, her father had lost his tools and therefore his livelihood. Before the Communist victory, Yulin had picked up rags to sell to makers of cloth shoes. Sometimes she sat with her father on a square of paper by the curbside, selling matches. Sometimes the family was reduced to eating weeds. She told me about her little nephew Peiquan who had been sold to an opera troupe to keep the rest of the family from starving.

After the party took over, Yulin went to high school, the first person in her family to do so. She was a star student and joined the party when she was fifteen. She was a stubborn girl who could hold her own in an argument, and didn't believe in giving in when she thought she was right. After she graduated from high school, her diligence and quickness at study, combined with her uncomplicated working-class background, had made her a natural choice for the sensitive job at the Broadcast Administration.

At the end of our evenings together, I walked Yulin back to her quarters at the Golden City Inn, an old-fashioned Chinese-style hostel that had been taken over and converted into living quarters for Broadcast Administration cadres. Because of her important job, and the fact that she frequently had to work at night, she had a little room all to herself. But we would bid a polite farewell at the doorway and I would head back by tram for the Lane of the Fried Dough Twists.

After a few weeks of this, my friend Wen Jize pulled me aside, suggesting a quiet walk and tête-à-tête. Number two at the Broadcast Administration, second only to Mei Yi, Wen Jize was a genial, energetic, fussy sort of man who was kind to everyone. I had liked him ever since we were neighbors in Yanan and knew him to be honest and uncomplicated.

"I have noticed that you and Wang Yulin have become friends," Wen Jize said midway through our walk. "I know her well and I want to warn you. She is very negative on the whole idea of getting married because she has been promised she will be sent to Moscow to train to be a TV engineer. Twice, I have noticed that when a young man begins to chase after her, she immediately cuts him off."

"But I have no such intentions toward her," I protested. "We're just good friends."

He brushed my protests aside. "Let me be your adviser," he said. "I know you Americans write love letters. But let me tell you, don't under any circumstances write Yulin a love letter. It will scare her away. Now don't worry," he added. "She will get used to the idea of marrying you. Just don't be forward or aggressive with her."

Marry Yulin? It was only just then, when Wen Jize warned me off, that the idea occurred to me. And suddenly I realized I wanted to spend the rest of my life with her. We had fun together, we argued and laughed and joked. She was cheerful and upbeat, direct and unpretentious. What's more, she was a good, solid party member with a faultless proletarian background. She was

Mei Yi's private secretary and cleared to read secret documents at the highest level. I could trust her, I thought, to keep me on the straight and narrow path. I had already decided I needed that kind of partner to keep me out of trouble.

That night I sat down and wrote Yulin a love letter. I told her I was glad we had become friends. I said I hoped the relationship would develop into a solid one of love, and that we might eventually get married. I wrote the letter at night at my desk in the office, sealed it in an envelope, and put it on her desk before I went home.

The next morning, almost immediately after I sat down at my desk for the day's work, I heard familiar footsteps striding forcefully into my office and up to my desk; I could picture the straight back, the head held high, the defiant jet black pigtails swinging in the air as she walked. Yulin stood at my desk, dropped a note on it without a word, then turned away. There were two small sheets of paper folded to about an inch in width and then twisted together corkscrew fashion. It was the way the guerrillas used to fold their notes so they could easily be hidden or quickly swallowed when necessary.

Heart pounding, I unscrewed the note and smoothed it out to read. "Dear Comrade Li Dunbai," it began. When I saw the "Comrade," I knew I was in trouble. "I have never dreamed of the kind of relationship between us that you are proposing. I have never thought of us as anything but friends and comrades. Since you have other ideas, it is clear to me that the only solution is for us to discontinue our personal relationship completely. I wish you well in all your future endeavors. (signed) Wang Yulin.

"P.S. Since I agreed yesterday that I would accompany you to the Sun Yat-sen Park this evening, I shall, of course, keep my promise."

That night on a hill in Sun Yat-sen Park it was settled. I proposed, she accepted, and we were married six months later, on February 11, 1956, at the Chinese New Year holiday.

◆

Beijing was very beautiful in the winter, and very, very cold. The wind whirling down from Siberia whistled through windows and doors, and when snow fell, everyone piled up in the streets to clear it away. We bundled up in sweaters, overcoats, long johns, and flannel undershirts. Our offices were heated with the tiniest thread of steam wisping up from cranky, creaky radiators. It was only enough to take the worst of the chill off, and we all wore layers and layers of clothes, even indoors.

After we were married, Yulin and I sometimes went out to ride the trolley cars just to see the sights of the city. The thin dusting of snow softened the harsh lines of the big, rough buildings, built without any attempt at beauty, and rounded out the acute angles of the old storefronts and the rows of matchboxlike residential buildings for workers. Sometimes we walked along the old city wall that still ringed Beijing and threw rocks down into the moat below. Beijing still had many of the old gates built under the emperors' reigns. At Xidan in the west and at Dongdan in the east, there were red-and-gold-trimmed archways. The streets were only tiny alleyways between courtyard houses and a bus would barely squeeze between the stoops on one side and the thresholds on the other.

Sometimes late at night we still went out for a midnight snack of fluffy bean curd or hot dumpling soup. Or we took a stroll in Northern Seas Park or Sun Yat-sen Park, where we had sealed our engagement. But we spent most of our free time settling into a life of quiet domesticity. Right after our marriage we moved into Residential Dwelling #302, a two-bedroom apartment in a regulation four-story brick apartment building in the Broadcast Administration cadres' compound, only a short walk from the office where we worked.

By the standards of Southern living I grew up with—South Carolina houses with thick rich carpets, big kitchens, front and back parlors with pianos, wraparound porches covered with wisteria, and huge yards, back and front—my home in Beijing was Spartan. But by Chinese standards it was the height of luxury. Both the size of the apartment and its amenities—we had hot running water, which only China's top leaders were entitled to—marked this as the dwelling of persons of privilege.

Yulin cooked breakfast for us, usually rice porridge with salted vegetables and pears or tangerines. She learned to drink coffee with me. At noon we ate in the canteen where a Russian-trained chef produced his idea of Western cooking: chicken Kiev, beef Stroganoff, borscht, and veal or lamb cooked in vinegar. Then in the evening Yulin cooked a big dinner of Beijing-style fried onion cakes, chicken, spareribs, or fat stuffed dumplings.

Our house was close to the street, so the sounds of the city surrounded us. We could hear the hucksters' calls drifting up through our windows, the high melodic piping of the bean curd sellers, their trilling notes running up and down the scales. The knife grinder pushed his little handcart with his tools through the streets, shaking his metal rattles and shouting "Qiang jianzi leeeeee . . . Mo caidao . . ." Sharpen your scissors, hone your cleavers. . . . It reminded me of the cries of the tradesmen in Charleston when I was a boy.

In winter, we had shorter nap hours, knocking off at eleven-thirty and coming back at one. Sometimes I napped in my office, but most often I strolled the two hundred yards to my home. The winter air was sharp with the acrid smell of the high-sulfur coal that people burned in their homes, combined with the sharp odor of the ever-present outdoor latrines and with the smell of meat being cooked over street grills.

Under our windows city life teemed. In the first hours of dawn, workers from the late shift going home, or those beginning work especially early, would pass by loudly discussing the results of various basketball or Ping-Pong matches. Chinese tradition doesn't hold that it's rude to stare, nor does it say much about the need to keep your voice down when someone else is trying to sleep.

Before we were married, Yulin had planned to train in the Soviet Union; after our marriage that plan was abandoned. Still she got her wish for technical training. She was transferred to the technical side of the Broadcast Administration and was trained as a sound engineer, working with big open-reel machines made in Germany. The idea of being a party functionary had never pleased her. At heart, she was a craftsman, like her father. We were both happy at work and at home.

The prospect of our marriage had displeased many people, how-ever. Neither of Yulin's parents approved of her marrying a for-eigner. I had one lucky break when it turned out I had already met her father, whom I sometimes encountered in the bathhouse near my home on the Lane of the Fried Dough Twists. "He's very courteous and seems to treat everyone well," her father reported to Yulin when he finally gave her his permission to marry. She managed to get her mother's permission too, but neither would come to our wedding.

Mei Yi had tried to talk me out of marrying Yulin. "You've just come back into circulation and you need to take it easy," he said. "You two like each other, and she's a very capable person—one of the best. But I've seen too many people that like each other get married, and then find the cultural differences between them are too great. Then the marriage becomes humdrum and they're both dissatisfied and it affects their work. You want to talk about Shakespeare and she wants to talk about Peking opera, and you are both bored."

My supervisor, Zhao Jie, had opposed the match on the same grounds. A skinny, asthmatic old character who was the butt of constant jokes and teasing from everyone, Zhao had lost so much of his hearing that he often wasn't quite sure what was going on. Still he felt it his duty to try to talk me out of this marriage. "Marriages don't work when the two people are too far apart in education," he said. "You've been through university and have cultivated tastes. Wang Yulin is a simple Chinese girl, even though she is very able. It won't work. You'd better find some way to get out of it now."

Get out of it? That was the last thing I wanted. In the deeper meaning of culture and education, I felt that Yulin and I had many of the same interests, and that she had a lot to teach me and share with me. I was certain we would continue to enjoy being together and would get along well. But my supervisor's approval was important because there was a regulation that no one doing confidential work, like Yulin, was allowed to marry a foreigner. So the party committee had to write a letter certifying that I was a member in good standing, and the rule could be waived for me.

Talking with Yulin, I had raised some objections to our marriage myself. I wanted her to know what she was getting into. There was the matter of our ages, a twelve-year gap. I had been married twice before, a difficult fact for a young Chinese girl to swallow. And, I explained to her, there was my cultural and ethnic background. I was a Southerner and a Jew.

"What's a Jew?" she asked.

And then there was Wei Lin. Shortly after Yulin and I became engaged, Wei Lin's party branch secretary and mentor had approached me with the message that Wei Lin wanted to divorce her second husband and renew her marriage to me. The branch secretary counseled me to accept this offer and restore what had originally been a happy home.

My answer was no. If Wei Lin had waited for me, I explained, I would have stuck by her for the rest of my life. But she had chosen differently, I had completely gotten over my original attachment, did not love her anymore, and could not consider remarrying her. What's more, although I did not say it to the branch secretary, I did not like the woman Wei Lin had become.

Wei Lin herself had also commented on my choice. She had heard, she said, that Wang Yulin was a real troublemaker and had a hard time getting along with her leaders. "Too individualistic, too independent," she said. I had seen enough of the way Wei Lin's mind worked to discount what she said. Still I was a little disturbed. I went to my friend, Wen Jize, told him what had been said about Yulin, and asked him what the story was. He shook his head. "Wang Yulin is a good person," he said. "Her problems are ideological, not questions of character." And that was the end of that.

But Wei Lin was never completely out of our lives. I saw her every day at work, and sometimes we bumped into her when Yulin and I were walking from home to work and back again. Once, after we had been married several months, such an encounter caused Yulin pain. We were walking down the street holding hands when I spotted Wei Lin off in the distance. Instinctively, I dropped Yulin's hand. She was stunned. "Why did you do that?" she asked when Wei Lin had passed. Her face was clouded.

"I just thought she'd see how happy we are and feel hurt, and I didn't want to hurt her."

Yulin started to cry. "That's not it. You still love her, and you don't love me as much. You care more about her feelings than you do about mine."

Yulin cried and cried long into the night, and nothing I could say helped. In the morning things were better, and soon we were happy again. Still, I felt bad that I hadn't been more eloquent, that I couldn't find the right words to explain to her how much I loved her, and just how much she meant to me.

It was to Yulin, I felt, that I owed so much of my peace of mind. Although she didn't know it, I was still afraid that something had gone seriously wrong with me during my first year in prison, that my mind had gone awry. I feared each recurrence of panic and strove mightily to contain it. I was afraid of becoming hysterical again, of overtaxing myself and dropping back into that horrifying dark world of nightmares. In crowds or late at night, I would feel a moment of cold fear when panic began to grip me.

It was Yulin who had taken me by the hand and led me out of that world. Her loving care, steely pragmatism, and calm matter-of-factness brought me back, day by day, to everyday life. And when I did feel the panic coming on, it was the thought of her that held me, steadying me, letting me know that there was another world, a real, solid, comforting world that I could return to.

CHAPTER ELEVEN

The Golden Age

In 1956 the harvest had never been better and the stores were filled with produce. That summer merchants stacked their watermelons in the streets and people joked they were hoping someone would steal them. In October and November, we had shining persimmons from the western part of north China. The grape harvest was so lush that people joked about not accepting grapes even as gifts. That winter there were oranges and tangerines from Hunan and Guangdong and Fujian. People who hadn't had apples and pears regularly for years had them in abundance that year.

I felt that a golden age of democratic socialism had begun in China. The party was scoring one major success after another. The Bandung Conference had just finished, with major improvements in the relations between China and India, Indonesia, Burma. The Chinese Communists no longer felt isolated, but rather that they were in the ascendancy in world power. The movement to seek out hidden counterrevolutionaries was over, and with it the tension and daily meetings. There was a spontaneous outburst of relief and everyone seemed to come to work with greater enthusiasm. Perhaps it was only relief that the possibility of attack was over. But I felt it showed that these movements were correct. They did weed out bad elements, and did help liberate the energies of the rest.

The collectivization of agriculture had produced big gains for the farmers, by banding together those too poor to buy an ox, tools, or even fertilizer on their own. It was also a time of relative artistic freedom. The old jazz clubs in Beijing and Shanghai re-opened and young people went out to dance at night to the high wailing pulse of trumpets and saxophones. There were acrobats and Peking opera, and playwriting and cinema flourished.

We all participated in the public health campaigns that swept the country. One day our entire office trooped down to the People's Hospital to take a blood test. We were told that a new method had been discovered for the early detection of cancer. Later, a ranking official at Radio tipped me off to what was really going on. We had all been given a Wassermann to test for syphilis. Yulin surprised me by grumbling. "They never tell us the truth about anything," she said. I was startled. Wasn't she supposed to be the loyal, unshakable party member? What was she doing voicing such heresy?

Very quickly after we were married, I discovered I had been wrong about Yulin in one major way. My devout, rock-solid proletarian Communist Party cadre wife was turning out to have a mind of her own. Not that she wasn't a loyal Communist. She was. She had seen what the party had done for the country, and for her own family. She had a firm sense of duty, and of obligation, and a craftswoman's single-mindedness about work. But, unlike me, she did not believe everything she was told. She was also troublingly uninterested in political theory. Rapidly becoming one of the best sound technicians at the Broadcast Administration, she had better things to do with her time than debate dogma.

Occasionally I was appalled at her low level of social consciousness. Once she took me to a Peking opera called *The Orphan Is Pursued and Rescued.* The orphan was the infant heir to the ancient throne of China who was rescued by loyal subjects from the pretenders to the throne. Coming out of the theater, I groused to her. "That story was terrible. All that fuss being made today, in a socialist society, about a little emperor. Who cares what happened to him? They were all a bunch of oppressors and exploiters who kept the working people trodden down. How can they still make him the focal point of theater-goers' sympathy?"

"Nonsense!" Yulin scoffed. "These are old, traditional dramas. Should we throw away everything precious in our artistic heritage just because most of it is about emperors and court ladies or Imperial scholars? You're being doctrinaire, which is a sure sign of stupidity."

This from my working-class bride? I argued back manfully, certain that I was correct. But Yulin wouldn't budge an inch in her view, so we just had to give up the argument after a while and talk about something else. It never worked to try to talk her out of something I knew she believed in strongly. Whenever I tried, I could see the stubborn set of the jaw that I had noticed the first day I met her. "Don't try to remold me," she would say. "Other people have tried but nobody has succeeded."

◆

The Cold War was raging. Red baiting in the United States was nearing a crescendo. The Sino-American relationship was hostile and we seldom officially uttered the word "American" without appending the word "imperialists." Personally, however, Americans were very popular. Most Chinese got along very well with them. The two groups shared the same raucous, adolescent sense of humor, the same directness with friends, the same lack of pretensions. As I had seen so clearly in Yanan, there was also a particular fondness for things American, for American movies, books, and music—provided it wasn't considered too decadent.

The Americans in Beijing loved the Chinese. Some of them were refugees from American McCarthyism, like Jane Sachs Hodes, whose father was Harry Sachs, of Goldman Sachs. She and her husband, a physiologist, had fled with their three children when their left-wing views had made Bob Hodes's university position untenable. Now they were both living and working in Beijing. Apart from the Soviets, in fact, Americans made up one of the largest foreign groups in Beijing. There were about a dozen of them—two dozen including spouses and children—who were mainly teaching English or working on English language publications.

But there was still a wall between foreigners and the Chinese. With only a few exceptions, like me and George Hatem, most non-Chinese were effectively shut out of the world they so loved. The Chinese Communists treated their foreign guests as Chinese had treated foreigners for a millennium. They made use of their skills—most of the expatriates in Beijing were teachers, language experts, or scientists—treated them with impeccable courtesy—and kept them strictly isolated.

Our party branch secretary, Zhang Hua, had explained to me the Broadcast Administration's guidelines about talking to foreigners. Say only what the *People's Daily* had published. Don't string together information from separate articles or give any interpretation. I had also studied directives that came through the classified documents room that said any Chinese wishing to meet with a foreigner had to request permission from his or her work unit beforehand, and then report back afterward. Most Chinese were thus understandably reluctant to get involved with foreigners. If you asked permission, it might be denied, and then you would come under suspicion.

While the Americans in Beijing didn't know the precise regulations behind their isolation, it burned them up. I once saw Bob Hodes, Jane's doctor husband, explode. "It's the bane of my existence. Just as my work is going great and I need help from my Chinese partners, someone comes along to call them to a political meeting, everyone drops what they are doing, and they all disappear. They never tell me where they're going, or how long I have to wait before they come back. My work comes to a stop and I have to sit there twiddling my thumbs, or else just call it a day and go home."

Still, they all loved China, loved the Chinese, loved socialism, and were passionately devoted to it as a cause. They, like me, felt that a new China was flowering around them. To combat their feeling of isolation, they banded into study groups to study political theory, share their problems and concerns, and horse-trade in the little knowledge that did become available to them.

One such group met Saturday afternoons—the time when Chinese work units held political study classes—usually at the home of Josh and Miriam Horn, just north of the ancient Peace Gate. Josh was a left-wing British surgeon and his wife a Lithuanian-born nurse. The group also included David and Isabelle Crook, both Marxists, he British, she the daughter of Canadian missionaries, who were English teachers of long standing in China. Frank Su, another member, was an overseas Chinese from Philadelphia, who had run a small business there and returned to devote his skills to the motherland. His wife, Sonia, was an Austrian Jewish refugee from the Nazi terror. Then there were a few wives of Chinese, like Ione Kramer, a big, husky young journalist from Wisconsin who had married a Chinese chemist in the States and returned to China with him.

Asked to join the group, I looked forward to its Saturday afternoon meetings, partly for the freewheeling discussions in English. My own English had grown rusty through my six years in prison when I spoke only Chinese, and precious little of that. And partly I enjoyed the prominent role I quickly assumed. The other foreigners were starved for news and information, and my contacts, information, and clear status as an insider made me the star of the group. I never told them anything really secret, of course, but my sources of information were considered—and were—impeccable.

Mainly, however, I saw attending this group as one of my duties as a good party member. Every party member took upon him- or herself the task of doing social work among nonparty members, spreading the correct line, winning friends and converts—and keeping the party informed about them. No one prompted me. With Mei Yi's knowledge and blessing, I took on the foreign community in Beijing as my natural constituency.

One day in 1956 I was able to bring big news to the group. They were all stirring in their seats, exchanging glances or whispers, sipping their tea. There was an expectant feeling in the air as I rose to give them a preview of an important series of speeches that Mao Zedong was preparing. Months before the principal speech, called "On the Correct Handling of Contradictions among the People," was to be delivered, I—along with some scientists, writers, and political figures—had heard a tape of an early version of the speech in a secret relay.

I told the group that Mao's analysis of China's present situation was in keeping with the cheerful picture I saw around me. China, he said, was now entering a new phase of democratic socialism. The movement against hidden counterrevolutionaries like Hu Feng and his cronies had disarmed public enemies and raised public awareness. The Korean War with its menace to China was over. The international scene was relaxing and China had built a sound foundation for a planned socialist economy. At the same time, the attempted revolution in Hungary showed the dangers of a bureaucratic, insensitive, undemocratic party leadership.

China had created the conditions for progress, said Mao, by its use of the "dictatorship" side of the People's democratic dictatorship, the Chinese version of the old Communist idea of a dictatorship of the proletariat. Enemies had been smoked out and dangerous opposition suppressed. But now that period was over, and it was time to stress the democratic side of the equation: democracy for the great majority of the people. From now on, most of the "contradictions" or conflicts would not be with the enemy but among the people, and they would be handled by discussion and consultation. There would be no coercion.

Reading from my notes, I told the group that to be judged correct politically, one had to support the party leadership and the Socialist Road. But, I said, Mao made it plain that it was no crime to oppose those positions, and to argue against them, as long as no laws were being violated. In People's China, there was no such thing as an ideological crime, a crime of thinking. I warmed to the subject. It was precisely this democracy, this vision of peasants all over China debating their own policies, electing their own leaders using black beans in bowls, that I had found so appealing back in my days at Stanford.

Of course, I continued, quoting Mao, such democracy applied only to the people. There was still a tiny handful of enemies who would try to undermine the socialist state and they had to be suppressed. For them, not democracy but dictatorship. So it was to be democracy for the people, the great majority; dictatorship for a "tiny handful of enemies." More democracy than any Western country could boast, said Mao.

When I finished my presentation, Jane Hodes was the first into the fray. She had been a passionate fighter for civil rights in America. "But who decides who is an enemy and who belongs among the people?" she demanded to know. "If you keep switching people around arbitrarily, so that today's revolutionary becomes tomorrow's enemy, what good are the guarantees of democracy for the people? What good does it do to say that only a tiny handful of enemies are subject to dictatorship?"

Jane was speaking with the voice that I had so effectively silenced in myself in prison. It was a question that had painfully occurred to me when I had been called an enemy. I knew just the argument to silence her. It was the party that decided who was an enemy, I said, and the party in its wisdom would make the correct choice. We should have enough confidence in the Chinese party leaders to know that they wouldn't condemn anyone they weren't certain about.

My viewpoint was supported by prematurely white-haired Frank Su and his visibly shaky gray-haired wife, Sonia. He told how there had been some misunderstanding about him for a while during the last political movement, but it had all been straightened out and now he was treated very well. Sonia said she was sure that anyone whom Chairman Mao personally identified as a bad person had to be a bad person.

Rewi Alley grunted at this. He was a crotchety New Zealander poet and engineer, two hundred percent behind the party in public, testy and highly individualistic in private. He had adopted several Chinese children, now grown, and several of them had been wrongly accused during the movement against Hu Feng, he said. His implication was clear. Don't be too sure the party won't pin bum raps on people, especially those connected with foreigners.

At a certain level I knew what he was saying was true—why else had I been worried at the movement's beginning about being accused once again? But I could answer that one too. Here in socialist China, I said, the state belongs to the people. What motive could there be for the state to railroad a good person who hasn't committed any crimes or isn't an enemy? Of course, there are always mistakes. Good people don't question things like that —if they do, they play right into the hands of the enemy.

◆

During the first year of my marriage to Yulin, her parents had gradually come to accept me. Her father, who lived in a little adobe settlement just a few blocks away, used to visit us frequently, riding his bicycle over to our building. It was an Eternal brand bicycle made in Shanghai, and the old craftsman kept the machine well oiled and spotless. Yulin's mother, who lived about four hours away in the town of Shijiazhuang where Yulin had grown up, had never met me. She was too busy living with Yulin's third sister and brother, caring for their children. But early in 1957 when Yulin cabled her sister to escort her mother to Beijing, it was clear that we had priority on Mama's help. In about six weeks, we were expecting our first baby.

My mother-in-law and I got along well from the start. She gave her approval to Yulin with only one reservation: "He doesn't have much hair on his head, does he?" Yulin explained that Western men did not have as firm a hold on their original hair as did Chinese. From then on, I ate some of the world's most exquisite food as a routine matter. My mother-in-law was the kind of cook that Schubert was a composer. I never called her anything but Mama, finding in her the kind of warm, understanding mother that I had pined for when I was young.

When Mama discovered what an appreciative eater I was, I quickly became her favorite son-in-law and nothing was too good for me. And if I decided I was getting too fat and started to reduce, she would greet the decision with frowning disapproval. She lurked behind doors and around corners, waiting to ambush me with a delectable slice of fried eggplant stuffed with slivers of pork. As I came by, she said, "Dunbai, would you taste this for me, please?" and popped it into my mouth. Or it might be crisp, paper-thin egg pancakes, or tasty shrimp chips, or a little dish of sweet-and-sour spareribs cooked to such tenderness that I could eat the bones. Or doughnutlike Chinese pastry with a bowl of sweetened bean milk to dunk it in. Or an apple, already peeled. Or a tangerine. Or a sweet persimmon. "Reducing?" she said scornfully. "That's nonsense. How can you work as hard as you do if you don't eat and sleep properly?" Or, "Dunbai! A man is iron, but food is steel. Eat and be strong."

Before the Communist liberation, my mother-in-law didn't even have a name of her own. Few women in those days did. It wasn't worth naming them. As a child she was called "Ah Fu," meaning good fortune. It was a sardonic insult, since a girl baby was considered a sorry misfortune. She never went to school and so never received a school name. After her marriage to her cousin, my father-in-law, Wang Hanqing, she became Wang Lishi—"the wife of Wang from the clan of Li." She did not know the date of her own birth.

Her life had been anything but happy. At age five, her feet were bound. Four toes were crushed, the foot bones were broken, and both feet were bent backward and cinched with long cloth wrappings. They were kept bound and broken so they could never grow again. It was cruelly and permanently painful, and restricted her to a hobbling, unsteady gait. Her family was so poor that, she told me years later, before liberation she had had her hands on an apple only once. It was during the feast that her family was required to give for her wedding. The family borrowed an apple from some well-to-do relative and placed it in the middle of the little table on which nuts and sweetmeats were laid out to welcome the wedding guests. "It was still there at the end of the day," Mama said. "No one dared to take a bite out of it. The next morning, I took it back to the house of its owners and thanked them again for lending it to us."

The Confucian ideal held that women should obey their fathers when young, their husbands when married, and their sons when old. Mama told me once how she was bullied and beaten from the moment she entered the home of her bridegroom, whom she had seen for the first time on their wedding day. Her new mother-in-law, who was her husband's stepmother, treated her like a slave. Once when she was serving her mother-in-law some soup, she dripped a bit on the older woman's garments. Her mother-in-law grabbed the bowl of soup out of her hands and broke it over her head. The last thing Mama remembered was her own blood pouring down about her head as she fell to the floor and passed out.

Yulin's older sister was the original Yulin. She was twelve years older than my Yulin and had received the name when she arrived at school age. My father-in-law was a man of learning and had decided to give all his children school names even though they couldn't attend school. My Yulin was five, and still unnamed, when her older sister was murdered. She was a bright, pretty girl, engaged to marry a distinguished Chinese traditional doctor, when the Japanese army overran their village and a junior Japanese officer in shiny leather boots with high knee-guards tramped into their little hovel with a group of his men.

From the doorway, Mama had seen the soldiers headed their way and had hidden the girls in the back. When the Japanese stomped in demanding "Guniang! Guniang!"—Girls! Girls!—Mama waved her hand back and forth, palm forward. There's no one here, she was saying with her hands. No one.

But the officer found a photo of Yulin's sister in the room, and he and his men began to beat Mama unmercifully, still shouting "Guniang! Guniang!" When Yulin's sister could bear her mother's screams no longer, she finally came out into the room and the Japanese officer raped her repeatedly in full sight of her mother. The other soldiers held Mama back while waiting their turn and left the girl bloody and broken on the floor. She never recovered and later died. The death of her favorite daughter sent Mama out of her head for months, and she wandered the streets telling anyone who would listen, "Do you know? My second girl is coming home."

But Mama still had to work. The cigarettes the newly named little Yulin and her father sold from a mat weren't enough to feed the family, especially since both the Japanese and Kuomintang soldiers took cigarettes and swore if asked for payment. The job Mama found was as charwoman in a Japanese military hospital. Trembling with hatred, unable to repress the shivers of fear that came when she so much as heard patients and doctors chattering in the strange tongue of the invader, she had to scrub their floors, empty their bedpans, clean up their vomit, change their clothes. And she had to carry the fat corpses of Japanese officers down the narrow staircase and out to waiting army vehicles. "That was the worst thing," she would say, and then she would sigh and change her mind. "No, selling Peiquan was worse." Peiquan was Yulin's eldest sister's son, sold at age five to a Peking opera troupe for sacks of grain.

"Do you have any idea what happened to poor little Peiquan?" I asked Mama one day.

"We got him back," she said matter-of-factly. "After the people's government was set up, his mother told the story to the mayor of Nanjing. They put ads in newspapers all over the country and finally we got Peiquan back."

"And where is he now?"

"He's an engineer in a big military plant out in the northwest. His mother stays with him and his wife and child. He has won a lot of awards and commendations for his work."

Mama attributed everything good she had ever had in her life to the party. She got back her grandson, threw off fear, threw off poverty—even threw off her tortured marriage. When she decided in middle age that she could no longer get along with her husband, she separated from him. The arranged marriage had been miserable for both of these proud, stubborn people. And when the Communists came to power and proclaimed equality for women, she surprised everyone by making up a name for herself. She announced to the Liberation Army census taker that she was "Li Dani"—the big wench. A little tiny woman, she was taking her first opportunity to make a sardonic little joke of her own.

◆

Mama fed me and tended to her daughter until finally, on March 3, 1957, Yulin went into labor. We rushed to Beijing Union Medical College Hospital. The doctors sent me back home, to wait and phone every hour or so. It wasn't until the next afternoon that the nurse told me, "You have an eight-and-a-half-pound baby daughter, and both mother and daughter are fine."

I hurried to the hospital and ran to Yulin. "She's beautiful," Yulin said. "Go see her. She looks just like you." Luckily, that turned out not to be true. The nurse behind the glass went over to one of the cradles, picked up a little bundle of something in swaddling clothes, and brought it over to the glass partition for me to see. It was a lovely little girl who looked just like her mother. She stared straight at me, and sneezed.

We had decided that all our children would be given the gen-

eration name Xiao, written with sixteen strokes of the brush. It
was a kind of pun. Xiao means Dawn. It also means to know. But
another Xiao, with the same sound, written with just three strokes
of the brush, means small, and was commonly used in children's
names. The second character of her given name, Qin, means diligence. So her name was Xiaoqin, "she who knows diligence."

◆

And then, a Hundred Flowers bloomed in China.

One section of Mao's speech on "Correct Handling of Contradictions among the People" had contained a call to the Chinese
people to express their criticisms of the party freely without fear
of reprisal. He wanted to bring China's intellectuals, who had
been so badly traumatized by the campaign against Hu Feng, back
into the fold. "Let a Hundred Flowers bloom," he told writers
and artists. "Let a hundred schools of thought contend," he exhorted scientists and scholars. It took a while to take hold, but
when it did, the results were explosive. Years and years of pent-
up frustrations suddenly burst forth. Newspapers, periodicals, and
intellectual journals swelled with criticism of the party.

Every morning we rushed to the office and unfolded the day's
papers, almost unable to believe the force of the arguments that
had been unleashed. Old Yunnan warlord Long Yun, now an
honored member of the united front against Chiang Kai-shek,
complained that by leaning to the Soviet Union China had cut
itself off from Western contacts and aid. Zhang Bojun, chairman
of the Democratic League, demanded that instead of having one
party in power, there should be a rotation. Lo Longji, another
Democratic League official, said that the party committees should
be withdrawn from the universities so that they would have complete academic freedom. A Beijing University professor named Ge
Peiqi warned that if the party didn't mend its ways the day might
come when Communists would be killed in the streets of China as
they had been in Hungary.

The criticisms spread to government agencies. All over Beijing,
big-character posters sprouted on walls and doors inside government compounds with criticisms that became more pointed—and
more personal—aimed not just at party policies, but at specific
individuals. At the Broadcast Administration, the posters began to
appear on the downstairs wall. As they proliferated, special areas
were set aside and people were allowed to write what they liked.
One poster criticized Zuo Moye, a department head, saying that

he was arrogant, conceited, talked down to the masses, and a bureaucrat who sat on people's scripts for days. Then someone wrote that he had been seen on a workday strolling in Sun Yat-sen Park.

While the intellectuals—students, office workers, writers, editors, professors, and poets—were protesting, however, nearly everyone else was smoldering on the sidelines. To the great majority of the population of Beijing, such critics of the party didn't seem to be heroes crying out for intellectual freedom. To the contrary, they seemed to be selfish and ungrateful eggheads and city slickers, demanding democracy as a ruse to deprive the party of its leadership—leadership that ordinary people saw as vital to their own interests. Suburban peasants saw themselves losing control of the land if this educated elite came to power; the workers were concerned about their newly won eight-hour day and higher wages.

The workers' expressions of rage were palpable. When Professor Ge Peiqi's warnings about coming executions appeared in the *People's Daily,* his home at Beijing University had to be guarded to protect him from the workers who stormed up there to "debate" with him. At the Broadcast Administration, print shop workers refused to print the scripts of some intellectual critics who had been invited to state their views on the air. "We workers were only treated like human beings after liberation," they said. "We're not going to print these attacks on the party." I ran into Mei Yi on his way down to the print shop in person to persuade them.

At the peak of the criticisms, I asked my mother-in-law for her opinion. "Mama, what do you think of what these people are saying in the paper?" I said.

"What are they saying?" she asked.

"They demand that the Communist Party take turns with other parties in running the country, that the professors manage the schools without interference from the party committees, that farmers be allowed to sell their grain, cooking oils, and cotton on the free market. They're saying that the landlords should be given equal status and that those who were denounced as hidden enemies should be reinstated."

"Fang pi!" Mama snorted. "Farting. That's what they're doing, just farting. The landlords want to crawl up on our backs again and crap on us. No way! Their hearts are black, not red like ordinary people's. They cannot change in ten thousand years.

They used to ride on the peasants' backs. If they're going to be equal, the peasants will be ground down again."

The strange thing was, however, that the party and its members were silent in the face of these daily attacks. In fact, I had read a directive issued to party members of my rank and higher that ordered us to remain quiet and not to debate our critics. Weeks went by and there was no response from the party; still we were not allowed to discuss the attacks with the critics.

I was puzzled. I thought the critics were wrong. I thought as my mother-in-law did that they were selfish and misguided. But I also believed Chairman Mao had meant what he said, that a revolution could only grow and develop in struggle. I thought the critics deserved a response, and a debate, the kind of democratic exchange Mao had promised. But when I complained to Mei Yi, he silenced me. There will be an answer, he promised me. We will answer them when the time comes.

When the answer finally came, it was not at all what I expected. In July, a few days after I had talked to Mei Yi, I arrived at the office one morning to find a major article in the *People's Daily*. Running from top to bottom on the left side—the usual place for portentous party messages—was a headline: "Why Is This?" it read. On the surface, the story was merely about an elderly man who, after complaining that the critics of the party were ungrateful and unfair, had received threatening phone calls and letters. But as I translated the article at top speed for the day's broadcast, I was also taking in its message. Here at last was the opening salvo in the great debate that Mao had promised. By painting the critics of the party as unwilling to accept criticism themselves, the party had at last opened the door for the debate I had been waiting for. I was itching to talk back to them. I thought both sides would learn from a lively debate.

That afternoon, there was a special meeting for party members of my level on up to relay instructions for the debate. The Central Committee had set up a two-man committee—Mao himself and Party Secretary Deng Xiaoping—to take charge of the movement. Party critics were dubbed rightists, and each organization was to choose its own rightists for the Great Debate. The main topics were also set: Is it true that if it were not for the Communist Party there would be no New China? That was the title of a popular song that the rightists had heaped scorn on. Other topics were: Aside from socialism, was there any way out for China? Was the government monopoly on purchasing grain and cotton from the

farmers right or wrong? Was the movement against hidden counterrevolutionaries right or wrong?

A few days later Zhang Hua, the former schoolteacher who had
become head of the party in the English section, asked me to stay
late to help him sort through the English section dossiers to find
our rightists. The criteria for naming rightists had been clearly laid
out. They had to be people who had challenged the monopoly of
Communist Party leadership, attacked the party's foreign policy,
advocated Western-style democracy, or who were against the party's farm policies or the movement against hidden counterrevolutionaries. Not only did they have to have these views, they had to
have formulated them into a political program and actively prose-
lytized them in an organized way.

Zhang Hua and I spread the dossiers over the table in an unused
conference room. They were voluminous and included notes of
what everyone had said in meetings, what they had been writing
on big-character posters, what people had reported about their
attitudes. After carefully looking through all of them, we both
came to the same clear conclusion: no one in the English section
at the Broadcast Administration met the party's criteria for a rightist.

"Well," I said to Zhang Hua. "If we don't have one, so much
the better. We can just watch what other organizations are doing
and learn from them."

Zhang Hua shook his head. "We have to have a rightist," he
said. "This process is about reforming and remolding the bourgeois intellectuals. We hit hard at one target, completely discredit
him so that he stinks to high heaven, and then the others will
distance themselves ideologically from the target. That's the point
of mass political struggles. There must be a live target."

My heart felt like cold ashes. I suddenly understood. This
wasn't going to be a democratic debate at all. This was class
struggle all over again. We weren't going to be settling contradictions among the people the way Mao had specified, because Mao
had decided that the party critics weren't people at all, but enemies. A thought rose unbidden, breaking through the armor of my
loyalty to the party. How much longer would it be before the
party stopped pitting one group against another? When would the
democratic process that Mao promised begin?

Zhang Hua was my friend. He would listen to reason. "You
told me yourself," I said, "that there was no quota, nor any direc-

tive that says we have to conclude that wherever there are intellectuals there must be rightists."

Again he shook his head, a longish, round head shaped like a
football that he often tilted to one side as if questioning something.
"There's no way of educating and leading the English section
without the struggle against a live rightist of our own," he said.
"Let's look the dossiers over again and see who might qualify."

There was only one logical choice, and that was Gerald Chen.
Neither of us liked it, and it was going to be awkward. Gerald had
already been announced as a candidate for admission to the party.
Now we were going to attack him as a rightist. But he was the best
we had.

His real name was Chen Weixi, but he used the name Gerald,
a souvenir of his Western connections. He was the son of a
Chongqing businessman who had cast his lot with the Communists. Living in Canada in the home of Dr. James Endicott, a
well-known left-wing preacher who once taught school in China,
Gerald had grown close to the Canadian left wing and had returned to China after the Communist victory, a patriotic young
man who wanted to do something for his country.

Gerald's dossier revealed that he had echoed many of the views
of the rightists criticizing the party. He had agreed that party
committees should get out of the universities, since they didn't
know how to run schools. He had said he heard that the party's
purchase of farm goods depressed the peasants, since they weren't
allowed to sell their produce freely. He had talked about the
excesses of the campaign against hidden counterrevolutionaries.
The specific action that Gerald was accused of was plotting to
overthrow the leadership of the English section in favor of the
deputy head of the section, the flashy son of a Chinese-Canadian
minister and not a party member.

Gerald Chen was nervous and shaky when confronted with the
charges. But he wouldn't accept them. "I'm not a rightist," he
insisted. And nothing, it seemed, would change his mind.

The English section members shouted at him. They wrote diatribes against him. They pummeled him with questions and then
shouted down his responses. The debate was a travesty, as it was
everywhere. Skimpy evidence had been collected that could formally label Gerald Chen a rightist, but one thing remained: he
had to confess. But he would not confess. "I'm not a rightist," he
continued to repeat.

Finally I was chosen to talk with him. I invited him for a walk in Jade Pool Park near our building, and as we strolled along the paths around the man-made lakes, I exhorted him to look reality in the eye. There were several different categories of rightists, I said. If he held out and refused to confess, he would be assigned to the worst category and sent to a work farm, which was much like a prison camp. If he confessed, he would be given the most lenient treatment. He would be sent to an ordinary farm to work, but he would get better treatment and he could come home to visit. "Ten years from now, this will all be forgotten and no one will even know you went through this trial," I assured him.

Tearfully, Gerald insisted on his innocence. But gradually he realized that he had no choice. He confessed to being a rightist and was sent to a farm in Hebei Province.

I had not forgotten that I had once been in the exact same situation, charged with a crime I had not committed. And my old panic, which had begun to subside, flared up anew. My forehead felt as if a flatiron was pressing on it, my heart began rushing at odd moments, and I carried with me at all times a vague sense of alarm. A shocking thought flitted through my mind. This terror is the way they control people, and the terror is inside my head! But I suppressed the thought quickly. I knew enough not even to think such disloyal things.

Part of my fear stemmed from having stood up—if only briefly —for a friend. Zhao Jie, the deaf, nervous, asthmatic old man who was my direct senior authority, had been branded a rightist while attending the central party school. "I've worked with him for two years," I began to explain to the investigators who had come to dredge up material for the case against him. "I've always found him intensely loyal."

"His main trouble here," Zhang Hua chimed in, "is that he's hard of hearing and often sick, so he tends to be testy and impatient."

I agreed. "He's kind of an old fuddy-duddy, and he doesn't like a lot of back talk. But he doesn't punish people who disagree with him."

The two investigators looked condescending. One of them flipped through his notebook. "Let me read you some of his statements," he said. Citing a date, time, and place, he read what Zhao Jie had said in an argument with another student at the party school: " 'Cadres of worker-peasant origin do not necessarily enjoy a higher level of socialist consciousness than any other cadres.' "

Both investigators smiled pityingly, and one said, "Only see what hatred and contempt he has for the workers and peasants, the two basic revolutionary classes in China! Doesn't that show exactly where he stands, behind all his camouflage?"

Zhang Hua and I looked at each other. According to the rules of the grim game we were playing, Zhao Jie was doomed. Still, we had to try. "That doesn't sound bad enough to make him a rightist," I said.

"That just shows a lofty attitude," added Zhang Hua, "and that can be corrected."

The investigators put it all down, frowning. These two men were types we well recognized: intellectual-bashing peasants. Their language was crude and their country clothing was disheveled. Every few minutes one of them would walk over to the cuspidor and spit after a lot of noisy hawking.

"Are you suggesting that the worker-peasant comrades at the central party school are persecuting Zhao Jie?" one investigator asked with a scowl. "Are you saying that we are doing him an injustice?"

Zhang Hua and I both knew we had lost. In different ways we said that we had a great deal of faith in the party, and in the party school. And since we knew nothing about what went on there, all we could talk about was what we had seen here.

Zhao Jie was denounced as a rightist and sent home in disgrace.

According to the Communist view of friendship, your strongest attachment should be to the party. When there was a conflict between duty to a friend and duty to the party, the party always came first. We all knew that, and felt it strongly. Thus the party influenced the friends we made. When I first arrived at Radio Beijing after prison, part of Mei Yi's briefing to me was a warning not to socialize with people below my party rank. "You make your friends among members of the editorial board and members of the leading party group," he said. "Don't become intimate with people down below."

When people were promoted, it was quite usual for them to stop socializing with their old friends. What's more, as the movements against the counterrevolutionaries had demonstrated, close friendships laid you open to charges of forming cliques, betraying party secrets, or putting personal friendships above your love for the party. And if you got too close to others, it was always possible that they would betray you under pressure, or that you would be forced to betray them.

Still, not everyone bought the party-above-friendship stance. When I mentioned to Yulin that Zhao Jie had been sent home in disgrace, she challenged me. "Have you gone to see him yet?" she asked.

"Of course I haven't gone to see him," I said rather testily. "He's a rightist. Nobody's supposed to go see him, you know that." According to the rules, people were forbidden to see anyone who had been branded a rightist except on official business, and then only after securing the proper permissions. Zhao's wife, who worked on the *People's Daily,* was the only human being who spoke to him or had anything to do with him. Otherwise, he was in total isolation.

"But I thought you've been telling me all this time that Zhao Jie is your friend," said Yulin. "You used to tell me about what a good person he was, how considerate of you he was, and about all the trouble he had keeping up with what goes on when he can hardly hear."

"Yes, he was my friend," I said. "But you can't visit with a rightist just because he's your friend."

"Well, I don't think that's much of a friend if he doesn't go to see his friend when he's in trouble," said Yulin. "If his friends don't help him, who can he rely on?"

I was shamed, but torn, by this appeal to personal loyalty. I went to visit Zhao, but I didn't offer to help him any further. I still felt vulnerable myself. If I stuck my neck out any more, I thought, I was likely to get it chopped off again.

◆

So when the campaign against rightists at the Broadcast Administration ended in a struggle against my friend Wen Jize, I found myself again trying hard to toe the party line. Wen Jize was the man who had hastened my courtship of Yulin by advising me not to write her a letter. Like many old cadres, he was in ill health. While he was in a KMT prison in Shanghai, part of one ear had frozen and dropped off, leaving only a stump on one side of his head. And despite a painful tuberculosis of the spine, he was permanently optimistic. He was in charge of all the international broadcasts, and the leading cadre in charge when Mei Yi wasn't around.

At the beginning of the Hundred Flowers movement, I had gone to Wen Jize and given him my own sharp criticisms of his work as leader of the foreign broadcasts. I believed that it was the normal duty of a Communist toward all comrades, high or low, and I cast aside any worries about retaliation. Besides, I knew that Wen was not the type to strike back at well-intentioned critics.

But Zhou Yang, Mei Yi's boss at the propaganda ministry, had told him to get Wen Jize. Wen, who had never hounded or persecuted anyone, had dared to present some honest criticism of Zhou Yang's views, and this towering party authority wasn't about to tolerate that. Along with two vice directors of the foreign broadcast division, Wen Jize was accused of plotting to seize power at Radio.

I believed in rectification. I thought Wen Jize had a lot of problems with his work style that should be cleared up. But I certainly didn't believe he was guilty of conspiracy, and when I saw Mei Yi, I said so. "That's how much you know about judging these kinds of people," Mei Yi said. "You're too innocent."

But I didn't feel innocent. I was attending the meetings to criticize Wen, raising my voice with the rest of them. For the first time, I was going along with the persecution of someone—and a friend at that—who I couldn't really believe was disloyal to the party. I rationalized it by telling myself that it looked like his thinking, not his emotions, were antiparty. But I became depressed and worried about the future of the party.

"I can't believe all these people have conspired against the party," I said to Yulin every night when I returned home from work.

She was indignant. "Well, why do you keep going to the meetings if you don't think they're guilty?"

I just mumbled an answer. "I'll have to find some way to cope with it," I said. I knew she was right, but I couldn't do anything about it. My doubts were twisted with my zeal to do right by the party. Doubt tangled with loyalty. Dogma, pride, common sense, disbelief, certainty, fear, altruism, self-interest, and self-sacrifice all struggled within me and held me frozen in their thrall.

CHAPTER TWELVE

A Leap in the Dark

The nastiness of the campaign against the rightists opened a little crack in the armor of loyalty I had forged around myself in prison. Perhaps, given time and tranquillity, that crack might have widened sooner than it did. Perhaps space might have grown for me to see that the means that were being used to arrive at a new and better world were inconsistent with the end. Perhaps all of us might have come to see that a government that pits men and women against their fellows cannot endure. Perhaps our fatigue and distaste after seemingly endless class struggle might have been changed into active horror at its folly.

But as Mao had intended, none of us was left alone with our thoughts. None of us had time to reflect. For as quickly as the antirightist campaign had begun, it ended. And it was not many weeks later that new stirrings began to fill the air. Mao's active, restless, driving mind gave us no reprieve. He was thinking, scheming, planning, analyzing, preparing for a change unlike anything he had tried before. It had been over nine years since I had seen Mao Zedong, but even from that distance, he reached down and shook me. He grabbed all of us with a vision more beautiful, more dramatic, and more exciting than we could have hoped or dreamed for.

We were not only going to build a Communist society, we were going to build it now.

Communism, with everyone working according to their ability and receiving goods according to their needs, could occur only when necessities were available in such abundance that it would be wasteful to print money with which to buy them, and when people were educated to rise above narrow self-interest. Most people thought that progress from socialism to Communism had to be slow, methodical, and gradual. They were wrong, Mao said. Communism could be attained in our lifetimes.

It was early in 1958 when Mei Yi read us the relay of Mao's speech to the Supreme State Conference. He didn't use the words "Great Leap Forward" that day. But his message was clear and ringing. Just as we had won the victory over the Japanese, and then over the Nationalists, just as we had transformed the country-side and given the land back to the peasants, so too could we transform China's economy. The secret of this battle, Mao said, was the same one we had used to win our other victories: giving the common people a vision of a glorious future, and offering them the possibility of reaching that future much sooner than they thought.

Mao had already tested the outlines of this idea three years earlier. We should press ourselves to produce more, faster, better, cheaper, he said then. This time, he was codifying his idea into a systematic plan. By demanding the utmost of ourselves and of others, we could accomplish things we had never thought possible. The two marshals of a powerful economy, Mao said, are Marshal Grain and Marshal Steel. We should work hard to put those two marshals in command.

"If we fight hard for three years, we can change the face of the Chinese countryside!" Mao proclaimed. "In these three years, we can build dikes and canals, expand fields so we can plow with machines. We can recover new land from the sea and from the desert, spread scientific farming skills, restrain soil erosion, and push forward with the electrification and the industrialization of the villages." We could even bypass industrial countries. "What about the slogan 'Overtake Great Britain in steel output within fifteen years!' " he asked. "Is that unrealistic, impossible? Think it over, comrades. It seems to me that it can be done."

If these battles were won, it would bring about a fundamental change in the Chinese economy. And it could all be done by tapping the will of the people. No longer would the state planning commission strictly regulate everything. Rather, there would be not just one plan, but two, three, even four plans as each locality challenged itself to develop not only in accordance with the state plan, but also beyond it.

Mao was throwing down a gauntlet, and not just to the Chinese people. He was breaking, once more, with the Soviets, repudiating their stolid, disciplined, authoritarian construction of the Communist state. Mao was going to make revolution in China's own way, in his own way. He was going to show the world that he could achieve modernization better, and in a much more thrilling and inspiring way than the clumsy, dull-witted Russian Bear had ever been able to do.

Mao tossed aside the criticisms of "some comrades" who, he said, had objected to the slogans "more, better, faster, cheaper." They called such policies "Mao jin"—adventurist or out of control. I didn't know who he was referring to, but after the meeting, my old friend Xu Maijin told me they included Zhou Enlai and Chen Yun. "I never want to hear that word 'Mao jin' again," Mao said angrily. "People are like atoms. When this atom's nucleus is smashed, the energy released will have really tremendous power. We shall be able to do things that we could not do before." The key was to explode the atom bomb of the human spirit.

I couldn't have agreed more, and all my doubts and fears were washed away. The many years of class struggle had been for a purpose after all—as Mao had promised it would be. I had wholeheartedly supported the idea that individuals should subsume themselves in the collective. Here was the signal from Mao that the collective would now, in turn, support the flowering of the individual.

One day would be like twenty years! The cry of the Paris Commune in 1871 would be ours. I felt that nearly everyone in the Broadcast Administration was as excited as I was at the vision of the new world. Who could be so cold as to want to go on living and working in the old way? For the truth was that the old revolutionary fire was in danger of being snuffed out by bureaucracy and humdrum daily routine. In the decade since liberation, zealots like me had become increasingly frustrated by the poky pace of life, so different from the revolutionary fervor of the mountains.

Nowadays, in Radio Beijing's English section, I would watch my colleagues wander in at eight, grab a copy of the *People's Daily* and *Reference News,* fill their mugs with tea and settle in for an hour or so of browsing. A bit after nine, the covers came off the typewriters and the room filled with the spasmodic clack of hunt-and-peck typing. Then, at ten o'clock sharp, the loudspeakers in the courtyard outside blared forth with the overture to the official calisthenics music, and everyone dropped whatever he or she was doing and we all poured out of the office to do our daily exercise.

Except that very few actually did the exercises. Most of the women made a beeline for the neighboring state-run store to get an early place in line and buy whatever meat or vegetables they needed at home. Since there was no such thing as household refrigeration, whatever you needed had to be procured on a day-to-day basis. And since the store workers, being employees of the socialist state, naturally kept about the same hours as their brothers and sisters everywhere, you usually had to get what you needed during work hours. So instead of "Zhong Jian Cao," or "Calisthenics during Recess," the women referred to the breaks as "Zhong Jian Cai"—"Veggies during Recess."

Then it was back for an hour or so of work before lunch, followed by a one- or two-hour noontime nap. Most of the staff, who lived too far away to go home at noon, would simply stretch out on top of a table or a row of chairs. Some hardy souls just put their heads down on their desks and snoozed in that position until work resumed.

Another afternoon dash to the vegetable store, another hour of work, a half hour of end-of-day joking and teasing, and the long day was over. I usually figured our staff averaged about four hours work a day apiece. "Low nutrition level," I would explain apologetically to Jane Sachs Hodes, who was exasperated to find that these Chinese comrades were not as enthusiastic about work under socialism as she, an American comrade, was. "Poor housing, bad sleeping conditions, overcrowding, no hot water, too much noise," I said.

At the same time, there was a handful of people—"active elements" they were called—who were busy every minute. The whole operation of getting the programs out every day really rested on their shoulders. They worked long hours, thoroughly enjoyed their work, were proud of what they were doing, and had the élan and the conquering spirit that it took to put programs together and get them out on time. We had always had that problem—a few overworked volunteers surrounded by a sea of plodders.

The Great Leap Forward changed all that. Everyone became an

active element. We felt we were unstoppable. We planned grand, exciting projects. We would start up transmission in a batch of new languages that we had originally planned to begin over the next five or ten years. We would answer every listener's letter within twenty-four hours. We would start new, lively drama programs. We would train translators to write, writers to produce programs, and offer vocational studies in language, journalism, and in the politics, culture, and customs of each country we broadcast to.

Everyone would participate in productive physical labor. After all, the Great Leap Forward would produce the new Communist Man, versatile in all fields. Everyone should feel at home in industry, in farming, in his or her own professional work, in military pursuits, in academic studies, and in commerce. We were also going to take daily exercises seriously, form a glee club and all learn to sing. What's more, we were going to hold a competition on how many pages of Chairman Mao's works we could read by National Day—October 1.

Our enthusiasm made the meeting rooms at Radio Beijing seem like the revival meetings I had seen back home in the South. One after another we all rose to pledge our efforts toward leaping China forward. Jiang Guinong promised to improve her work as a group leader and editor, and to finish her work faster so that she could pinch-hit as an announcer. Xu Meijiang said he would spend every evening in the office brushing up on his English grammar and going over the corrections that the group leader and I made in his scripts. I promised to come to the office every evening during the night shift to support the comrades working at night. I also volunteered to write detailed comments on every story that I polished, so that the translator would know what had been wrong and why. By late spring, three-quarters of the desks at Radio Beijing were filled at night. Senior party members had to take it on themselves to shoo people out when the hour got too late.

Yulin and I were so excited by what was happening that we decided to commemorate it in a small way. When our second daughter was born in June, we named her Xiaodong—she who knows the East, and the East wind, which Mao said prevailed over the West.

Miracles were happening everywhere. The newspapers swelled with the stories of success. At the Anshan Iron and Steel Plant in Manchuria, production had doubled when, following Chairman Mao's call, workers began participating in management. "Learn from Daqing!" exhorted the *People's Daily,* citing similar spectacular achievements at the Daqing oil fields. At Radio Beijing, we were asked to find and emphasize similar success stories for our broadcasts.

So in July, all of us in the English section went out by bus to the village of Xiaolitun, on the outskirts of Tianjin, about three hours' drive from Beijing. There, we read in the newspapers, the village had tripled its grain production.

We were met by a corps of well-trained young guides. One of them, in blue creaseless cadre's pants, a white shirt with heavy piping and little Chinese buttons, and a wide-brimmed straw hat, briefed us on the commune and its achievements.

The commune, he told us, had accomplished these wonders by following the Chairman's call. The people had set their sights high and used scientific management. Their secret was dense planting, which, they said, was like getting masses of people to close ranks against the enemy. The thicket of wheat stalks discouraged insects, shut out weeds, and drew moisture toward the surface from the deep underground water table.

But after a ringing account of the phenomenal harvest they expected, the young man paused uncomfortably. There were a few individuals here and there who were cynical about their achievements, he said. Please be on guard against those who might spread rumors and cast doubts on them, he warned. Then he took us to see the wheat fields with the mammoth yield. What we saw was miraculous, but not what we expected. The outsized yield was not on all the commune's wheat fields, or even on a large portion of them. It was all squeezed into one Chinese mou of land, or one-sixth of an acre.

Still, I stood there fascinated by the thick growth of wheat, already more than knee-high and yellow in the ear. Long ropes had been stretched across the field from one side to the other, attached to long boards that stretched across the field between swaths of wheat every six feet or so. Village children at either side tugged on the ropes, activating the boards that fanned the wheat from side to side. Otherwise, one little boy in a blue cadre cap explained to me, the grain would die from lack of air and sunlight.

I was a bit troubled by the small scale of the experiment. But I pushed that thought away. I was more impressed by the implications for China. Just think, if other farms did this, how much wheat could be grown in China each year! If even twenty percent of the wheat-growing communes followed suit, there would be more grain than anyone could eat. And that meant the promise of permanent free food in the collective canteens. The Communist paradise of abundant food, shelter, and clothing was just around the corner.

◆

That summer in Beijing it seemed even hotter after dark than during the day. The heat stored up in the streets and adobe houses released itself in waves that shimmered under the street lights. Yulin and I often walked down the steaming little lanes at night, pushing our two girls in their bamboo carriage. Nobody was indoors. Everyone was out sitting on the sills of their mud-brick houses fanning themselves with huge bamboo or rush fans. Yulin objected to the lengths to which some people went to stay cool. "I hate to see these women sitting around on the public street in their underpants," she said.

And indeed, that's just what they were doing. These Beijing back-alley ladies, so fastidious about not leaving so much as a forearm bare for most of the year, were wearing nothing but their big, ballooning, flowery printed underpants, which came down to their knees. And they looked us right in the eye as we passed with defiant righteousness. It was just one of the peculiarities sanctified by custom. It was even considered quite proper for the primmest Beijing lady to show a length of flower-print underpants through the side slit in the modest indigo-blue gowns they wore.

Since light bulbs were small and dim, and early risers needed their sleep, each city lamppost became a center of activity at night. Old men in sleeveless vests and trousers rolled up above their bony knees sat on the curb playing the ancient Chinese variety of chess, each surrounded by his circle of kibitzers. "Can mo," the Chinese called them: staff advisers. Some people were gathered around old-style yarn-spinners who would hold forth with thrilling serial adventures from ancient days, like *The Tales of the Three Kingdoms,* or *Outlaws of the Marshes.* And when school was in session, most of the lampposts had one or more students sitting propped up against them, using the light to do their assigned reading or their written homework.

In the busy market districts the night was heavy with cooking smells. There were the pungent odors of the thick sesame sauce and pickled garlic around the hot pots of the boiled lamb vendor; the spicy smell of crispy, slightly scorched chili peppers around the hot bean curd wagon; the sweet aroma of onions crackling in an iron pan; and the steamy fresh odor of sesame seed cakes baking around an iron grill.

There were special cool dishes for summertime: spicy Sichuan noodles soused with ice-cold water and eaten cold; the cool gelatinous pasta made from green soybeans and served with shredded cucumbers and sweet garlic; big pots of cold rice porridge with green beans; the cooling, slightly acidic, and vitamin-rich concoction brewed by steeping dried haw skins in water; and paper-thin rice pancakes sandwiching pressed walnuts, honey, dates, and a kind of cooling medicinal root.

During that hot August, everyone at Radio Beijing—editors, translators, announcers, writers—became steelworkers. We had all read about the ambitious steel production targets for 1958. The year before, China had produced eleven million tons of steel. This year we would produce eighteen million tons. The difference would come mainly from backyard steel furnaces set up by villages and urban work units.

The Great Leap Forward office of the Radio party committee assigned us an empty lot just south of the radio building, along the shores of the moat that encircled Beijing. The lot was intended to be the site of China's first television station. But for now it was a storage space for huge, hulking, unidentifiable items of imported heavy metal equipment, which lay there through sun and rain ignored by the busy managers who had pushed, shoved, and finagled a year earlier to get the stuff bought and paid for. For us, there was a special thrill in setting up our baby steel furnace next to these rusting machines. We were shoving aside the bureaucrats and their waste and taking matters into our own hands. The steel that we made here would go into the huge melting pot that would bring China's steel output in line with that of Great Britain, if not the United States.

Our furnace was made of grayish brick, about shoulder height, and about eight paces long by six paces wide. It was lined with yellow fire-resistant brick, and it had a long, low mouth at the eastern end. Stacked alongside the furnace was a pile of raw material. The call had gone out for everyone to volunteer some piece of iron for our patriotic steel drive. We had collected pots and pans, old tools, and a long stretch of heavy iron chain that had fenced off an area for stacking equipment outside one of the radio warehouses. Yulin and I contributed a cooking pot.

There were eight of us in all, taking turns at whatever work had to be done at the furnace mouth. When I arrived, someone handed me a long rod and a pair of thick leather gloves that reached halfway to the elbow. "Stir it!" was the order.

"What is it?" I asked.

"Steel!"

I seized the long iron rod, poked it through the mouth of the furnace, and began to stir the incandescent mass that rested on top of the flames. Holding those long iron rods and making anything inside move with them was very tiring.

We sang songs as we worked there in the twilight. Some of the better English speakers in the English section had learned Western labor songs like "John Henry" and "Drill Ye Tarriers Drill." We sang them together, and I felt the thrill of being one of the people who didn't just talk about changing the world, but actually did something about it.

People brought us cold drinks and salt tablets to help stave off dehydration. Over in the next yard, Yulin and a group of women workers were building their own facility, called the March 8 Women's Steel Furnace in commemoration of International Women's Day. Chairman Mao himself was known to be keeping tabs on our daily progress toward our goal.

We switched to singing about the Great Leap Forward:

Socialism is good!
Socialism is good!
In socialist countries
The people are powerful!
What they say they can do—
They do!

Our furnace chief handed me a pair of smoked goggles. "Put these on," he said. "Watch the fire. When it glows a dull red, evenly for the whole furnace, then it's time to pour the steel."

After a few minutes' watching I cried out, "It's ready to pour!"

The chief handed me a rod with a hoe on one end. "Pour the steel," he said, pulling over a sort of flat pallet and placing it under the mouth of the furnace. I took the hoe and began to scrape the glowing red mass out of the furnace and onto the pallet. To my amazement, it didn't pour, and it didn't look like any steel or any metal that I had ever seen. It looked like a kind of granulated, black mud.

"Is that steel?" I asked.

"That's steel," said the furnace chief. "Now we send it to be refined. When they get through with it, it'll be fine. It all looks like this at first."

Late that August Yulin and I took Xiaoqin and Xiaodong for a week's vacation at the seaside resort of Beidaihe. As the train chugged along, north of Beijing inside the Great Wall, we watched what was going by our window. The fields looked quite different from the last time I had passed this way. Back then, most of the heavy tilling and planting was being done by men. Now I could see only women, young children, and very old men. I knew why. All the robust young men had answered Mao's call to go to the hills to prospect for more iron ore.

As darkness fell, we could see the red lights from the furnaces dotting the countryside. Every field, every hill glowed with the light of the homemade ovens turning out steel in places where not a thimbleful of metal had ever been produced. Yulin and I were proud to be part of the great chain, from the peasants hunting for ore up in the hills to the sturdy workers at the big steel plants who would turn our peculiar-looking product into real steel. With more steel, we gaily told each other, we can make more textile machinery and farming tools. With more tools and machinery, there will be more food and clothing, and people will laugh about the times when we used to have coupons for cloth and for rice.

◆

Shortly after we returned from vacation, Mei Yi suddenly informed me that Anna Louise Strong was about to arrive. She was returning to settle in Beijing indefinitely. My first thought was to spare her the knowledge of my imprisonment, and the connection with her arrest in Moscow. I wrote a letter to Premier Zhou Enlai, proposing that none of us tell Anna Louise about my six years in prison. At her age, I argued, she should be spared shocks like that. She had already been bitterly disappointed at Soviet socialism; why shake her faith in Chinese socialism too?

Toward the end of September, Anna Louise arrived and was given a choice suite at the Beijing Hotel. Yulin and I were invited to a small welcoming dinner hosted by Premier Zhou. We took the elevator upstairs to her room, knocked on the door, and were confronted with the towering figure of Anna Louise in the doorway.

"Anna Louise!" I exclaimed. "It's good to see you again."

She took my hand. "Comrade Zhou has been telling me about what a hard time you went through because of me," she said, "and how proud of you they feel because of the way you conducted yourself."

I looked at Zhou Enlai. "We Chinese Communists," he said, stressing the second word, "could never make a mistake that harmed a friend of ours and then keep the mistake secret. I have told Comrade Strong all about what happened to you, that it was our mistake and that you behaved very well."

I sensed the rebuke, but also felt a deep sense of pride at the integrity of a man who wouldn't shrink from admitting the party's errors.

Zhou Enlai regaled Anna Louise during the meal with stories of the Great Leap Forward. Chairman Mao had been traveling around inspecting the new form of organization that was springing up around the country—the People's Commune. In the commune, not only were the people pooling their labor to make work faster, more efficient, and more pleasant, but they were doing away with the stultifying division of labor that entraps so many in the same occupation for life. In the commune, everyone was learning to do everything, and people would rotate by turns as doctor, bookkeeper, worker, farmer, teacher.

The communes were already providing free canteen food for members, and in some places they were providing free towels, toothbrushes, and toothpaste. Without directly referring to the Soviet Union, Premier Zhou made his point: "Chairman Mao is working out the way to build socialism in a revolutionary way, not in an ordinary everyday way."

Liao Chengzhi was at the dinner too, old "Fatty Liao," who used to head the media section in the caves of Yanan. Now he was vice director of the foreign affairs office of the state council. It was the first time I had seen him since he hugged me and sent me off for a jeep ride along the river to jail. The dinner ended suddenly, as Chinese banquets are wont to do, with the host and all the guests standing up and bidding an abrupt goodbye. Liao put his cap and jacket on and started for the door, pulling me after him by the arm. "It's time you started circulating," he said. "Why should you hole up at the radio all the time?"

To start me off on a more public life, Liao soon afterward escorted me to an official reception in honor of Mexico's ex-president Lázaro Cárdenas, an old friend of China. In his big Red Flag limousine on the way to the reception, I asked Liao the question that I had saved up for nearly a decade. "That morning way back in 1949, when you escorted me to the jeep that I thought was going to take me to Beijing, you told me, 'Just don't be like Liu Bei when he entered the city of Jingzhou, and everything will be all right.' What did you mean by that? I couldn't figure it out, because I couldn't remember what happened to Liu Bei in Jingzhou. So what was it?"

"He went to pieces, that's all," said Liao with a chuckle. And that was all I ever got out of him on that subject.

◆

The word had been spread at the start of the Great Leap Forward that the just-concluded campaign against the rightists would be the last such massive class struggle in China. But that didn't stop some people from trying to start little struggles on their own.

There was, for example, the battle of the suggestion boxes. The party branch in our Europe/Americas broadcast department offered a prize for the one who made the most suggestions for improving our work. So Jiang Meiyong, a timid little Cantonese girl who had risked isolation and disgrace by marrying Gerald Chen just after he had been labeled a bourgeois rightist, saw her chance. She decided to prove her diligence and loyalty by winning the contest. She stayed up one night scribbling suggestions on bits of paper and stuffing them into the box.

When Wei Lin heard of this, she was incensed that a backward, nonparty member, the wife of a rightist, might win an important party contest like that. As party leader she swung into action. She rousted Zhou Hong, the newest party member, from her bed, and had her return to the office to begin writing suggestions of her own. All through the night the two women labored, Little Jiang writing down suggestion after suggestion, the sleepy-eyed and scatterbrained Zhou Hong struggling to make up for lost time. In the morning, the clear winner was Little Jiang. But it was almost a Pyrrhic victory. Wei Lin accused her of deliberate conspiracy to make the party lose face and tried to start a struggle meeting against her. Little Jiang threatened to drown herself sooner than appear before a struggle group.

Outraged, I went to the leading party committee and protested against Wei Lin's scheme. The plans for the struggle meeting were dropped. And few of the suggestions were implemented.

◆

Meanwhile, we were transforming the face of Beijing.
Early in 1959, the papers announced that ten major construc-

tion projects would be completed by October 1, the tenth anniversary of the People's Republic. The projects were grandiose: a magnificent new hotel, a new railroad station, a museum of Chinese history, and a museum of revolutionary history. The centerpiece was to be an enormous meeting hall, built right in the middle of the city. A nationwide contest was held for designs and people followed the results as if it were a football match. A young boy in Sichuan sent in a model. One of the oldest and most famous architects in China sent in his model. A committee was set up to evaluate the designs and choose a finalist.

When the model was finally chosen, people talked about it for days. You could hear them on the streets marveling at how big and impressive this building would be. There was going to be a banquet hall that could seat five thousand people, an auditorium that could hold ten thousand. There would be a reception room honoring every province in China, each room a different color and furnished with that province's native products. The columns in the meeting hall would be of marble brought all the way from Yunnan Province in the south. And the technology would be the most modern and up-to-date, with each place provided with simultaneous translation. I hardly believed it could be done in the time allotted. They didn't even break ground until April.

It was going to be our hall—the Great Hall of the People. What's more, we were going to build it ourselves. Except for some skilled workers who would give guidance and do technical work, the hall would be built with volunteer labor. Every neighborhood committee, every factory, every work unit sent contingents of workers. First an area in Tiananmen Square had to be cleared, and then the streets widened. Yulin spent a week working on the roof, coming home shining-eyed and enthusiastic with tales of spirited labor and singing and camaraderie. It was just one more example of how the Chinese people, working together, could achieve the impossible.

◆

On June 1, 1959, I pulled out of the old Beijing railroad station heading south on the Peace Express to make a two-week-long inspection tour of communes and factories, and to report on the great achievements of the Great Leap Forward for Radio Beijing. It was the first time I had been back to the area I visited as a UN observer thirteen years ago. Through the train windows I could see how socialism, and now the Great Leap Forward, had lifted the country out of its misery. We passed field after rolling field of golden winter wheat. The area was suffering from drought, just as it had the year I visited for the United Nations, and some of the growth of wheat was stunted. But I could also see, lacing the fields, brand-new networks of irrigation canals, built collectively under the Great Leap Forward campaigns.

When the train arrived at Wuhan, I remembered my last visit and how we had had to wait for hours to cross between the Hankou side of the river and the Wuchang side. The trains had to be broken up and ferried across the river. This time, we chugged straight across on a huge new bridge. Artists from all over China had been invited to compete for the designs of the forty-eight wrought iron panels in the parapets. No two were alike. There were birds, flowers, leaves, deer. It was a beautiful structure, built at high speed, with Chinese materials, designs, and builders.

I talked to an eighty-year-old man who lived on the riverbank not far from the bridge on the Wuchang side. He told me he had dreamed of seeing a bridge there for half of his life, and he had vowed that if anyone built it he would walk across it barefoot.

"And did you?"

"Mei cuo!" he chortled. "You got that right!"

At the great Xin'an River dam, the first dam built entirely by the Chinese, I saw the local people fired with the enthusiasm of the Great Leap Forward, rushing to finish the dam that would run turbines to provide power to the area. Young men and women were running with their barrows along the treacherous top of the dam, apparently oblivious to the heat and the danger.

"Could I ask them why they're running with their loads of dirt?" I asked.

"Sure!" said my guide, a bright young engineer named Zhong Boxi, and motioned the nearest worker over.

"Why are you running?" I asked him. "It isn't required, is it?"

"No," he grinned and shook his head, mopping his brow with a towel tied to the handle of the barrow.

"So why do you run?"

"We are having a socialist emulation competition," he said. "Our team challenged the other teams in our brigade, and our brigade challenged the brigade next to us. The whole work site will come to a big meeting to applaud the winning team, and all the winning team's members will receive towels with the name of the dam written on them."

"Do you get more pay when you go faster and do more work?" I asked.

"Not on this project," he said. "But we get water for our farmlands and protection from flooding."

From Wuhan, I flew into Changsha in Hunan Province, Mao Zedong's home province. From the windows of the plane I could see the startling changes the People's Communes had wrought. The rich red earth was no longer carved up into a patchwork of tiny plots. Under the commune management, the tiny plots had been joined together and now big expanses of land were covered with thick green growth. The landlords who survived the land reform struggles had been given plots of land of their own to farm, which they did under surveillance. As I traveled around, I could see these men coming out of the doors of their houses, ringing a bell and shouting to the empty street, "I am going to the north field to dig yams."

The foreign adventurers were gone. The Austrians who had fed themselves with wheat ground in dark sheds by peasant children were gone, chased back to Europe after 1949. The speculators who had hoarded grain while hundreds of thousands starved were gone too. I knew that many of them had probably been beaten to death during the land reform movement. But thinking back on the scenes of hellish misery they had helped to cause, I couldn't feel sad about their fate. Ou Guan, the oily prefect who had stolen the relief grain, was gone too. I heard that he had been shot.

I drove down a branch of the same road that thirteen years ago had been choked with refugees and littered with the corpses of children. This time, I was heading for the Long Bridge People's Commune, about thirty miles from Changsha. There, the children played in a clean, sunny collective nursery while their parents worked in the fields. People looked well fed. I saw the grammar school. I saw the public dining room, where everyone could eat free. I saw the commune-run home for the aged.

In their smart new brick office, the commune leaders told me of their achievements. The output of rice had more than doubled from 1958 to 1959. Where they used to plant two crops of rice a year, now they were planting three. Their main problems, they said, were trying to find enough places to store the grain. But they were busy building new granaries to solve that problem.

I ate one of the best meals I had ever had in my life, the fiery hot Hunan food prepared in the commune kitchen. There were strips of pork cooked with chunks of red peppers, and chicken cooked with peanuts and pepper sauce. Unlike the meal at the monastery thirteen years ago, I thoroughly enjoyed this one. It was food raised and cooked by and for the people themselves, and there was plenty for everyone. I liked to think that many of the people I could see working, safe, and well fed were the same ones I had passed on the road with their bowls outstretched, begging for food. I liked to think that the party had been able to put out the frantic light in their eyes.

I was not the only visitor to this commune. The commune leaders told me I had just missed a visit by General Peng Dehuai, who was making an inspection tour with the governor of Hunan. I knew that Hunan was General Peng's home province, and I thought he must have come through to help document the successes of the Great Leap Forward as I had.

When I got to Mao's home near Changsha, which had been turned into a kind of museum, I decided to write a poem in Chinese commemorating my visit. After all, Chairman Mao had said that in this new world everyone could be a poet. I wrote about the contrast between the horror of a road filled with corpses and that road today, covered with carts bringing fruit and vegetables and grain into the city:

The yellow road littered with corpses
and the little cart laden with treasures.
One in the hell of yesterday,
the other in the beauty of today.

I felt something bordering on euphoria during my inspection tour, and when I returned to Beijing I was full of enthusiasm and eager to share what I had seen with my comrades, and with the world. Jin Zhao, the vice director, asked me to prepare a series of talks to be delivered to several hundred people in the foreign broadcast section. Then I planned a series of broadcasts to be aired over Radio Beijing. I sat down to write immediately.

A few days later, when I was well into preparing my scripts and my talks, I went to consult with Mei Yi. I bounded into his office full of enthusiasm for what I had seen. I had brought him some of the famous Gegai wine, which had a high-mountain rock lizard curled in the bottom. It was much prized for its medicinal properties and I knew Mei Yi liked it. I bubbled on about my trip and began to tell him in great detail about my plans for speeches and broadcasts. But to my surprise, Mei Yi received the news with a grim face.

"I think you'd better wait a while for that," he said.

I was flabbergasted. "But everything I'm going to say is very enthusiastic about the local successes. I want to tell everyone about the achievements I have seen."

Mei Yi looked very serious. "This isn't a good time to say anything one way or another about the Great Leap Forward," he told me. "Some comrades have raised doubts and criticisms of the movement. The central leadership is working on this issue right now, but better not say anything about what you saw for the time being."

CHAPTER THIRTEEN

The Great Hunger

It was late in 1961 when the symptoms appeared, affecting first the young and the old, but before long reaching the more hardy ranks of the working population. People began swelling around their necks and going through the day in a listless haze. It was a virus, some said, a virus that is slowing the city to half speed with people dragging themselves from home to work on legs that ached from the strain. It was an astrological disturbance, older, more superstitious people claimed. Or maybe it was something in the water. Everyone seemed to want to believe that the ailment was inexplicable, a disease without a cause. But as the months wore on, it became increasingly difficult to overlook the real reason for people's distress. It was malnutrition.

We had all watched the food begin to vanish from the shops late in 1960. First meat became hard to find and expensive. Next fruit dwindled down to small piles of wormy and rotten apples, then none at all. The food in the canteen ran short and people who arrived late for meals had to do without. Often they got only porridge, not cooked dishes and rice. When Yulin and I went out on our evening walks looking for bean curd or Sichuan noodles, we found that the street stalls were gone and the night market had closed up completely.

It was when the grain rations were cut that the swollen necks began. Thirty pounds of rice a month, then twenty-eight, then twenty-five. In the group meetings everyone was being asked what they could do without. But even after Beijing had acknowledged its pain as hunger, the people still shrank from its cause. "Three years of natural disasters," the papers said. There had been flooding and drought and the harvests had been poor.

The party's ranks held firm. Zhou Enlai ordered all party members to stop eating meat for three months to guarantee an adequate diet for those doing hard physical labor. Nor were party members to stand in line to buy fresh vegetables. A line meant there wasn't enough to go around, and if there wasn't enough to go around, party members should yield what there was to nonparty members. Liu Shaoqi repeated his favorite Confucian quotation: The cultivated person is the first to endure, the last to enjoy.

Yulin and I knew a woman named Fan Cailan, a returnee from Indonesia, who was caught standing in line to buy cabbage for her three small children. She was a party member and I attended a big meeting a week later at which she made a tearful public apology for behavior unbecoming a Chinese Communist. But if anyone thought of criticizing Mao or the party, they didn't think it aloud. No one asked what had happened to the bumper harvests of the Great Leap Forward, or how the conditions that had produced those record crops could have also produced such famine.

Party leaders had their own answers. If we were hungry, they told us, we should blame the Soviets. Whatever good harvests there had been were being enjoyed now by the revisionist rulers of the Soviet Union. For during the two years since the end of the Great Leap Forward, Beijing had broken with Moscow.

Back when I had been in Yanan, I had realized that the Chinese and the Soviets were not as close as their common political ideology would have suggested. There were tensions that stretched back for years. Wang Ming, a Soviet-backed challenger, had temporarily ousted Mao from power in the early days of the party. Stalin and his followers derided Mao's Chinese strategy and tactics and scarcely hid their distrust. Stalin had later supplied arms to the Nationalists, but not to the Communists. Both Chiang Kaishek and his son Chiang Ching-kuo got their training in Moscow. Later, when the People's Republic was formed, Mao put his pride in his pocket and went to Moscow seeking aid, returning with much less than he had asked for. Mao, I knew, was still smarting from the slights. I knew too, from the document that Zhou Enlai had given me to translate in Yanan, that the Chinese resented attempts at domination by the Soviets and were secretly encouraging the Eastern Europeans to resist it.

Still, ever since I had been released from prison in 1955 China had been officially in a state of general adulation of Lao Da Ge— Old Big Brother—and his immense technological contributions. Most large work units had a resident Soviet expert. At the Broadcast Administration, Comrade Babinko was chief Soviet adviser. The newspapers had also carried stories of criticism of hapless Chinese managers and other bureaucrats who had slighted the opinions of the Soviet experts, and had therefore fallen behind in their output quotas. Wherever there were Soviet experts, the host unit was supposed to set up an office to record whatever wisdom Big Brother had imparted for future study.

During the Korean War, the Soviets had supplied military hardware to the Chinese Communists. In the 1950s, they had provided hundreds of millions of dollars in economic aid. The Chinese were dependent on the Soviets—the only industrialized country that was helping them—for this steady stream of money, military help, and technical assistance.

Officially the Chinese people loved the Soviets. "Moscow-Beijing! Moscow-Beijing!"—a popular hit tune—rang out from radio sets all over the place. "Ode to Stalin" was translated and glee clubs all over China learned to sing this dirgelike, mournful tune. Beijing brimmed with Russian culture. The Moiesseyev Dancers and the Red Army Song and Dance Ensemble had performed there. Galina Ulanova herself came to dance *Swan Lake* and tour the country.

But privately, many Chinese disliked the Soviet advisers. Some of their distaste was because of the special privileges exacted by the Soviets, far outstripping those accorded other foreigners. The work units hosting Soviet experts had to supply each one with a Russian interpreter, and they had to be served by cooks trained to prepare such Russian delicacies as borscht, beef Stroganoff, chicken Kiev, and blini Imperial. Not only their housing but their offices were plush. At the Broadcast Administration, Comrade Babinko held court in the only room in the entire building that had a carpet. Not even Mei Yi's office could match it.

Even the austere Central Committee concerned itself with the comfort of its Russian guests. When prima ballerina Ulanova threw up in Canton after learning she had just eaten snake, a local favorite, the Central Committee issued a document decreeing that the so-called Elder Brothers and Sisters must never be served snake without being informed of it beforehand.

The behavior of the Soviets themselves caused anger. While other foreigners, like me, had access to motor pool cars, Americans and Europeans tended to be more democratic, sharing cars, sitting up front and chatting with the driver, and using our privileges to do favors for our colleagues. The Soviets, on the other hand, swept about town, each riding in the back of his or her own chauffeured car, black curtains drawn against the prying eyes of the Chinese. I once witnessed a low-level Soviet expert throw a temper tantrum on the steps of the Friendship Hotel when in a particularly busy period he was asked to share a car with a fellow Soviet.

The heavyweight wives of the Soviet experts shopped at the exclusive store for foreigners and at Beijing's finest Wangfujing department store. There they comported themselves with an arrogance that made the proud Chinese shopclerks wince. A Soviet woman calling out "Tongzhi!"—Comrade!—to attract the attention of a busy clerk sounded like nothing so much as the good old boys of my hometown Charleston crying out "Boy!" to summon a grown black man to their service.

But because of the official adulation, people didn't speak openly of their personal feelings about the Soviets. They hid their distaste lest it be read as a sign of low socialist consciousness. I myself had nothing to hide in that department. As a former American Communist Party member, I was enamored of the Soviets and saw a Sino-Soviet alliance as only natural. Indeed, I believed the Chinese were clearly junior partners in such an alliance. In my eyes, the first homeland of socialism was the standard-bearer of world socialism.

But then one beautiful day in 1959, I heard a top secret message that made it clear that the Chinese attitude toward the Soviets was drastically different from what appeared on the surface. Zhu Xuezhi, the middle-aged woman who had taken over as Mei Yi's secretary when Yulin left to work as a sound engineer, called. I was to report to the big studio in the basement in ten minutes to hear an important relay. Ordinarily she would have announced such a meeting by carrying around a printed notice on a clipboard. A phone call meant that something big was afoot.

I had long since grown accustomed to attending these high-level, top secret meetings. Once in Beijing, the Communist Party organization that had so effectively led our comrades safely through the Taihang Mountains had metamorphosed into a complex and ponderous bureaucracy. The key to negotiating that bureaucracy safely was knowledge. Information was hoarded like gold.

The big studio where we gathered that morning was used for children's programs, musical groups, and other broadcasts that needed a hall. I walked down the stairs from my office on the second floor. There was a guard at the door and I showed him my little red passbook with my photograph on one side, and my name, nationality, and status as a foreign expert on the other. The studio was big enough to seat about a hundred people. On that day, folding chairs had been placed to accommodate about twenty. I looked around me. Judging from the faces I saw—Gu Wenhua, who was deputy director in charge of domestic broadcasts, and Jin Zhao, deputy director for international broadcasts—this was to be a high-level message indeed, only for central government bureau chiefs and above. Occasionally I was invited to hear relays intended for officials with a higher level of clearance than mine. This was one of those times. Nearly everyone in the room was a Grade 13 cadre or more.

The chairs were arranged in a narrow column running from the back to the front of the room, with wide aisles on either side and an empty performance stage behind us. Mei Yi hurried into the room and stood before us without a lectern. We all sat, our habitual little black or dark red notebooks open on our laps, pens and pencils poised. Mei Yi looked tall and impressive at the front of the room, his long thin face impassive. But we could tell he was holding in some strong emotions. Whenever he was excited, he would stutter a little and bat his eyelids. As he stood there waiting to begin, his eyelids were fluttering like butterfly wings.

"Today," he said, "I am relaying to you a very important statement on the world situation made by Chairman Mao at an enlarged meeting of the top party leaders." That kind of meeting, I knew, would have included the heads of the six Central Committee bureaus in the six subregions of China—north, northeast, east, northwest, southwest, and south central. Party secretaries in key cities like Shanghai and Tianjin also sat in, as would the key figures from the major propaganda organs. That was why Mei Yi had been there.

"This message is vitally important," Mei Yi continued, making his characteristic emphatic gesture, hand chopping against out-raised palm. Not only were we not to take notes and not to breathe a word about the message outside this room—a standard feature of these meetings—we were not even to reveal that a meeting had taken place. Anyone who was caught leaking information would immediately lose his or her party membership. That kind of warning would stick, and the party was very good about tracing leaks. So that was the reason for the phoned summons instead of a written document, I thought.

Mei Yi pulled out his own little notebook and he began reading us Mao's own words from the meeting of the top party leaders. The world scene was rapidly changing, Mao had said. From now on, China confronted not one main enemy—American imperialism—but two main enemies: American imperialism and Soviet revisionism. That in itself was an electrifying message. As far as the world—and we—knew, the Chinese and the Soviets were still the closest of allies.

Mei Yi continued. It may be, Mao had said, that our greatest threat will come from Khrushchev and Soviet revisionism. We may see the day when the Soviets and the Americans will combine against us in the United Nations. A process of polarization will take place in the whole world Communist movement. In the end, every single individual will have to make a choice, either to go with Beijing or with Moscow. This may sound frightening to some, Mao said, because it means the breaking up of the socialist camp, but it was an excellent thing, because the fight against revisionism is the preparation for the victory of the world revolution.

There was a standard, official-sounding intonation that people like Mei Yi habitually adopted when reading top-level pronouncements, stripping their voices of human tones in order to underscore the importance of the message. This relay needed no such augmentation. It was the biggest bombshell I had ever heard in one of these meetings. Mei Yi in a few brief minutes had completely changed the shape of the worldview we had been operating with for years. We could hardly imagine the implications. But all around me the only reaction I heard was coughing and the shifting of feet as these seasoned old cadres took in Mao's words and considered how they would adjust. Long years of painful experience with such abrupt turns in party policy had taught them not to show their reaction, either positive or negative, to anything.

When we filed out of the studio back to our own desks, there was no chattering among ourselves. Nor did we discuss Mao's pronouncement when we met later. There were so few of us who had heard it, and there never seemed to be a time or a place when we were together by ourselves, without someone who wasn't authorized to know what was going on at the top.

I never even told Yulin.

After that, little by little, the myriad differences between Beijing and Moscow began to harden and the debate between Mao and Khrushchev took on a sharp edge. The two leaders' worldviews differed in the most fundamental ways, but underlying it all was the clash of Mao's proud nationalism with the patronizing, superior Soviets. Just as he had with Stalin, Mao butted heads with Khrushchev, and as time went on, those clashes became more frequent and more bitter.

I accidentally witnessed the aftermath of one. It was the night of October 3, 1959, at the celebration of the tenth anniversary of the founding of the People's Republic of China. It had been a festive day, following a military parade two days before that was bigger and grander than the one I had seen shortly after coming out of prison.

The Great Hall of the People now dominated Beijing's Tiananmen Square. Built with volunteer labor in less than a year, it had opened on schedule in time for the anniversary. So the highlight of the day was a grand celebration in the hall to honor the foreign dignitaries who had flocked into Beijing for the occasion. There was singing and dancing by folk troupes from all over China. China's best acrobats took the stage, their twisting limber bodies contorting into impossible positions. Around the hall women in flowing silk gowns twirled, scattering rose petals among the audience.

I was sitting in the balcony with a group of foreign experts, overlooking a sea of Chinese officials and delegations from other socialist states. At the intermission, a friend, an Indian professor from Singapore, and I walked out into the foyer to stretch our legs. The hall was as grand as we had been told it would be. Wide, sweeping white marble staircases with thick red carpeting were flanked with marble pillars several stories tall. Ringing the mezzanine level were meeting rooms, their formal entryways shielded from view by carved wooden screens. I saw the USSR's elder theoretician, Mikhail Suslov, walking about looking grave. Cambodia's Prince Sihanouk strolled by. The North Korean leader, Kim Il Sung, was there too, and I was astounded by the sight. I had never seen a public figure so fat, his vast round stomach blending seamlessly into a thick jowly neck. He looked nothing like his pictures.

My friend and I were enjoying ourselves milling about among the crowd of dignitaries when suddenly two great doors right by our side crashed open and out strode Mao and Khrushchev. Khrushchev was on the left and Mao on the right, one short and fat, one tall and stately. The rage on the two men's faces was palpable. Khrushchev's was twisted into something between a scowl and a sneer, and he flashed a look at the people milling about him as if his anger took in every citizen in China. As for Mao, I had never seen him so angry. Usually, his anger was controlled, sarcastic, biting, needling. But at that moment, his fury was unchecked. His face was black and tense and the atmosphere all around him snapped and crackled at the force of his emotions. The two men strode side by side, but a million miles apart, back to the hall where they, unspeaking, resumed their seats.

I had no idea at the time what that scene portended. But later on Lu Dingyi, the propaganda minister, told me a bit about what had happened that day. And many years later, Mao himself recounted his version of events. During their meeting in between the festivities, the two leaders had clashed on every single topic that had been raised. Khrushchev had arrived in Beijing following his trip to Camp David to confer with Eisenhower; Mao saw the meeting as a gross betrayal of world Communism. Khrushchev had also met with Nehru in New Delhi; Mao accused him of encouraging India to attack the Chinese border. The two men talked about revolution in Third World countries. Mao felt such local battles ensured world peace by drawing America into enervating conflicts; Khrushchev feared they could explode into a conflagration that would engulf the world.

A bare six months later, the conflict between Mao and Khrushchev broke out into the open. In the summer of 1960, the Soviet Union suddenly withdrew its experts from factories and work units all over China. Suddenly, Old Big Brother was gone. The engineers were gone, the technicians were gone, the advisers were gone. And with them they had taken as much of their technology and equipment as they could carry. Even those who wanted to stay were forced to leave. At the Broadcast Administration, Comrade Babinko showed Mei Yi a letter he had written asking to be allowed to stay and finish out his contract. His request was refused.

Chinese industry was crippled by their flight. But worse, the Chinese leaders told us, were the Soviets' inhuman demands. After the split, they said, the Soviets now demanded repayment for all their military aid to China during the Korean War. That aid from Stalin had never been intended to be repaid, the Chinese said. But China, although poor, was a proud country and remained indebted to no one. We would pay off the debt—much of it in food —no matter what suffering it cost. If we were hungry, they told us again and again, it was the Soviets who were to blame.

Few in China knew the truth until decades later. The Chinese were not just hungry, they were starving, starving to death in the countryside by the tens of millions. Fewer still knew the main cause: not bad harvests, not the Soviet debt—although both probably played a role—but the Great Leap Forward itself.

The same enthusiasm and all-out effort that had built the roads, the dams, the irrigation projects, the Great Hall of the People, the backyard steel furnaces, and the bridges had also devastated China's agriculture. The ill-conceived hunt for ore that had pulled able-bodied peasants from the fields had ruined the harvests. Just as I had seen on my ride to Beidaihe, fields all over the country had been left to the care of old men, women, and children unequal to the task. The crops had rotted and the people were dying of starvation.

I knew that Mao had been having trouble with overenthusiastic comrades taking the policies of his Great Leap Forward too far. I had heard a relay of a speech he made at the central party leadership's Nanchang conference, in which he acknowledged that peasants had been prospecting for ore at the expense of cultivating and harvesting their crops. What's more, Mao said, some accomplishments of the Great Leap Forward were being exaggerated.

Later on, I heard about the extent of such exaggerations, and even deliberate deception. The model commune I had visited near Tianjin the year before, for example, had been revealed to be a hoax, the thick wheat assembled from fields elsewhere and replanted in one spot for show. Mao's explanation, which I readily accepted, was that such problems were local ones caused by zealous local cadres misinterpreting Mao's words. If such exaggerations and unwise enthusiasms weren't contained, he warned, "The Chinese will die out. Perhaps all of them—or maybe only half." I felt he himself was exaggerating for effect to try to bring unruly comrades into line. The problems, Mao explained, and we all agreed, came from mistaken interpretations of his policies. No one dared challenge the Great Leap Forward itself. But Mei Yi's un-expected warning to me when I had returned enthusiastically from my inspection tour of Great Leap Forward successes signaled big changes. Shortly afterward, the exuberance and euphoria of the Great Leap Forward melted away as quickly as it had sprung up.

Even so, none of us had any idea that the problems were as serious as they later proved to be. Because the worst devastation was in the countryside, far from our view, most of us in the city knew nothing about it. All we knew was that something had gone wrong, and that the leaders were like tigers in the mountains fighting. None of us knew exactly what they were fighting about. But when tigers fought, the best thing for everyone was to keep a safe distance.

Only later did we hear Mao's version of that fight. I heard a hushed and shaken Mei Yi deliver a relay informing us that a senior party leadership conference had just ended. There, at a balmy summer resort high on Mount Lu, some of the senior party leaders had dared to criticize Mao Zedong and the Great Leap Forward. Defense Minister Peng Dehuai, whose path I had crossed in Hunan, had not been on a routine inspection tour at all, but rather had been systematically collecting evidence that the country's headlong drive for development was wrecking the econ-omy. What's more, he hinted in a mild and circumspect private letter to Mao, the problems were caused by Mao's own petit bour-geois romanticism. And surprisingly, nearly all the party leaders had showed sympathy for Peng's views.

Mao had invited the criticism himself. But when it came, he lashed out in fury. Even though Peng was one of the Ten Marshals, even though he had been commander-in-chief of the Chinese forces in Korea, even though he had the support of Zhu De and Mao's ideological aide, Chen Boda, such treason couldn't be sup-ported. Marshal Peng Dehuai, Mao charged, was using the prob-lems of the Great Leap Forward as weapons to try to usurp the leadership of China.

So Mei Yi's message to us was grim. The blunt Marshal Peng Dehuai had been removed, replaced as defense minister by the wily Lin Biao. Everyone else was forced to apologize. In the doc-uments room at the Broadcast Administration, I later read an abject letter to Mao from Marshal Zhu De. I even heard a tape of a two-day, full-dress self-criticism by Zhou Enlai that he had deliv-ered to an auditorium full of party leaders. In it he apologized for his doubts about the Great Leap Forward, attributing it to the limitations of his background. He came from a family of petty officials of the old empire. Still, the failures and excesses of the Great Leap Forward were too enormous to ignore and its policies and programs gradually faded away. But its most tragic legacy, the great hunger, was now devastating China's cities and countryside.

◆

Between the end of the Great Leap Forward and the beginning of this great hunger, I hadn't been at the Broadcast Administration much. In early 1960 Mei Yi had called me to his office and told me, with a scowl, that I was being borrowed by the Central Committee for a special task. A team was being formed to translate the new fourth volume of Mao's works into English, and to revise the old translations of the first three volumes, which had been published in the early 1950s.

A new addition to the works of Mao was an earthshaking event in China. Mei Yi didn't like losing me one little bit, but for me it was a great honor. I was excited at the prospect of being part of an elite translation team, involved so closely in bringing Mao's words to the outside world. I was just as glad to be relieved of my responsibilities at the Broadcast Administration. I was getting tired of my job. The glamour of being an important part of China's voice to the outside world that had so entranced me in Yanan had begun to wear thin, finally eroded by the mind-numbing contents of the broadcasts, and by the implacable bureaucracy that governed them.

The stirrings of rebellion that I had begun to feel during the campaign against the rightists were still simmering under the surface. The Great Leap Forward had temporarily deflected them, but now my thoughts began to trouble me again. In the back of my head were doubts. I wondered if the use of class struggle, brutal as it was, wasn't also cynical, and if it would ever end. More doubts were intensified when, just after the Great Leap Forward ended, a dear friend and I both became targets of struggle meetings.

The Lushan conference at which Peng Dehuai had been removed was followed by a campaign against right opportunists. That meant anyone in the party who had expressed doubts about the Great Leap Forward. At the Broadcast Administration, one of the first targets was my gentle friend Ding Yilan. Capable, kind, and almost painfully honest, she had made the mistake of sharing her diary entries at a party meeting. In her diary, she had fretted that the aging Mao was losing control of himself, growing increasingly arbitrary and dictatorial, and even losing his ability to listen to other people's opinions. After a struggle meeting, she was sent to a farm in Hebei Province for a year of hard labor.

At about the same time, I had drafted a memo criticizing the foreign newscasts. Anyone should have known it was a bad season to be critical. But I was delighted with the opportunity to blast the poor quality of the broadcasts, and the stuffy, bureaucratic leadership at the Broadcast Administration. Still, I couldn't believe it one morning when I was ambushed. I walked into a meeting to find my colleagues, the department heads, armed with prepared speeches attacking me. If the leadership at the Broadcast Administration was wrong, they said, then the party was wrong, since all the leaders were working under party authority. My attack must be a veiled attempt to grab power, my motive must be ambition, they charged. I tried to rebut the accusations, but I couldn't. They were not going to let me defend myself until they were good and ready.

It was the first time since prison that I had been subjected to anything like that, and the old panic flashes returned. I went home for lunch, where Yulin held me steady. "Stick to your guns," she said. "Just tell them the truth, no matter what they say."

That afternoon, the same faces were assembled around the table, but the atmosphere was completely different. The leader of the session apologized, in tears, and asked me to forgive them. I was saved, not by the valor of my arguments, but by a deus ex machina. The party propaganda chief, Lu Dingyi, had got wind of what was going on and angrily phoned Mei Yi to stop the sessions against me.

So I was safe once again, but shaken. It was just another example of how bad the party bureaucracy had become, I thought, this stifling, stultifying, infighting bureaucracy that was perverting Mao's policies and keeping us from realizing the land of democracy, learning, and plenty that we were all working for.

◆

The first meeting of the translation team for Mao's works was held in the former French embassy, an elegant building in the old legation district south of Beijing's Wangfujing shopping area. As soon as I entered the building with its thick carpets, carved furniture, and paintings in gilded frames, I was transported into a much more rarefied world than the routine, bureaucratic, backbiting one

I had left. I couldn't tell anyone where I was working, and people didn't ask. If anyone noticed I wasn't at the Broadcast Administration anymore, I just told them I was working somewhere else and that ended the discussion.

We were truly an elite group: the foremost scholars, economists, and English speakers in China. There were fourteen members of the team, nine Chinese and five foreigners. Our leader was C. Y. W. Meng, the veteran economist with whom I had walked much of the way from Kalgan to Yanan in the fall of 1946. He was China's leading expert on the American economy and spoke excellent English. The second-ranking member of the team on the Chinese side was Tang Mingzhao, who had been active for many years in left-wing politics in New York and now headed the work in the English language areas of the Central Committee's liaison department.

Next was the legendary Ji Chaoding, scholar, collector, politician, humanist, calligrapher. He had done the cover calligraphy for Joseph Needham's Cambridge series on Chinese science and civilization. Ji's younger half-brother, Ji Chaozhu, probably the foreign ministry's best Chinese-English interpreter, joined the group a little later. Other Chinese members included Xu Yongying, former chief of the foreign ministry's America-Oceania department; Wu Wentao, director of the Foreign Languages Press; Professor Qian Zhongshu, Oxford scholar and noted Chinese authority on Shakespeare; Qiu Ke'an, chief of the foreign ministry's translation section, an Oxford graduate; the famous Chinese history scholar Chen Hanshen; and Cheng Zhenqiu of the Foreign Languages Institute, another Oxford graduate who acted as the team's secretary and general factotum.

There were two other Americans besides me. One was Frank Coe of Virginia, a Marxist economist who had risen to an important post in the U.S. Treasury Department during the New Deal and World War II, had later become secretary of the International Monetary Fund, and had chosen exile in China after defying the McCarthy investigations. The other was his close friend Sol Adler, who was born British, had been a noted Cambridge economist, and had become a naturalized American citizen while working for the U.S. Treasury Department in World War II.

The British member of our team was Michael Shapiro, who had once represented the British Communist Party in London's Stepney town council and was now a foreign expert for the New China News Agency, polishing English-language releases. And then there was Israel Epstein, the left-wing China historian, an impish, erudite senior editor at *China Reconstructs* monthly, who had been born in Poland, brought to China as an infant, and raised in American schools in Tianjin.

For nearly two years we worked together, six days a week, eight hours a day, and, altogether, we translated about five hundred pages of Mao's works. Volumes one through three, which had been published in England between 1951 and 1956, contained Mao's writing through the end of the war with Japan. The new Volume Four consisted of documents from the final civil war with the Kuomintang up to the founding of the People's Republic, including Mao's speech on the people's democratic dictatorship, his essays on the U.S. State Department's white paper on China, and some important military writings.

I felt as if I had been chosen to translate a fifth gospel. We were going to bring a new body of experience from the Chinese Revolution to the rest of the world. And we were under orders to work as quickly as possible because Mao was anxious to release these documents. He had already gone over all the Chinese texts, and the Central Committee had approved them. The Chinese were beginning to advance the idea of Mao as the Lenin of our time, the true standard-bearer of world socialism. Edgar Snow had first called him the Chinese Lenin, way back in the 1930s. But now, with the break with the Soviets, the Chinese were more anxious to contrast Mao favorably with Khrushchev as the true messenger of socialism.

We weren't the original translators. The Chinese team that did the basic translation worked apart from us in a guest house in a Beijing suburb. They were the best available from the foreign ministry, the Broadcast Administration, the New China News Agency, and the Foreign Languages Press. But we outranked them. We were polishers, called the Finalizing Group. We had the last word on the style, accuracy, clarity, and fidelity of the translation. We could challenge anything and change anything. Some of our members, like Meng, Tang, and Ji, were minister-level officials.

As secretary of the group, it was Cheng Zhenqiu's responsibility to drive out to the suburbs every few days to pick up the latest translations from the Chinese team. They were always ahead of us. Each worked on a different typewriter, so the legal-sized sheets of paper were all in different fonts. The translators worked from handwritten documents that had been cleaned up and put in printed form. We worked from their typed translations, stapled together to form a single document. We were also given the original Chinese texts. Told to prepare a literal translation of Mao's works, word for word, the Chinese team was competent, but the style and diction of their translations were often inadequate, or the English renderings of some of Mao's concepts were not accurate.

Our job was to remedy those shortcomings and our procedure was simple. We all sat around a long table, our covered cups of Chinese tea before us, while Old Meng, who as leader sat at the head of the table, laid out the plan for the day's work and led the discussion. Cheng Zhenqiu noted each of our decisions as we made them. We took the translated pages and went over them line by line, phrase by phrase, word by word, passage by passage. First we worked in pairs, thrashing out individual problems. Then each pair reported their findings and questions to the entire group, and the entire group repeated the whole process line by line, phrase by phrase, word by word, passage by passage, debating each point as we went. Often, if we got through half a page in a day's work, we considered it a good day. Sometimes, particularly with Mao's philosophical writings, we would complete two lines a day and that was it. We wrangled constantly.

Some of our debates stemmed from the different ways we had been schooled. Ji Chaoding, Meng, and Tang had all spent a lot of time with Americans and so their English was more Americanized. The Oxford scholars tended to side with British usages. They were more precise about subjunctives than we were, for example, and less free about using indirect quotes.

On other matters, we tended to split into two camps, literalists and stylists. Ji Chaoding, the best revolutionary propagandist of the lot, focused on how to make the English translation smooth, appealing, and convincing to the Western reader. Tang and Xu Yongying were less troubled by literary style than political content. Xu frequently tangled with others over a word or a phrase. Some old-timers who had known him back when he worked on the *Overseas Chinese Daily* in New York told me that the paper frequently couldn't go to press because of such doctrinal disputes.

I was one of the more troublesome characters on the team. I was a literalist. Confident in my own savvy in the political language of both continents, I held out for what I considered an absolutely accurate rendition of Mao's meaning and style, sometimes filibustering against a reasonably accurate translation in better style but

less literally accurate than the one I wanted. Hard-headed prag-
matist Tang Mingzhao once lost his temper at me and accused me
of displaying "an extremely bad style of work." But my view was
that the outside world should read and know exactly what Mao
had written and spoken without having the translator stand between the reader and the writer. Once when we were arguing
about the interpretation of a complicated sentence of Mao's I
blurted out, "The translation should not be any clearer or less
ambiguous than the original text." Some of the others glared at
me, and I wondered if their expressions indicated outrage at my
denigration of Mao's clarity.

Sometimes we asked Mao himself what he meant. We sent our
messages via Meng, who passed them on via the central authorities. The answers we got back didn't always help much. Once we
asked Mao about a statement he made in a document about land
reform. "Don't kill too many people, and don't kill wildly at random with no aim," he said. How many people is too many? we
asked. His answer—if you kill one person too many, then that's
too many—wasn't really an answer at all.

Sometimes our hardest battles were fought over the tiniest
things. When we retranslated Mao's essay "On Contradiction,"
we fought hard over how to express the Chinese term "mao dun."
They are the two Chinese characters for "spear" and "shield" that
together make up the word "contradiction." But Chinese words
don't have a specific plural form. So was it "contradiction" or
"contradictions"?

Some of us, including me, argued that "contradiction" implied
the state of being in contradiction or the general concept of contradiction. The essay was concerned with showing that the universe was full of contradictions. It was not written to show the
essence of the state of contradiction. We could accept the singular
form in the title, but not generally in the text. The other side
argued that the concept of contradiction was Mao's focal point,
and that the singular was therefore the only choice. After arguing
for days, we finally concluded that we should look at each individual use of the word and decide whether the singular or the plural
was more appropriate.

Sometimes Mao's homely, folksy style tripped us up. In a speech
urging cadres not to make long tedious speeches, he used a country saying from his native Hunan. Such speeches, he said, were
"like a lazy woman's foot-cloth: long and smelly." A majority of
the team supported using the word "slut" for "lazy woman." I

insisted that "slut" meant prostitute or loose woman in America, and that the word would be an unacceptable alteration of Mao's original meaning. If he had meant "slut," he would have used a comparable Chinese slang term like "broken-down shoe" or "wild chicken." The right word for the phrase, I insisted, was "slattern."

The Oxford dictionary backed up the "slut" supporters; *Webster's Collegiate* supported my argument. Our passions became so inflamed that we shouted until our faces grew red.

In order to win my argument, I not only had to filibuster, I also canvassed a group of Americans in Beijing, including Frank Coe's wife, Ruth, all of whom agreed with me.

Mao's writings were interesting to work with. Unlike the writings of some other Chinese theoreticians—like Chen Boda—that fell apart when analyzed too closely, Mao's logic was taut and his thought process elegant. He cut his teeth on Confucius, went through high school with Locke, Rousseau, Benjamin Franklin, and Thomas Jefferson among his favorite writers, and accepted Marx and Lenin after World War I. All his political life, Mao dreamed of building a new and better world in which the human race would understand—and be able to harness—the laws of nature and of society that governed it, regardless of their individual wills. "Freedom is the understanding of necessity and the use of that understanding to transform the world" was one of his favorite sayings, "Serve the people" his most frequent injunction. Aside from being a brutally practical politician and general, he was also a man of dreams, of ideals.

Still, in my own mind the tiny wisps of other thoughts, long suppressed, were beginning to emerge with greater force. I began to see things in Mao's works that I had never seen before. Gradually, his emphasis on questioning everything, on research, on self-reliance, on testing theories, and on planning and revising actions based on reality began to strike me as not just a political prescription but a personal one.

Ever since I had been released from prison, I had made unquestioning fealty to the party my sole aim. But here I was translating the works of Mao himself in which he argued for precisely the opposite. He advocated fighting persistently for what you thought was right, not obeying wrong leadership, testing and judging everything for yourself and not following blindly.

I translated a famous passage from Mao that demanded that Communists make a distinction between "obedience to the leadership as a matter of discipline, and adherence to truth as a matter of principle." In the passage, I used the word "obedience" deliberately. In the Chinese original, "fu cong" literally means "to obey."

Tang Mingzhao vehemently disagreed. I simply didn't understand a most basic tenet of Mao's, he said. Party members, he explained, are required by party discipline to go along with orders they consider wrong and not to oppose them in public. But they are also expected to stick to their own opinions and to continue to argue the point inside the party whenever possible. "Obedience" was too passive, Tang said. It didn't stress the individual Marxist's devotion to principle and the interaction that should take place between the leader and the led. The proper word was "compliance." Tang's view carried the day.

After that, passages in which Mao stressed independent thinking fairly leaped out at me. "A Communist should ask 'Why?' about everything," he wrote. "He should absolutely not obey blindly." I could also see from my own observations how Mao had set the example in his own political activities. He had defied first Stalin and then Khrushchev, although for many years he never made public his struggle with them except in the highest circles of the party hierarchy. To be a true student of Mao Zedong, I finally decided, required critical thinking and a fight to uphold the truth against all comers.

Despite our disagreements, everyone on the translation team became very close. We couldn't help it, working in such tight quarters, banding together to support our views, debating each other, and sharing our meals. Sometimes we relaxed together too, going as a group to Peking opera or to see a play.

For my part, I fell under the spell of classical Chinese furniture. It was the great love of Ji Chaoding, a calligrapher and himself a collector of the finest Chinese pieces. The beautiful furniture of the Ming dynasty had been the inspiration of all the great European designers. I now recognized the influence of its flowing lines and graceful carving on the Sheraton- and Hepplewhite-style furniture my mother filled our house with in Charleston.

Beijing's antique stores were still full of lovely old pieces, but Ji had a great fear that they would all be bought by foreign diplomats, who could ship them home with their household goods. His own house was stuffed with furniture—tables under tables, coffee tables under his bed, pieces piled on pieces. Whenever he could, he bought some perfect item and tried to convince all his friends

I studied Chinese at Stanford University in 1943, hoping for a short tour of duty in China and a return home at the end of the war. Instead, appalled by the conditions I found there and eager to help in any way I could, I joined the Chinese Communist Party (the only American citizen allowed to do so) and remained in China for thirty-five years—sixteen of which were spent in prison in solitary confinement.

After being released from my first term in prison, falsely accused of being an American spy, I joined the Broadcast Administration in the English-language section at Radio Beijing. There I met Wang Yulin and overheard her declare that she—unlike my ex-wife—would never divorce her husband simply because he was in prison: "Otherwise, what do you mean by love?" We were married soon after.

Everyone worked enthusiastically to bring China into the modern age during Mao Zedong's Great Leap Forward. I tended a "backyard" steel smeltery at the Broadcast Administration; Yulin helped build the Great Hall of the People in Tiananmen Square. And along with a group of volunteers from the Broadcast Administration, I spent several weeks planting trees in the mountains near Beijing.

Mandatory breaks for exercise were still an important part of the Communist work ethic in the early 1960s. By then, the Great Leap Forward was an unacknowledged failure and the growing Communist bureaucracy was stifling individual initiative and new ideas.

Yulin and I posed with our three daughters in our apartment in Beijing. Because of my position, we lived a life of comfort and privilege. Our apartment was filled with my collection of priceless Ming dynasty furniture, which I later gave to the Palace Museum.

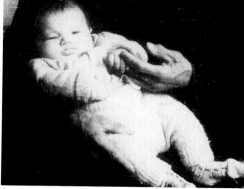

Our last child, and only son, was born in 1966. He was doted on by both his grandfather, a cabinetmaker who lived nearby, and his grandmother, who lived with us and helped raise our children. Like most of the women of Old China, Yulin's mother had had her feet bound and had been given no real name. Yulin's older sister had been raped and murdered by Japanese soldiers, and the entire family had endured terrible hardships during the war.

I made a sentimental
return to the caves of
Yanan in 1966. It was
there that Mao had
spearheaded the
Communist revolution that
toppled the Old China.
There I had first met Mao
and others who now ruled
the People's Republic. And
it was there that I had
finally convinced them of
my sincere dedication
to the party and to
the people of China.

With the advent of the
Cultural Revolution in the
late 1960s, I became an
outspoken activist and
advocate of returning
power to the people. Here
I am exhorting the Rebel
Regiment to Defend Mao
Zedong Thought in
Tiananmen Square,
without the least suspicion
that this new revolution
was a cynical strategy by
Mao—and his wife, Jiang
Qing—to foment unrest
and rebellion and to vastly
increase their own power.

As one of the stars of the Cultural Revolution, I was asked to join Mao and the other top Communist leaders for the October 1, 1966, celebration of National Day in Tiananmen Square. Mao signed my copy of his Little Red Book, the collection of sayings that was the bible of the Cultural Revolution. A year and a half later, I was in prison again, accused of spying.

I should have known I was in trouble when this photograph was reprinted in the *Beijing Review* and my likeness blacked out (here, I am shown second from right, second row from the top). Mao can be seen in the front row center with Lin Biao, his designated successor, to the left and Zhou Enlai second to the right. Jiang Qing is sitting next to Anna Louise Strong (front row, second and third from left). I had run afoul of Jiang Qing and her cronies—later dubbed The Gang of Four. After Mao's death, the group tried, and failed, to seize power and Jiang was sent to the same prison where I was being held.

While I was in prison, my family was also locked up. Then relatives took in our daughters, and Yulin was beaten, forced to serve as a washroom attendant, and finally sent to a labor camp in Henan Province, where our son, then only five, joined her.

True to her word, Yulin waited for me, and after my release from prison our entire family was almost miraculously reunited. But I had come to see the harsh reality of the old idealistic world I had once believed in; I couldn't accept the corruption of the new world under Deng Xiaoping. All my children adopted American names and became citizens and the whole family moved to the United States: from the left, Yulin, Toni, Jenny, Sunny, and Sidney, Jr.

关于李敦白同志的平反结论

李敦白，男，一九二一年生，美国籍，原任中央广播事业局专家。一九六八年二月二十一日被错误关押审查。一九七七年十一月十九日释放出狱。

李敦白同志一九四**五**年到中国以来，为中国人民做了许多有益工作，对中国人民的革命事业是有重要贡献的。李敦白同志在"文化大革命"期间，被诬陷为"特务"，有"现行反革命活动"，长期关入监狱审查，纯属冤案，应予彻底平反，恢复名誉，恢复工作，恢复原待遇，补发审查期间停发的工资。其家属王玉琳同志及子女受株连被隔离，也一并予以平反。

撤销公安部一九七七年十一月十九日《对李敦白同志的审查结论和处理决定》和一九七九年三月十三日《关于李敦白同志问题的审查结论》。本结论向李敦白同志所在单位群众公开宣布。

公　　日

For years after my release, Yulin fought to have my name completely cleared, and finally in 1982 she succeeded. The document cites my "major contributions to the revolutionary cause of the Chinese people," and describes my imprisonment in 1968 as a "pure and simple case of wrongfully accusing an innocent person."

Now in the United States for more than ten years, Yulin and I are working together as consultants to American companies doing business in China. Looking back, I have no regrets about the years I spent in China, even my years in prison. I was motivated then, as today, by an unquenchable desire to support the Chinese people in their quest to taste the responsibilities and rewards of freedom.

to do the same. Eventually, he planned to donate his collection to the Palace Museum in the Forbidden City.

I had never had an interest in furniture before, but with Ji's instruction I soon fell in love with the finely crafted Ming pieces. After work I often went with Ji to scout the antique stores, the old Marco Polo shop on the southern extension of Wangfujing, the Liulichang furniture shops, and the antique furniture warehouse outside Chongwen Gate. I readily agreed to Elder Ji's plan. I would buy as many perfect pieces as we could find—and I could afford—and Yulin and I would keep them in our home as a display of the beauties and civilization of China for our many foreign guests to admire. And then when the time came, we too would donate our collection to the museum.

I was ideally suited to help carry out Ji's plan. Not only was my house roomier than those of all but the most high-ranking Chinese, but because I was a foreign expert, my salary was higher than that of any Chinese, including Mao and Zhou. Where my colleagues earned about eighty yuan a month—or about thirty-seven dollars—my monthly salary was six hundred yuan. But just as in Yanan, my needs were simple, so I had saved enough to be able to spend thousands of yuan on furniture.

Yulin and I filled our house with my acquisitions. We bought a three-drawer buffet piece, long and low, with a serpentine molding framing the back of the top and curving down into armlike borders at the two ends. We found a high lute table in yellow rosewood carved to look exactly like beautifully fluted bamboo with every knot exactly in place. You could not tell from three feet away that it was really made of rosewood. In the living room and the dining nook, we placed several heavy eight-place tables, called Tables of the Eight Immortals after mythical Chinese figures, and four pairs of heavy carved chairs. It was all the most beautiful furniture I had ever seen. And when I came home tired, late at night, I used to sit there in the half light, just enjoying the quiet grace and beauty of these works of art.

◆

The world outside the walls of the former French embassy and my serene apartment was far from beautiful. By late 1962, when our translation of Mao's works was completed and I returned to the Broadcast Administration, I was forced to confront the painful reality of the great hunger close up. Our elite translation team had seen the special meals prepared for us grow more and more sparse. But still the food we were served every day by special cooks was more than adequate. Back at the Broadcast Administration I saw firsthand the way other people were suffering from poor nutrition.

More than two-thirds of the people at the Broadcast Administration were afflicted by the swelling caused by protein deprivation. Shortly after I returned, many had grown so sick that they could work only every other day. As people began showing up with dark puffy patches on their legs and around their faces, and feeling faint and nauseated, they would be sent home to rest. The English section was operating with a rotating staff. People spent one day at work and the next at home in bed recovering from the exertion. On any given day, I would look around the newsroom and see half the seats empty. It reminded me of my days in the mountains with the New Fourth Army in 1946 when so many people suffered from malaria that only a third to a half of them could attend any given meeting.

Yulin was at school, learning English at the Foreign Languages Institute. One weekend she too came home with her face and forehead swollen and her arms and legs puffed up. Her grain ration had been cut by twenty percent and meat eliminated completely from the students' diets. She and her fellow students were subsisting on less than a pound of rice a day and a little bit of cabbage. The most serious sufferers of the edema were given an emergency ration of a tablespoon of soybeans a day.

People went around poking a finger in each other's foreheads, cheeks, or arms. It was the test for edema. If a depression appeared in your face when it was poked, but immediately filled out again when the finger was taken away, you were normal. If you were suffering from the swelling, it would take quite a while before your face filled out again.

People ate what they could get. One weekend Yulin and I went out with a group to spend the morning using long bamboo poles to knock leaves down from the trees. We then took the leaves to the Broadcast Administration's canteen, where they were stewed into porridge or cooked with noodles in place of vegetables. Yulin was one of the experts on this expedition. She never forgot how she went out as a child with her mother and sisters to collect edible weeds to feed the family during the famine years of Japanese occupation.

Still, incredibly, party loyalties prevailed. There was little corruption and almost no complaints. Even those who had suffered at the hands of the party stood firm. At the height of the hunger, Gerald Chen, still laboring in the countryside after having been exiled as a rightist, was given permission by the party to go to Hong Kong to visit some relatives. "That's the last we've seen of him," I thought to myself as he left. But back he came, on precisely the date he was expected.

And Yulin, despite her obvious discomfort, stubbornly refused to break ranks with her fellow students. My foreign-expert status entitled me to a much richer diet than hers, more than enough to stave off malnutrition. So several times I packed up a bundle of fruit and bread and some cooked meats to take up to her. She would not accept them. "I'm secretary of the student party branch," she said reproachfully. "How can I put myself on a special diet while the other students and the teachers are suffering?"

I hadn't been looking forward to returning to the Broadcast Administration. Once again, I found the lack of energy and enthusiasm and creativity stifling. And it wasn't just hunger that was causing it. More profound than that, it was the product of the same stifling bureaucracy that had made me glad to leave in the first place. Side by side with elitism was a leaden egalitarianism. If sixteen pages in Chinese came in to be translated, I had to divide the job up, two pages to each of eight people. Of those eight, maybe four had less than minimal translation ability. So the translations that came back were unusable. I couldn't throw them out; that would be considered undemocratic. But when I finished correcting them, there were so many balloons and lines, fixes and margin notes that the translators were hurt, complaining that only a word or two of their original text was left.

"Give the work to the good translators," I argued to the department heads. "It will be faster. The work will get done better." But it never happened. Their argument was that they needed to train new people, but they also did it to keep harmony in the office, not to be seen to favor one person over another. So we were always bogged down doing stupid work, trying to take something unusable and pretend that it was usable.

I saw people around me—talented, enthusiastic people—trying to write interesting radio scripts. One after another they were shot down. "This is a sensitive subject," they would be told. Or, "This is something the foreigners won't understand." Or, "We don't know the proper line on this."

The longer I was out of prison, the more my head began to

unfreeze and I found myself unwilling to say that anything the party wanted to say or do was great. I looked over our broadcasts and realized there was no content to our stories, few facts in our economic news reports. We were like a court gazette, leading off our daily newscasts with bulletins about the happenings of the royals. Mao met this world leader. Zhou Enlai went to the airport to see this visitor. Liu Shaoqi hosted this delegation.

And what about me? More and more I thought back to my early years as a labor organizer in the South, teaching Marxist economics to mill hands, exhorting white women workers to rise up and support their black sisters during the Merita Bakery strike, spending time in Bull Connor's jail for what I believed in. I had been a world-changer, a mover of hearts and stirrer of souls, an activist, an organizer, a proselytizer, an educator. What was I here? A pencil-pushing bureaucrat. I didn't want to spend the rest of my life translating crop yields at the Broadcast Administration. I wanted to reach people, to be where the real action was.

CHAPTER FOURTEEN

The Inner Circle

True to his word, my old friend Liao Chengzhi had offered me a path out, and with his help, I began to emerge as a public figure in my own right. He not only reintroduced me to the diplomatic world of the senior party leaders, he also smoothed my way to a more influential role in party activities.

I had already had long experience as an informal political worker for the party. Mei Yi had always approved and supported my work with the foreigners' study groups. But because of my duties at the Broadcast Administration, I had been reluctant to involve myself too deeply in such outside activities. Liao knew of my work and had whispered a few words in the right ears, giving me authorization from the very top to do something that no one had done before: to play a bold, independent role in expanding as widely as possible the Chinese Communist Party's influence among the foreign community in Beijing, and through them to influence the worldwide contest between the Chinese and the Russians for the loyalty of revolutionaries everywhere. I was delighted with my new mandate. I was back in business, I thought, once again in an important, organizing role.

The party really needed me. The split with the Soviets was threatening all the alliances and working relationships with other countries that China had built up since the revolution. When the

Soviets went home, everyone else had to choose: go with the Soviets or stay and remain as friends of the Chinese. For the Chinese government, it was critical that as many alliances be preserved as possible, and that foreign experts remain living and working here. The pullout of Soviet experts from factories had crippled Chinese industry. The loss of too many foreign experts who helped with translating, polishing, and language training would just as surely cripple our propaganda work. So just as the party was fighting a desperate battle to wrest the loyalties of the Communist parties around the world from the Soviets, I began to fight a battle to maintain personal loyalties.

With some, of course, it was a losing cause. Those with the closest ties to the Soviets, like the East Germans and the Spaniards, went home when the Soviets did. The Jordanian Arabs pulled out, forcing the Broadcast Administration's Arabic section to scramble to find a mullah from China's northwest to take over the job of polishing and translating. But others were on the fence. The Canadians and Australians wavered, some going with the Chinese, some the Soviets. Giorgio Zucchetti, an Italian Communist from Perugia, was ordered by his party to return home, but refused, after reassuring himself through me that the Chinese would guarantee him a position. It was my job to nurture the loyalty of the foreigners who chose to stay in China, whatever their nationality.

Mei Yi enthusiastically supported my new endeavor. My successes would redound to his credit. What's more, influence and information could be a two-way street. If I kept him abreast of goings-on in the foreign community, he might use the information as an asset in his own advancement.

Although Mei Yi remained my boss, he gave me permission to operate virtually autonomously. "There aren't many people who can speak as freely as you can, or be as influential as you can be," he said. "Go ahead and do whatever you think you should." He told me I could be free about interpreting policy and taking whatever steps I felt were necessary on my own. "If you make mistakes, we'll just spank you and then you'll know better next time, that's all. If I'm in a meeting, get my secretary to call me out. If the English section is upset by your outside activities, I'll take care of it."

At the same time, the Sino-Soviet split gave me a different view into Chinese circles of power—one that I had never seen before. After the split, the Communist Party began issuing a numbered series of polemics attacking Khrushchev for toadying to the West, for revisionism, for expansionism, and for imperialism. But the Chinese leaders, quite rightly, didn't trust their own press, or the press in other countries, to translate such sensitive materials accurately. So they put together another elite team. The Mao translation team had included several foreigners, but this time I was often the only foreigner cleared to work on the translations while they were still not in final form. Alone among foreigners qualified for such work, I was a party member and thus could be entrusted with party secrets. These were not trivial issues. China and the Soviet Union were fighting for nothing less than control of the world revolution, which they saw as including leadership over the Third World countries. At the same time, the Chinese leaders, among themselves, were also working out their own differences on these same vital issues.

The physical secrecy was much greater than when I had worked on the Mao translations. The translation of the polemics was done at the Xinhua News Agency, and I was whisked in and out of the agency compound in a car with curtained windows. I worked in a back office with other specially cleared translators. I wasn't allowed to walk through the rest of the compound. If any of my friends at Xinhua happened to spot me, I was not to tell them what I was doing there. At lunch and dinnertime, meals were brought to me in enameled boxes, so that I would not be seen eating in the Xinhua canteen.

Once I began working on the translations, I immediately realized the reason for the secrecy. Unlike the Mao translations, which had already been revised, read, and approved by the Central Committee before we ever saw them, these polemics were being sent to us directly from the drafters. And as we translated each successive draft, with corrections, emendations, arguments, and conflicts clearly laid out in each Central Committee leader's distinctive handwriting, it was as if I was sitting in on the debates myself. Often I could see Mao's style and arguments creeping in bit by bit until finally they nearly overwhelmed the original document.

One early polemic was called "On Nehru's Philosophy." It was about the Sino-Indian border conflict, and was written to demonstrate that the Chinese road—not the Soviet one, which was becoming too revisionist—was the right one for the Third World. We began to work immediately on the translation, but before too long, the emendations were pouring in.

The polemic went through more than two dozen drafts. Zhou

Enlai's measured comments were written in a neat, controlled, circular calligraphy. His writing was regular and easy to read, each character in its proper square on the special paper designed for Chinese writing, which wasn't lined like Western paper, but rather marked out in faint blue boxes. Zhou would sometimes support one side of the argument and sometimes the other. Then there was Liu Shaoqi, Mao's second-in-command and anointed heir. He wrote like a scribe, conventional in most cases but occasionally indulging in flourishes and inventive styles.

Mao, on the other hand, wrote in a classical flourish with attention to the differences between thick and thin strokes, and to the hooks and embellishments appropriate to each character. His style was the easiest of all to recognize, and sometimes the hardest to read. His characters were of uneven height, some of them less than a quarter of an inch high, some more than an inch and a half high, bursting out of the line.

Through successive drafts, more and more of the document was covered with Mao's florid calligraphy until, in its final version, to my eye it was all Mao. And the blunt, withering, dogmatic style of the original draft had been replaced by something more sophisticated, more subtle, and at the same time more biting, more sarcastic, and much more finely crafted. The original began as a blistering attack on Nehru. The final version was a caring little sermon, which angered the Indian leaders even more than a frontal attack would have.

◆

By the summer of 1963, the worst edge was off the great hunger. The Broadcast Administration canteen had begun serving enough food to go around. Grain rations were slowly restored, and it took fewer coupons than before to buy rice and wheat. Yulin's face was still puffy and swollen, but it seemed to be getting better. Little by little some pork and green vegetables were reappearing in the meals served at her school. That summer when we went for our evening walks on weekends, we noticed that some of the restaurants that had been closed for almost a year were beginning to reopen, serving simple but adequate dishes. By the end of the summer, the vendors of foods from the night markets were returning to the streets.

People still railed indignantly about the Soviets. But internally, we were enjoying an unexpected bit of peace. The political mass movements had gone still. Whatever battles were being fought by the leaders up in the mountains were being fought in secret. A people battered by an unremitting series of shocks and attacks didn't ask too many questions, or wonder too much at the calm. Everyone just took it as a gift and enjoyed it.

My family had grown. We now had three little girls. The youngest had been born in 1959, in what was then the Sino-Soviet Friendship Hospital, but which after the split had been renamed simply the Friendship Hospital. She had been born at a time when the world was agape over Sputnik and fascinated with the power of rockets. So we called her Xiaoxiang, using a character that means "to soar." She was a strong-willed, impetuous little girl from the first, a bit of a rocket herself. Yulin never made it onto the maternity ward, but delivered her right in the examining room.

Yulin was still in school in 1963, living there six days a week and coming home only from Saturday night to Sunday afternoon. And when she was home, we frolicked like kids. She loved sunflower seeds and, like all Chinese, loved cracking them open at the movies or the theater. She had perfected the art of positioning a seed between her teeth and opening the shell with one bite to get at the kernel. Whenever I tried it, the seed dropped to the floor. "Poor man," she would whisper in a loud sotto voce. "Coming from a land of such high technology and he can't even open a sunflower seed." Giggling, she would crack open a few and hand them over.

We went to the Temple of Heaven Park and at the shops there bought red lion dogs and paper tigers for the children. We stood at opposite ends of the famous echo wall and tried to pick out our words from among all the whispers and calls being passed back and forth between dozens of other couples.

Yulin put her face to the wall and whispered, but down the line I shook my head. She whispered again. Again I heard nothing. Stepping back from the wall, she shouted, "I'm saying, 'Hello, Sid!' Can't you hear me?" Then she tried again and suddenly I heard her voice echoing along the length of the curving wall: "Li Dunbai is a turtle egg"—a bastard, a son of a bitch. I immediately jerked upright and glared in her direction.

Yulin was doubled over laughing. "You see," she gloated, "you can hear me just fine."

With Yulin gone during the week, Mama played a major role in raising our girls. In the evenings after supper, I would watch her sweeping the floor with a long-handled broom while one of the girls followed behind sweeping with a little whisk broom to the great encouragement and admiration of her grandmother. Mama would never allow any child to be abused or even shouted at. "They're too little, they don't understand," she said. "You can't just scold them. You have to start from where they are and coax them around to where they ought to be. Don't let them cry. They'll cry their eyes out. I had such a hard time, and I'm not going to let them suffer."

When our number two daughter, Xiaodong, at age two, nearly died from a sudden and inexplicable seizure, it was Mama who kept her calm. "Don't worry," she said serenely as we fearfully rushed off to the hospital. "Children don't die in the New China. Xiaodong will be all right."

By age two, each of our girls went off to nursery school. On Monday mornings, their grandfather, who still lived in a little adobe house down a small lane not far from us, wheeled his bicycle over to our house and planted each girl in her own spot on the bike. With one on the seat, one on the crossbar, and one on the handlebars, he then walked the bicycle from our house to the nursery school, which was near the senior leaders' Diaoyutai guest house. On the way, he told them the classical *Tales of the Three Kingdoms*.

There was a camel stand directly in front of the girls' school. It was the end of the same camel trail that snaked down from Xinjiang in the remote northwest, across the desert and through the darkness in front of the caves in Yanan. Even in the New China, camels made that long and difficult journey into the heart of modern, bustling Beijing.

The city came alive, and on weekends my whole family would stroll out together, taking the blue-topped East German trolley buses to one of the many parks. These parks, formal, symmetrical, and relatively sedate in cold weather, were now alive with activity. There were all sorts of acrobatic and circus performances; minstrels who sang the Chinese Homeric tales accompanied by their own drumbeat or a Chinese lute or dulcimer; singers of political pop tunes, with lots of love songs smuggled in under cover of political lyrics. There were magicians and jugglers. Once in the Working People's Palace of Culture, right beside the Forbidden City palaces, a young magician cast a hook, line, and sinker at me and pulled a wriggly little fish out of my right front trouser pocket, to my eternal mystification.

Girls and young women blossomed out in skirts and dresses,

the men in short-sleeved tailless shirts and sandals. There were thousands of people everywhere: old men swinging bird cages, young men pedaling by to a remote place to release their homing pigeons for a flight back, elderly single men shuffling along singing, hands clasped behind their backs, trailing long wisps of haunting Peking opera in their wake.

Children were kings and queens in Beijing, and in summer the popsicle was the royal scepter. Every family, including our own, had to negotiate with their tots about whether they were or were not going to be bought popsicles, and if so, how many. Middle-aged women and elderly men and women added to the family income by pushing the omnipresent little four-wheeled cabinets containing vanilla, cream, and haw-fruit popsicles wrapped up in thick quilts against the blazing sun. It was a happy time for me and my family. The great hunger was behind us and we had high hopes for what might lie ahead.

◆

When I did go to the Broadcast Administration, usually in the morning, I squeezed as much work as possible in the shortest time possible. But my heart wasn't in it. I took less care with the features than I had in earlier years, and often didn't bother with the thankless, and nearly impossible, task of trying to make the programs interesting. The interesting part of my day began at eleven-thirty when I hopped a ride with one of the Latin American comrades, heading up to the Friendship Hotel and to lunch. It was there that my political work began.

The big dining room for foreign experts at the Friendship Hotel was an arena of cliques, klatches, and table-hoppers. There was a table for Dr. George Hatem with the German Dr. Hans Mueller and his Japanese wife, his Singaporean friend Chet Lim and Chet's Australian wife. African-Asian-Arab friends and the Maoist Latin Americans made up other tables. There were Chileans, Brazilians, Colombians, Uruguayans, one lone Paraguayan, Argentineans, Peruvians, Venezuelans, and Bolivians. There were Cubans you could spot by their cocky macho walk even before you met them, and a mystically romantic, quietly ardent black Haitian with beautiful deep saintly eyes. At the West German Marxist table, there was much stiff humor, stacks of meat and potatoes, and battalions of beer bottles. When I showed up, I sat with the people I needed to talk to the most, and table-hopped around to the others, saying whatever I had to say. Often, one big table would be formed by putting several together, and a great gang of people would eat and talk around it.

We told Khrushchev jokes, like the one about the man who was sentenced to ten years and two days for running through the streets shouting, "Khrushchev is an idiot!" Why such a bizarre sentence? the prisoner asked. "Two days for slandering our leader, and ten years for revealing state secrets," replied the judge. We would howl and slap our thighs with delight.

All of the joking and raconteuring was to set the mood for my political work. I took very seriously my job of briefing the foreigners intimately on the latest revisionist crimes in the Soviet Union. To Latin Americans, for example, I told stories of how Khrushchev utilized the blockade against Castro to force Cuba into a dependent position, both politically and economically, and how the Soviet agreement to buy the embargoed Cuban sugar squeezed blood out of the Cuban economy in return.

For Africans, there were stories about how the Soviets toadied to the reactionaries in their countries in order to sell arms and gain UN votes, while refusing the African revolutionaries the guns and the support they needed. For Americans I stressed issues of revolutionary principle and made fun of the ridiculous way in which the Soviets treated foreigners in Moscow as well as those in transit through Moscow airport on their way to China or Vietnam.

It was delicate work, knowing exactly how much to say, how far to push, and then retreating and having the patience to wait until I was asked for more information. And underlying it all was my own understanding of Mao and Mao's brand of Marxism. Think for yourself, I would tell my comrades from other countries. No need to follow this line or that line. Here are the facts, make up your mind yourselves. Good Communists must learn to think for themselves.

No one was telling me what to say. By then I thought I knew the Chinese Communist line more intimately than perhaps many people far more senior than I and I believed fervently in what I told my foreign comrades.

Then suddenly, in August 1963, I was boosted into even greater prominence. I was sitting in my office at the Broadcast Administration when Ding Yilan poked her head through the door. She had been exiled to the country during one of the last movements against the counterrevolutionaries for daring to write in her diary that the Great Leap Forward was making her worry about Mao's sanity. Recently she had returned, exonerated and rehabilitated.

"I have some great news for you," Ding Yilan said, her soft face all lit up. "You are going to be received by Chairman Mao. You have to leave right away because you might be late."

There was no time to go home and wash up or change clothes, and indeed there really was no need. "There's a car ready for you and its license number has already been reported to Zhongnan-hai."

Roman candles went off in my head. I didn't have a clue why Mao wanted to see me, but I knew it must be important. I hadn't seen him since before I was imprisoned.

The driver who was waiting for me at the gate was one I knew. He was specially cleared to drive into the Central Committee's compound at Zhongnanhai. We swept down the street, were waved into the compound, and drove up to the state council meeting hall, the Qin Zheng Ting—the Hall for Diligence in Government Affairs—a wood-paneled pavilion, stately and elegant. There I was met by an attendant who walked me down a long corridor with antechambers on either side. We stopped before one and he motioned me to go in. It was a small room just large enough for six to sit comfortably, three on each side. Frank Coe was there, smoking a cigar. The American Marxist economist and I were friends from our days on the Mao translation team.

"What's happening?" I asked.

Frank said, "Mao is receiving some African guerrilla leaders and is also going to answer a letter from Robert Williams." A black preacher from Munro, North Carolina, Robert Williams was an ardent fighter for black rights and favored arming blacks for self-defense against the Klan and lynch mobs.

"They want us to go over the English text of the letter, and Mao wants our opinion of the contents," Frank said. And sure enough, just as he was talking, someone from the foreign ministry entered the room and brought in the text of the letter, typed out in English, that Mao was going to read. That night, the official told us, the text would be transmitted over the Xinhua news service. Frank and I sat down and hurriedly polished the text. The translation wasn't bad, but some awkward points needed smoothing over. The only change we suggested was the addition of American Indians to a list Mao had offered of American ethnic groups struggling for equality.

We were then escorted into the main meeting hall. Mao himself greeted us at the door, shaking hands, murmuring, "Thank you for coming." He looked just as I had remembered him, better perhaps, now that the strain of fighting a war was behind him. His shining black hair was untouched with gray. His soft eyes still had the odd androgynous quality I remembered from our days in Yanan.

The African guests were already assembled in the hall, standing just inside the open door. There were about twenty people, none from an independent African state. They were all from various nationalist organizations or guerrilla movements. More than half of them were in traditional African dress, long loose gowns with gorgeous purple and gold and green fabric billowing out around them. Some wore headdresses to match. I knew that a few of them were receiving military training in China. I recognized a cherubic young student who had once told me he was learning from the People's Liberation Army how to use small arms, hand grenades, land mines, and booby traps.

The room was arranged in standard Chinese meeting style, side-by-side overstuffed chairs for Mao as host and for the guests of honor, flanking wings of overstuffed chairs for lower-ranking honored guests, and rows of smaller chairs for everyone else, including secretaries and note-takers. There was also the usual bleacherlike wooden contraption for group picture taking. We all mounted in rows for the obligatory group photo. While the picture was being taken, Mao assured the group that the photo wouldn't be printed, since many of the guerrilla leaders were meeting here secretly. Then he sat down in the center of the hall. Frank and I were ushered to our places on the side.

"On behalf of the Chinese Communist Party, and of the People's Republic of China," Mao began, "I'd like to welcome all our friends and comrades-in-arms from Africa." He was giving a standard diplomatic opening. "The first thing I would like to do is read this letter," he continued. It was the letter that Frank and I had worked on. By this time, everyone in the room had a copy, a stapled sheaf of papers. Mao began to read, but in the middle of the first sentence he stopped and looked quizzically at the diminutive young woman who was secretary of the meeting. "I can see that everyone has a copy. Do I have to read this whole thing?" The secretary hurriedly assured him he did not.

Then Mao relaxed, leaned back in his chair, and lit a cigarette. After the meeting Frank told me he had counted: eight cigarettes in the one-hour meeting.

"I know you are having a very difficult struggle in Africa, and you've already scored many successes," Mao said. "Many battles remain to be fought, but Africa is coming alive. It is making its presence known. Here in China, we knew little about Africa. Then as you fought for independence and were successful, your countries came and made their presence known to us. Now, before I say any more, I would like to hear what you have to say."

A young visitor from Southern Rhodesia, a big, strapping, square-shouldered man in his mid-twenties, stood up. "I have a question I would like to ask Chairman Mao," he said. "When I am lying there in the jungle at night, I worry. Do you know what I worry about? I don't worry about the white colonialists or the lion or the rhinoceros. I worry because there used to be a red star that burned over the Kremlin. The Soviets used to help us, and then the red star went out and they don't help us anymore. On the contrary, they sell arms to our oppressors. What I worry about is: Will the red star over Tiananmen Square in China go out? Will you abandon us and sell arms to our oppressors as well? If that happens, we will be all alone."

I felt the young man's worry was justified. Khrushchev, with his fear of thermonuclear war, had abandoned the Soviet policy of supporting armed revolutionary struggle in favor of negotiation and accommodation with the United States.

Mao took a few puffs on his cigarette. "I understand your question," he said. "It is that the USSR has turned revisionist and has betrayed the revolution. Can I guarantee to you that China won't betray the revolution? Right now I can't give you that guarantee. We are searching very hard to find the way to keep China from becoming corrupt, bureaucratic, and revisionist.

"We have already taken a number of measures," he continued. "We try to teach our cadres to listen to what the masses are saying. We have various systems like requiring every officer in the army to spend one month as a private in the ranks, and requiring office cadres to go down to the countryside at least one month a year, so that they don't lose touch with the masses, and so that they can learn about the lives of working people. We advocate having factory workers take part in the management of the factory, having managers take part in physical labor. But are all these measures sufficient so that we are guaranteed against revisionism? No, I don't think we have solved this question."

I was intrigued. It sounded like Mao was worried about the very things I was worried about: bureaucracy, stagnation.

"We are very disturbed," Mao continued, "when we talk to our children and grandchildren and we find that they don't understand the bitterness, the hardships of the Revolution, and what sacrifices it took to get where we are today. We are disturbed that they don't feel the need to keep the Revolution going. We are afraid that we will stop being a revolutionary country and will become a revisionist one. When that happens in a socialist country, they become worse than a capitalist country. A Communist party can turn into a fascist party. We've seen that happen in the Soviet Union. We understand the seriousness of this problem, but we don't know how to handle it yet."

Mao took a few more questions. Then he turned in my direction, startling me. "Here is our good friend Comrade Li Dunbai," he said. "Comrade Li Dunbai, will you stand up please?"

I stood.

"Now please look at him," Mao said. "He is an American. He is a white man. Are you afraid of him?" The Africans in the room all burst out laughing. Mao laughed too, throwing back his head and roaring in the way that I remembered from back in Yanan. "There's no need to be afraid of him. He is an American, but he is our friend. He understands us, and we understand him. He is an internationalist fighter for Communism."

I remained standing and Mao went on. "It's very important for you to know this. Who is Chiang Kai-shek? He is a Chinese. His skin is yellow, just like mine. Chiang Kai-shek, this yellow-skinned Chinese, is our enemy, while Li Dunbai, this white-skinned American, is our friend. Not all white people are your enemy. It is very important to unite with as many friends as possible. We have a saying in China. Narrow your circle of enemies to the smallest possible, and enlarge your circle of friends as widely as possible."

I liked what Mao was saying. He was saying that nationalism was fine, but limited, and that racism was poison for the Revolution. Underlying his words was a single message. Only Marxism, which unites all people of all nations and races, can solve your problems.

For all of the next day back at the Broadcast Administration, people came running up to me excitedly to point out the story of the meeting in the *People's Daily*. And there I was, right in the story.

After that, I saw Mao, Zhou Enlai, and the other leaders at least once or twice a year. Because of the new formality of government in the big city, our meetings weren't as relaxed and casual as they had been during our days in the caves. But in many ways our relationship was closer. My time in prison had tested me, proved me loyal, given me a shared experience with many of their best revolutionaries. I could clearly feel that I was one of them in a way that I had never been in Yanan.

Sometimes our meetings were social. Anna Louise Strong's birthday parties in November were the event of the season. The Chinese still loved and revered her. Several of the most senior leaders would always turn out for her birthday banquet. But often these social meetings were occasions on which Mao would reveal some news or policy tidbit. In January of 1964, he hosted a dinner for the group of us who had translated his works, a kind of thank-you meal. It was in the same place as my last meeting with him and the Africans, the old Qing dynasty Shrine for Diligent Government.

Frank Coe, Sol Adler, Israel Epstein, and I arrived together in a group at about two P.M., along with Anna Louise Strong, who had also been invited. Mao was standing in the doorway to the hall, waiting to greet us. Qi Xiyu, the high-strung but talented interpreter from the English section of the central liaison department, was at his side. Mao greeted each one of us by name and asked after our wives.

The furnishings of the long rectangular room in which we met were the same as in plush party meeting rooms everywhere: over-stuffed easy chairs with lace antimacassars, little tea tables arranged in front of each chair, and strategically placed plump porcelain spittoons. There were some small Chinese paintings on the walls, and the east end of the room was hidden behind a dark red velvet curtain. The easy chairs were arranged in a semicircle. Mao took his chair in the center of the arc with Anna Louise to his right and the rest of us distributed on both sides.

Mao greeted Anna Louise warmly. "When you were in Yanan and the bombing started, you wanted to stay, but we wouldn't let you," he told her. "We were wrong. If you had stayed, you wouldn't have been arrested as a spy in Moscow and had all that trouble. And we wouldn't have caused all that trouble for him. He was implicated by your case." Mao nodded in my direction. "We made a very bad mistake in his case. He is a good comrade and we treated him wrong."

"I had a good experience," I said.

Mao looked at me as if I was crazy. There was an instant of silence and suddenly an old feeling returned, the feeling that had first struck me in Yanan. This man doesn't like me, not one little bit. "Yes," he said, a bit coldly, I thought, "you had the experience of sitting in the slammer."

He turned away from me. Then he gestured at a tense, unsmiling man nearby. "Khrushchev says that I am full of empty talk," Mao said. "I'd like you to meet Comrade Kang Sheng, my Minister of Empty Talk." Kang looked about the room with a supercilious gaze, almost a leer. I had never seen him before and found little to like about him in this meeting. He seemed cold, distant, plotting, suspicious, only unbending to pour flattery over Mao. But it was evident that he enjoyed Mao's favor. Mao's introduction was clearly intended as a complimentary one. He was telling us that even though Lu Dingyi was minister of propaganda Kang Sheng was in charge of the polemical articles that were coming out, and that I was helping to translate.

Then Mao turned the conversation to Khrushchev himself and made a startling revelation. "Khrushchev came here secretly," he said, referring to a meeting that none of us had ever heard of before. Mao turned to address Israel Epstein. "I sat where I am sitting, and he sat where you are sitting, and we talked. Khrushchev said that the relationship between the Chinese party and the Soviet party should be strengthened."

Mao lit a cigarette. "Then he proposed that we agree to establish a composite Sino-Soviet Pacific fleet. If we agreed to that, Khrushchev said, then he would give us the vessels to make up the Chinese part of the fleet. We were to allow this fleet to use the port of Dalian, and we would set aside an area there for the Soviet navy, which would be governed by a Soviet commandant, and which would fly the Soviet flag. Also, we would designate two other ocean ports that the Soviet navy would be allowed to use."

We were all astounded by this news but we kept silent. "They also wanted missile bases," Mao said. "They wanted us to give them bases where they could put Soviet missiles aimed at American bases in Japan." He had a gleam in his eyes as he continued. "So then I said to him: 'Suppose I give you the whole China coast and all our ports. How would that be?' " Mao paused, waiting to deliver the punch line. "Khrushchev just looked at me puzzled and then he said: 'But if you do that, then what will you do?' And I said: 'Me? Oh, I would just go back to Yanan and be a guerrilla leader again and organize guerrilla warfare. But I just want to remind you that historically we Chinese have always driven aggressors into the sea, and we will drive you into the sea as well.' "

Mao threw back his head and roared with laughter. Then he looked around the room disingenuously. "You know," he said, "Khrushchev got very angry with me. He said: 'But this sort of comradely relationship is the normal relationship that we have with our fraternal parties in Eastern Europe.' And I told him: 'We have observed that. That is why we aren't going to have it in China.' "

Mao lit another cigarette. "Khrushchev wanted us to conduct the fighting according to his rule book," he said. "But," he continued, wagging his finger, "never fight a battle according to your enemy's rules. We used to say in the war with the Japanese, 'You fight your way and we'll fight ours,' and you have to do the same thing fighting the revisionists. All people whose thinking is retrograde share one problem in common: they overestimate themselves and underestimate the people's forces."

Underneath all this talk, there was something on Mao's mind. Something was pressing him, keeping him restless and dissatisfied. He kept circling back to a topic that I had last heard at the meeting with the Africans six months earlier. The subject was revolution. It seemed to be a topic much on his mind.

"Some people think that when you get to socialism, the revolution is over," Mao said. "Don't believe for a minute everyone in China is for socialism. That's not true. We have people here who are against socialism. There aren't many, but they exist. I don't believe there is such a thing as an end to revolution. To make the transition from socialism to Communism will mean a revolution. Even after we get to Communism there will be a revolution. It seems to me that there will always be revolution, even ten thousand years from now. Otherwise what will people like us do? We'll be unemployed."

Again, Mao threw back his head and let out gales of laughter. But I knew he was dead serious and had already decided that the only way to prevent revisionism in China was to have another revolution. But how? And when? And against whom?

Just then, Mao spotted his wife emerging from behind the velvet drapes. "Ah, Comrade Jiang Qing is inviting us to dinner," he said, rising. The drapes were drawn to reveal a long table set for our meal. Mao seated himself at one end of the table, Jiang Qing at the other. We continued our conversation for several more hours, but Jiang Qing, facing her husband, sat silently through the entire meal.

CHAPTER FIFTEEN

The Good Life

My star was rising. Over the next two years I was more and more at the center of things, more and more called on to perform sensitive and delicate tasks, more and more appreciated and lionized for my efforts.

Everywhere I was in great demand. At Chairman Mao's personal request, I set up a network to translate and circulate Anna Louise Strong's *Letters from China.* I began a whirlwind, one-man campaign to set up the translation network in Beijing and recruited a translator from nearly every major language group. There were Yemenis who spoke Arabic, Indians who translated into Hindi. I recruited French, Italians, Portuguese, Indonesians and Malaysians, Thais, Japanese, Albanians, and a Yugoslavian to translate into Serbo-Croatian.

From then on, we had a sizable network that helped nurture anti-Soviet splinter Communist and left-wing nationalist groups in many countries. We were also an effective conduit for strategic leaks, like the time when Foreign Minister Marshal Chen Yi told Anna Louise "in confidence" the three conditions under which China would enter the Vietnam War in force, demanding secrecy of her and knowing that, loyal as she was, her uncontrollable urge to get news out made her a perfect pipeline to the American authorities.

Many of these expatriates became my friends. There was Amadou of Niger, a devout Muslim who would enter the dining room at the Friendship Hotel carrying a silver teapot filled with holy water. Tall and striking in his white robes, he would bow to all he passed, murmuring courteously: "Bonjour, bonjour." He held elegant little tea parties and invited our daughters to attend. Mario Arencibia, who translated into Spanish, was a famous Chilean bolero singer, who from time to time entertained us with his haunting tunes. I held a study group for many of these people in my own home, holding forth on Maoist theory and the latest topics of current interest. Then we would all laugh and joke, and eat wonderful meals that either Yulin or Mama prepared.

Apart from these gatherings, I spent less and less time at home. The polemics against Khrushchev were coming at a more furious pace than ever before, and I worked long hours translating them under very great tension. I was considered a crack translator. I was fast, but I still checked meticulously as I went along, because I was such a purist about finding an exact correlation between the Chinese and the English.

The central leaders' schedules added to the tension. I often worked all day long translating the latest polemic. Then around five P.M., as I was about to break for supper, a new version would suddenly arrive and I had to start all over again. Late in the evening, more new versions or revisions would begin to pour in and I tried to keep up with them before stumbling home to bed. Just as they had in Yanan, the central leaders worked from around nine P.M. until close to dawn. Most of them, like Mao, had insomnia and needed very little sleep. They went to bed between three and five A.M., slept until lunch, worked in the afternoon, and then, after meeting with foreign dignitaries at dinnertime, began work again at night. All their retinue, their secretaries, messengers, nurses, and translators like me had to adjust to that schedule.

Meanwhile, the editors and translators at the Broadcast Administration were always frantically trying to get my help in untying some particularly obscure phrase. Often, they couldn't find me in the daytime, so they called me at night, sometimes in the middle of the night.

Ring, ring, ring. Sleepily, I would pick up the phone to hear a frantic questioner. "The House of Representatives has set up an oversight committee on spending in the judicial branch. Doesn't oversight mean something that you didn't catch? Does that mean that it is a committee to catch mistakes?"

Ring, ring, ring. One A.M. "It says here: 'I thought they were putting me on.' What does that mean?" "There's a story here about a judge who is a 'competent authority' over a certain area. What does competent authority mean?" After the Cuban Missile Crisis, a Washington official said that the two sides were "eyeball to eyeball, and the other fellow blinked." My callers thought they knew what that meant, but they weren't certain.

Yulin wasn't often home herself during this period, since she was still living at her school six days a week. But when she was home on weekends, she was cross at the interruptions. "Don't those people know how to use a dictionary?" she would grumble when the phone interrupted our sleep for the third time in a night. "They're just being lazy."

But it was more than just my translation work that kept me busy. Through my translation network, I had become not only a celebrity in Beijing, but a bit of a gourmet and theater buff as well. People were seeking out my company, not just for the inside political information I could be counted on to dispense, but also for my intimate knowledge of Beijing's attractions. Night after night, weekend after weekend, I set up restaurant parties at the request of whoever wanted them—Latin Americans, Italians, French, Belgians—and, of course, very frequently, Americans. In a country without advertising, the only way foreigners could learn about a good restaurant was when someone in the know, like me, told them. I knew the spots, I knew what each specialized in.

I steered my guests away from the most famous Peking duck restaurants, the Chuanjude chain, in favor of two lesser-known places whose food was more savory. Sometimes I suggested the wonderful little Shanghai eatery in the Lane of the Goldfish Sellers that was called the Three Tables because there were only three big tables that seated fifteen each.

Or perhaps I chose the Xinjiang restaurant, with Uigur shish kebab, Gobi Desert Muslim bread, and marinated whitefish in vinegar. Or the Tongchunyuan, where you could munch huge Shandong fried pancakes, wrapped around green onions dipped in plum sauce. I often recommended Donglaishun, the Muslim restaurant near the end of Wangfujing Street, where, it was said, the fire never went out under the Mongolian hot pots. There you could simmer your own paper-thin strips of lamb to eat with sweet pickled garlic, shredded cabbage, spinach leaves, small pancakes for a wrapping, and crisp sesame seed cakes.

Sometimes I would take parties to the Peking opera, or to the local vernacular operas, which were less stylized, were often comedies of manners, and were sung in more popular musical modes. I would translate the show for my guests in great detail, stories like that of a stupid Imperial scholar saved from disgrace by a feisty wife; or of a Han dynasty scholar who refused to turn against his master; or of an ancient general who returned after eighteen years in the emperor's service to test his wife and find her still faithful. I often took groups boating on the lake at the Summer Palace, sightseeing in the Forbidden City, or climbing around the temples in the Western Hills, where I translated the ancient inscriptions with great pride. Important work, a devoted family, good friends—I couldn't imagine a happier life.

◆

The tigers in the mountains were still fighting. The Great Leap Forward was over, but its effects were not. Finally, the errors of the Leap had come home to roost on Mao and he had decided to beat a strategic retreat to what he called the "second echelon" of leadership. He had resigned as president of the People's Republic. The more pragmatic and practical Liu Shaoqi and Deng Xiaoping were running the show now, trying to restore order.

Meanwhile, a new political movement—called the Four Clears —was getting under way. At the Broadcast Administration, the campaign took its usual form, with selected individuals chosen for criticism, long struggle meetings, and self-examinations. Aside from going after graft, malfeasance, and gross waste, the main targets in the foreign broadcast sections were things like bourgeois individualism—trying to stick your head up above your fellow workers.

Over the previous few months, I had been absent from the Broadcast Administration more than I had been there. My political work was just too important to be interrupted, I decided. But when the Four Clears movement began, it was mandatory for every party member to participate. I was ordered back to work. Confident in my new role, I took a bold step. I defied the party committee at the Broadcast Administration. I refused to return.

They tried to get me to change my mind. Sometimes when I went to the Broadcast Administration in the morning for a bit of work, Wei Lin would accost me and attempt to talk me into returning for the afternoon's meetings. I refused. Assistant Branch Secretary Ye Jidong also buttonholed me for a similar talk. I brushed him away too. Then Meng Jiefu, the department head, told me the party committee at the Broadcast Administration had decided that I, like all other party members, had to return to participate in the Four Clears movement. This was serious business. If I refused such an order I could be disciplined by the party. Still I refused. I was sick of these movements, sick of the waste of time, sick of the fear and the unfairness. I told Old Meng I simply had too many outside obligations, and that I would come if I could. But I never did.

I not only ducked the party, I openly challenged it. I wrote a letter to Mei Yi, detailing my complaints about Radio Beijing. The problem wasn't the individuals doing the work, I said. It was the mind-set of the leadership. The whole structure of the Broadcast Administration determined that party officials, not real journalists, controlled the news. Mei Yi circulated my memo, with a caustic little note attached. "It's good for us to hear even very different opinions," he wrote.

But for all my newfound cheek in challenging the party organizations, inside I was still a rock-solid Communist. The further I got from prison, the more I could challenge what I saw. I was still unable to question what I believed.

Then one day, I was sitting in the classified reading room at the Broadcast Administration, poring over documents, when I came across a note from Mao about the Four Clears movement in the countryside. The document, contained in a red letterhead cable, made clear what Mao considered the real nature of the Four Clears movement to be. It was not just to root out corruption, but to revive class struggle. The document described how a village in Hebei had solved its problem of corruption by treating some erring village cadres as class enemies. A note from Mao, printed in extra large boldface just below the letterhead, was approving. "Class struggle," he wrote. "All you have to do is take hold of that, and it works immediately."

As I read the note, suddenly my head rebelled. Yes, it works, I thought. But is it right? The landlords had been overthrown and there was scarcely a noticeable difference between village cadres and other poor peasants. Often the cadres in the villages worked harder than anyone else, and what was called corruption was often very minor stuff, like accepting small gifts. To stir up hatreds among the peasants by calling for class struggle might work in the short run. But it was like inciting a lynch mob.

Would class struggle really solve the problems of rural corruption, political apathy, inequity, and tyranny? Just as quickly as that thought emerged, I tamped it down. What the hell do you know? I angrily asked myself. This was Mao talking. This was Central Committee policy. Did I know more about policy than they did?

Underneath my self-censorship was the old fear. I knew this query of mine was heretical. I also knew, from experience, what powerful means the party had for making people talk. I would be loath to conceal anything from the party if I were now asked to reveal nonorthodox thinking. Whatever was inside me, I would tell. The only way to be safe, then, was to suppress the heretical thought myself, before it even had a chance to develop into a full-blown idea. In fact, this sort of self-coercion and self-suppression by the majority, stimulated by ruthless struggle against a small number of vulnerable targets, was what the whole system of ideological control rested on. I knew that and still wanted more than anything else to be correct politically—and safe. My challenges to the party so far were ones of practice, not of dogma.

I believed wholeheartedly, and I suppose I always have, that the enlightened individual should be ready to make sacrifices for the well-being of the masses, since that was the highest good. I kept trying to convince Yulin of that when she complained about the hours I was keeping. Although she was still away at school, weekends she devoted to the family. More and more these days, I didn't. On weekends as well as week nights, I was off at a meeting, or doing a translation, or escorting a group to a new restaurant. "You should pay more attention to the family," Yulin complained. "You haven't spent any time with the children in weeks."

"I'd love to be with the family," I argued, and indeed I meant it. "It's just that the most important thing is our work. You aren't thinking straight," I said.

I always considered Yulin's complaints on this score as a sign of her continuing political backwardness. People should never put concern for themselves and their families first. We were working for the overall picture, for the people. The people were more important than family.

She wasn't buying it.

One afternoon, when we took our Ceylonese friend Kandaswami down to lunch at Wangfujing, Yulin let her bitterness spill over. "I'm really upset with him," she told the portly, dark, white-gowned man. "He spends so little time at home. It's always work work work. Even Saturdays and Sundays. He's either at work or off with his foreign friends all the time."

Then it was my turn to be upset. Not only should I not be

criticized for my behavior—and certainly not in public—I felt I was due praise. I was more dedicated, more committed, and a much better Communist than she was. Her petty complaining wasn't revolutionary, I decided. Despite her good, proletarian class background, it was just ordinary wife stuff.

◆

One day in October I was informed that I had been selected for yet another important task. If I was willing, I could be sent as a member of a delegation to an international conference to support the Vietnamese war for independence.

Willing? It was another sign to me that I was being groomed for ever more important tasks. It was my dream to take on an international role representing the Chinese position to the outside world. I would be opposing the wrong, immoral position of the U.S. government, but I would be taking the position of a true American revolutionary. I thought the Vietnamese in their drive to throw off their oppressors were like the American patriots in 1776, and I heard the American leaders talking about the Vietcong the way the British commanders had talked about Washington's men. I felt that the Vietnamese were fighting a just war against unprovoked aggression.

When I arrived in Vietnam, I was in my element. Ho Chi Minh himself had asked me to introduce a young boy to the conference, a boy who had been scarred and disfigured by American napalm blasts. I really cared about this little boy in his plain blue pants and white pressed shirt with a red scarf. His face was a mass of welts from the napalm bombing. "Tested by his scars," I said, "anyone who supports the struggles of the Vietnamese people to drive out the aggressor and free their country is a true friend."

At the same time I found myself shocked and disillusioned with the Vietnamese Communist Party. I thought they were lying to their own people about major policy issues, and were duplicitous and manipulative with their friends. I didn't feel, as I did with the Chinese, that these people were trustworthy.

When, a few months later, Anna Louise and I returned to Vietnam, we had a chance to visit with some American prisoners of war. It was largely Anna Louise's idea. She thought she might be able to help be a conduit for mail between these prisoners and their families back home.

We never saw the prison camp itself. We were introduced to two men, who were brought, one by one, into a reception room to meet us. The men looked gray and drawn, very tense, eyes staring, ill at ease. They stood at attention in front of the little table set up for them until ordered to sit. Then they sat stiffly waiting to be questioned.

Anna Louise spoke first. We had come out of concern for their well-being, she said, and were trying to arrange to send messages home for them. Would they like that? They visibly brightened. One gave his wife's name and address. "Tell her I love her," he said, "and I'm fine and in good health and I live for the day when I can return home and be with her again."

The other prisoner asked if Mr. Rittenberg was among the group. Startled, I identified myself. He said that he knew of me, and had read some speeches by me in the periodicals they were given.

Then Anna Louise asked them how they understood their mission when they first came to Vietnam. They both said they had been told they were coming to enforce the provisions of the Geneva Agreements on Indochina and to help South Vietnam repel an invasion from the North.

"Have you ever read the Geneva Agreements?" I asked.

Both of them said no, and I asked if they hadn't thought it strange to bomb and strafe a people to enforce an agreement they knew nothing about.

One looked awkward and didn't answer. The other spoke up. He had found the picture in Vietnam quite different from what he had been led to believe, he said. He thought Americans had come to defend our allies and our friends. But after being in South Vietnam for a while, he said he doubted anyone here really liked us. Following his capture and on the way to the prison camp, the North Vietnamese had shown him farms, schools, hospitals destroyed by American bombing raids, and he had been distressed. He bore the Vietnamese no ill will, and all he wanted now was to go home.

We asked how they were treated.

Under the watchful eyes of the guard, one answered briskly, but carefully. We are treated very well, he said. When we are sick, we get medical care. I am allowed exercise outside my cell for twenty minutes a day. I am given progressive literature to read, so that I can learn the true situation in the world and reform my attitude.

To Anna Louise and me, the message was clear. He was telling us that he was in tight confinement, allowed out only for a brief period once a day to move around a little, and that he was given no reading matter whatsoever except for the propaganda materials that they decided would be good for him.

At least we might be able to get mail in and out for them, we thought. But when we got back to Beijing, the Chinese refused to let us do that on Chinese soil.

◆

The year 1965 dawned clear and full of hope. The hunger was behind us and once again people's bellies were full. Pork—real pork, not just pork fat—was back in people's lunch tins. Grain was plentiful once more. By midyear, the shops overflowed with fruit and vegetables, and the lines vanished. Schools and clinics were both much improved. The economic news in the papers was good. Factory production was rising and overall the climate was one of recovery.

Everyone was much more relaxed. It had been six years since the Great Leap Forward, and most people now felt free of the kind of scrutiny and harassment that a mass movement inflicted on them. In the cities, the Four Clears movement had turned out to be mild, and with few major victims. Once again, there was a feeling that the era of chasing enemies was over, that it was finally safe to express opinions. The year before, Mao had come out with a statement that from now on people shouldn't be labeled leftist or rightist. Everyone should feel that the period of attacking and putting labels on people was over, and that we were in a new epoch of unity.

At the Broadcast Administration, Xu Meijiang, who had been criticized for his independent translation work, got out his dictionary and began studying English again. I was happy and busy, seeing to the translation and circulation of Anna Louise's letters, still doing official translations for the Central Committee, and coming in to the Broadcast Administration to do whatever work was needed. I was more and more confident of the new policies, and of my own role.

Whatever new developments I saw, I felt were very positive. One day I came into the newsroom to see two or three people gathered around an announcer named Li Xiaodong. They were poring over a little volume bound in red. "It's a collection of quotations from Chairman Mao," the girl said. "I got it from a relative in the army." For the first time, she said, soldiers were being encouraged to study Chairman Mao's works themselves in the form of brief quotations, rather than just hearing political lectures that interpreted them. It seemed that this was Lin Biao's idea, to bring study of Chairman Mao's works directly to the army personnel. The old slogan used to be "Learn from the Party." Nowadays it was changing to "Learn from the PLA."

I had admired Lin Biao as a brilliant commander. Still, I had my own suspicions about him, starting back when I first saw him at a Saturday night dance in the autumn of 1948 a year and a half after we had evacuated Yanan. He was a man with little presence, with a thin wizened face, and a chalky white complexion.

I got the impression that he was arrogant and ambitious. Once at our New China News Agency headquarters, I had picked up a copy of the *Northeast Daily,* put out by the northeast bureau of the party, which Lin Biao headed. On the front page, in the most important position, was an editorial that said everyone should learn from Chairman Mao's strategic thinking, and from Comrade Lin Biao's tactical thinking. I had never heard of any other leader —not the other marshals, not the theoreticians, no one—raised to a level parallel with Mao. That kind of editorial couldn't have been written without Lin Biao's support. I felt his self-aggrandizing was unseemly.

Still, this new program seemed valuable. Maybe he wasn't so bad after all. I thought it was a great idea to ask people—ordinary people—to study Chairman Mao on their own.

Then there was Jiang Qing's opera reform. The Chairman's wife had always been involved in the arts. She herself had been an actress in Shanghai before joining the revolution. Back in Yanan, she had invited me to visit her experimental movie studio. These days, she was busy producing Peking operas on contemporary themes.

All the operas and ballets and music are still based on old themes, she complained in statements published in newspapers. They still focus on the exploits of emperors, generals, scholars, and damsels. She wanted more operas on contemporary themes, on the struggles of workers and peasants, on the glories of revolution. She sponsored eight works, including two ballets and six Peking operas.

When I went to see Jiang Qing's works, I was pleased. I liked operas like the *Chronicle of the Red Lantern,* the story of a revolutionary railway worker's family and their tribulations during a strike. I thought this kind of cultural reform was good. But not everyone agreed. I once met with my old Shanghai friend Xu Maijin, the Peking opera aficionado. He had recently returned from the home of Chen Yun, one of the party vice chairmen. "Chen Yun has just read Jiang Qing's work in an internal document," said Xu Maijin. "He thinks there's only one problem with the new operas. The old ones were better."

With Chairman Mao now somewhat in the background, his conservative comrades were pushing through more practical and pragmatic policies. Mao hadn't been seen in public for several months. Indeed, he hadn't even been in Beijing for some time. Thus it was that on a stormy day in November 1965 Yulin and I arrived at Beijing Capital Airport. The rain was pouring down around us and the wind howled. But we were excited. We were going to Shanghai to see the Chairman.

At least we hoped so. With Chairman Mao, you never could tell. The occasion was Anna Louise Strong's eightieth birthday. The Chinese revere the aged, and eighty years was a particularly important milestone. The Chinese were hosting a birthday banquet for her, and Yulin and I and a dozen or so of her closest friends were being flown down for the occasion. As part of the festivities, we had been promised that the Chairman would probably be able to receive at least a few of us.

Why Shanghai? The Chinese press naturally had mentioned nothing about Mao's absence from Beijing. In fact, I had only learned about it from reading the American press, which was full of articles about the Chairman's mysterious disappearance. Still, I didn't think much about it, because I didn't think much of anything the American press wrote about China. Something was going on in the top leadership that meant Chairman Mao had to be in Shanghai, that was all. Why should that trouble us? In any case, we were all in a jolly mood. And Yulin in particular was keyed up. She had never met Mao before. She had never even been in an airplane.

Yulin had had a lot of trouble finding suitable clothes for the trip. Six and a half months' pregnant with our fourth child, she was a perfect example of why the Chinese call pregnant women "aircraft carriers." They didn't have specially styled maternity clothes. They just depended on bigger and bigger jackets to cover their bulk. But that wouldn't do for a trip to visit the Chairman. Finally Yulin borrowed a copper-colored maternity jacket from Frank Coe's wife, Ruth. She couldn't button her pants, so under the jacket she had tied them up with a cotton sash.

The China Peace Committee, Anna Louise's official hosts, had chartered a Viscount for us. Yulin and I, Anna Louise, Israel

Epstein, Frank Coe, Sol Adler, Rewi Alley, the Chilean artist José Venturelli and his wife, Delia, the American writer Julian Schuman and his wife, Donna, a pair of American teachers, David and Nancy Milton, Dr. George Hatem, and Liao Chengzhi all clambered aboard. The storm continued for the entire trip to Shanghai. The plane bucked and pitched and rolled from side to side. Luggage dropped from the overhead rack and we were all alternately protecting our heads from flying objects or hanging on to keep from being tossed from our seats.

Meanwhile, poor Yulin was miserable. I couldn't blame her. It was just about the roughest flight I had ever taken, even much worse than my midnight ride over the Hump into China. The excitement, her condition, and the dreadful flight had all gone to her stomach. Almost from the moment the plane took off, she began to vomit. She used her airsickness bag, then mine, then George Hatem's, and finally Anna Louise's. Liao Chengzhi, seeing what sad shape she was in, ran back to the galley and returned with a glass of water. But nothing helped. Yulin threw up all the way to Shanghai.

We stayed that night at the Jinjiang Hotel. It was the best Shanghai had to offer, although its prewar elegance had long since faded. The velvet carpets were threadbare, and the sofas and chairs showed unmistakable signs of the thousands of heads and trousers that had rested there.

No one knew when Mao would be available, or if indeed he would receive us at all. So to fill some time the next morning, our hosts ushered us all into Red Flag limousines for a visit to a nearby steel rolling mill. We had barely arrived when a secretary came running breathless from a back office. A phone call had just come in. The Chairman was ready to receive us and we were to return at once. Frantically we piled back in the limousines for the dash back to the hotel.

Chairman Mao was to receive us at the Jinjiang Club, an old social club near the hotel. We arrived at about ten-thirty A.M. Mao was waiting for us in the doorway of the club. He already knew Frank and Sol, Israel Epstein, George Hatem, and me. He greeted us by name. When he got to Yulin, I could see that she was nervous. Meeting Mao wasn't just like meeting the President. It was like meeting God. When you met Mao, you were meeting the father of the country and the liberator of mankind.

Mao disarmed Yulin in no time. "I haven't met you before, have I?" he said, holding her hand and looking directly at her. I saw it again, that gift of focusing directly in on the person he was speaking to, shutting out the entire rest of the room, and the rest of the world. "Where are you from?" he asked her. "Who was your father? When did you join the Revolution?" Within sixty seconds, I could see that Yulin was just standing there talking to a man named Mao. She was completely relaxed and was chatting with him without reserve.

Along with Mao and his entourage, we all filed into a meeting room, which had overstuffed sofa chairs pushed along the walls on three sides. The ever-present lace antimacassars and red-velvet hangings gave the room a garish look. When Mao received heads of state, he hewed strictly to protocol. On other occasions, however, he was much less formal. Rather than taking the proper place exactly in the middle of the row of chairs on the short end of the room, he sat down a bit left of center. Then he pulled out a cigarillo, Gongzi brand. Most of us were on pins and needles, sitting stiffly in our chairs. Mao was a genius at breaking down that stiffness. He waved the slender cigar in the air. "Are most of you smokers or nonsmokers?" he asked.

No one replied.

"Who here smokes and who doesn't smoke?"

More silence.

"I'll tell you what," Mao said. "Everyone who is a smoker hold up a cigarette, and nonsmokers keep your hands down." He looked around the room, toting up the number of cigarettes in the air. There were very few. "The nonsmokers are in the majority," he said. Then he turned to Liao Chengzhi and said dryly, "It seems on this point too I am in the minority."

All of us chuckled politely and the ice was broken. But from my vantage point alongside Mao, I could see the entire room. And at that remark, I saw Wu Lengxi, the head of the *People's Daily,* and Yao Zhen, a vice chief of propaganda, turn chalky white, stop taking notes, and go rigid. Something about what Mao had just said had frightened them. Something about the whole atmosphere was odd.

Mao looked around the room. "What shall we talk about?" he asked.

Frank Coe answered. "Let's talk about the world situation."

"First, I'd like to hear your views," Mao said. But nobody would answer. "No, no, no," we all murmured. "We want to hear from you first."

Then Mao sat and puffed and looked up at the ceiling. "Well," he said finally, "so it looks like you've all had a meeting in advance and passed a resolution on how to deal with me. You've decided that the way to deal with me is no one will talk until I talk." He threw his head back and laughed. It was the laugh of an infant. Every part of his body seemed to be laughing. He was really enjoying it. But as I looked around the room, I saw that nobody else was laughing.

Then Mao began to talk about the world situation and his mind seemed even more driving and skittish than the last time I had seen him nearly a year earlier. He circled around the globe, flipping from country to country, ranging from topic to topic in seemingly random order. He talked about Indonesia, where a huge massacre of Sukarno's followers and Indonesian Communists had just taken place. "In 1927 our party was wiped out by Chiang Kai-shek," he told the Indonesian representative in our party. "Then we had fewer people than you have now. But twenty years later, we took power." He talked about Latin America. He talked about Iraq, where Abdul Karem Kassim had come to power on a left-wing program. "In the world today, the East Wind prevails over the West Wind," Mao commented. "If the people of an oppressed country have a correct revolutionary line and unite and fight and stick together, they are bound to win."

Underlying all his talk was one central thing. The world has entered a period of revolution, he was telling us. The world has changed. The balance of forces has shifted in favor of the people, if only the people take bold action. Get up on your feet, unite and fight, and you can win. Over and over he kept saying, "The worst thing in the world is to have dead water. The worst thing in the world is a stagnant pond. When you have a stagnant pool, you have to find some way of stirring things up. Otherwise there is no progress. When you have the right line, you can win so long as you persist in the struggle."

But, Mao added, don't worry about failing. "Don't think you won't make mistakes from time to time," he said. "Don't think the Chinese Communist Party doesn't make mistakes. There's one of our mistakes there," he said to Anna Louise, pointing at me. "He was one of our good friends, but because he was implicated by your case, we put him in jail, and kept him in jail for a long time. That was our mistake."

All the while he was talking, I noticed that Mao's entourage never seemed to relax. They kept looking around nervously as if they weren't quite sure what he was going to say next. He had talked for about an hour and a half when, as usual, Jiang Qing appeared. And, as usual, she was the quiet, retiring hostess. Wearing a dark suit with a lapel, she looked a bit matronly.

"Ah, Comrade Jiang Qing is inviting us to lunch," Mao said, as he always did.

Over lunch, Mao spoke of his talks with Soviet Premier Aleksey Kosygin, who had met with Zhou Enlai en route to Vietnam and with Mao on his way home. Often, while the Soviet Union and China were exchanging polemics, the *People's Daily* would print the full text of the Soviets' message. *Pravda*, however, printed nothing of what the Chinese said, and the Chinese taunted them about it unmercifully.

"When Kosygin came here to see me, he said, 'Let's call a truce in the polemics,' " Mao remembered. "And I said, 'I can't understand why you should ask us for a truce in polemics. You have all of Marxism-Leninism, and all I have is empty talk.' " Then came the laugh again, head thrown back. "And then I told him I would stop the polemics—but only in ten thousand years, not a day before."

Both probing and in jest, I asked him, "Wouldn't you agree to stop the polemics in only 9,999 years, provided the Soviets' behavior was good?"

Mao, about to go for a dish of pickles in the center of the table, stopped instantly with his chopsticks in midair. Looking straight at me with his eyes wide open, almost glaring, he replied very seriously, "No, we could not do that. When you make a commitment, you must always live up to your commitment. Even though he is the enemy, if you promise him ten thousand more years of polemics you must live up to your word. It must be ten thousand years, and not a year less."

I was a little surprised that Mao would use my little joke to make a serious point about being uncompromising toward the enemy. From that I drew the conclusion that he intended to stress "No compromise" to the world in general. And as usual, I noted that things I said to him tended to be bounced right back at me.

During the latter part of the lunch, Mao got quite testy. I had never seen that before. "Quit looking at your watch," he snapped at Liao Chengzhi. "You're trying to hustle me away. I'm not done here yet. I haven't even finished my tea and cigarettes!" He glared at Liao, and Liao, a man of enormous courage, grinned sheepishly, ducking his head and hunching his shoulders like a scolded schoolboy.

Mao continued talking. Finally, after a few more minutes he doused his cigarette and got up abruptly from the table. "All right. All right," he said. "Liao won't quit putting pressure on me. I'm leaving." And he stalked away.

The Chairman had barely left when Tang Mingzhao came running. "I have good news," he said excitedly. "Premier Zhou Enlai is coming in from Beijing this evening, and he will be hosting a birthday banquet for Anna Louise." The premier in Shanghai too! That was unusual, but we were glad we were going to benefit from it. We went back to our rooms to rest and wait.

That evening at six P.M. we were driven to the main banquet hall of the city of Shanghai. We were met inside the door by Zhou Enlai, and by the first party secretaries for the east China region and the city of Shanghai, as well as the mayor. Many other local officials—about twenty people—were also waiting to greet us, as was Dr. Guo Moruo, famous writer, archaeologist, and president of the Chinese Academy of Sciences.

The room set aside for us was huge and entirely filled with banquet tables, with a stage facing the entryway. The seating arrangements were a bit strange since, in addition to our group, the premier was hosting a big posse of Japanese youth who had come to China to explore the prospects for Japanese tourism. That huge group, some two hundred people in all, was seated off to the side and received little attention. Our party was arranged more intimately toward the center of the room, a head table with Anna Louise at the premier's right, and four or five tables facing them.

There was much laughing and joking. The Chinese truly revered and admired Anna Louise, and she was especially fond of the premier. They toasted her work, and Guo Moruo made a joke about her being not eighty, but rather forty metric years old. Just as the dessert was being served, the members of a local army choral group filed in, and Liao Chengzhi announced that they would sing to entertain us. The piece they chose was the *Long March Suite,* a lengthy elegy that had been produced under the direction of Xiao Hua, the chief of the general political department of the army, and a close friend and ally of Zhou Enlai. I had heard snatches of it on the radio, but I had never heard the whole thing sung at once.

The chorus started off, a young officer wielding the baton. Stanza after stanza they sang, ringing out all the by now famous episodes of the party's flight from the Kuomintang, across the Tibetan plains, across the arid grasslands.

Suddenly in mid-performance, Zhou Enlai jumped up from his place of honor. "Why have you skipped a stanza?" he shouted.

We all started. The young officer conducting looked befuddled.

Standing at his place, Zhou cried out again, "Why have you skipped a stanza? The stanza about crossing the Great Snowy Mountains of Yunnan. Why aren't you singing it?"

The young conductor seemed struck dumb. "We don't know it," he said. "I'm sorry."

"Not know it?" Zhou cried out. "That stanza was written personally by Comrade Xiao Hua. How can you not know it? I want you to sing that verse."

Now the officer looked embarrassed. "But we haven't rehearsed it," he said.

"Never mind if you haven't rehearsed it," Zhou said. "We'll sing it anyway. If you can't lead them in it, I will." He strode from his place to the front of the choral group, and using his hand for a baton began the stanza in a clear tenor voice. It was a tragic verse about a period when the party had suffered heavy losses crossing the Great Snowy Mountains of southwest China.

The conductor stood stony-faced. But as Zhou was singing, the chorus joined in. No matter what the conductor said, it was clear they knew the stanza perfectly well and they sang it with him right to the end.

When that verse was finished, Zhou returned to his seat. He looked angry. The conductor looked upset. The piece droned on for dozens of more verses. But none of us was really paying attention. We were mulling over the peculiar scene we had just witnessed. Why was Zhou so angry? What was so important about that verse?

Soon, such strange stirrings were everywhere.

From a distance, far out of the sight or understanding of ordinary people, something was disturbing that stagnant pool. Over the next few months, the newspapers were filled with veiled attacks. The stage, the screen, even musical pieces sprouted that, like the odd episode with the choral group in Shanghai, said one thing but meant another. But just what did they mean? No one quite knew.

I got a hint about the Shanghai incident from a secret cable in the documents room. Luo Ruiqing, a friend of Xiao Hua's, had been removed from his post as chief of staff of the PLA. Had Zhou Enlai, by singing that stanza in Shanghai, been trying to show his personal support and protect his friend Xiao Hua from a similar attack? If so, from whom? And why?

In article after article suggestions appeared that Mao was once again chafing at the bit. I kept hearing hints that harked back to our talk in 1964. Revolutions, he had said, would always be necessary. I was convinced Mao was concerned that this revolution was faltering, that some comrades were undermining our progress, and that unless we did something about it, this country would go rotten from within.

Mao seemed to be struggling, as I was, with the stultifying bureaucracy that this revolution had become. Over and over I heard the same cries. A revolution is a big leap, not gradual change. Progress comes through struggle. The fight is between a revolutionary working-class outlook and a selfish bourgeois world outlook. Are you tired of revolution? Are you just into soft living? Then you aren't fit to be a Communist cadre.

Somehow, the new stress on a battle between two world outlooks—between selfish egotism and selfless devotion to serving the people—made me feel that new revolutionary storms were approaching, much-needed storms, long overdue.

I looked at myself, and I wondered.

Then one morning in February 1966, an assistant group leader, Jiang Guinong, came up to my desk at the Broadcast Administration with a *People's Daily* article in her hand. "There's a terrific story here you should read," she said. It was a big story, nearly two pages of type and pictures. I sat down at once with my tea and began to read. And as I read, I felt more and more chagrined and humiliated.

It was a feature story about a party secretary for Lankao County, in dirt-poor, flood-ravaged southeastern Henan. This man, Jiao Yulu, was a living example of all the things I had originally thought the party wanted us to be. He didn't just sit in his office. He spent all his days walking the dusty country roads, listening to the peasants, asking them their problems, carefully checking out the terrain, climate, crops, soils, figuring out how to give them the leadership they needed to get out of their poverty and helplessness. And he went right on working for them even after he himself was deathly ill. Despite a painful and debilitating liver cancer, he kept at his post helping others until the day he died.

When I finished reading the article, I felt tears running down my cheeks. That's what being a Communist is supposed to be, I thought to myself. That's serving the people. He's a human being; I'm a human being. He's a Communist; I'm a Communist. But what a difference!

I was swept up in a feeling of tragedy. Suddenly, the last few years of my life seemed selfish and venal. I looked down at the big belly protruding over my belt, the product of the last few years' good living. I had been spending my time preening before high officials, cavorting with other foreigners, eating well and living well.

The system was becoming corrupt, and I had allowed it to corrupt me. The party had let the necessary special privileges of the mountains in wartime run wild into an unconscionable elitist system. We were living in special quarters, eating special food, driving in special cars. We kept ourselves apart from the masses. I had even allowed myself to be talked into eating well during the great hunger when other people were suffering.

Now what was the result? I had a big office and I had a big gut. Look at what I have turned into, I thought to myself in disgust. I hate self-serving bureaucrats so much, but I have turned into a damn fat lazy bureaucrat myself. Again, I felt a big surge of remorse. Is this how it was all supposed to end? For twenty-six years, since my college days, I had thought of myself as a Marxist, someone who served the people. Did I want to end my days as a damn bourgeois elitist? I hadn't been living up to my revolutionary ideals. I was in danger of ending up what I had always despised: a hypocrite and a phony.

The very next day, I moved out of my private office. I found an empty desk in the newsroom and moved my teacup there. The distant rumblings were unsettling me. I could feel some kind of new revolution brewing. I didn't know what and I didn't know how. But I wanted to be ready. I started to keep a diary, showing the work done each day, analyzing how I spent my time and how effective I was. I began writing self-criticisms, circulating them among my friends, sometimes posting them on the notice board for comment.

I went on a crash diet. I ate mostly grain, and very little of that, with only a tiny bit of meat and lots of vegetables. I began to jog for an hour a day, and to do push-ups five times a day. The weight fell off me. In less than two months, I went from 185 pounds to 132 pounds, and when I arrived at work someone would invariably meet me at the door. "You must stop this dieting at once, Old Li," they scolded. "Your skin is hanging on your bones."

The reporters and translators were jubilant about my reappearance in the newsroom. "This is really convenient, Old Li," they said. "Anytime we need to ask you something, you're right here." But some parts of my transformation made people very unhappy. When I demanded a fifty percent cut in my salary, the party fought me, until I said I would open a bank account and deposit half anyway under a false name. When I took to eschewing the motor pool, instead riding my bicycle back and forth to the Friendship Hotel, a security department head came to see me to talk me out of it.

He was an old pal from the countryside. "You know that if some nut hits you on the back of the head with a brick, I'm going to spend the next five years writing self-criticisms," he said. "If you won't take the car, I'm going to have to post security people all along the route. It's going to take all those people and all that time."

I wasn't impressed. It seemed to me yet another example of the bureaucracy standing in the way of my trying to do the right thing. "You do what you have to do," I said. He left looking glum.

The party organization was also furious when I decided to return to regular manual labor, digging on the subway line across from the Broadcast Administration. "This is a security problem for us, to have one of our foreign experts doing construction work," party member Ma Ruiliu complained, relaying the organization's opinion. "There are former landlords doing work on that project under surveillance. If you go down in the pits, one of us has to go too, to watch you." I wasn't having any of it. If I wanted to do construction work, I felt that was my business. If they wanted to come with me, well, so much the better. Hard work would be good for them too. Ma Ruiliu accompanied me from then on, grumbling all the way.

My next move was more serious. I gave away our beautiful antique furniture. Ji Chaoding, the connoisseur who had helped me buy it, had died two years before. From that time on, I had already begun to think of carrying out our plan and donating what we had acquired to the Palace Museum. Now my thoughts came stronger and faster. This beautiful furniture belonged to the Chinese people, and for me to keep it for my private enjoyment was every bit as corrupt as for it to be in the homes of the nobles who had paid to have it carved.

So when Yulin returned from school one Saturday evening, the furniture was gone. A team of experts had come and, their eyes wide at the beauty and value of the Ming dynasty treasures I was offering, had taken it away, all but one rebuilt piece. In its place was the standard, utilitarian furniture issued to all foreign experts and high-ranking cadres: a beige overstuffed sofa and easy chairs, and a plain black wooden dining room table.

It was the worst quarrel we ever had.

"You gave the furniture away," she said as if she couldn't believe it. "It's all gone."

"Yes," I said defensively. "It's what we agreed on."

"I didn't agree to give it all away," she said.

"Yes you did. We talked about it." We had, in fact, talked about giving it away. She had resisted, but finally had agreed to donating some of the pieces to the museum. I knew she had agreed only under pressure, and now she felt betrayed by my going ahead and doing it anyway.

She was angry, really angry. The next morning she returned to school without speaking. The following weekend, she didn't come home and I went up to the school to find her. She came out and agreed to talk, but she was still fiercely angry. I had given away the furniture without her consent, she said. It wasn't fair. I wasn't respecting her wishes. It wasn't democratic.

I apologized. Maybe I had been too impetuous. I thought she had agreed, but perhaps I hadn't troubled myself enough to find out her real feelings. She came back home the next weekend, but she stayed angry for a long time.

Meanwhile, the big discussions in the press were about culture and literature. The debate seemed to center on whether intellectuals, artists, and scholars had lost sight of the Revolution. My old friend Deng Tuo and two of his colleagues were being denounced almost daily in the press for a column they had written that appeared to be a veiled attack on Mao. "Bourgeois intellectualism," their critics sneered.

I could see the faint outlines of another battle being drawn. Old party activists like Propaganda Minister Lu Dingyi said develop new art forms, but keep the old. Jiang Qing—with Mao behind her—wanted to throw away the old ones because they were capitalist and feudal poison. In May, a committee called the Cultural Revolution Group was formed to oversee the change. Still, no one thought this particular controversy was very serious. It was only art and literature, after all.

Everyone went to see the new works. That May Day, Yulin and

I took the two older girls to see *Harbor,* an opera about stevedores in a port city. We were sitting near the front of the auditorium at the air force headquarters, Yulin and I in the middle and a little girl on either side. There was a row of empty seats in front of us, and the opera had just begun when suddenly Zhou Enlai and his entourage swept in. Zhou shook hands with Yulin and me, patted the girls on their heads, and then settled in the row in front of us.

Almost immediately, eight-year-old Xiaoqin started to complain. "I can't see anything," she said. "The uncle in front of me is blocking the stage." As Yulin and I were frantically trying to hush her, Zhou swung completely around to the right, picked her up in both hands, and lifted her over the back of his seat to his lap.

She sat there happily watching the opera. But her little sister wasn't about to suffer such inequitable treatment. Seven-year-old Xiaodong began to whine and complain. "I want to sit in Premier Zhou's lap too." Once again, Yulin and I tried to hush her. Just then, Premier Zhou turned to his left this time, and swung little Xiaodong over the seat too, depositing her on his left knee. Yulin got up and went around to the premier's row to call both girls back. But Zhou waved his palm back and forth sideways in the air and said, "That's all right, that's all right. Just let them sit here and enjoy the show." And there they sat right up to the intermission, one on each knee as quiet as mice.

On a windy day late in May, I was bicycling back from the Friendship Hotel with a features editor. We had been working on a piece together, and we were riding side by side and talking about our work. It was a tough ride. The funny thing about Beijing was that the wind reversed itself exactly at noon, so that both the ride up to the hotel and the ride back were against the wind. Sometimes in the wintertime I wore a gauze mask against the grit, but today was warm and I didn't bother.

The streets were not crowded. There were few cars traveling the road, and at that hour factory and office workers were still at their jobs. The only cyclists around us were high school students returning from classes that had just gotten out. We came to the junction at Muxudi, where the north-south road joins with the main street that is the extension of the Avenue of Eternal Peace. There a small knot of cyclists passed us, crossing over the moat heading west. They looked like ordinary clean-cut high school kids, but their clothes were a little different from ordinary students' clothes. They were wearing khaki pants and tunics, and on their arms were red armbands with gold inscriptions. They looked a little like army uniforms. "What's that?" I asked my colleague.

She seemed a bit cautious about replying. Some high school students have said that they are being prevented from exercising their right to revolutionary criticism of the school leaders, she told me. So they are organizing themselves into groups to defend their rights. It was the elite students in each school who were organizing, she explained, the kids with the best proletarian class background. Her own daughter was in a school with such groups, but because the child's grandfather had been a banker in Shanghai and her parents were not party members, she wasn't allowed to join.

I looked again at the insignia on the students' armbands. There were three words, hand-stitched in Chinese characters: Hong wei bing.

Red Guards.

◆

At the end of the month, I made my first trip to Yanan in seventeen years. Foreign experts were entitled to a trip every year, and this year, a group of us decided to make it a study tour. Our first stop was in Lankao County, near Kaifeng, to see the home of the model party secretary, Jiao Yulu. From there we took a train to Xian to visit two famous pagodas and an archaeological site—a Neolithic village that had been uncovered just outside the town.

That night, we all stayed in a modest little guest house in the center of the city. With nothing to do after dinner, we congregated in each other's rooms, chatting and thinking over the day's events, listening to the news on the transistors we brought with us. It was Radio Beijing with its usual collection of meetings and encomiums, nothing to startle us. Suddenly Edmundo Palacios, a Chilean foreign expert, came bursting into the room. He had been listening to the Voice of America on his own transistor in the next room. "You won't believe what they're saying!" he shouted. "Peng Zhen, Lu Dingyi, Yang Shangkun, and Luo Ruiqing have been arrested!"

Everyone but me began to shout and babble. I stayed calm because I didn't believe it. "That's impossible," I said. "You know how the Voice of America is. Every ten minutes they are reporting that Mao has died. This is just another one of their little games." The room quieted down and everyone listened to me. After all, I was a member of the party, the one with the inside contacts. I was the one who knew what was going on.

Peng Zhen was the second-ranking man in the secretariat, I explained, and the mayor of Beijing. Yang Shangkun and Luo Ruiqing were director of the central party office and army chief of staff. As for Lu Dingyi, the propaganda minister, I explained that I knew both him and Peng Zhen personally and that they were both good comrades. Even if they did make any mistakes, they would correct their errors. To arrest them would be unthinkable. Everyone went to bed greatly comforted and the next morning we left early for our flight to Yanan.

I hadn't seen Yanan since I had ridden out of it, terrified of the bombing, in Liao Chengzhi's truck. Since then, there had been a lot of building. There was a modest little inn and much of the village had been redone. I went to see my old cave. Peasants were living there, growing corn outside the door. That made me happy. Feeling nostalgic for the old days of millet and rugged living, I told my friends how easy it had been to see Mao and Zhou, how people had formed close friendships, how nobody in Yanan had stood on ceremony or title. Everyone had been equal in Yanan, I said.

That night in the little inn, we once again tuned in to Radio Beijing. This time, I was the one who was shaken up. A party functionary at Beijing University had put up a big poster accusing the university leadership of revisionism. The leaders at the university had tried to suppress the protest, and some people at the very top of the party had supported that suppression. Such suppression is wrong, the *People's Daily* reported. In ringing, almost visionary language, the paper announced the beginning of a new revolution in China. The way a country goes rotten is from within, the broadcast continued. There are revisionists in the party, people who would suppress, control, lead us down the wrong road, and even attack Chairman Mao himself.

Don't let that happen in China! The high tide is now rising! A new day is dawning! Think for yourselves. Revolutionaries, arise! Think of the words of the Great Chairman Mao. Ignore all orders that conflict with that. It is right to rebel.

The words were electric. Ever since the party was born, had tramped here to Yanan and stood off first the Japanese and then the Kuomintang, its members had lived and died by an ideal that demanded complete obedience. It was obedience to the party in the name of this ideal that had helped me overcome my fear of the bombs, that had kept me hopeful through my years in prison. It was obedience that led us to endure rectifications and movements, to endure hunger without complaint through the bad years. It was obedience that had brought us to where we were today.

Now an article in the *People's Daily*—which I was sure could only have come straight from Mao—was telling us to throw it all away. Many in the party were seeking to deceive us and only we could flush them out. Oppose orders that you believe are wrong, the paper said. Rebel!

With great excitement, I translated the newscast, line for line, for the other foreigners. Suddenly I was my own man again. The party had bound me, and now the party was setting me free. I could break loose the bonds that had so chafed me, use my own judgment, and work once again for what I thought was right.

As we left Yanan by bus the next morning, my perceptions had been altered in many ways. Flying in the day before—the first time I had ever approached Yanan by air—I had seen the landscape for what it was. We had always talked of living in the mountains —on News Mountain, on Emancipation Mountain. But Yanan was not mountainous at all. In fact, the area surrounding Yanan was a vast, flat plateau. What I had taken to be mountains were actually the sides of deep gullies, carved by eons of rains and rivers. When we climbed up the mountains, we were really climbing up the sides of canyons to the flat plains above.

The party hadn't been forged in the mountains, I realized, but in the ditches.

CHAPTER SIXTEEN

Arouse the Masses

When our train pulled into Beijing station after the long trek to Yanan, there was a bus from the Broadcast Administration waiting to drive us back to our apartments. My friends scattered for home, but I went straight to the office. As I walked across the courtyard, a friend spotted me. "Old Li!" she said. "You won't believe what has been happening since you were gone. Go to the music hall. There are big-character posters everywhere."

She was right. The hall fluttered with posters. They were hanging from the walls, or from clotheslines strung out across the room. Some were written on sheets of unused newsprint, others on newspapers themselves. The sheets were pasted together so that the tails of the longer ones dragged on the ground. Most were painted in big, thick black Chinese brush strokes. Each one spoke of a new era at the Broadcast Administration. Each one attacked its director, Mei Yi.

"Down with Mei Yi," the posters read. "Mei Yi is against Chairman Mao." "Mei Yi is a revisionist." In smaller print, each poster detailed some specific crime of Mei Yi's, from violations of party policy to being an opportunistic leader. I walked around the music room. It was empty except for one person. Mei Yi.

He looked pale and drawn and frightened, carefully walking up and down, reading each poster. Most of them were signed by people we both knew.

I went up and shook hands with him. "I'm back," I said.

"Did you have a good trip?" he asked. But he was distracted, not paying much attention to me. He had a notebook in his hand, and he didn't stop taking notes to talk with me. We passed a few moments in silence.

"Well," I said, "I'll see you later."

"Yes," he said and kept on writing. He knew what was happening to him. He knew his days at the Broadcast Administration were numbered.

I agreed with many of the criticisms. I thought Mei Yi had harbored a stultifying bureaucracy at the Broadcast Administration, and deep down in my heart I knew he had helped unjustly persecute some people. But I felt sorry for him standing there in such obvious misery. I liked him. He had always been an ardent revolutionary, and he had always been good to me and to Yulin. But then too I was ecstatic at the idea that reform was in the wind. Finally, those in charge were beginning to realize that our revolution was being frozen by a bureaucracy that stressed order and control rather than progress and efficiency, and that stifled individual initiative and suppressed democracy. I stood ready to judge Mei Yi based on what the party and the masses thought, not on our own personal relationship.

I left the music hall and went right to the office of Meng Jiefu, the director of my department. He wasn't there, but his executive assistant, Wang Zhenhua, was. "You're back," he said, standing up to shake hands.

"Yes," I said. "What's going on here? I've been to the music hall."

"A lot has happened since you went away," he said. "Sit down. I'll tell you about it."

I was glad I had found him in. Besides being executive assistant to Meng, Wang Zhenhua was also party branch secretary for our department. He was a nice, straightforward man, son of a former underground party member. He had gone to the university in Moscow, learned Russian and English, and was a devoted party member.

"The Great Proletarian Cultural Revolution is in full swing," Wang began, using the formal name I had heard before. "This is a big movement that touches the soul of every one of us, not like anything that has ever happened before. All our comrades are very aroused and active," he said. Wang wasn't an effervescent type, but this time I could tell he was excited.

"But what about Mei Yi?" I asked.

"Mei Yi is a representative of the Black Line, going all the way back to the 1930s."

For months now, I had been reading snippets in the papers about followers of the Black Line. They were people who back in the 1930s, the early days of the party, were considered by Mao to be weak and conciliatory toward the Nationalists, and to have abandoned revolutionary principles. I knew that Mei Yi had been in Shanghai with the party in those days. I had no idea that he had ever been suspect.

"How can you know for sure?" I asked.

"There's no question about it," Wang said. "Zhang Pinghua himself came to Radio to tell us while you were gone. He's now standing vice minister of propaganda."

Zhang Pinghua in charge of propaganda? So it was true. The radio report that we had heard in Xian had been right after all. Lu Dingyi, the minister of propaganda, had indeed been ousted. Then the others—Beijing's Mayor Peng Zhen, PLA Chief of Staff Luo Ruiqing, Director of the Central Party Office Yang Shangkun—must be out too. That was unprecedented. Unlike their Soviet counterparts, the leadership of the Chinese Communist Party was very stable. I had never heard of a whole body of leaders being ousted overnight.

"Mei Yi hasn't been formally removed yet," Wang Zhenhua continued. "But he has already been suspended. He won't be allowed to work anymore, and he's being told to make a self-criticism."

"So who's in charge at the Broadcast Administration?" I asked.

"It's Ding Laifu," he said. "He's already been told that he's in charge."

Ding Laifu was political commissar, the general manager of the entire political structure at the Broadcast Administration. I had only spoken to him once, at a banquet a year earlier, and I had thought he was okay, a kind of bluff, hearty man. But I knew that some people didn't like him, or what he stood for. He was a general who had come to the Broadcast Administration just a few years before from one of the armies guarding Beijing, bringing with him a batch of army officers he seeded throughout the Broadcast Administration in different departments. They knew nothing about the work, and some people resented their presence.

"There's more," Wang said. "There have been some big changes at the top. There's a new Cultural Revolution Group." Mao was moving back in. Peng Zhen, Deng Xiaoping's number two man, had been removed, and the committee he had chaired, along with other moderates, had been dissolved. "Peng Zhen and his group were revisionists," Wang Zhenhua explained. "They tried to limit the Cultural Revolution to just an academic debate."

The new Cultural Revolution Group favored direct revolutionary action, like Mao. Their chairman was Chen Boda, one of Mao's chief ideologues, Jiang Qing was the first vice chairman, and Kang Sheng was adviser.

I had known Chen Boda since Yanan. Back then, I had tried to translate some of his works and found them shoddily constructed and completely lacking in logic. But in recent years, he had impressed me with his position on communes, which, he said, should make up the basic unit of organization everywhere, not just in the villages. I felt that Chen Boda, for all his faults, was a progressive, forward-looking man.

Jiang Qing, Mao's wife, I had only known as a dancing partner and a gracious, retiring hostess. She must be sitting with the group as a representative of Chairman Mao, I thought. As for Kang Sheng, during our one encounter with Mao in 1964, I had found something cold and vaguely sinister about him. At the same time, having heard Mao introduce him as "my Minister of Empty Talk," I realized that this man had the Chairman's ear—and his confidence.

Over the next few days, the trappings of the Cultural Revolution started to enfold me. I was issued a Little Red Book, Lin Biao's palm-sized collection of Chairman Mao's sayings. Everyone else was being issued one too; I could see them stacked up in big piles around the newsroom. We marveled at the quantities. Where was the paper coming from to print in such volume? How were they getting to us with such speed?

A few people in our office began showing up at work wearing tiny badges, busts of Chairman Mao rimmed in a gold color. They created quite a stir. No one had seen anything like them before and everyone wanted to have one. I brought back and handed out great quantities from the Friendship Store, exclusively for foreigners.

Eager to participate in the Cultural Revolution, I found myself barred from the room where the big-character posters were mounted on the grounds that if they let me in they would have a problem explaining it to other foreign experts, who were not allowed in. I was furious. I took the issue to the leading party committee and finally got the ban against my participation lifted.

In the secret documents room, I was handed fat files containing papers going all the way back to February that I had never seen before. There was a speech that Jiang Qing had given to a military conference on literature and art, issued with Mao's approval and a covering note from Lin Biao. The speech promised a major battle to save the Revolution from the evil influences of those who would subvert it—the revisionists who had been hiding in our midst since the 1930s. The Cultural Revolution thus wasn't just an artistic matter, but a serious, all-out power struggle.

There was also a report of a meeting on May 18, 1966, a joint meeting of the political bureau of the Central Committee and the Cultural Revolution Group. That seemed a bit strange. That kind of joint meeting had never been held before. It was placing the Cultural Revolution Group on a very high level indeed. The results of the meeting were even more startling. The documents revealed that Lin Biao, the minister of defense, had been named number two man in the party and anointed as Mao's successor instead of Liu Shaoqi. None of us had any idea that this was in the cards. I thought it was terrific. I had had some reservations about Lin Biao back in Yanan, mainly about his personal ambition. But I knew that it was he who was distributing the Little Red Book so that people could read Mao's works for themselves in small doses and think about them. And it was he who was stressing the study of theory, not just for theory's sake, but for improving practical work.

The documents also had the text of the speech Lin Biao had made at that meeting. It sent electric shocks through me. "This revolution," he said, "is a revolution against our last revolution. In 1949, what we had was a military takeover. There was no arousing of the great masses in their millions to get up and free themselves. We took over most of the government personnel from the old regime and kept them at work. We didn't have an opportunity to deal thoroughly with the old viewpoints and the old culture.

"Now we must crush the Four Olds—old ideas, old culture, old customs, old habits—and make way for the Four News." The battle, Lin said, was between selfishness and public service, between addiction to material goods and the overall best interests of the great majority, between soft living based on parasitism and hard work, frugal living, and comradely mutual aid and cooperation, so that the whole of society grows and prospers together.

It was a battle between the Capitalist and the Socialist Roads.

◆

The first meeting to criticize Mei Yi was held in the theater of the television building. Mei Yi sat up on the stage behind a table, holding his notebook and a microphone. At the top of the curtain, running from one end of the stage to the other, was a great red streamer bearing the keynote slogan for the meeting: "Criticize the Black Line in Literature and Art! Criticize the Representative of the Black Line in the State Broadcasting Administration—Mei Yi!"

My feelings were complicated. Mei Yi had been my sponsor, protector, boss, counselor, and friend. I had not liked him when we were in Yanan, but as we had worked together over the years, I got to like him better. I thought he genuinely cared about the Revolution and was very professional. On the other hand, I thought he was harsh on those who might be considered threats to him.

I had personal worries too. Many people knew I was close to Mei Yi. I worried that I might be accused of being an accomplice, or of deliberately withholding information in order to protect him. Finally, I decided to speak, but to say something harmless. About two-thirds of the way through the meeting, I asked for the floor. I went to the microphone on the right of the stage. "Mei Yi," I said, "denied the need to have a special separate radio station to handle international broadcasts. He said that making the party's achievements known in China and abroad were just two sides to the same job.

"That is wrong," I continued. "It's difficult to put the Chinese data into a form that the foreign listener could readily understand and accept. It's not just a matter of language and editing. Mei Yi's attitude shows a lack of understanding of the importance of delivering the message of Mao Zedong Thought to people in other countries."

After the meeting, a colleague in the English section told me, "Old Li, your exposure of Mei Yi was okay, but you looked a little shaky and your voice was quivering. Next time you should do a little better, don't you think?"

Many people were happy about the new freedom to criticize those who had previously been immune. "This is a great movement," said one translator happily. "It's different from all the others. People can write whatever criticism they have about anyone. They can argue about the political system and theory. Everyone is taking part. Everyone is getting an education."

Not exactly everyone. I had been notified that no one was allowed to criticize me, a foreigner. I told her so.

"Well, Old Li," she said, "you ought to take a good bath yourself. Nobody is perfect, you know."

She had struck at my very thoughts. If no one would criticize me, I would do it myself. I went into my old private office with her, and a few other people helped me. We pasted together some newsprint and I wrote a self-critical poster in my own chicken-scratch brushwork.

"Li Dunbai must get rid of his bourgeois elitism," I headed the page. I listed my own shortcomings. I led a special elitist life. I sat in a private office, separating myself from the masses. I got cranky sometimes when I was called in the middle of the night. I didn't do enough to help my comrades improve their skills.

The head of my department, Meng Jiefu, was flatly opposed to my putting up the poster. "You don't want to get involved in this thing if you don't have to," he said. "You don't know where it will lead." Wang Zhenhua was also dead set against it. "It isn't necessary," he said, looking worried.

I was adamant. I put the poster up. Still, I was full of fear and trepidation. Self-criticism could open a Pandora's box, I thought. Once I had criticized myself, I could be bringing on a storm. I knew that there were sharp-tongued and envious people who would be glad of a chance to use my self-criticism as an opening, but I felt I had to do it. If I didn't take criticism upon myself, how could I say I was transforming myself? And how could I criticize others?

I slept fitfully that night, and the next day I waited until late in the afternoon to visit the big-poster room, fearful of what I might find. What I saw shocked me. I had become a hero. "Learn from Li Dunbai" the headline on one poster read. "Look what a good example Li Dunbai has set for the old cadres" read another. I was the only one who had come forward with my own problems, and I was the only one coming in for praise. People stopped me. "I liked your revolutionary action," they said, pumping my hand.

The next day my translator friend came into my office. "You can think it over and dig a little deeper than that," she said, but she was grinning. I had passed a test. I had made it.

I was in the Cultural Revolution.

◆

Behind the scenes, always restless, always on the move, the tigers in the mountains were still fighting their own battles, and as the Cultural Revolution progressed, their fights became our fights. For the last few years, Mao had been strangely silent, his questing experiments held in check by his more conservative, pragmatic colleagues. But he was maneuvering his way back to the fore. In Shanghai we had seen his restless brilliance champing at the bit. Now, gradually, we watched events unfold that could mean only one thing. Mao had regained supremacy.

"Did you hear what happened last night at the Radio Institute?" asked Little Li when we bumped into each other very early one morning on the way to fill our first teacups of the day. He was peering through his thick lenses as if hoping I hadn't heard. A young country boy who was training to become a production assistant, he was excited and wanted to talk. There was only a handful of people about; it was early and the morning shift hadn't yet arrived. Still, before Little Li began to talk, he pulled me along to my office and closed the door.

The Broadcast Institute was a university where announcers and editors were trained for radio stations all over the country. I hadn't heard about anything in particular happening there. But I did know that schools and universities were in turmoil. Yulin had been coming home every weekend with tales about events at her school. The original leadership of virtually all the universities had been removed under a storm of criticism. Mao was supporting a radical faction of students who wanted students to run the school. The moderates, on the other hand, had sent in work teams from the Central Committee to fill the vacuum and try to keep order.

"Everything was pretty quiet at the institute last night," Little Li began. "People were just meeting or resting. Then all of a sudden, there was a big commotion at the front gate. My friends couldn't help hearing it. No one could help hearing it. There were people shouting and milling about." Li explained that he had been visited early that morning by friends among the students who told him what had happened.

A caravan of large curtained cars had stopped by the big iron gate to the institute, which was locked and barred by orders of the work team. The gatekeeper refused to open the doors. Then, Little Li said, a senior military cadre got out of the lead car. "Do you know who's in this car?" he shouted. "It's Comrade Jiang Qing."

That in itself was enough to cause a commotion. Since the Yanan days, few had seen the Chairman's wife in public. Now she was second-in-command of the Cultural Revolution Group. And with her was Chen Boda, the head of the group, and Kang Sheng, their adviser.

"She was very angry that they wouldn't let her in," Little Li continued. "She sent her guards to tell the gatekeeper that if he didn't open the gate right away, she'd have it smashed and drive in anyway." The gatekeeper, frightened, opened the gates at once and the caravan drove into the school.

Once inside, Little Li said, Jiang Qing summoned Li Zhefu, the head of the work team, and Ding Laifu, who had taken over after Mei Yi had been forced out. Then Jiang Qing sent for some of the radical student faction who had been opposing the work teams. The best known were a young woman from Manchuria named Cao Huiru, and a young man named Yang Yipeng.

When everyone was assembled, Jiang Qing asked the rebel students to tell their story. The students angrily related how they had been harassed, surrounded, and shouted at by the students supporting the work teams, and then finally hauled off to detention where they were forced to write self-criticisms under guard.

"When she heard these students' stories, Jiang Qing started to cry like rain," Little Li said. "She walked over and put her arms around their shoulders." Then she turned to school and Broadcast Administration leaders and said, "Look at you—you great generals in the uniforms of the Liberation Army. Are these children your enemies? Is this the way you treat the sons and daughters of the Revolution? Is your heart so hardened that you have no sense of compassion whatsoever for these revolutionary children?"

Next Chen Boda began to speak. "The Cultural Revolution is a movement to rid the party of the Capitalist Roaders who are in power now, and who have sabotaged Chairman Mao's proletarian revolutionary line," he said. "You can't just do it by exposing and removing the leaders from the top down. You need the sharp ears and clear eyes of the masses—and especially of you Little Revolutionary Champions. Revolutionary change has to be accomplished from the ground up, not from the top down. That's why the Capitalist Roaders are trying to stifle you. It's to protect themselves.

"Who are the masters of the Cultural Revolution?" Chen Boda cried out.

"The party!" the students roared back with one voice.

"No!" he cried. "No, not the party. It's you! You, the people, are the masters of the Cultural Revolution. You have to do it. You have to arouse yourselves, organize yourselves, take revolutionary action, educate yourselves as you go along."

Then, turning to the radical students gathered around the platform, Chen Boda said, "You are about to find yourselves in new circumstances. You have been an oppressed minority. Very soon you will be recognized as the genuine left wing and you will win the support of the majority. Then it will be your turn to make mistakes, so be careful!"

Word of Jiang Qing's visit to the institute spread rapidly around the Broadcast Administration that day. Work ground nearly to a halt as little clumps of people gathered at desks and in hallways, their discussions growing progressively more heated. Some of the more rebellious-minded at the Broadcast Administration exulted over the unexpected elevation of the rebels. Others were disturbed by the attacks on the work team. Yet others worried about the blow to the prestige of the party.

I overheard one heated argument, among two men and a woman at the central news room. "The students are wonderful!" the woman exclaimed. "Look how brave they were! They held on to Chairman Mao's line even after there were thousands of posters up denouncing them, even after they were put in detention. Now Comrade Jiang Qing has said they were right after all."

"But look at what a hard time the work team had," one of the men argued. "This is new territory. They're old party cadres. When they saw the students attacking the party, naturally they thought this was something dangerous that should be contained."

"If all these young people run around just shooting their mouths off about everything, how will the party function?" the other man chimed in. "If everybody is allowed to go around attacking the party, how can you tell good people from bad people?"

I felt emancipated. I loved to hear these discussions. I loved to hear the voice of the people freed once more. I agreed with everything that Chen Boda had said. The party was supposed to be the servant of the people, not their master. Now the people were master.

The next morning we awoke to find Mao Zedong himself back in the fight. The headline in the *People's Daily* was of a size that other newspapers might have used for wars or coups d'état. RIDING THE WIND AND BREAKING THROUGH THE WAVES the headline read. And underneath in slightly smaller type: OUR GREAT LEADER CHAIRMAN MAO AGAIN SWIMS THE YANGTZE. Indeed, he had. There was a picture of the Chairman, his head bobbing out of the great river. And alongside that picture was another of the Chairman, a bath towel slung over his shoulder, hale and hearty and full of spirit. He looked like life eternal.

The message to all of us was clear. Here I am, Mao Zedong was saying. I may be seventy years old, but I am full of vigor and vision, ready to lead you wherever the battle takes us.

Almost immediately, the Broadcast Administration began to break up into factions. There still weren't any formal divisions as there were in the universities. But the views of the little knots of people discussing Jiang Qing's visit to the Radio Institute began to harden. Gradually—and largely behind the scenes—people began associating with like-minded people. Some favored the highly demagogic, democratic-sounding program laid out by Jiang Qing and her colleagues and followed by the student rebels. Others began to form into a group to protect the status quo.

Strangely enough, I began to hear rumors about Wang Zhenhua. As party branch secretary, he was a likely candidate for the conservative side. But I was told that he had been quietly slipping off to meet with rebels from the People's Liberation Army program section at the Broadcast Administration. Sometimes they were joined by liaison agents from the *Liberation Army Daily,* the military newspaper that was quickly getting a reputation for being the center of radical ideas, directly connected with Lin Biao, Jiang Qing, Chen Boda, and the Cultural Revolution Group.

One day I approached Wang Zhenhua. "Is there some kind of rebel organization forming at the Broadcast Administration?" I asked. "If there is, I'd like to know about it."

"Well, a couple of us have been meeting to talk things over," he said. He was reserved, guarded, not tipping his hand. But a few days later a young man from the Spanish section approached me quietly when no one else was around. "Ever since you posted your self-criticism, we have been watching you," he said. "We think you are a good, forward-looking comrade. There's a group of us who are interested in making some big changes at the Broadcast Administration, and we have been getting some material right from the center. Would you like to read some of it?"

The blue-streaked mimeographed sheets that he handed me were hard to read, but they were dynamite. This shadowy group, whoever they were, had great contacts. I was seeing top secret papers that weren't even appearing in the secret documents room at the Broadcast Administration. This half-hidden rebel group was almost certainly being fed information straight from Jiang Qing and the Cultural Revolution Group.

In the texts of the documents I could hear the voice of the old, biting, sarcastic Mao Zedong that I had come to know. It wasn't he who wanted the work teams sent in to destroy the students' initiative, he averred. It was conservative, frightened, undemocratic elements in the party leadership. "Why did you have to act in such haste?" he chided Liu Shaoqi, Deng Xiaoping, and others. "Why prohibit free speech and free criticism in the universities? Why not let students put posters up around the Beijing Hotel? Are you afraid that foreigners will read the posters and think that China has problems?

"I have been thinking about constitutions," Mao continued. "Every socialist country from the USSR to Eastern Europe to China has a constitution, which guarantees to all the people freedom of speech, press, assembly, and much more. But none of us has ever carried it out. Don't you think it is time we started to carry it out? The first thing we should do is withdraw the work teams and announce to the students that they can march where they want, put posters where they want, and say what they want."

I was ecstatic. The people were going to be free at last.

Then we heard Liu Shaoqi and Deng Xiaoping apologize. Everyone heard it. No one had a choice. A note had gone around informing us that a tape was to be played and everyone was to listen to it. At the Broadcast Administration, groups of a hundred people were organized to hear the recording of the meeting that had just been held in the Great Hall of the People. We all filed into the audition room of the central news section to listen to it.

Liu's voice on the tape was high-pitched and squeaky. "We are in a situation today where old revolutionaries are faced with new problems and we haven't learned how to handle them," he said. "In the period that's just ended, we handled them the old way. We thought that sending in work teams was the right thing to do. But it turns out it isn't the right thing to do."

So that was it! The work teams had come from Liu Shaoqi. If Mao and Jiang Qing were against the work teams, and Liu Shaoqi was for them, then obviously there were some big problems at the top.

"So we've invited you today to discuss how the Great Proletarian Cultural Revolution should be conducted," Liu continued. But, he said, "If you ask me how it should be done, I'll tell you honestly, I don't know." That too was unprecedented. Party leaders never said they didn't know.

I heard something new in his voice. The Liu Shaoqi I had known in Yanan was a man used to laying down the law, an arch, intellectual, commanding personality. But this voice belonged to a man who was bewildered, at a loss, adrift in a sea not of his making.

Deng Xiaoping made a similar apology. His voice was clearer, stronger, but he too said he had been wrong. Then, all of a sudden, on the tape we could hear Liu Shaoqi shout at the top of his lungs, "Long live Chairman Mao." And voices began to roar, "Long live Chairman Mao! Long live Chairman Mao!"

CHAPTER SEVENTEEN

Smash Everything Old

Monsoon season was coming on in Beijing. The days alternated with uncomfortable regularity: a day or two of stifling, muggy heat, a day or two of downpours. There was the kind of electricity in the air that comes before a storm.

The past few years had been calm, regulated, as Mao sat on the sidelines while Liu Shaoqi and Deng Xiaoping struggled to put a normal, regular face on our Revolution, and to undo some of the damage of the Great Leap Forward. But now that Mao had returned to Beijing, a real, full-scale battle was shaping up. He had been in retreat, and now he was attacking. Deng and Liu were being positioned as revisionists who would hobble the Revolution that could make Mao immortal and China great. Mao was now poised to vanquish them.

Beijing took on the air of a city under siege. The *People's Daily,* which had tried to hold out against his passion, was now in hands friendly to the Cultural Revolution Group. Chen Boda had gone in with troops to take it over. When we passed by, we could see armed guards at the door. We could feel Mao's aggressive, restless, unruly touch everywhere. He was egging on the Red Guards, encouraging them to rebel. "You Red Guards are great!" he wrote. "You express rage and indignation against the crimes committed by the exploiting classes."

Another member of the shadowy rebel group approached me. A woman from the German section quietly passed me more material. "Here," she said, "you will be interested in this." It was the text of a poster that Mao himself had written and posted in the Zhongnanhai compound where the top leaders lived and worked. "Bombard the headquarters!" he wrote. Expose the poisonous plot within the party. Rise up. Rise up even against those who once led you, for they are not who they seem.

Then I was slipped yet another document. It was Mao's guidelines for the Cultural Revolution, and to my ears they sounded like the guidelines for the American Revolution: elect your own leaders, assemble your own organizations, print your own posters, publish your own newspapers. This, I thought, was a program for the end of party dictatorship.

Underneath, I could feel something else, however. Ever since the Great Leap Forward, the restless seeking part of Mao had been stilled. Now it was breaking free, and the Mao who thought he saw the possibility for backward China to leap into first place in the world was again coming to the fore. Let's let things break forth, he was saying, let's remove the controls and let the contradictions rise up. Let's take the lid off this big simmering pot and let what is inside boil over, so that we can understand the forces it contains and learn to drive them forward.

But there was a frightening side to this kind of freedom.

Before the Cultural Revolution, the party controlled everything —every factory, every government office, every village, every hospital, kindergarten, and army battalion. What line of products should an iron foundry produce? The party committee would decide. Should a rural commune grow high-priced vegetables and melons and enrich itself, or grain and cotton to meet the state's needs? The party committee would decide. What songs should a kindergarten teach? The party branch at the school would rule on the correct ratio of play songs to political songs. Appointments to jobs, promotions, marriages, housing, schooling—the party had a voice in it all.

But more than that, the party told us what to think. If an army commander found his men uninterested in training for war, he would immediately launch an educational program stressing the difference between just and unjust wars. Party publications told people which works of art to cherish and which to reject, which individuals should be honored and which criticized. The party newspapers kept us up to date on which foreign governments to support and which to oppose. The party committee or branch in the work units even told us whom to befriend and whom to shun. There was little to puzzle our minds, as long as we kept ourselves current with party thinking.

Then suddenly all that was gone. The Cultural Revolution scattered it like dust. Lin Biao cried out to sweep away freaks and monsters, and the men who had led us for decades were gone. Jiang Qing declared that enemies had been subverting the Revolution for years, and the clear voice of the party became murky and occluded. Then Mao himself cried out to bombard the headquarters of Liu Shaoqi, who had supervised day-to-day party work for years, and the party itself evaporated.

All at once, there was no one to trust, no one to tell us what to do, how to think, whom to like, what to believe. We all had to think for ourselves, to decide was this good, was this right, was this revolutionary. Did it follow Mao's teachings? It was perplexing, exhilarating—and terrifying.

Young people struggled to find their way. It was shortly after seven A.M., and steamy from a predawn shower, when I saw a young girl I knew riding alone on her bicycle across the courtyard that separated my apartment building from the Broadcast Administration compound. She had a tan raincoat over her shoulders; beneath it, she wore the khaki slacks and tunic typical of the Red Guards. When she saw me coming toward her, she jumped down respectfully and stood by the side of her wheel.

"How are you, Uncle Li Dunbai?"

"How are you, Morning Dove?" That was the name her family and friends still used, from back in the days when she was an infant in Yanan. Her father had been a musician there, playing in the string-and-winds ensemble at our dances. Her mother was an announcer.

"I'm sure that you're being a good daughter of Chairman Mao," I said. I knew that she was studying composition at the Central Conservatory of Music. But instead of beaming, as I had expected, she burst into tears.

"What is it, little Morning Dove?" I asked anxiously, putting my arm around her shoulders and peering down into her face through the hands that tried to cover it up. "What's the matter? You know you can tell me about it. After all, you peed all over my army overcoat and I didn't say anything, did I?"

There was a ripple of giggles through the crying. It was an old family joke. When she was less than a year old, I was keeping her occupied while her mother prepared to go on the air. I put her down on my beautiful black overcoat, thick fur under a blue silk lining, and noticed to my horror a widening puddle spreading out from where she sat.

"So what are you so upset about?" I asked again.

There was pain in her voice when she told me she had had to choose among three groups at her conservatory: a wild, anti-intellectual faction made up of angry service workers; a radical faction that wanted a complete overhaul of the school and the right to run everything themselves, with the old musical authorities staying on only as hired hands; and a moderate faction that wanted an overhaul, but stopped short of wanting to purge the old leaders.

Morning Dove was elected chairman of the conservatory's first Cultural Revolution Committee and took a moderate position. "I want the flaming red world of Mao Zedong Thought just as much as anyone," she sniffled. "It's just that I don't think the old cadres should be crushed like that." They were good people, experts on Western and Chinese music, she said. They should be allowed to correct their mistakes and go on.

But when Jiang Qing declared the rebel radical minority the true revolutionaries, Morning Dove's Cultural Revolution Committee collapsed. She was thrown out of the Cultural Revolution leadership at the school and became the butt of mockery and criticism. Now she was crushed, ashamed of having been so timid politically. "I feel bad because I let Chairman Mao down in the Cultural Revolution," she said.

I sat her down in the guardhouse at our gate. It didn't matter, I said. "Everybody makes mistakes in the Cultural Revolution. That's how we all learn."

◆

"Chairman Mao is going to receive the Red Guards in Tiananmen Square today!" the deputy editor of the English section newsroom said with excitement. "There's a big script to be broadcast tonight." It was August 18, and people in the newsroom were buzzing in anticipation.

I wanted to see as much of the demonstration as I could. So as soon as I had helped set up the day's programs, I headed for the square. As I walked down the Avenue of Eternal Peace from the Broadcast Administration, I saw endless detachments of Red

Guards, each school represented, carrying a red silken banner and a huge portrait of Chairman Mao on a pole before them. They were marching and singing, heading toward the square.

By the time I had reached the ceremonial southern gate to the government offices, more than half a mile from Tiananmen Square, I could go no further. The square was jammed with Red Guards. There were contingents from Beijing and the suburbs, and from as far away as Sichuan and Guangdong provinces, several days' journey on the train. Most of the people must have been waiting since the previous night.

The ornate cast-iron lampposts up and down the boulevard had all been wired with massive loudspeakers. Over the loudspeakers I could hear the full, resonant voice of Xia Qing, one of our star announcers, whose delivery was measured and well paced. "Now the meeting at which Chairman Mao receives the Red Guards has begun!" he proclaimed in a ringing timbre. The meeting was obviously being broadcast into every office and home in China.

Like a commentator calling the plays of an important match over the loudspeakers, Xia Qing told us what he saw. "Tiananmen Square today is a sea of red," he said. "Everywhere we see red banners, red armbands, red insignia on the collars of the army men and women. And everywhere we see these upturned shining faces looking up at the Red Sun in their hearts." All around me I could see those same shining faces.

Xia Qing went on. "On the gate we see our great leader, Chairman Mao Zedong, his close comrade-in-arms, Vice Chairman Lin Biao, and also Premier Zhou Enlai, and other responsible leading comrades." At the mention of Chairman Mao's name, the cry began to go up: "Long life to Chairman Mao, our Great Teacher, our Great Leader, our Great Commander-in-Chief, our Great Helmsman." I could hear it over the loudspeakers and all around me at the same time.

Lin Biao spoke first, his words filled with praise for the Red Guards. "The world belongs to you," he said. "The Little Champions of Revolution are the most sensitive, the most loyal, the most obedient of all the followers of our Great Leader." But as his speech proceeded, it was clear that the praise was only a prelude to a set of instructions. "We in this Proletarian Cultural Revolution are determined to smash the Four Olds!" he cried out. "Old ideas, old culture, old customs, old habits—until they are destroyed, we cannot move on. As our great Chairman Mao says:

'Without destruction, there is no construction. Nothing can be built up until something is torn down!' "

"Long life to Chairman Mao!" the students shouted. "Chairman Mao is the Red, Red, Reddest Sun in our hearts!"

Above the shouting, Xia Qing kept up a running commentary over the loudspeakers. "Our Great Leader, Chairman Mao Zedong, wearing the uniform of the People's Liberation Army, is now standing and waving to the crowd." That in itself was unusual. Before the Cultural Revolution, I had never seen Mao in an army uniform, not even in Yanan. "His comrade-in-arms Lin Biao is also saluting the Red Guards," Xia Qing said. "Chairman Mao is the one who loves the Red Guards the most and who cares about them the most in his heart!"

Suddenly a loud commotion rang out over the loudspeakers, and a cheering and shouting began that lasted for several minutes. When the announcer could be heard over the disturbance he explained. "A Red Guard representative is approaching the Chairman carrying a Red Guard armband." Then there was another deafening ovation. "Chairman Mao has accepted the Red Guard armband and has put it on."

As I returned to the Broadcast Administration, the cheers of the crowd followed me back. "The revolutionary Red Guards are good soldiers of Chairman Mao!" "Carry the Cultural Revolution through to the end!" "It's right to rebel!" "Long live our Great Teacher, Great Leader, Great Commander-in-Chief, Great Helmsman Chairman Mao!

"Long Live! Long Live! Long Live! Long Live!"

From that day on, the word on everyone's lips was "rebel." But it was an odd sort of word that Mao had used. The word was "zao fan" and it meant to turn all control and authority upside down. It was a word that might be used to describe a servant in a squire's house who ran amok, setting fire to the stables and smashing all the crockery. I had never heard it used before except in a destructive sense.

One morning in late August, a translator in my office burst in shouting, "The Little Champions of Revolution are on Wangfujing! They're getting rid of everything feudalistic and capitalistic."

Wangfujing was Beijing's main shopping district, and I decided on the spot to go there. I also decided to bring along some of the other foreign experts. I had fought my way into the Cultural Revolution, but they had not been so successful. Most didn't read or speak Chinese and so couldn't read the big-character posters. Without the secret channel to inside information being leaked from the top via rebel organizations, these foreign experts were almost completely shut out. I rounded up Edmundo Palacios, the Chilean Marxist, our friend Kandaswami from Ceylon, and Meme Galliano and Jaime Martens, both Brazilians. We set off on foot for Wangfujing, about three miles away.

After the rally in Tiananmen Square, the city had been transformed. There were big-character posters lining the street from the Broadcast Administration building all the way down to Tiananmen Square. They were pasted on fences and doors and telephone poles. They covered the long walls. Some were on ropes, strung between two sticks. I translated the posters for my friends as we went along.

Some were pleas from Red Guard groups. A rebel group from a factory in Chengdu in Sichuan Province appealed to colleagues for help in overcoming persecution from their leadership. A group of revolutionary coal miners from Shaanxi Province complained that reactionary mine heads were torturing their leaders.

There were political essays and tracts, analyses of Marxism and analysis of Mao Zedong Thought. They all boiled down to one point: it is right to rebel. But perhaps the most strongly worded posters were being put up by the organization that had formed to defend Liu Shaoqi and the other old cadres who were being attacked. "You dog spawn who dare to lay your foul hands on our old revolutionary cadres," such posters read, "you beware, you pig droppings, because retribution will be swift and terrible."

We walked slowly down the street, partly because of the hot muggy weather and partly because most foreign experts weren't used to such long walks. Kandaswami, for one, had a large, barrel-like belly. Sweat rolled down his neck and into the folds of his long white gown. When we finally arrived at Tiananmen, we found political speakers scattered all over the square. Each held forth on some topic, with their followers, or merely curious lookers-on, clustered about them, arguing and posing questions. Some were going on and on about their personal problems at school or at work. Some were bemoaning the fact that since the work teams had been withdrawn, the schools were out of control and nothing was being done about reforming education. Some were complaining that they had been falsely accused.

A few were real political stump speakers, calling their fellows to revolutionary action. Before each speaker began, someone would grab the microphone and, in a threatening voice, warn all the bad elements away. "Are there any of you little bastards from the five black categories around? Any landlords, capitalists, revisionists, counterrevolutionaries, or criminals?" the person shouted. "If you are here, you'd better get out before we find you." But in spite of all the crudeness and narrowness my friends and I saw, we were all happy and excited. This was revolution, it was free political expression. We had never seen anything like it before. We strolled Tiananmen Square, stopping here and there to chat with a speaker.

When we arrived at Wangfujing, we discovered that all hell had broken loose. Following Lin Biao's instructions, the Red Guards were sweeping away the Four Olds. Red Guards in mock army uniforms were pulling the brightly colored wooden or neon signs off the buildings and smashing them into pieces. They were tearing the doors off the shops and clambering up to scrape the paint off the sides of the buildings. Anything old and fancy that suggested bourgeois consumerism was being knocked apart. Shops with luxury goods, the Peking Duck restaurants, old street signs and shop signs with names that smacked of the old good-luck superstitions or of admiration for the old aristocracy—all were being shut down or smashed up.

The Red Guards had posted a hand-lettered sign that spelled out a new set of regulations, their own rules for the Cultural Revolution. Nothing that encouraged consumerism, nothing merely decorative would be permitted. The posters explained that parasites were wasting too much of the working people's time prettying themselves up. That would no longer be tolerated. As pedestrians passed by, the Red Guards—mostly high school students—would grab them and "process" them according to those regulations. Women with hair longer than regulation shoulder length had their braids summarily snipped. Men whose trousers were too tight had their pants clipped at the knees.

All of us watching this scene felt the same way about it. These were children, really, high school age or under. They had no guns, no weapons, no real strength. If any of the people they were harassing had decided to fight back, these kids couldn't have defended themselves. But none of us saw anyone fight back or even try to defy the Red Guards. Everyone did exactly what he or she was told. All these grown men and women stood by while children smashed their signs, clipped their pants, cut their hair. It was Mao, of course. His assumption of supreme authority authorized their attack on all other authority. Somehow it didn't seem entirely real. It had a touch of comic opera.

It was comic opera. But tragedy flowed in its wake.

I was in the newsroom when one of the translators, a party member, approached me. In very even tones, he told me politely that he was going to leave early and wouldn't be in the next day. "It's because of Little Yang," he said, referring to his wife. "Her mother and father were killed last night."

"Killed?" I asked, puzzled. I thought they must have been in some accident.

When the translator told me what had happened, he very carefully avoided any expression of judgment or any language that might have been construed as anger or pity. He spoke coolly, and I could see he was nervous. "Yes," he said. "They used to be shopkeepers in the old days and in recent years they worked in a small state-run shop near Wangfujing. Last night, some of the Red Guards who were sweeping away the Four Olds came to their room in the middle of the night and started to question them. I don't know why, but they beat them to death."

I was shocked and horrified. I didn't understand why he wasn't more upset than he was. I guessed that he feared trouble for himself and his wife if he showed sympathy for the exploiting classes, or laid himself open to charges of wanting revenge. Lin Biao's call had brought out, not only the Little Champions of Revolution, but the little tigers. There was a violent, ugly under-current to this rebellion that no one was prepared for.

Then the violence spread to the Broadcast Administration.

Ever since Mei Yi had been removed from power, we saw him every day, sadly coming into the building, settling into an empty conference room and working on the self-criticisms he had been ordered to write. But a few days after Lin Biao's speech, all that changed. I was in the English section when someone stuck his head in the door and shouted, "They are struggling with the freaks and monsters inside the front gate."

The room emptied out as we all rushed to see what was going on. I ran down the stairs leading from the front doors of the building to the vast cement courtyard outside. There I saw a gro-tesque and hideous sight. About ten of the old cadres were in the courtyard, surrounded by a group of mostly young people.

Ever since the old cadres had been deposed, these old revolu-tionaries had spent their time quietly writing self-criticisms and going to meetings. Some had been allowed to continue working. Now Lin Biao's speech had spurred the young people to treat them much more harshly. The day before, Beijing Red Guards had unmercifully hazed a group of distinguished artists and writers, as a result of which China's best-known writer of fiction, Lao She, lost his life.

Among the group in the courtyard were Mei Yi and my old friend Ding Yilan. Their heads had been shaved. Mei Yi had only half of his gray hair left; Ding Yilan had half of her soft black hair dangling down over her face, which was white and frightened, every line stretched taut.

Was this truly revolutionary action? Among the young people in the courtyard I recognized a recording engineer, someone I knew was disgruntled with Mei Yi. She had taken one of his cloth shoes and was beating him about the head. His glasses had been knocked to the ground. Pale and terrified, he was quivering violently from head to foot.

Then a couple of the young people made little speeches about the black gang at the Broadcast Administration. "These are the Little Khrushchevs who have been sleeping by our side," they said. "They would walk a revisionist road. But the Cultural Revolution has exposed them." Next the young people hung large wooden signboards around each of their victims' necks. I could only read one. "Mei Yi is a counterrevolutionary black gang member," it said.

They herded the old cadres from the center of the courtyard over to the eastern end and made them kneel down along the edge of the stone porch just outside the front doors to the radio building. From this elevated position, the old cadres faced the crowd. Holding their shoes aloft—they were not allowed to lower their arms—they one after the other were ordered to sing out the inscriptions on their placards. "I am counterrevolutionary revisionist Mei Yi," I heard him quaver.

"Louder!" shouted a young rebel. And Mei Yi was forced to repeat it several times.

I wanted to throw up.

I couldn't denounce the rebels. No one could. The crowd was too big, the mood was too ugly. Besides, ugly as it was, I couldn't help seeing the revolutionary spirit in it. These young people had gone overboard, it was true. That, perhaps, was the price for setting free a people who had no experience with freedom. Given time, they would learn, I thought. Meanwhile, I didn't believe anything should be done to risk crushing the newly awakened vigor of the masses.

Mao said that in a revolution everyone had to choose: a place with the revolutionaries or a place with the oppressors. I had made my choice. Still, I vowed that our rebels wouldn't be like these young rowdies. We would eschew violence. Not just eschew it, but work against it. The crowd disbanded and I returned to my office. But from then on, I saw Mei Yi, Ding Yilan, and the other old comrades every day, mournfully doing yard work, picking up the garbage in the Broadcast Administration courtyard.

To me, however, the real issue wasn't the behavior of these young hooligans. To me, the real issue was democracy. The control the party had exercised was over. Now who would rule in its place? Would a new dictatorship emerge? Or would each organization—as I hoped—evolve into a true democratic community, electing its own leaders, setting its own policy, solving its own problems?

I asked Little Shi that question. "We can set up our own organizations with whomever we like," she said, eyes flashing. She was a pretty young matron with large light brown eyes and long lashes, usually very quiet and proper. Now she was caught up in the cause of free speech, and free criticism.

"But who sets up the organizations and how do you join?" I pressed.

"It's simple," she replied. "You just join up with anyone who shares your own viewpoint. The organizations are set up by people with a viewpoint in common. It may be a group of a thousand people or it may be only five. Upstairs in the African department there's even an organization called the Independent Thought Combat Team, which is only one person. He has his own viewpoint, so he hasn't joined with anyone else in an organization."

Ever since 1949, no one had been allowed to set up any sort of organization without the approval and control of the party. People who buddied up in twos or threes or even two couples who hung out together were often criticized for forming a "little clique" separate from the party and the masses. I had heard our acting party branch secretary comment back in 1957 that two women in her overseas Chinese broadcast section were a little clique. The proof? "They are always together, and there's nothing they don't talk about between them."

Now, all of a sudden, there were no barriers. For these people, it was the first time in their lives they could meet, form organizations, speak, and publish freely. For China, it was an earthshaking change.

◆

On the first Wednesday afternoon in September, I was walking home from work when I noticed a big meeting going on in the TV theater. "What is it?" I asked someone coming out.

"The rebels are holding a meeting to discuss the Ma Wenyou incident," he said. "Ma Wenyou has taken over the meeting and is questioning Peng Bao on the stage."

I had no idea what the Ma Wenyou incident was, or even who Ma Wenyou was, but I wanted to see Peng Bao answering questions. He was the director of the Broadcast Administration's security department, our own political police.

I picked a seat next to a friend in the Portuguese section, someone who had been quietly funneling me rebel literature. "What's all this about?" I whispered.

"Ma Wenyou is a technician," he whispered back. "Poor peasant family, party member. He is one of the early rebels at the Broadcast Administration, and he has been agitating people in his department. The leadership decided that he was dangerous and should be confined in our detention center. But because of his family origin and party membership, his department can't send him as an inmate. They arranged with Peng Bao to send him over as a guard. But really, it was to get him out of the way. Now Ma Wenyou is accusing Peng Bao of this, and Peng Bao is vowing it's not true."

Peng Bao was seated on a chair at center stage, smiling sourly as if his liver ached. He was a tall, slouching peasant type with a prematurely wrinkled face. To me, he seemed like a typical flatfoot, plodding, trying to do his job, gifted with more loyalty than brains. His accuser, Ma Wenyou, striding back and forth in great diagonals across the stage, was very much the man in charge. He was of medium height, wearing a cadre's uniform with the blue pants rolled up to his knees to reveal a pair of red flannels underneath. He had a large head with tousled hair, and a broad horsey peasant face, heavily freckled.

Ma Wenyou was throwing questions at Peng Bao, who was clearly vexed at having to turn his head and neck to follow his questioner. "Isn't it true that you sent me over there so that you could get me out of the technical department and keep an eye on me?" Ma accused. "Didn't you do it to shut my mouth?"

"Of course not," said Peng Bao. "How could we do a thing like that?" His tone was unctuous. "Why, Comrade Ma Wenyou, you are our own class brother. You're a member of the Chinese Communist Party, from a laboring family." He was droning on and on. "Why ever would we do a thing like that to you? It would be against the policy of the party—"

Wham! A loud noise in the middle of the row just in front of me stopped Peng Bao in midsentence.

Someone had pounded the chair back with his fist and then leaped to his feet. "Peng Bao! Peng Bao!" he cried. "You're lying! You're lying!" He was holding up a piece of paper in his right hand, shaking it in the direction of Peng Bao, who now looked like a man in shock.

I recognized the man who had leaped up and was now making his way down the aisle. He was Yuan Zhe, Peng Bao's confidential secretary. He marched up onto the stage and grabbed hold of the central microphone. "You're lying, Peng Bao," he said. "You think you're lying to protect the party. But I'm going to tell you, I'm not going to lie for the party anymore. I have told my last lie for the party."

A gasp went up around the room.

"All this time I've been lying to people to protect the good name of the party," Yuan Zhe continued. "But now my mind has been freed by this Cultural Revolution that Chairman Mao started and I can see very clearly that we have been suppressing people, taking away their rights, and all in the name of protecting the party. I'm not going to be a part of that any longer."

Yuan waved the sheet of paper in his hand. "You see this paper?" he asked the crowd. "This is a copy of a letter that Peng Bao sent to the head of the detention center. Let me read it to you all, so you can judge for yourselves whether Comrade Ma Wenyou is being suppressed."

Peng Bao went purple as his secretary read the letter. Ma Wenyou is a dangerous troublemaker, he had written. Because of his good family background, it wasn't convenient to send him to a detention center directly, so he was being transferred as a guard. The head of the camp was instructed to assign people to watch him, to impose the proper restrictions, and to see that he didn't stir up any more trouble.

There was a roar of indignation from the audience. The cry went up, "Peng Bao, tell the truth! Tell the truth!" Peng Bao's jaw was set and he sat there grimly. Nothing was going to shake his loyalty.

Then, in the back, about a dozen men leaped to their feet. "We're from the security department and we are forming our own rebel group," one man said. "The entire department has decided to join with us, and we want to be accepted into the rebel regiment!"

Thunderous applause greeted this announcement. As for me, I felt as if shackles had just fallen from my body. Like Yuan Zhe, I too had covered for the party when talking to nonparty members, thinking that it was in the people's interest. Now, as I watched Yuan Zhe's insurrection, I felt both released from the obligation ever to do that again, and at the same time ashamed of myself for having been blindly loyal.

I thought to myself, if this isn't a real rebellion, I don't know what is. This is my kind of fight, the fight for civil rights, for the right of the people to be protected from arbitrary treatment by the big bosses. This is the kind of fight I was proud to have been a part of in the South during the civil rights movement and my days as a labor organizer.

I began to read the rebels' material regularly. They had developed a whole program for the Broadcast Administration. These young people wanted to build a new society, the kind of society I had originally envisioned when I joined the party. They wanted a kind of town hall democracy, with everyone having a say in selecting their leadership. They wanted complete freedom to express their views, to organize, and to meet. And they wanted complete and total civil rights. No more dossiers, no more checking into people's backgrounds. "Your history only explains your past," they wrote. "Your actions explain your present."

These were my kind of people. I started to attend their meetings regularly and to bring my other foreign expert friends along. I began to learn more about what had been going on at the Broadcast Administration. The people who had been in the party's internal security apparatus were now in the rebel regiment and leaked out information. Recently, I found out, someone had denounced me to the public security ministry. I was now on a list as one of the three most dangerous elements at the Broadcast Administration. Who had denounced me? My ex-wife, Wei Lin.

I was called into the office of my boss, the vice director in charge of foreign broadcasts. When I got there, he looked grave. "I don't want you to misunderstand some of the things you have been reading and hearing," he said. "There are some bad people here at the Broadcast Administration who are fomenting dissension and stirring up hostility to the party leadership. You should not associate with such people."

A year ago I would have obeyed. But I was a changed man. I told him I would associate with whomever I pleased and left his office.

◆

October 1, 1966, was the seventeenth anniversary of the People's Republic and I was on top of the Tiananmen Gate Tower, waiting for Mao Zedong to appear. It would be the first time I had seen him since the Cultural Revolution began. How had he changed?

I had been notified to attend the celebration only at noon the previous day by a call from the foreign experts bureau. Foreign experts had never before been invited to review the annual parade with Mao. The half dozen of us foreigners who were chosen for the honor were driven to the Friendship Hotel where we spent the night, and by nine that morning, one hour before the parade was to begin, we were escorted up a ramp from the Forbidden City and placed near the fourth column on the east side of the gate.

The square before us was already jammed with Red Guards. I saw a sea of blue uniforms, laced with beige and khaki, punctuated with red armbands. The huge balloons at the edges of the square trailed long slogan-streamers: "Long Live Our Great Teacher, Great Leader, Great Commander-in-Chief, Great Helmsman Chairman Mao!" "Long Live the People's Republic of China," and "Long Live the Great Proletarian Cultural Revolution."

On top of the great crimson gate was a pavilion covered by a roof with flying eaves like a temple. There were twin ramps from inside the walls of the Imperial Palace that led up to the top. Small chairs and tables were set up in the pavilion with larger chairs along the walls. To watch the parade, however, everyone had to stand.

At the stroke of ten, the huge People's Liberation Army band in the square struck up "The East Is Red" and Mao appeared in the center of the reviewing stand. At his side was the shrunken, chalky-white Marshal Lin Biao, and behind them, Premier Zhou

Enlai, Tao Zhu, the number-four-ranked minister of propaganda, Deng Xiaoping, Kang Sheng, Liu Shaoqi, and Chen Yi, the minister of foreign affairs.

Mao looked completely different from when I saw him last. I was used to a thoughtful, laughing, relaxed leader. Today, he looked stiffly self-conscious in a starched People's Liberation Army uniform, waving his right hand back and forth slowly. He removed his army cap and waved it in a slow arc at the crowd below. They roared up at him, "Long Live Chairman Mao! Long Live Chairman Mao! Long Live Chairman Mao!"

As I glanced around, I realized everyone looked a little different. Zhou Enlai wore an army uniform like the other leaders, but he was no longer the dashing young general I had met in Fresh Flower Village in 1946. His green garments looked rumpled, and age and stress had thinned, dried, and slightly twisted his mouth. I started when I saw a thin, gray-looking man come toward me in ordinary cadre dress. It was my old friend Marshal Chen Yi, and I barely recognized him, he had shriveled so much.

Liu Shaoqi, still nominally the president of the People's Republic, was standing with Mao, waving at the crowd below. Suddenly, he turned and looked about at the people behind him, as if he was searching for a friend. I was shocked by what I saw. He had been the most patrician of all the old leaders, with calm, cool eyes and a strong chin. I remembered seeing him one day in 1948 walking along the road in the Taihang Mountains, a brown woolen scarf wrapped tightly around his head. His wife, Wang Guangmei, was walking behind him, two paces to the rear, one to the left, and I thought, Communist or not, there goes Confucianism. Now the eyes that seemed desperately searching for a friend were beady with fear. He licked his dry lips from time to time. He had never been one of my favorite people, but now he looked pitiable.

There was silence while the band played the national anthem. Then the parade began down below. Tens of thousands of Red Guards and members of rebel groups from Beijing and all over the country marched through the square, shouting "Long Live Chairman Mao!" All the young people in the sea of faces below were holding aloft their Little Red Books. The leaders of party and state stood watching from their high perch, saying very little to each other.

At around eleven, I went to the reception area at the rear of the pavilion where you could sit and sip a cup of tea or a bottle of the local orange pop. There, I found Deng Xiaoping hunched over a table by himself, shunned by all, holding a bottle of orange pop with a straw stuck in it, but not drinking. He was just sitting there, his left elbow on the table and his forehead resting on his left hand. He looked lonely and ill at ease.

I got a bottle of pop and approached his table. "Comrade Deng, I am Li Dunbai," I said, offering him my hand. I thought he might not recognize me. I had met him, but we had never spent time together.

"Oh, yes, yes, yes," he blurted out with an apologetic little smile. "Yes, indeed, I know." He rose to shake my hand and then we sat together in silence, while I tried to think of something to say. He looked so forlorn that after a while I realized there was nothing I could do to reach him. I excused myself and quietly left his table.

Everyone seemed skittish and more deferential than usual of the Chairman. Sometime around eleven o'clock, Mao turned his big frame around from the reviewing stand and lumbered toward a line of comfortable chairs with red-velvet seat cushions at the rear of the pavilion. He seated himself and lit up one of his Gongzi brand cigarillos. After a moment, Premier Zhou Enlai joined him and they chatted while I stood off to one side, watching.

Suddenly, I saw Mao mutter something, looking not at Zhou but straight ahead. Immediately, the sixty-five-year-old Premier leaped to his feet and charged full speed from the enclosed rest area to the reviewing stand, shouting out the name of the Beijing garrison commander: "Zheng Weishan! Zheng Weishan!"

I saw Zheng Weishan run up to him. Zhou whispered in his ear and pointed to Mao, who was slowly getting himself to his feet and moving toward the reviewing stand. Zheng Weishan shouted orders to his left and right, and then hurried over to escort Mao. Zhou Enlai, rumored to have a weak heart, had jumped up and raced about like a young boy simply because Mao had said he was ready to leave the rest area and go back to reviewing the parade.

I had gathered long ago that Zhou, after being defeated in the early 1930s when he supported policies that Mao opposed, had given up any idea of developing his own strategy for the Chinese Revolution and had submitted to Mao as the helmsman and prophet. He fought for tactical points that he considered important, but yielded to Mao on strategy—and worked long and hard as his chief of staff to implement his policies. I had just seen a picture of Zhou's dedication to Mao, even at the risk of his own health. It seemed highly exaggerated, yet I knew it was real.

Near twelve o'clock, the end of the parade, there was a sudden move among the foreign guests to get Mao to autograph their Little Red Books. Anna Louise Strong was one of the first. My old friend Liao Chengzhi brought her forward to see Mao. I soon followed, doing some pushing and squeezing through the crowd to make sure I got my autograph too.

When I came up to Mao, he was standing there bareheaded. His army cap was gone. "Chairman," I began, the habitual manner in which he was addressed.

"Rit-ten-berg," he said, articulating the syllables slowly in English, after which he grinned broadly as if proud of himself. "I have studied English for a very long time, but I never seem able to get it."

"Well, your pronunciation of my name was fine," I said. "Would you write in my Little Red Book?"

He took the book out of my hand, and took my little pen in his other hand, and stood there looking quizzically down at the writing in the front of the book—my signature in Chinese, Li Dunbai. "What do you want me to write in your book?" he asked, making me feel like a tiny boy as he loomed over me.

I should have asked him to write some new directive for the masses, or one of his famous poems, or a personal message to me, or something for the American people—but my mind went blank. All I could think of was to say, "Just write your name."

And that's what he did. He wrote Mao Zedong in a beautiful hand vertically down the edge of the page, large bold characters, each flowing into the next without a break.

At twelve o'clock sharp, the parade ended and a sonorous voice declared the celebration over. Mao, Lin Biao, and Zhou left first, followed by an orderly withdrawal of the others in the pavilion. Below, in the square, the crowd filed out column by column in silence. I left the gate and went straight back to the office. Because it was National Day, there was only a skeleton staff and just five or six people in the English section. As soon as I walked in, the program editor looked up. "Old Li!" he cried. "We saw you up there on the gate. We were watching it on TV. Did you shake hands with Chairman Mao?"

I had pushed my way through the crowd to the Chairman at least partly for these people. "Yes," I said.

"Have you washed your hands?" someone asked.

"No," I laughed, and they crowded around me to seize my hand. The cult of Mao was in full swing. Before the Cultural

Revolution, he was a hero. Now he was a god. Shaking hands with a man who had shaken the hand of Mao was something to tell your grandchildren. One of my colleagues ran down the hall to spread the news, and soon people in all the different translation groups were pouring in by threes and fours, from the German section, the Russian section, French, Vietnamese, about forty people in all. And there I stood, the man who had shaken hands with Mao, shaking hands with everyone who could press in close enough.

CHAPTER EIGHTEEN

Seize Power

And so Mao turned me into a personage, someone valuable, someone to be courted by both sides. For by now at the Broadcast Administration, the battle lines were drawn. It was the new world versus the old. Just as Lin Biao had said, the Cultural Revolution was a revolution against our old revolution.

It was easy to tell the two groups apart. The conservatives defending the status quo were largely older cadres or uneducated workers and ex-soldiers. Even though Mei Yi had been deposed, these conservatives were still in control. Ding Laifu, the old army man now in charge, was like the other conservatives struggling to maintain law and order, to keep his ruling party committee afloat, and not to rock the boat.

The conservatives had come along a hard road, often a grim one. Veterans of one mass movement after another, many of them suffered from insomnia. They were knee-jigglers, finger-drummers. Even though they commanded their battered bodies to sit up long hours bending over their work, their efficiency was as low as their energy level and their minds balked at any innovation no matter what the source. Professionally, the only thing they were really good at was tailoring the programs so they would not offend political sensibilities. "Bu qiu you gong, dan qiu wu guo" was an old saying people used to describe them: "I don't seek achievement, but only not to do anything wrong." They were a dogged, hard-bitten, change-resistant crew.

The rebels were younger. Aside from one retired army man, none was over thirty-five. They had all grown up after Liberation; many were party members. They were loyal to the Communist Party as they thought it should be—not a conservative bunch of power-holders, but a truly revolutionary party that kept society in a constant state of innovation and rebirth.

The conservatives wore their standard blue cotton cadre's suits. The rebels mimicked military wear. The old cadres were family men and women, given to Monday morning grousing about household tasks. The rebels, who had never actually lived in Yanan, were fascinated by its mystique and were dedicated to the good old revolutionary virtues of the Yanan days—frugality, hard work, simple living, staying in close touch with the masses.

Because many of the conservatives were, like me, in their forties and fifties, veterans of Yanan and of our campaign against the Nationalists, they naturally assumed I would support them. They spoke to my devotion to the party. "You are a living Dr. Bethune," they gushed, referring to the much-revered Canadian doctor who had died while setting up China's first-ever field hospitals for the People's Army. Because of my history, I should understand the position of the old leaders, they said. I was an old revolutionary too. "You are our old comrade, an old friend from the Yanan days." The party had appointed Ding Laifu. I was a loyal party member. Therefore, I should help keep him in power.

But I wasn't interested. It was the rebels whose cause attracted me. They were fighting for Chairman Mao's revolutionary line, and against the reactionary bourgeois line of which Liu Shaoqi and Deng Xiaoping were accused. They envisioned a China in which a vibrant party would build a thriving, prosperous, democratic socialist society.

I knew which side I was on. After one of the rebel meetings, I climbed onto the stage to greet the leaders. "I'm ready to help the rebel regiment in any way I can," I said.

"You're welcome to come to our meetings," a rebel leader said.

I did. And a few days later at a rebel meeting I was accepted into the organization. They pinned a red armband on me that read: "Regiment to Defend Mao Zedong Thought." The rebels also resurrected a title for me, dug up from the secret reports of my meeting in 1963 with Mao and the African guerrillas. I was Li Dunbai, the internationalist fighter for Communism.

I found the rebels to be real freedom fighters. They fought against the systems the party had used to control us. One evening in early November, I was coming home late when I was surprised to see the main gate of the Broadcast Administration building open and what looked like a platoon of soldiers guarding it. Facing the soldiers was a milling band of students wearing Red Guard armbands. I walked up to the gate. A stocky, red-cheeked girl with one shock of hair tied up in a ribbon was haranguing the soldiers. It was Cao Huiru, a girl the Chairman's wife had called out of detention at the Broadcast Institute.

"This is a struggle," she was shouting. "Feudal landlords and capitalists are on one side and the working class and poor peasants on the other." She jabbed her finger at the chest of the platoon commander. "You are the People's Army," she cried. "You should be supporting us."

The Broadcast Administration was always well guarded. The leadership feared that the mouthpiece of the Dictatorship of the Proletariat would fall into unfriendly hands. This evening, however, it was particularly heavily defended. "We have orders not to let in anyone who doesn't work in this building," the platoon commander said.

"Enough of this nonsense," Cao Huiru shouted. Turning to her band of students, she waved toward the gate. "We are going in!" she yelled. The soldiers leaped forward and trained their guns on the students. But she was all brass and bravado, shaking her finger in the face of the lead soldier and stomping her foot. "Who do you think you're pointing your guns at? For shame! Are we the enemies you're supposed to guard against?"

Cao Huiru startled the soldiers just enough to win one moment of hesitation. She seized it, and she and her band stormed the gate. I followed behind. The Red Guards knew exactly where they were going, straight to the sixth floor and the dossier room. The files in that room had become politically explosive. Lin Biao had ordered all dossiers kept on rebels during the Cultural Revolution sealed or destroyed; the conservative forces were stalling.

Cao Huiru, sounding like Patrick Henry, began to lecture a political officer who was blocking her way into the room. "We are ready to die for our democratic rights," she shouted. "You are violating the decisions of the Central Committee. We are here defending the Central Committee, not attacking it."

"But we have no instructions," began Li Zhefu, the old army staff officer who was now deputy director of the Broadcast Administration and head of its political work department. She didn't let him finish. She drew herself up, crying, "The time has come to sacrifice for the people!" and flung herself at the door.

A huge military security man, loyal to law and order and the existing regime, blocked her way. One of the students sank her teeth into his arm, through several thicknesses of clothing. And while he was shaking her off, ten students charged the room and began pulling at the doors of the cabinets containing their files.

The deputy director was chalky white. The two sides tussled over the documents. It was bedlam. Finally, the students withdrew from the sixth floor to the third-floor conference room to plan their next moves. I went with them, and while we were talking, two leading members of the Central Cultural Revolution Group, Vice Chairman Zhang Chunqiao and principal scribe Yao Wenyuan, suddenly appeared in the main editorial offices, demanding to speak to Ding Laifu. A rebel on the office staff was there and later told me what happened.

Speaking with the awesome weight of the Cultural Revolution Committee, Zhang and Yao chastised the Broadcast Administration leaders. They had behaved disgracefully. The students were right. The dossiers were to be sealed, pending final destruction. And the Cultural Revolution Group members didn't let it go at that. They demanded that a public meeting be called the next day, at which Broadcast Administration leaders were to make a full apology to the students and the students were to tell their story for the entire staff to hear.

The conflict ended, but not, I heard, before Zhang Chunqiao asked for me: "Where is our old friend Li Dunbai?" The young rebels who reported that fact were filled with awe. I, however, was simply startled. When I heard that Zhang had asked for me, I realized with a start that the person I had been reading about in the newspapers, the person third in command at the Cultural Revolution Group, was the same little man I had known in Kalgan and while we were in the mountains. Now, including Jiang Qing and Chen Boda, I knew five of the ten members of the Central Cultural Revolution Group.

I got up extra early the next morning to be ready for the meeting. I wanted a seat near the center of the action. The meeting was scheduled for nine A.M. Word had spread about the pending public apology, and by eight A.M. the twelve hundred seats in the TV theater were full. There were people in the aisle, sitting on the stage, maybe two hundred more in total, and even more packed around the outside and in other halls where loudspeakers had been set up.

The deputy director made his apology: "We are old revolutionaries in a new revolution," Li Zhefu said, copying the phrase from the self-criticism I had heard on the tape recorded by Deng Xiaoping. "We don't know how to handle it. We are out of our depth. I'm sorry I didn't treat the students better."

It wasn't exactly a great apology, but the triumphant students could afford to be magnanimous. Cao Huiru took the microphone and accepted the apology. "We never intended to create a disturbance," she said. "We were forced into it because you rejected the central leadership's instructions to give us the material collected against us."

Then the heckling began. The conservatives defending the existing leadership began taunting her: "Chairman Mao says you must fight with words not with weapons!" one cried. From around the room, more shouts rang out: "You bit a Liberation Army man! You broke through the gate! What will happen if everyone runs wild like this?"

The rebels' supporters leaped to their feet to counter the accusations: "The students broke in because the leaders wouldn't obey the law! Comrade Jiang Qing says follow closely after the Little Champions of the Revolution!" The atmosphere grew tense. Around the theater, people began to square off, and it was easy to see that in about two minutes a fight was going to break out. In that packed room, a brawl would be ugly.

My heart was pounding. I was thinking, here, at last, is something I can do for this revolution, something more than translating texts and passing on propaganda. Because I am an American, a foreigner, a popular figure, I can get all the warring factions to listen to me. I can be the conciliator. But I had to move fast. I was really worried we were going to have a riot.

I leaped on the stage. Suddenly there was dead silence. I asked the girl, Cao Huiru, if I could say something. She gave three quick nods, and with a look half fearful, half hopeful, handed me the mike. "Comrades!" I cried, pointing to the students. "Who are these people?" I waited to let the words sink in. "These are our successors!" It was a quotation from Mao and it acted like magic. Everyone in the room burst into applause and the atmosphere changed just like that.

"According to what I saw," I continued, "the students were moderate, well behaved, and careful not to hurt anybody. They

took good care of public property. All they did was to put themselves in a position where they could reason with the leaders who
had refused to reason with them.

"What's different about the Cultural Revolution," I said, "is
that the leaders don't get to refuse to reason with people who have
opinions. They have to give them a hearing. Why do some people
want to disrupt? What is it that they are afraid of? If they think
the truth is on their side, why won't they let the students speak?
Chairman Mao says that this is where freedom of speech, of asso-
ciation, of publication is now going to be carried out for the first
time in Chinese history."

All around the room, people leaped to their feet, applauding. It
worked, I thought. I brought them together.

When I returned to the office after the meeting, everyone was
full of praise for me. You really came through in a pinch, they
said. That took guts. That afternoon, I heard the secretaries listening to a tape of my talk. By the next day, the big-character posters
were going up. "Comrade Li Dunbai told it the way it was," one
said. "This American friend took his stand courageously with the
minority students fighting for real democracy and defied the powerful bad elements who were trying to start trouble."

Within a few days, I heard that the tape of my speech was being
played all over the country. I began getting letters and phone calls
from schools, factories, institutes. All over China people were talking about the drama at the Broadcast Administration and the part
I had played in it. I had done what was right, and it had worked.
I can be accepted, I thought. I can make things happen the way I
used to in the South. I can be a part of changing the world.

Largely because of that speech, I became known as a rebel
advocate all over China. People recognized me on the street, and
I could block a whole line of traffic simply by agreeing to stop to
autograph one Little Red Book. If I wrote in one, I would quickly
be surrounded by hundreds of young people. When I took a
domestic flight, as I did not long after, the attendants treated me
with such respect that a British courier pulled me aside. "May I
know your name, sir?" he asked. "You are obviously some great
person, and I didn't know there were such foreigners in China."

When I attended meetings, I would be escorted ceremoniously
up to the front of the room and seated on the rostrum in the place
of honor among fellow dignitaries. Schools, institutes, international friendship associations, high-level rebel meetings—everyone wanted to associate themselves with me and my influence.

♦

In those heady, hypnotic days, we all did strange, sometimes outrageous things. How could we have been so carried away? I later wondered. How could we have forgotten ourselves like that? But back then it was real, vital, necessary. We were caught up in a trance of excitement and change.

There was no heat inside the Beijing Workers' Gymnasium when we piled in for the Big Criticism and struggle meeting. We kept our coats, hats, gloves, and mufflers on. The huge circular gymnasium was packed. Some in the audience were student Red Guards. The rest were people from the various news organizations like Xinhua, the *People's Daily,* and the Broadcast Administration. There were reporters, editors, technicians, print shop workers, service and maintenance staff.

This was indeed Big Criticism. The big meant both large-scale —there were over fifteen thousand people in the gymnasium— and uncompromising, a criticism that minced no words toward anyone. And the meeting targeted those at the very top: Lu Dingyi, the deposed minister of propaganda whom I had known in Yanan; Wu Lengxi, former chief of the *People's Daily* and the New China News Agency; Zhou Yang, propaganda ministry czar over literature and art; and Mei Yi, director of the Broadcast Administration. One of the banner slogans running around the walls of the gymnasium read "Beijing News and Propaganda Group Big Criticism Meeting against Counterrevolutionary Revisionists Zhou Yang, Lu Dingyi, and Wu Lengxi. Another read "Overthrow the Devil's Den—Liberate the Little Demons!"

As I walked down the aisle toward the podium, I came face-to-face with Lu Dingyi. I had always liked and respected him, and found him witty and intelligent. He was wide-eyed and staring, but he showed no sign of recognition. A Red Guard was grasping each arm, raising it up and backward so that he was forced into the twisting crouch known as the jet-plane position. Another Red Guard had his hand on the top of his head, pressing it toward the ground. Like the other targets of the meeting, he was dressed in black prison garments, cotton-padded, with no cap.

I was escorted to my seat on the rostrum along with the dignitaries. I sat down beside Mu Xin, who had been a reporter back in Yanan, a war correspondent. I thought he was a swaggerer and I had never liked him. Now he was the head of the *Guangming Daily,* and a member of the Cultural Revolution leading group.

As each target was dragged in, a stentorian male voice led the crowd in shouting slogans. "Down with counterrevolutionary revisionist Lu Dingyi!" "Wu Lengxi, bow your dog's head down!" And we sang a battle song, a direct quotation from Jiang Qing set to music: "When anyone dares oppose our Great Leader Chairman Mao, we will smash his dog's head!" Then the voice read out an indictment against each man as his turn came, accusing him of having followed an evil, revisionist line, and sabotaging Chairman Mao's work. The indictments were punctuated by a full-throated cry from the audience: "Bow Your Dog's Head Down!" Then the young Red Guards pushed down on each man's neck and pulled up and back on his arms, twisting his body even more.

The roars of the crowd volleyed and thundered around the gymnasium. The people in the audience seemed to be enjoying themselves. There were smiles all over. People were amused at the sight of these old crocks who had only recently wielded such unbelievable power over them, but were now reduced to disgrace and misery. None of the targets was allowed to speak. Every so often, one of them—like Zhou Yang—screamed in pain when his arms were pulled back too far, or when a Red Guard cuffed him.

From the rostrum, I shouted and raised my fist along with the others. The masses were being aroused, awakened, by leading them in struggle against the representatives of the old dictatorship. They were being taught to hate the old regime and everything associated with it. And that would lead to reforming our revolution, workplace by workplace.

Still, I found the violence of the whole process repulsively cruel. I turned to Mu Xin. "Isn't this in violation of Chairman Mao's policy?" I asked. "Didn't he say to make the Cultural Revolution with words, and not with force?"

He smiled an oily smile. "This is just one of the traditional ways the masses have of handling contradictions," he replied. "It's not really violence." So it was only violence if the enemies of the people did it, and not if the masses did it? I thought it was a self-serving argument, but I kept quiet. The next time I saw Mu Xin, however, he was in a gymnasium himself, in the jet-plane position. "Down with Counterrevolutionary Revisionist Mu Xin," a big banner read.

◆

All over China, in nearly every large organization, the leaders were falling. At the Broadcast Administration, we began to set our sights on Ding Laifu. The rebel group had gone back and forth on the question of what to do with him. At first, our group had tried to win him over. If he would only make a self-criticism and agree to mend his ways, he could go with us into the new world of revolutionary democracy.

I went to see him, to persuade him. But he refused. "If I admit I'm wrong, then I'm okay. If I don't admit I'm wrong, then I'm not okay. Is that right?" he said with a grin.

"That's what I think," I said. "You have to have faith in the masses. If you do a good job of self-criticism, you will win the understanding of the masses, and you won't have a problem."

"I can't really agree," he said. "Your problem is that you don't understand that this is a different kind of movement than we have ever had before. Look around you. Do you see a single place where the leadership has acceded to the demands of the masses and then wasn't overthrown?"

He was right. I couldn't name one. But I still believed the rebel leaders were sincere. If Ding Laifu made the self-criticism the rebels asked for, I told him, I personally would guarantee to give him my all-out backing. As it was, we couldn't excuse or support him.

Big-character posters began to appear denouncing Ding Laifu for his actions, and mutterings grew louder about the callousness of bureaucrats. The pressure was building. The rebels trying to unseat Ding Laifu were boring in harder and harder, attacking his weak spots in meetings and in big-character posters. Meanwhile, Ding Laifu further incriminated himself by sponsoring the formation of a quasi-rebel conservative group that defended him. They called themselves the Dare-to-Die Brigade, and they were counterattacking, trying to undermine the power of the rebels, to break them down and destroy their organization.

Who was right? Who was wrong? It was all so different from the days of absolute obedience. The party could give us no guidance. The party itself was divided. We had to think for ourselves, and it wasn't easy. At dinner one night at the home of an American friend, I grew teary-eyed thinking about it. "I wish I could figure out what Chairman Mao wanted me to do," I said. "If I knew the answer, I would just do it and life would be very simple."

On December 12, we bowed to the inevitable. Our rebel group planned a meeting and there, for the first time, we would unfurl our slogan: "Down with Ding Laifu."

We invited everyone, not only the workers at the Broadcast

Administration, but also the radical students from the Broadcast Institute. The students, with their more developed rebel organization, would be especially important in reinforcing our efforts. But as our preparations proceeded, we heard that Ding Laifu's friends at the top had mobilized troops to support him. We heard through the grapevine that the regimental commander for the west city garrison had moved his headquarters nearby and was ready to ensure that the students didn't get into the Broadcast Administration compound.

That morning, we awoke to find soldiers everywhere. A whole extra platoon had been brought in. Soldiers were manning every gate, with the back gate leading to the theater especially heavily fortified. The meeting was scheduled for three. At two forty-five, I went out to the back gate. There stood about thirty of our people from the rebel regiment, being faced down by about twenty armed People's Liberation Army soldiers outside the gate. The same area was choked solid by about a dozen big men from the conservative Dare-to-Die Brigade, the protectors of Ding Laifu.

We stood there, two hostile phalanxes. Both sides held Little Red Books. Suddenly, the battle erupted—into quotations. "Be resolute, fear no sacrifice, and surmount every difficulty to win victory," we roared. Little Red Book: page 182.

They, in turn, raised their Little Red Books. Page 7: "Policy and tactics are the life of the party!"

"It is right to rebel!" we shouted. "It is right to rebel!"

It was Mao against Mao. There was no authority, no universally acknowledged party secretary, no one to interpret for us which of these quotations from Mao applied to this situation.

The standoff continued, quotation against quotation, regiment against brigade, until finally our side gave in. Those of us who worked at the Broadcast Administration, and thus had to be admitted, walked into the theater, leaving the students behind. We were disconsolate even though the theater was already packed with rebel supporters.

But as I sat there on the podium, I noticed a ruckus near the entrance. A ripple of applause began in the foyer and rose until it broke into a roar of acclamation. Down the aisle marched two flag-bearing columns of the Broadcast Institute student Red Guards. In front were Yang Yipeng and Cao Huiru, the two students who had spoken with Jiang Qing when she visited the Broadcast Institute. They marched to the rostrum and ranged themselves on either side of the steps leading to the stage.

"How did they do it?" I whispered to the person next to me on the rostrum.

"The leaders climbed in over the walls before the soldiers got here and have been hiding out in some empty rooms," he chuckled.

The meeting began with ringing denunciations of Ding Laifu, punctuated by shouted slogans. "Down with Ding Laifu!" "Build a Flaming Red Broadcast Administration that can teach Mao Zedong Thought to all China and to the whole world!" "Long Live Our Great Leader Chairman Mao! Long Live! Long Live! Long Live!"

After the first few speeches, an intermission was declared to give the leaders a chance to confer. But just as we walked outside the theater, a group of soldiers pounced on the Red Guard students and tried to drag them away. The courtyard erupted into a melee of pushing and fighting. Then, up on the wall surrounding the compound, I saw a head appear. It was the ferocious-looking regimental commander, who had climbed up to see his troops. He was shouting at the students at the top of his lungs. "You are wrong!" he screamed. "Yesterday you were wrong. Tomorrow you'll still be wrong. You'll always be wrong!"

The soldiers weren't armed, but they were strong. Right in front of me, one of them had grabbed a young Red Guard and was trying to pull him toward the gate. The student was pulling back. Round and round they went in a circle, neither able to pull the other over.

When I saw the student falter, I yanked out my copy of the Little Red Book, autographed by Mao. I grabbed the soldier's arm and flourished Mao's vivid calligraphy under his nose. "See this?" I shouted. "Chairman Mao supports us. You're making a mistake!" The soldier's eyes clouded over with confusion, and for an instant he let go of the student. By the time he had recovered, the young man was darting up the steps to the theater and it was too late.

I saw another soldier tussling with a student and ran over to them, deliberately getting close enough to take a solid blow from the unwitting soldier's body. I immediately fell over and lay there. Six or seven people, both soldiers and students, rushed to pick me up and I heard someone scolding, "Now, see what's happened as a result of all this mess?" I shook myself free, and the pushing and shoving ended.

◆

In every battle, even an internal one, one of the most important prizes to capture was the press. Chairman Mao himself had taught us that years ago. And in this fight, hadn't Chen Boda immediately secured the *People's Daily*? Wasn't the Broadcast Administration an important strategic prize? Perhaps we should have thought more closely about the aims of those at the top who supported us. Perhaps we should have questioned whether they were truly seeking a flaming red world of radical democracy—or simply consolidating their own hold on power. But we were too intoxicated to question. All we saw in those top leaders was support for our side. And all I saw in my access to the top was a chance to be influential in a cause I thought just.

December 18, a few days after the tussle at the Broadcast Administration, I was sitting on the rostrum at a meeting held in the giant Workers' Stadium to support the war in Vietnam. The Vietnamese ambassador was there, as was a representative of the South Vietnamese Liberation Front, the Vietcong.

We had formed a receiving line in the anteroom before the meeting. I was standing next to the Vietnamese ambassador, murmuring polite nothings to all the people as they filed in. Then in swept Zhou Enlai, along with Kang Sheng and Jiang Qing as representatives of the Cultural Revolution Group. When Zhou Enlai, moving down the receiving line, came to me, I decided in a flash to break protocol and make a bid to get help for our beleaguered rebels against the formidable power that Ding Laifu had amassed against us. "The people at the Broadcast Administration really need help," I told him. "Ding Laifu is using the army to suppress the democratic forces."

Zhou's head jerked up as if from an electric shock. Without a word, he pulled me out of the receiving line, leaving the Vietnamese guests of honor stunned, with their hands still awkwardly out in the air. Over in a corner, Zhou asked, "What's going on?" And I told him everything: how Ding Laifu had ordered the gates sealed against the students, how the students had broken in, how garrison troops had been used against them.

Again Zhou looked shocked. He shouted across the room, "Xiao Hua! Xiao Hua!" The chief of the general political department of the People's Liberation Army, Xiao Hua had written the stanza Zhou sang that evening in Shanghai. Obviously he was still safe.

"Xiao Hua," Zhou said when he ran over to join us, a tiny ball of energy. "Some of your troops are interfering with the rebels. I want you to get in touch with them immediately and make sure that comes to a stop. The rebels have a complete right to make a Cultural Revolution at the Broadcast Administration, and the students have the right to use the theater. It is walled off from the studios."

"I can't believe it," said Xiao Hua on hearing the full story. "Generally speaking our troops are good. If such a thing really did happen, I'll take care of it immediately."

I felt very good about what I had done. I had used my privileged position in a good cause, clearing away a big obstacle for the rebels at the Broadcast Administration. When I got to my seat on the rostrum, I looked around and realized that I was just two seats behind Jiang Qing. I had been successful with Zhou Enlai. Now she too was within reach. I decided to press my advantage. As the speeches droned on, I composed a little note.

The Broadcast Administration, I wrote, is the voice of the whole country to the outside world, and I was concerned that the representatives of the reactionary bourgeois line were suppressing the Cultural Revolution movement. The only way we could turn the Broadcast Administration into a school for Mao Zedong Thought was with the right kind of leadership. Could she help us?

I passed the note to Jiang Qing and, a few minutes later, noticed a young girl sitting beside her get up and leave the rostrum. When she returned and took her place, a big man in an army uniform followed behind. He bent down over me. "Please stay here after the meeting is over. Comrade Jiang Qing wants to invite you to dinner to talk with you about the situation at the Broadcast Administration. She wants you to bring with you the two best representatives of the rebel regiment at the Broadcast Administration."

Now I was not just a conduit to the top, I was a kingmaker. I thought carefully about whom to pick for the visit. I bypassed some personal friends and, instead, immediately named Wang Ziqiang and Cao Renyi. In my opinion they were the straightest, most reliable of the influential rebel leaders. Their jaws dropped when I told them where we were going. I had just made their careers.

A car came at six and drove us to the west wing of the Great Hall of the People. In Cultural Revolution style, the meal and the setting were Spartan. We were escorted to a large conference room, not a banquet hall. And the dinner I could see on a table in the center of the room was nothing more than a pile of meat-filled buns and orange soda.

Li Na, the daughter of Jiang Qing and Mao, met us at the door. I hadn't seen her since Yanan, when I gave her piggyback rides. Now she was a young woman in her mid-twenties, wearing a snappy army uniform, but looking worried. "You're very good, Uncle Li," she said. "I'll give you one of my best buttons." She pinned a golden Mao Zedong button on my lapel.

"Are you very busy in the Cultural Revolution?" I asked.

She looked disgusted. "I wanted to go around the country with the other Red Guards but *she*"—a special emphasis on the word, jerking her head over her shoulder in the direction of her mother —"she wouldn't let me. She made me join the army so I couldn't go around with the others."

The others in the room were Chen Boda, the head of the Cultural Revolution Group; Yao Wenyuan, a prominent member of the group; Yang Chengwu, the chief of staff of the armed forces; Liu Zhijian, the deputy chief of the general political department; and Zheng Weishan, the commander of the Beijing garrison troops, and his deputy, Fu Chongbi.

But the person who riveted my attention was Jiang Qing. I had been hearing tales of the militant new person she had become, but nothing prepared me for the change I found. I had danced with her many times, and had been struck by her vulnerability and her carefully cultivated femininity. At the informal dinners with Mao, I had seen a soft-spoken, retiring hostess, more matronly than girlish. I could find no traces of either in the woman who stood before me now. She was wearing a People's Liberation Army uniform, green khaki and a cap with a red star. Her stance was pugilistic, her face hardened into an aggressive, hostile sneer. What fury had her modest demeanor been concealing all these years? Where had it come from all of a sudden?

Jiang Qing looked down at the red armband I was wearing. "Aren't you a little old to be a Red Guard?" she asked. I was forty-five years old; my companions were in their mid-twenties. "But Chairman Mao is older than I am," I replied, "and he put an armband on. Besides, this is an armband of the Rebel Regiment to Defend Mao Zedong Thought at the Broadcast Administration. It's not really a Red Guard armband."

Little tables with platters of steamed buns were placed in front of everyone. Jiang Qing opened the conversation. "Comrade Li Dunbai has been our old comrade-in-arms ever since the Yanan days," she said. "He is our good friend and he has been very active in the Cultural Revolution. He is a member of our party."

I felt flattered enough that the next part of her speech didn't jar me as much as it might have. "Of course," she continued, "we distinguish between Chinese and foreigners. The Cultural Revolution is a Chinese Revolution, and even though foreign comrades should be able to take part in the Cultural Revolution, still . . ." She didn't finish the sentence, but I got the message. As useful and special as I might be, she didn't approve of equal treatment for foreigners.

Then she began to recite an embellished version of the situation at the Broadcast Administration, and it was clear that she was completely familiar with it. I had heard that as a screen actress she was second-rate. Acting in this overblown political drama, she was dynamite.

"Originally, we were thinking of calling in Ding Laifu for a talk with the Cultural Revolution Group, showing him the error of his ways and giving him a chance to correct himself," she intoned. "That's the way we handled Comrade Hu Yaobang and the Communist Youth League. But now I see that we cannot do that with Ding Laifu. I cannot call him Comrade Ding Laifu. He is our enemy. He is a representative of the revisionist bourgeois line in opposition to our Great Leader Chairman Mao Zedong. Ding Laifu is a Capitalist Roader! He cannot lead our revolutionary radio station!"

In denouncing Ding, her voice had risen to a shriek and now she barked, "You people in the rebel regiment. You arrange a meeting to criticize Ding Laifu. I will attend it, and we will settle the question of Ding Laifu."

Jiang Qing raged on, her voice gaining in power and stridency. "We have made up our minds that we are going to smash all these bureaucratic structures all over China to bits. Ding Laifu has put up a big wall all around the Broadcast Administration. If we have to, we will smash that wall to bits. What is the wall for? The most dangerous thing is not the people outside the Broadcast Administration. The greatest danger is the revisionism inside."

Then she began to recite a version, again embellished, of the story I had already heard of her visit to the Broadcast Institute. "You know when I went out there to your school," she said to the two students present, "they wouldn't let me in. They shut the great iron gate right in my face. They were insulting! And I told them, 'You don't want to let me in—fine! I will go right back to Zhongnanhai and get my cadre rebel column, smash your iron gate, and smash into the school!' "

Everything was smash, smash, smash. I could hardly believe what I heard. These people at the very top were truly planning to destroy everything they had built up over the past two decades, to smash and build something new. It was exciting, and yet I had a chilly sensation. Jiang Qing was telling us that if we didn't play ball with her, if she couldn't get what she wanted out of the Broadcast Administration any other way, she would smash it down. And everything else in China.

Then she turned to the army commanders present and asked venomously, "And what is the army doing persecuting the follow- ers of Chairman Mao's line at the Broadcast Administration?"

Yang Chengwu, the chief of staff, began to answer. "Our men are trained in not interfering, and by and large they have a very good record. Occasionally there will be some mistakes and mis- understandings—"

Jiang Qing broke in shouting. "I want you to remember that the Chinese People's Liberation Army is the army of Chairman Mao Zedong, and his reputation depends on this army, even though Comrade Lin Biao is . . ."

Another sentence she didn't finish. And again, I heard some- thing between the lines. Even though she and Lin Biao were work- ing closely together, they weren't of one mind or she wouldn't have spoken like that. Chinese political language is very sensitive. She wouldn't have introduced a negative note in connection with Lin Biao's name unless she truly meant it.

Then she turned to Liu Zhijian, a high-ranking general. "We have reports that the Cultural Revolution is being suppressed in some of the army schools and academies. Is that a fact?"

"Comrade Jiang Qing," Liu began, "in most of the schools, the movement is healthy and the real revolutionaries are winning sup- port. There may be some problems in some of them—"

Once again, Jiang Qing broke in, not allowing him to finish. "I want you to report to me immediately, in writing, the situation of the Cultural Revolution in all the army schools and performing troupes. I suspect that you have been using the reactionary bour- geois line to repress revolution in every school, and to repress Chairman Mao's line."

It was one of the few times I had ever seen a grown man go completely white. Liu was not only a high-ranking general, but a Long March veteran as well, and he knew that Jiang Qing was powerful enough to bring him down.

She turned from Liu to the students, asking them to describe the scene in detail the day the army prevented them from going to the Broadcast Administration meeting. Cao Huiru told her about the clash at the gate, the tussling, how the army had harassed them, pushing her down and pulling her hair.

Jiang Qing became livid. "Find out who that was shouting from the wall!" she demanded. "It may have been an active counter-revolutionary."

Deputy Garrison Commander Fu Chongbi spoke up softly. Pink-faced, white-haired, he did not seem scared. "No," he said. "It was my chief of staff. He's okay. He's not a bad man. He's just a bit hotheaded."

But Jiang wasn't listening. "I want him arrested immediately," she shouted. "He's a counterrevolutionary. How can we permit such a vicious tiger to wear the uniform of our Liberation Army?"

In the space of an hour, Jiang Qing had denounced three people as enemies, not one of whom she had a scrap of evidence against.

◆

The three of us from the Broadcast Administration met separately after that remarkable performance by Jiang Qing, and we agreed we would say nothing to our fellows about her calls to smash things up or her cries to grab and arrest. Instead, we held a meeting to announce our victory. Jiang Qing and the Cultural Revolution Group had certified that we were the true revolutionaries, I said. So let the rebels and the conservatives come together and work to oust Ding Laifu.

Soon afterward, my ex-wife, Wei Lin, came to visit me. She looked chagrined. "I want to talk with you about my denunciation of you," she said.

I had seen posters around the Broadcast Administration recently, criticizing her for denouncing me. "The masses are angry at me for the letter I wrote to the security ministry accusing you of being a spy," she said. "Now they are going to struggle with me. There is a big meeting all set up to attack me for this. You know I have trouble with my nerves. I don't think I can take it." She looked tired, and very old.

"What made you do it?" I asked. "I really don't understand."

Wei Lin hung her head and said nothing. Then she looked at me again and said: "I hope you can help me. Can you tell them not to have a struggle meeting against me because of my health?"

I didn't hate her. But I had lost respect for her over the years. I saw her as one of the petty bureaucrats the party had created who had made their way up the ladder over the fallen careers of inno-cent people they attacked without giving the matter a second thought. Here was Wei Lin, not showing the slightest sign of being sorry, worried only that she had been caught, hoping that our old ties would save her.

I was colder than I needed to be. "I'm afraid that's not in my power," I said. "What you did was wrong. It's natural that they are angry. What you need to do is think carefully back over what you have done, and why. That's your job—not worrying over what may or may not happen because of it."

I left her and went straight to the rebel regiment headquarters. There I told both the head, Wang Ziqiang, and Wang Zhenhua, the ex–party branch secretary, that it would be a bad idea to criticize Wei Lin. "She's too weak. She can't take it," I said. I proposed instead that someone appropriate hold personal talks with her to see if she could be brought around to understand that what she had done was wrong.

I did not tell Wei Lin that I had interceded in her behalf.

◆

There wasn't enough room in the TV theater to handle the crowds that poured in to hear Ding Laifu denounced. But it wasn't Jiang Qing coming to do the job. It was Tao Zhu, the number four man in the Central Committee leadership, the chief of propa-ganda, and a supporter of Ding Laifu. He had somehow gotten wind of Jiang Qing's plans and had come to get the jump on her, to do the job first, and in a milder, more controlled way than she probably would have.

There were people on the stage, in the aisles, and crowded outside the doors. We had arranged for loudspeakers to carry the meeting into other conference rooms to handle the overflow. I was the lead speaker, and I delivered a fiery South Carolina political stump speech in Chinese. We had tried to reason with Ding Laifu, I said, but he was unreasonable. He had been cruel and unfeeling in suppressing his critics. Now, he had to be removed from the leadership.

Tao Zhu rose to speak, looking right at Ding Laifu. "Obviously Comrade Ding Laifu cannot continue to lead the proletarian radio administration one day longer," he said. "As of today, he is sus-pended from his post and will devote himself to making a thor-oughgoing self-examination."

The audience just about tore the house down. Ding Laifu was

finished, he was out. The rebel regiment had won the day. So great was the shouting and cheering that we barely heard Tao Zhu appoint two of Ding's colleagues to carry on where he had been forced to leave off.

The two men lasted only a week and the battle for control of the propaganda machine became even more serious. The *Liberation Army Daily* was firmly in the hands of the Cultural Revolution Group, but other newspapers—and the Broadcast Administration —were not.

Almost from day one, the two men appointed by Tao Zhu proved ineffective. They refused to broadcast news of the Cultural Revolution that the rebels believed should be aired. Our broadcasts had been reduced to trivia, hunks of unrelated material pulled out of the newspapers and from the New China News Agency.

We were also getting word that Tao Zhu was on his way out. Jiang Qing and the Cultural Revolution Group were gunning for him the way they had gunned for Lu Dingyi, his predecessor. And if Tao Zhu was being exposed as a hidden revisionist, how could his choice to lead the Broadcast Administration be correct?

Then Wang Ziqiang went to a meeting at the propaganda ministry and found all the other media representatives heaping scorn on him. He came back red-faced. "We have no standing," he said. "They said, 'You have no leadership! Who are these two guys running the Broadcast Administration? No one knows them.' "

The telling blow came on the last day of the year. I was in the newsroom when it happened. The only true, certified revolutionary publication was the army paper, the *Liberation Army Daily,* which was run by Lin Biao and watched over by Li Na, Mao's daughter. Other papers had recently been hiding their bourgeois sentiments behind army material. They would get the midnight proofs of the paper, and then simply reprint its articles in order not to be out of line and exposed. So the *Liberation Army Daily* was giving the midnight proofs only to trusted revolutionary organizations. Up until now, we were on that list. That night, the courier sent to fetch the drafts came back empty-handed.

We were all frantic. How could we operate? What does this mean? "It means that the PLA paper doesn't trust our leadership to be loyal to the Cultural Revolution," said the newsroom chief. It was alarming. Us? Unreliable revolutionaries? Our station in the hands of bourgeois leadership?

A dozen of the leaders of the rebel regiment began to caucus.

This was the most serious thing that had happened to us yet. What were we to do? Mei Yi had been a representative of the Black Line; Ding Laifu had followed Liu Shaoqi's bourgeois line; the men appointed by Tao Zhu were ineffective. The voice of the proletariat was being silenced. One of the representatives of the drivers for the Broadcast Administration, who had been quiet up to that point, spoke up. "Why don't we just take power and set up our own leadership?" he asked.

No one had ever seized power at a central government operation. The thought made us nervous. We decided to seek the approval of the Cultural Revolution Group first. Wang Ziqiang went for the red phone number.

The red phone system was a separate, secure system that connected high-level operations directly with the Central Committee. The lowest-ranking official with a red phone was a bureau chief. Mei Yi's office had one and it was used to check on important policy matters. When I was being attacked in 1959, Lu Dingyi had used the red phone to tell Mei Yi to have it stopped. When the Khrushchev-Eisenhower summit meeting was called off after the U-2 incident, Mei Yi had used it to call the minister of propaganda to ask how to play it.

Wang Ziqiang obviously had important army connections. He had the secret phone numbers that would make the red phone work. Three of us went into an empty office to make the call. Wang asked for Yao Wenyuan, a member of the Cultural Revolution Group. A secretary answered the phone. The Cultural Revolution Group is in a meeting, she said.

Wang suddenly felt timid and just stood there holding the phone. Cao Renyi grabbed it. "Can you go into the meeting and ask a question?" he said. "We are in a critical situation and we need guidance. We are the rebel regiment, we are the people who are loyal to Chairman Mao's revolutionary line. We feel we have to take power at the Broadcast Administration. Can you go ask Yao Wenyuan if the Cultural Revolution Group will support us?"

The three of us waited without saying a word. The phone hung silent in Cao's hand. Two minutes went by. Three minutes. Five minutes. We were becoming more and more tense. What if they turned us down? It was cold in the room, but I could feel the sweat rising on the back of my neck. Finally, I heard a voice return to the other end of the phone. "Comrade Yao Wenyuan says you have to make your own decisions," the secretary said.

We jumped up, elated, and pounded each other on our backs.

We were okay. We had the go-ahead. "Let's go take power," said Wang Ziqiang.

It was ten o'clock in the morning on the last day of 1966. A half dozen of us from the rebel regiment leading council, to which I had been elected, walked down the hall to the office where one of the two men appointed by Tao Zhu was sitting reading the paper, a steaming mug of tea before him. "Please come across the hall to the central editorial offices," Wang Ziqiang told him curtly, but not impolitely.

We all filed into the suite of offices that Mei Yi had once occupied. Wang Ziqiang stood in the center of the room. "Everybody, stop what you're doing and listen," he said. "The Rebel Regiment to Defend Mao Zedong Thought has decided to take power at the Broadcast Administration. We have called the Cultural Revolution Group and discussed it with them. You will all continue to work at your posts for the time being, but you will take your orders from us and will work under our supervision."

He spoke in a gruff, Henan Province, country accent, but he was a nice young man and not too good at sounding fierce. He gave the impression of being reasonable, approachable, responsible. "There had better not be any slackening in your work or any sabotage of Chairman Mao's proletarian revolutionary line," he said. "We will meet with you this afternoon to hear your reports on current work, and to work out plans for the immediate future. Are there are any questions?"

There were none.

Then we pasted a big-character poster on the door of the central editorial office: "All power at the Broadcast Administration is now assumed by the rebel regiment, which is reporting directly to the Cultural Revolution Group. We intend to make the Broadcast Administration a great school of Mao Zedong Thought."

And that was that. The Mouthpiece of the Proletariat, the voice of the party to its own people, and to the world, had fallen into our hands.

CHAPTER NINETEEN

Hold Power

It is easier to take power than to wield it well. The party had taken seventeen years to learn that lesson. Our rebel group learned it almost overnight.

We came up with a beautiful program of civil liberties for all. We promised freedom to everyone to organize, to debate—real debates, not the loaded trick debates of the campaigns we had all been through—and to elect a management attuned to the people. We promised to end bureaucracy, waste, and mismanagement, to listen to the people, to listen to our audience. But at the first challenge to power, the rebels fell back on the tactics they had been raised on. When they were seeking power, they abhorred oppression. When they were in power, they practiced it.

We tried hard to deliver on our promises. One of the first things we did was seal the party committee offices and suspend all remaining party operations. Then we sealed the dossier room where the secret folders on everyone were kept. There would be no spying and secret record keeping under our administration. We organized a provisional editorial leadership group and elected a twelve-man council, including me as adviser. We kept the old leaders in place—no purges for us. We told them they would continue to do their jobs under our leadership.

Everything was going our way. On New Year's Day, Wang

Ziqiang, now head of the Broadcast Administration, got a phone call from Wang Li of the Cultural Revolution Group. Congratulations on taking power, he said. You have made a wise move. I was visited by the head of the garrison troops, who apologized for having kept me on the list of the three most dangerous people in the Broadcast Administration.

My fame was growing. I attended a big meeting for scientists and engineers in the Great Hall of the People. I was supposed to sit on the presidium, but I was late and Zhou Enlai had already started speaking. I slid into an obscure seat at the rear of the platform. But someone noticed me enter and went up to whisper in Zhou's ear. He stopped in midspeech, left the speaker's platform, took me by the arm, and led me down to the front. Then, using the epithet that by now had become familiar, he introduced me as Li Dunbai, the staunch internationalist freedom fighter. The audience roared its approval.

The time was now ripe for real revolution. All over China, people rose up against the leadership. The watchword became "take power from below." The Shanghai commune was the second after us to seize power. Now, there was no stopping anyone. From then on in China it looked as if all power truly did belong to the people, with nothing to keep it in check. But behind the scenes at the Broadcast Administration, everything began to fall apart right from the start.

We didn't know the first thing about running a radio and television station. The democracy we had promised quickly melted into near anarchy. Old professional workers wanted to keep their heads down and get their work done. The people who had supported the old guard dragged their feet. Other independent-minded people refused to get involved at all.

Everyone was enjoying their new freedom and the independence, and everything was chaos. The technical people were in revolt against the editorial people. One engineer in the biggest technical department announced one morning that he was taking power. He was the son of China's most revered left-wing author, the novelist Lu Xun. In Shanghai in the 1940s, when he was a boy, I had given him a radio amateur's handbook. I was sent to negotiate with him, lest we find ourselves facing an alien power center in our own midst.

Meetings dissolved in factionalism. Everyone had an opinion. Everyone had an argument. The minute we tried to hurry up the work, we were accused of arrogance, of not listening carefully to the masses. It was a bitter blow to some who had long dreamed of power and influence.

One good-hearted young man had been a driver in the car pool. The first to suggest taking power, he was now running the whole logistics division, including the car pool. Short, round-headed, thick-set, and tubby, he made crude jokes and loved the melee of revolution. When we were in the minority and thought there might be rough stuff, we called him in as our protector. He loved it. "I'm making revolution with my head hanging on my belt," he said. "I am playing with my life, but who cares?" And he really meant it.

But a couple of weeks after we took power I ran into him. Beads of sweat were ringing his round forehead. "Old Li," he said, "I've always dreamed of becoming a great official one day, of being in a position where I get to make the decisions and order other people to carry them out. I've had that experience now, and I've had enough of it."

"What's the problem?" I asked.

"It's so hard," he said. "Everybody is free and independent, everybody talks back. You can't just tell drivers to go pick someone up. You have to tell them why it is necessary and revolutionary. Every time you have to get something to move, it's a separate case. This is democracy, and it's wonderful, but I can't handle it."

The rough little man started to cry. "I've had enough. Every dispute, every argument, every complaint, it all comes back to me. I'm on the phone all day long. I get anxious and excited, and then they jump all over me. They say, 'What kind of attitude is this? Are you going to be just like those Capitalist Roaders?' I want to go back to driving my car," he sobbed.

◆

Almost immediately, people began to turn against their new leaders. At first, the dissatisfaction came mainly from young people who banded together, complaining that editors and other newsroom people were hogging all the best positions. Then the complaints grew more serious, charging us with taking over fancy offices and treating everyone else like underlings. Quickly, these small knots of complainers coalesced into groups, the groups into factions. Then the factions decided to take control on their own.

Our rebel group had been in power less than a week when we got the news from the Beijing city station across the street that a new rebel group had seized the keys, marched into the offices, and tossed the old rebels out. Now we are in command, the new group said. Our rebel group was alarmed. If the new rebels across the street could toss out the old rebels, it was just a matter of time before our hold on power was threatened too. Some of the advisers over there were obviously coming from within our own ranks. As we walked the halls, we could hear the same type of complaints echoing through the corridors of our building. Clearly a new rebel faction was forming over here as well.

We had to do something. I thought the new rebels had a good point. Despite our good intentions and good start, we hadn't handled ourselves well since taking over. Maybe we could do better. Our group asked me to conciliate with the new rebels, and to win back our position. From what I saw of them, I thought they were a wholesome, hearty bunch. Clean-cut and earnest, they really believed in the ideals we had fought for. They wanted to participate in the leadership, not just take orders from a new group of leaders.

Chairman Mao Zedong wanted unity too, I was sure. His "Newest Supreme Directive," as all of his pronouncements were now called, said so. "The rebels at the Broadcast Administration have seized power," he wrote. "Very good. Now they're arguing among themselves. And then there's the Beijing city station. We should counsel solidarity."

I would take Mao's case to them. And once more I felt the useful peculiarity of my position. I was a foreigner, not Chinese, not part of a vested interest group. But I was accepted, trusted, a member of the inner circle in a way no other foreigner was. If anyone could bring the two sides together at the city station, I could. I returned to the Broadcast Administration rebel headquarters with the news. I had counseled both sides, I reported, and got them to consider sharing power among themselves. If both sides could work amicably together, I thought, we would be well on our way to a real democratic leadership.

It didn't work the way I planned. Almost immediately, I found myself at odds with my own rebel group. Mao Zedong's Supreme Directive notwithstanding, when I returned to my leadership group I found not appreciation, but anger. "You should have backed the rightful rebels those kids stole power from," said one of our twelve-man committee. "Now you've made the usurpers feel legitimate. The first thing to do is to restore the rebels to power there," he said. "Of course, we'll give those kids plenty of room to take part in the Cultural Revolution and to play a responsible role."

"It won't work," I argued. "Those are good kids—bright, clean, dedicated. But the old rebels are being sulky and demanding that the new rebels surrender. I think we can get unity, but not if one side has to surrender first."

Wang Ziqiang was more thoughtful. "Once rebels take power, can other rebels seize power from them? If so, how will anyone be able to set up a Cultural Revolution leadership that has a chance to show what it can do?"

That was the question.

If it was right for us to rebel, then why wasn't it right for other groups to rebel? If one group took power from another group only to be overturned itself, how could a radio station, a school, a factory be run? And if the members of a new organization had to immediately face challenge and possible overthrow, what was to stop them from attacking dissidents as they themselves had been attacked?

For all the discussion, it seemed to me that, for my colleagues at the Broadcast Administration, democracy ran a poor second to keeping themselves in power. When factions began to form that were critical of us, the old rebels' leaders closed ranks and drew up a list of tactics to use against them. First, they denied the new rebels the use of the larger meeting halls so they couldn't arouse broad support. They also set up a surveillance system, assigning people to tail the new rebels, find out who they were meeting with and what they were talking about. The old rebels also seeded spies among the new rebels. They even sent young rowdy types out in posses at night to cover up the big-character posters of the new rebels with opposing ones from our side.

Meanwhile, I was turning from a valued adviser into a major problem for the old rebels. Over and over I took them to task. "Don't you see?" I asked them. "Don't you see that they are rebels just like us? Don't you see that democracy doesn't just mean that we get our say, but that they do too? The majority should rule, but we have to respect the rights of the minorities. Don't you see that some of their criticisms are valid? Ding Laifu lost power because he refused to make a self-criticism. Let's not us make the same mistake."

I got the distinct feeling my words were falling on deaf ears.

As the different groups jockeyed for power at the Broadcast

Administration, or tried to keep it, they sought allies from on high. Each group sensed those who were sympathetic and appealed to them. At the same time, people from the top sought us out. Even as we were using them, they were using us.

Jiang Qing had told me that she intended to come to the Broadcast Administration. But I wasn't expecting her when she and Chen Boda just showed up suddenly one morning in mid-January. Someone in the corridor collared me. "They're in the receiving room," he said. "You'd better get there."

I headed quickly for the Distinguished Guests Reception Room on the ground floor of the east wing of the Broadcast Administration building. It was a long rectangular room, heavily carpeted, and lined with overstuffed sofas and easy chairs in crimson with the usual lacy white antimacassars. There were little end tables for tea. The room was reserved for foreign guests or for Chinese celebrities and bureaucrats above the rank of vice minister.

When I arrived, Wang Ziqiang had just finished telling Jiang Qing about the trouble the new rebels were making for the old rebels. Jiang Qing sat in a big easy chair at the center of the room, with Chen Boda in a similar chair on her right. Wang Ziqiang was surrounded by his close cronies in the rebel regiment. I saw a flash of tension cross his face when I entered the room.

I shook hands with Jiang Qing and Chen Boda, and sat in the easy chair directly facing Jiang Qing, which someone yielded me. "Comrade Li Dunbai, what is your opinion of what has been going on here?" she asked. "We knew nothing about it. We just happened to be in this area and I've been wanting to drop in and visit the revolutionary comrades at the Broadcast Administration for a long time. Remember? I said when we last talked that I was coming."

"Yes, I remember," I said. If Jiang Qing wanted my opinion of what was going on here, I would tell her. And when I thought of the bright promises with which we had taken power and what had happened since, I boiled over with pent-up anger. "Since taking power, the rebel regiment has become bureaucratic and high-handed," I said bluntly. "They've won the right to criticize, now they are denying everyone else the right to criticize."

I saw Jiang Qing's eyebrows go up at once. Suddenly I had gone from her ally to her opponent. She gave a little indulgent half smile and creased her forehead at me with the air of a governess hearing an exaggerated tale from a child in her care. "Can it be that bad?" she said. "They've only been in power for a few weeks.

Didn't you say they were very good? I think they are loyal to Chairman Mao's revolutionary line, don't you?"

"Yes," I said. "But I think they are becoming arrogant rather than modest and democratic, and they are not careful to listen to everyone's opinions, no matter whether they agree with them or not."

"Well," she said, "you have to remember that once the revolutionaries seize power, the task confronting them is to consolidate power. If they can't consolidate power, they won't be able to hold their ground." It was clearly a rebuke to me and I was stung by the implied criticism.

Just at that moment there was a commotion outside the door. Someone was trying to get past the guard and was being restrained. One of the east wing attendants appeared in the doorway. "Comrade Li Juan insists on seeing Comrade Jiang Qing," he said. "What shall we do with her?"

"Let her in!" said Jiang Qing. "Let's hear her out."

Li Juan was a beautiful young woman, a popular, twenty-two-year-old Chinese-language announcer. "So what are you so agitated about that you have to talk to me right away?" Jiang Qing asked her, half teasing, half scolding.

"I just want to tell you," Li Juan said, "that if the rebel leaders keep carrying on the way they have been, we won't be fit to call ourselves the Mao Zedong Thought combat regiment." With that, she began to cry, one hand to her eye to stem the big tears rolling down her cheeks.

"Now, now, now," said Jiang Qing, "it can't be that bad. Just calm down and tell us about it."

Li Juan confirmed my story: the bullying, the threatening, the harassing that the old rebels were using to silence their opposition. In their defense, Wang Ziqiang commented lamely that there were some hotheads who might have gone a little too far in their use of language, but he hoped Comrade Jiang Qing understood that they were motivated by concern that the new red regime at the Broadcast Administration was being threatened, and that the enemy would take advantage of this.

"Call together all of the Broadcast Administration's staffers," Jiang Qing said imperiously when she had listened to all she wanted to hear. "I will bring them Chairman Mao's greetings."

The entire staff was assembled in the television theater. The focus of all eyes, Jiang Qing began to speak. "Comrades!" she shouted in her high, slightly quavering, intensely dramatic crowd-speaking voice. "Comrades! Comrade Chen Boda and I only wanted to come here today to bring you revolutionary masses at the Broadcast Administration warm greetings from Chairman Mao. We didn't expect to find you going at it hot and heavy!"

There was a roar of laughter in the packed theater.

"Comrades," the high-pitched nasal harangue continued, "in our struggle against the enemy, solidarity is our weapon. You fight amongst yourselves and Ding Laifu is tickled pink. Talk out your problems! Will you do that? Will you meet together, this very day, and talk out your differences through democratic consultation? Will you promise me to do that?"

"Yes!" The whole theater roared back at her in acclamation, including those in the audience who had nothing to do with any side.

Oddly, her message was quite different from the words she had uttered to me just moments before about consolidating power. Now she appeared to be in agreement with me about what had to be done. But it didn't turn out that way.

I should have seen that our rebel leaders were helplessly ambivalent and inexperienced, tossed about on the ebb and flow of the surging political currents around them. They wanted to be democratic, but they didn't know how to do it. I should have seen that in China, few understood the tradition of democracy well enough to understand that democracy meant, not just the rule of the majority, but the protection of the rights of the minority.

I should have seen that our rebel leaders followed instructions from on high just as long as it helped consolidate their own power, but tried to undermine anyone who threatened that power. I should have seen that those at the top were manipulating those of us below as deftly as chess pieces, wielding us like weapons in their own battles for power. And in particular, I should have seen that Jiang Qing listened to my advice and praised me to the skies when it suited her plans, but turned her face from me when I opposed her views.

But I saw none of these things. Hardly any of us did. We were caught up in a shining and powerful drama. Our hopes for a future of democracy and freedom were so bright that they blinded us to the realities around us. It didn't seem like a wild, violent, terrifying high-stakes political battle. It seemed like the birth pangs of a new world. Everyone seemed to share in some glorious vision. But even as we struggled to achieve our goals, the alliances, missions, and strategies of the top leadership were shifting in ways that we could not fathom, or even guess at—ways that would profoundly affect our lives.

◆

While Jiang Qing had turned away from me for daring to criticize the old rebels she backed, another member of the Cultural Revolution Group, Wang Li, made it clear that he supported me. Perhaps because the old rebel leaders had insulted him at an earlier meeting, Wang Li had turned against them.

One day his secretary pulled me aside for a private talk. "I have been authorized to say that the party center knows you and has confidence in you," he said. "The Central Cultural Revolution Committee wants you to know that. When the right moment comes, these people are going to be removed from power. It will not be long. They aren't capable of carrying out Chairman Mao's revolutionary line."

The secretary counseled me to bide my time and wait on the sidelines until the old rebels were overthrown—advice that I could not take. I was not going to keep silent while my old rebel colleagues were being set up for a fall. I wanted them to mend their ways, not lose power completely.

Among the other top leaders, even Zhou Enlai, who was counseling unity and restraint, seemed transformed by the events of the Cultural Revolution. I saw him that January of 1967 at the Beijing Workers Gymnasium, preparing for a conciliation meeting with the many factions that had sprung up all over the city. Zhou walked in and waved when he spotted me. I went over to shake his hand. "How are things going at the Broadcast Administration?" he asked.

"Now that we have taken power we should be able to put out better programs," I said. "Everyone is thrilled with the new liberties they see, but our foreign broadcasts still have nothing specific or moving to say about the Cultural Revolution. How are we going to win friends all over the world when our programs have no appeal to foreign listeners?"

"Yes," Zhou said, suddenly becoming highly animated and gesturing with both hands as he spoke. "Look at these big-character posters. People can put them anywhere they like, and write anything they like on them. This is a scene of popular liberties such as no other country has ever had. Does Lyndon Johnson allow students to paste up sharp criticisms of him in the White House? No other country can do that. But we can do it here, and we *are* doing it. People can criticize anyone at all, except for our Great Leader Chairman Mao, and his deputy commander-in-chief, Vice Chairman Lin Biao, and the Central Cultural Revolution Group. Some people have said that no one is allowed to criticize me, but I have told the Red Guards that this isn't so. Of course they can criticize me."

Zhou's words, usually very restrained, were full of enthusiasm. "We should broadcast this great democracy so that listeners all over the world know about it," he said. "We are setting up a group to study ways of improving foreign propaganda and I will see to it that you are with them as a fully empowered member."

I had never seen him speak about anything with such excitement. I felt that this was a subject very dear to his heart. Also he intended to put me in a higher, more trusted, and more important position than I had ever held before. And he was very serious about it. "Wang Li!" he shouted, and the ponderous pundit of the propaganda media for the Cultural Revolution Group came pounding across the carpet from the other side of the room. "Tell Comrade Kang Sheng," Zhou said, "that I want Comrade Li Dunbai to serve on that new committee to reform foreign propaganda as representative of the Broadcast Administration."

I was getting in deeper and deeper. It was not only the two original factions at the Broadcast Administration who found me, and my prestige, useful. Many different leaders at the top obviously did too—for many different reasons.

◆

The Cultural Revolution Group and Lin Biao were now in command all over China. In February, Mao Zedong shut down the Politburo of the party. Now Jiang Qing, Chen Boda, Wang Li, and their colleagues were an absolute directorate it was forbidden to challenge or even criticize. Their words, shielded by the Supreme Directives of Mao, became the highest law of the land.

Still, they too were having trouble wielding the power they had seized. The situation at the Broadcast Administration was a microcosm of the state of all of China. Factionalism had broken out everywhere—in some places much more violently than at our organization. Members of opposing groups were attacking each other with bottles, rocks, sticks, even with real weapons, while Jiang Qing, Wang Li, and the others were frantically trying to control the fires they themselves had set. The *People's Daily* carried daily cries for rebel unity, warnings against anarchism, and pleas for proletarian discipline, now that the old bourgeois discipline had been successfully smashed. But the difference between good and bad discipline now escaped most of the rebel leaders. What they had learned was that "it is right to rebel." They had developed a taste for it that was not to be deterred, even by Supreme Directives.

One morning, I came into the rebel regiment headquarters at the Broadcast Administration to find the old rebels gloating over some diaries they were reading. There were piles of them, little notebooks, hard-covered in cardboard or leather, black, gray, red, and blue. One member of the leading council was talking excitedly with Wang Zhenhua. "It's all here in their own words," he said. "They are plotting together for a new seizure of power!"

"What's going on here?" I demanded. "Whose diaries are these?"

"They belong to those little bastards who are trying to take power from us," the council member gloated. "Now we've got the goods on them." The night before, he explained, some of the rebel regiment tough guys had broken into the desks and dormitories of the new rebel group and seized their notes and diaries. "Just listen to this," the council member said, reading from a scrap of paper. " 'This bunch is no good. They're conservative and bureaucratic. If we want to carry the Cultural Revolution through to the end at the Broadcast Administration, we have to take charge ourselves.' "

That's all there was. But this hothead insisted it was enough to prove the new rebels were plotting to seize power. And since our seizure of power had been approved by the Cultural Revolution Group, that meant the new rebels were plotting to seize power from that group—a heinous offense indeed. The old rebels were going to do something about it.

The next day, I was on my way home when someone stopped me to tell me that there was a big meeting going on in the music hall. "The old rebels are confronting the new rebels," my friend said. I hustled over to the music hall to find it packed with people from my rebel regiment. Wang Zhenhua was presiding over the meeting. I looked around, and with the exception of the small handful of new rebels who were obviously under attack, the entire hall was filled with old rebels.

Wang Zhenhua, microphone in hand, was sitting at a table in the center of the stage looking magisterial. "What do you talk about among yourselves when you talk about seizing power?" he shouted at one of the new rebels.

No answer.

"You must answer this question!" Wang shouted again. "You must. You can't keep silent!"

I jumped up on the stage and went over to Wang Zhenhua. "Who says he has to answer the question," I hissed in his ear. "Does one revolutionary have the right to coerce another because he disagrees with him?"

Wang went red. "Okay," he told the new rebel, "you don't have to answer it. But I advise you to talk because it will be better for you."

That night, I told Yulin what had happened. "They are digging their own graves," she said, frowning angrily. "They have no right to treat people that way, and they won't get away with it."

The next afternoon, the meeting in the music hall continued with the old rebels still hammering away at the new rebels, trying to force them to back down. Suddenly, in the middle of the meeting, Wang Li's secretary arrived and told Wang Ziqiang, who was again presiding, that he had brought a directive from the Cultural Revolution Group. The old rebels gave him the rostrum, a hush fell over the house, and he began to read, standing there in his Liberation Army uniform with a more-than-solemn look on his face. All coercion must stop, the directive read. The two sides were to sit down and iron out their differences. All true revolutionaries must unite together.

He finished reading and began to leave the stage. To my horror, I saw the old rebels get up and begin to fill in the aisles, jostling and pushing their way into a solid wall of people. They were angry. They had taken power and were not about to have their power undermined—even by a member of the Cultural Revolution Group. If necessary, they were willing to go over his head.

Wang Ziqiang grabbed the microphone. "This is a message from Wang Li," he said. "It's not a message from the Cultural Revolution Group. We know good and well that this doesn't represent our dear Comrade Jiang Qing's views. She knows how important it is to consolidate power. She said so herself the last time she was here."

The secretary tried to work his way through the crowd but it was impossible. The old rebels filling the aisles blocked his way. He was trapped. "Go to the red phone and call Comrade Jiang Qing," Wang Ziqiang shouted in the microphone. "Ask her to come here and settle these issues in person, once and for all. We don't trust the decision of Wang Li."

Looking angry and frustrated, the secretary finally turned and went back up on the stage, where he stood silently in one corner, flanked by those who refused to let him go. I couldn't let this continue. Infighting was not what I had joined this revolution for. I elbowed my way onto the stage and took the microphone from another old rebel who was preparing to speak.

"Comrades!" I shouted over the din. "Comrades! Why did we take power from the Capitalist Roaders?" The room began to quiet down and I continued. "We did it because we felt they were not following Chairman Mao's revolutionary line in running the radio station. Now, after we take power, if we also don't follow Chairman Mao's revolutionary line, and if we treat people we disagree with worse than the Capitalist Roaders ever did, then what right did we have to take power in the first place?"

The last time I jumped up on a stage—to soothe tempers after the Red Guards had stormed the gate seeking the secret dossiers —I had been met with a storm of applause. This time, things were different. The hall was deathly quiet; the faces looking up at me were taut and grim. Still, I continued my impromptu speech, chastising the old rebels. "Now we have been so carried away by fear of having our own power challenged that we have forcefully detained a representative of the Cultural Revolution Group, someone direct from Chairman Mao's proletarian headquarters, a People's Liberation Army cadre. So how can we call ourselves supporters of Chairman Mao's revolutionary line? What are we doing with this power that we took in the name of serving the people?"

The faces of the old rebels around me tightened. After all, I was supposed to be one of them. Now I was steadily alienating them. I saw myself as trying to conciliate. They saw me as a traitor.

As I continued to talk, I noticed that I had no way out. The stage was in the back of the auditorium. The way between me and the doors was packed with people, and they didn't like what I was saying one little bit. The hall was filled with cold stares and hostility, and it was now all directed at me. Suddenly, I didn't care. I didn't give a damn what they thought or whether I got out. I knew what I was fighting for, and that made everything simple.

"Where did people learn to behave this way?" I said with passion. "Putting people in the jet-plane position, beating them, killing them. These are all tactics that the exploiters used, the people who oppressed other people. These were the ways of the rulers of old China. Is this why we overturned them? Is this why we swept out the Four Olds? Is this part of the Four News? To use tactics that tyrants used against innocent people, and to use them against people in our own ranks? I am deeply ashamed. Deeply ashamed!"

The hall was completely silent. My comrades from the leading council were huddled off in one corner of the stage. No one else moved. Then, out from the huddle came Wang Zhenhua. "You're free to go," he told Wang Li's secretary. "We just wanted you to stay long enough to hear our case."

Then the way parted for both of us to leave. I left the hall alone. I walked to our apartment and was greeted in the doorway by Yulin. She kissed me. As I was taking my jacket and sweater off, I told her what had happened. "It's all over for me now at the Broadcast Administration," I said. "In ten minutes, I've gone from the most popular member of the majority to a minority of one."

"Have you eaten?" she asked.

"No," I said.

"What would you like?"

"How about some fried rice?"

We ate quietly together, both aware that I had lost. I was sure to be bitterly attacked, even struggled against in the coming days. Yulin put her small round hand over mine on the table. "It doesn't matter," she said. "You stick to the truth, and I'll stick with you, whatever comes."

We went to bed that night and slept well.

◆

The next morning, the visitors began arriving before eight A.M. Some of them were from the foreign broadcast section where I worked, some were from the technical department where Yulin had worked. Some were people I didn't know.

Everyone came bearing the same message. I was to be the new head of the Broadcast Administration.

Somehow the program that Wang Li's secretary had hinted at had been accomplished while I slept. Overnight, the Cultural Revolution Group had distributed leaflets carrying the unanimous decision of the whole group—including Jiang Qing—to commend me for my stand. Wang Li himself had called the Broadcast Administration security department to make sure I was safe. The old rebels—still clinging tenaciously to their hold on power—had been discredited. The new rebels had won. And I had been chosen to head the new leadership. Big-character posters had appeared in

several spots at the Broadcast Administration: "Comrade Li Dunbai is the man we can trust," they read. "We want Comrade Li
Dunbai to lead the Broadcast Administration."

Before I woke up, the new leadership had already been informally cleared with the Cultural Revolution Group. There was to
be a committee of three with me as its head. The other two members were Kang Shuji, a reporter who supported the new rebel
group, and Li Juan, the young announcer who had stormed into
our meeting with Jiang Qing.

That morning our living room overflowed with people. They sat
on chairs, on the floor, on dark red cushions on the window seat,
or just stood in whatever space there was. It was like a party. Yulin
and I poured them tea and coffee, passed around dishes of candy,
and fixed little sweet pancakes and bean puree buns. Everyone
was in a mood to be my friend. One very proper young woman, a
diehard supporter of Ding Laifu, sat there sipping coffee and
munching cakes. "Old Li, we have disagreed with you," she said,
"but we always knew that you were a good-hearted man and that
when the time came to stand up for justice you would be there."

I accepted the office on one condition. For public consumption
I would assume the lead, but I would cede to Kang Shuji the
secret post of the chairman of the Committee of Three and the
actual power to run the Broadcast Administration. Mei Yi's warning of a decade earlier still rang in my ears. A foreigner shouldn't
hold executive office.

The next morning, our Committee of Three met for the first
time. We set up a head office, named a half dozen people to new
leading positions, and began trying to figure out how to lead. I
was all for continuing the work of conciliation that the old rebel
group had prevented. I wanted to get the two groups to come
together, figure out how to share power, and work out the democratic leadership we had all been aiming for. The old rebels had
betrayed their promise. Now it was up to the new rebels to fulfill
it. But it wasn't one day before they broke their promise too.

I had known Kang Shuji only slightly. He was a country boy
who had become a provincial radio reporter. When we first over-
threw the leadership at the Broadcast Administration, he had been
a part of our old rebel group. But he had quickly broken away to
join with the new rebels and had been chosen for this new job
because he had recently posted many much-admired, strongly
worded big-character posters criticizing the old rebels for violating
the rights of the new rebels. But unknown to me, he also hated

Wang Ziqiang and the other rebel leaders. He thought he was smarter than they were, and more capable of leading.

When I began to talk of conciliation meetings, joint leadership, and alliances, Kang Shuji waved me off. "My buddies and I planned this whole thing back in November," he boasted. "We decided that Wang Ziqiang was incompetent, and that we could take power from him. It was back then I decided that I would be the person who ran the Broadcast Administration."

"But what about the old rebels?" I asked.

"Our real job now is to wipe out the old rebels' organization," he said.

I couldn't believe what I was hearing. For the second time in a row the oppressed had turned into the oppressors the instant they were handed power. No, I told him. No, we can't do that. Our mission is to conciliate. Our job is to build a democratic leadership. I turned to Li Juan for support. After all, it was she who had risked herself and her reputation to go before Jiang Qing with her complaints about the old rebels. She agreed with me, but wasn't ready to go against Kang. As for Kang, clearly I was someone useful to him, someone to take advantage of because of my visibility and prestige, but not someone whose opinions were to be taken seriously. I lost the argument.

That very day, Kang renamed the new rebels' core group the Red Iron Cavalry, drew up a list of loyal people, and removed the old rebel leaders from power in all departments. There was nothing I could do to stop him. So I decided to appeal directly to Wang Li himself. All along counseling conciliation, Wang Li had tried to get the old rebels to negotiate with the new rebels. He had backed me when I criticized the old rebels. And now that the new rebels had power, surely he would back the right of the old rebels to participate too.

I dialed Wang Li's secret number on the red phone. "Kang Shuji is acting in direct opposition to Comrade Wang Li's orders to conciliate," I told the secretary who answered the phone. "He's abusing the old rebel group's rights and trying to destroy their organization."

Wang Li's secretary left the phone and kept me waiting a long, long time. When he returned, he had a message for me: "Comrade Wang Li says there is no need for you to contact him directly any longer," he said. "Any messages you have can be passed through Comrade Kang Shuji."

Power Prevails

I should have quit then and there. It would have been the moral thing to do. Our people had given us a mandate to unify the factions, not to grab power and smash the old rebels. Once Wang Li had tacitly approved crushing the opposition, our three-person committee was hypocrisy. And when Wang Li's secretary cut me off, I realized immediately that my usefulness to them had ended. I had been tricked. I had nominated Kang for the leading role. Now he had sewed his link with the Cultural Revolution Group and stitched me out of the tapestry.

But I didn't quit. Partly I feared crossing Wang Li. Partly the Cultural Revolution had me in its seductive clutches. I didn't want to relinquish a hard-won position of power and influence. I felt that surely over time I could give Li Juan the confidence to take my side, and the two of us could outvote Kang Shuji.

And despite my discouragement with the chicanery at the top, I thought the Cultural Revolution had made a good start. No one in the history of China had ever been able to publish opinions freely. Now, everyone could. The Chinese had never been permitted to set up their own political organizations. Well, the factions were fighting, but at least they existed. The Chinese had never really elected their own leaders before. Now each department chose its own head. True, the liberties were limited, and they were being abused. But compared to anything else in the history of the country, they were magnificent. If we kept fighting, I genuinely felt that there was a chance that we could still accomplish real democratic reforms. I decided to hang on to what power and influence I had at the Broadcast Administration.

As it turned out, what power and influence I had was no longer there. I still went to executive meetings and argued with Kang Shuji, and I tried to keep ties to both the new and the old rebels. Now that I was in power and they weren't, the old rebels looked to me as a conduit to help them at least survive. But conciliation was impossible, no matter how hard I tried. Often, I found myself merely being the messenger of bad tidings to the old rebels. My power wasn't great enough to accomplish anything else.

Instead, I found a whole new sphere of influence outside the Broadcast Administration. I became again what I had been in my youth in the South: a public speaker, a mover of masses, a stirrer of souls. My specialty: denouncing blind obedience to the party. My vehicle: a condemnation of Liu Shaoqi's book, *How to Be a Good Communist.*

I had wrestled with the issue of obedience ever since my arrival in China. Back in Yanan, when I had read Liu's book, I had been repelled by the idea of complete, unquestioning obedience that it espoused—and at the dance in Yanan, I had told him so. In prison, I had decided that I was wrong, and that my selfishness, my inability to turn my own will over to the discipline of the party and the service of the masses were what kept me from being a good Communist.

During the 1950s, I had forced myself into unthinking obedience, pushing away my questions and doubts. But during the 1960s, gradually throwing off the influence of prison, I had turned completely around. I decided that Mao Zedong's ideal was a questioning, questing, striving party member who "must always ask, 'Why?' " And now in the Cultural Revolution, I wanted to help free everyone from those bonds of unthinking obedience to the party.

Because of my fame, and the mixture of my all too obvious zeal with my foreignness, I was a speaker in great demand. I spoke at Beijing and Qinghua universities, and the institutes of Geology, Post and Telecommunications, Aeronautics and Rocketry, Foreign Trade, Diplomacy, Public Security, Mining, Metallurgy, and on and on. I lectured to the powerful state science commission, to a huge meeting of the Shanghai rebel forces, and once before a mass meeting of more than a hundred thousand people at Nankai University in Tianjin.

Twice I was even invited to address the High Academy of Military Science, the school where Chinese generals were trained. It was so secret that its very existence was supposed to be hidden from foreigners. To reach it we had to pass through sentry post after sentry post in the Western Hills outside of Beijing. A huge portrait of Chairman Mao was hung in the center of the wall behind the rostrum of the academy's open-air amphitheater. The rafters were strung with red bunting, and a slogan-banner ran from one end of the stage to the other. "Firmly criticize and overthrow the vicious revisionist poison of the insidious Black Self-Cultivation," it read, using the rebel term for Liu Shaoqi's book.

Despite the festive air, the audience looked skeptical. These were mainly men in their late thirties and forties. Most of them must have gone through the Korean War. They were seasoned and hardened, and they were intensely loyal to the Communist Party of China. But today, they were having trouble identifying the party to which they were loyal. Had there been all along two parties—a party of Liu Shaoqi and one of Mao Zedong? If so, had their loyalties been misplaced? How could anyone account for the gulf that had suddenly opened in the top party leadership? My job was to help them understand as best I could.

Holding my Little Red Book in my hand, I began to speak in a very low voice to show that I was overwhelmed by being there and called on to speak. Then I made use of a Cultural Revolution ritual. I asked my audience, in gradually rising, gradually bolder tones, for permission to wish the Great Leader, Great Teacher, Great Helmsman, and Great Marshal of the working people of the whole world—Chairman Mao—Eternal Life without End. I repeated this at the top of my lungs three times in all, while the audience waved their Little Red Books and thundered back in unison.

I had learned this low-to-high voice technique back in the South from a fiery black Baptist minister who had led a column of striking sharecroppers out onto the public highway in Mississippi. Southern stump speaking worked in China too, I could see. The audience was with me.

I acknowledged their confusion and blamed Liu Shaoqi for having confused the party and the country. "Liu Shaoqi has built up a one-party dictatorship of his reactionary revisionist faction,"

I said. "Is this Marxism? No! Marx and Engels themselves had very different ideas. They said that the first task of the working class after seizing power was to carry out democracy."

And so, they had become slaves, I told my audience. "Liu's regime has demanded slavish, unthinking discipline, and that has produced slavish, uncritical, unthinking cadres. But wherever there are slaves, there are bound to be slave-masters. Just look at the party hierarchy from the bottom up. All you can see are tier upon tier of slave-masters who depend for their existence as slave-masters on enslaving those below them."

My voice grew higher and louder. "And when you look at the top of this pyramid, who do you see? You see the biggest slave-master of all, the master of all slave-masters, wielding power over all the many layers of slaves. That is what they have made of our daring, vibrant revolutionary party!"

The applause was deafening. The men leaped to their feet and gave me a rousing standing ovation. I left the stage and walked down the aisle through a sea of applause and hands stretched out with Little Red Books for me to autograph. As the car took me home, I leaned back against the cushions with the feeling that I was doing what I was intended to do. I was using all my knowledge and talents to spread the sparks of Chairman Mao's proletarian revolution, which might kindle new flames of revolutionary action, clearing away the old world so a bright new world could grow. Whenever I open my mouth these days, what comes out is Mao Zedong Thought, I thought to myself in some amazement.

But the applause thundering in my ears had deafened me to something I should have been listening to. What I was saying was not Mao Zedong Thought at all. Mao had said it was right to rebel, but only under the conditions he had set—to serve his purposes. Those conditions were now changing. With each passing day, I was more and more a rebel alone.

◆

I never thought my problem lay in the fact that I was a foreigner. Wasn't I a party member? Hadn't Chairman Mao called me an internationalist Communist fighter? And anyway, the Cultural Revolution itself had started off with a grand éclat of internationalism. Hatred for imperialist countries was part and parcel of the Cultural Revolution, but it was the first time that foreigners were made to feel welcome in a Chinese movement.

Little Hamidou, a foreign expert from Niger, had spent most of his time in China exquisitely sensitive to slights. If he asked for a brand of cigarettes in a store and they told him they were out of it, he was sure it was because he was African. One day, I saw him in the dining room at the Broadcast Administration, happy and beaming. Red Guards had set upon him and clipped his pants at the knees. "They treated me just like one of them," he said ecstatically. "Just like a comrade."

A few of the Americans got together and penned a big-character poster demanding that foreigners be given equal status in the Cultural Revolution. Mao himself read it and penned a marginal note. This big-character poster is right, he wrote. This is the Great Proletarian Cultural Revolution. There should be no distinctions made between Chinese and revolutionary foreigners.

The poster was copied and sent out all over the country. And soon, the foreigners in Beijing had formed a rebel group of their own called the Bethune/Yanan Brigade. By the summer, the brigade had about seventy members and was meeting once a week. Its members tended to support the most radical, most democratic factions.

And the foreigners, too, broke up into factions. There was a conservative minority—including George Hatem—who believed that foreigners should keep strictly out of Chinese politics. After all our years as good friends, I made a mortal enemy of George over that issue. He couldn't forgive me for taking a leadership role at the Broadcast Administration. "You have no right to tell the Chinese what to do, to criticize their leaders, to get involved in their politics," he said. And he hardly spoke to me again after that.

◆

Liu Shaoqi was not on the Tiananmen Gate on May Day, 1967. He was in confinement at the party headquarters. Deng Xiaoping wasn't there either. He too was in detention. Instead, the gate tower was crowded with Cultural Revolution heroes. By this time, I counted myself among that number. I was—publicly at least— the acknowledged spokesman for the Cultural Revolution at the Broadcast Administration and also well known for my speeches and writings throughout the country.

There was no parade this year, no floats celebrating production gains, no displays of military might. The square was too crowded. There were even more Red Guards present than in October, massed in formation in the square and its feeder avenues, looking up at the gate tower and listening.

For the first time Red Guards were allowed up on the gate tower itself. In seemingly endless file, they trudged up the east ramp from the Forbidden City to the rear of the gate tower, and then marched rapidly in a single file between the two rows of parapets at the front of the tower, passing right in front of Chairman Mao. They held aloft their Little Red Books and their chanting was bold, rhythmic, almost religious in its fervor. "Long live Chairman Mao! Long Live! Long Live!"

We could scarcely hear the speakers over the din. First Lin Biao spoke and then Zhou Enlai. As usual, both speeches were short. As usual, Lin Biao focused on the Cultural Revolution while Zhou spoke on the tasks of government. Then came the short, sloganized speeches as people from the model Daqing oil fields, the Dazhai agricultural brigades, and the Red Guards got up to speak.

After the speeches, Mao retired to the refreshment and rest area at the rear of the tower. I followed to see what would happen. He sat down to chat with Jonas Savimbi, the Angolan rebel leader, and I overheard Savimbi compliment Mao on the changes the Cultural Revolution was bringing to China.

"I have done nothing. It isn't me, it's them," Mao said, waving his hand toward the square. "They do it all. All I have done personally is to write a few poems." He looked bluff, hearty, much the man in charge.

A few minutes later, I noticed that Mao had not yet returned to the parapet. I strolled back to the rest area and what I saw startled me. Mao was sitting in one of the chairs that faced west, alone and looking miserable. His face was charged with such hatred and despair that I stopped where I was. I was standing eight or ten yards away from him, with only a ceremonial armed guard between us. He looked at me without seeing me. His face was puffy —puffy eyes, puffy cheeks, puffy skin. He looked old, but that wasn't what held me in amazement. It was the look of abject despair, something I had never for an instant seen cross his face before.

Why? What was it about? What was causing his distress? Was it that in his mid-seventies he was seeing the danger that his empire might be torn apart by the torrent he had unleashed and hurled against his foes? Whatever it was, it was more than enough to frighten me out of any idea of approaching and speaking with him.

Not wanting to just stand there and stare, I went back to the western side of the tower by the parapet. Sometime later, I saw

Mao come back to his front-and-center position and resume waving his hand in slow arcs to the huge crowd below.

That day Zhou Enlai looked different too, I decided—even different from the last time I had seen him three months earlier. The recent stresses had obviously taken their toll. The bright, witty man full of easy repartee was gone, replaced by a man serious, verging on grave. As for Lin Biao, he looked nervous and anxious, darting frequent beady-eyed glances at Mao as if trying to read something there.

The past year had also wrung out my friend Marshal Chen Yi, the foreign minister. He looked like a ghost. His body was frail and emaciated, his wrists like tiny sticks. This once hearty man seemed shrunken and gray. I had heard that he was having a very hard time during the Cultural Revolution. Zhou Enlai was protecting him, but it wasn't enough. The Cultural Revolution Committee was gunning for him, and he was losing. We walked together along the eastern parapet and I inquired anxiously about his health. He assured me, unconvincingly, that he had stripped the weight off on purpose and was feeling fine.

◆

One very steamy afternoon soon after the May Day celebration, I returned to my office at the Broadcast Administration to find about fifteen young student Red Guards from the city of Wuhan waiting for me. When they saw me coming in through the double glass doors, they jumped to their feet and "encircled" me, which was one of the approved techniques for Red Guards during the Cultural Revolution. They formed a ring around a target and refused to let him leave until they were finished. "We have come to ask you to talk to us about the international situation," a round-faced young man explained.

"I can't tell you about the international situation," I said. "I'm not prepared, I haven't been following it closely. I couldn't—"

"No problem! Of course you can! You're too modest!" they shouted insistently.

I was trapped.

"Look," I said, "I don't mind just sitting around and chatting with you informally about world events, but only on one condition. You have to guarantee me absolutely that not a word of what we say here today will be passed on or printed."

A whole chorus arose: No problem! This isn't for the paper, it's

just for us. We guarantee that no one not in this room today will
know a thing about it.

We all went up one flight of stairs to the Broadcast Administration's third-floor conference room. We sat down around the long
table and I began to talk. To tell the truth, I enjoyed holding forth
to the young people. I felt that I was in my element. Believing
their promise of privacy, I spoke about the revolutionary situation
in the world, how it appeared that students all over the world—
in Hong Kong, in France, in America—were all moved by the
same kind of revolutionary fervor.

And that led me to Vietnam. I had recently read in the Chinese
press of the sudden death by heart attack of the principal leader
of the South Vietnamese resistance. I knew he was a friend of
China and in favor of fighting the war through to the end. I also
knew, from having visited North Vietnam, how powerful the
forces were for accepting Khrushchev's plan for conciliation. As
soon as I heard of this man's death, I connected it with another,
recent death by heart attack, that of the former Vietnamese ambassador to Beijing. He too had been a staunch opponent of accepting the deal proposed by Khrushchev.

Don't those two deaths seem very odd, I asked the Red Guards?
I told them of what I had learned from my experience in Vietnam,
that the leaders there lied repeatedly and with total unconcern
both to the outside world and to their own people. I thought it
highly probable that they were killing off those among their own
leadership who were implacably opposed to making a deal with
the Soviets.

"A party that lies to its own people is bound to fail in the end,
even if it wins momentary victories," I warned the Wuhan Red
Guards, growing angrier and angrier as I spoke. "Genuine revolutionary elements are sure to continue to grow in the Vietnamese
party, and sooner or later they will make themselves felt."

Afterward, I felt as if I had gotten a load off my chest. That
feeling didn't last long.

I came to my office the next morning to find that the Wuhan
Red Guards had printed my entire little speech in their newspaper,
circulating thousands of copies with banner headlines on the front
page, trumpeting the story. Overnight, I heard, Wang Li had
ordered trucks out to find and destroy every copy of the paper,
lest it fall into the hands of the Vietnamese.

That afternoon, Wang Li's secretary came to find out what had happened and I soberly realized how serious my error had been. I had twice been on an American people's delegation to international conferences in Hanoi. The Vietnamese knew that I belonged to the Chinese party and might easily construe what I said as representing the inside views of the Chinese Communists. This was a matter that could affect a life-and-death war, as well as China's struggle with the Soviet Union for influence over the course of events in Vietnam.

I told Wang Li's secretary how sorry I was, and how I would do anything to make amends. He gave me no comfort. "This is a bad business," he said, shaking his head.

◆

In Beijing, thousands of Red Guards and other rebels were laying siege to Zhongnanhai, the compound where the senior leaders lived and worked. Inside, Zhou Enlai was struggling to keep Liu Shaoqi and his family safe and protected. The mob camped outside the gates, however, was demanding that Liu be handed over to them.

One night, Sol Adler and I went strolling down to see what was going on. Sol, the retired economist who once worked for the U.S. Treasury Department, had his rakish Irish hat perched on his head and a big cigar in his mouth. When we arrived at our destination, he stalked about with his lean frame bent over slightly at the waist, peering into the eyes of the young people there.

The whole street that skirted the western end of the Forbidden City, where a number of entrances led to the central government's offices and quarters, was jammed with Red Guard units from Beijing schools. Each unit had set up a service booth on the sidewalk, which acted as a liaison and supply center. A long streamer had been set up high in the air above the gate to the central government offices: "We firmly demand that China's Khrushchev, Liu Shaoqi, be dragged out, criticized, and struggled with!" It was signed, "Beijing Revolutionary Rebel Meeting to Drag Out the #1 Capitalist Roader, Liu Shaoqi."

It seemed to me that the person behind the scene was Jiang Qing. The Red Guards told me that one of her scribes, Qi Benyu, had appeared several times at the gate to say that "the will of the people is bound to be done."

Three or four young men in paramilitary uniforms from the Geological Institute were lolling about on the sidewalk across from the western gates to the state council offices. When Sol and

I stopped to chat, no one seemed to recognize me under the street lights. "Do you think Liu Shaoqi will really come out of there?" I asked them.

They were in very casual dress—pant legs rolled up to their knees, shirts and socks in disarray, looking tired and at loose ends. "If we hold out long enough," one of the students said, glancing around at the others.

"If that happens, what will you do with him?" I asked.

"Oh, we'll hold big public meetings to criticize him," said another of the students. "Why should he not come out and face the people like the others? He's only a counterrevolutionary revisionist. Why shouldn't we hold big meetings against him?"

Despite the ferocity of the slogans, the roars of the crowd, and the clenched fists, Sol and I couldn't escape the same feeling. This was no angry, out-of-control mob. It was a crowd full of merriment and good humor. Everyone was relaxed and friendly. It was as if roaring for Liu Shaoqi's head was the most amusing, most natural thing to do.

Not so elsewhere in China. The country was dissolving in civil war. There was no government. There was no authority. Every group had its own sponsor, every powerful figure supported his or her own group. Factions fought factions, not with words this time, but with real weapons. I heard a horrifying eyewitness report that the Red Guards at Qinghua University's high school were capturing and torturing high school students from other factions, recording their screams for their own members to hear, to toughen them for battle.

I saw films of factory workers battling each other with spears made in their own factories. I talked with students from Wuhan University. One showed a long ugly gash in his leg, from ankle to thigh, which had been caused by a spear-wielding worker. A young student friend went to Hunan Province and found both big factions were fighting with weapons taken from army arsenals. Then in the mail came a picture of my friend, lying dead with a machine-gun bullet through his neck.

Wang Li went to Wuhan to try to negotiate between warring factions. One group there kidnapped and tortured him. The area military commander was behind Wang Li's detention, and Wang was furious. The night of his return, he came to lecture us angrily at the Broadcast Administration. "Grab the tiny handful of revisionists in the PLA!" he said. Those who had detained him were typical of a hard-core group of counterrevolutionaries in the armed forces who were now exposing themselves one after the other.

Wang Li said he hadn't been frightened, but I saw the marks of his ordeal. He looked pale and drawn, walked with a limp, and had on his chest and arms little black wounds where the rebels had stabbed him with sharpened pencils. Only the intervention of Zhou Enlai, who had flown down to Wuhan, had saved him.

A few days later, however, I heard that Wang Li had been removed from the Cultural Revolution Committee. Mao had put his foot down. The military was sacrosanct. It was the only really obedient force that Mao had left and it contained his only functioning party organization. "Hands off my Great Wall," he roared. No one could attack the army. Wang Li had dared, and he was gone.

This was no longer comic opera to me; it was grotesque and saddening. I still thought we could rise above the disruptions and disorders to create and manage democracy. But my hope was now seriously laced with doubt. We were being consumed by chaos, not conquering it.

Then in August came a new Supreme Directive. Mao Zedong had just returned from a trip through the south and east of the country, and had brought with him four pages of instructions. All factions must conciliate and unite in one great organization at once, he declared. All the revolutionary cadres must be returned to the fold.

At the end of the month, everyone at the Broadcast Administration was ordered to attend an evening meeting. We had earlier proposed to the Cultural Revolution Group a new management slate—still including me—and we expected to have it approved. Despite being shut out of the real circle of power in our three-person committee, I had continued working with them and attending meetings. I was as eager as everyone else to know the decision.

Mao's headquarters sent Li Guangwen, their man in charge of news, to deliver the message. With a bald head fringed with dark hair, he resembled the manager of a pool hall. He looked cynical and talked in a rumbling voice, intoning the announcement from the rostrum, reading through from beginning to end, with no pauses or comments. The Committee of Three was dissolved, he said, and it was replaced by a much larger directorate, which included many members of the old rebel group. He read the list of new leaders. I was not one.

Then right after reading the list, almost as an afterthought, Li read another announcement: The Central Cultural Revolution Group was immediately transferring Comrade Li Dunbai out of the Broadcast Administration to a special assignment.

Tears came to my eyes. So this is the end of me here, I thought. After all these years from Kalgan to Yanan to Beijing, I am to leave the Broadcast Administration. I was sad to leave, sad to lose my friends, sad not even to have been consulted about the move.

But I was also excited by the possibility of moving on to something better and more important. Several of my friends crowded around me to congratulate me on my new assignment.

Early the next morning, I was still asleep when the phone rang. It was Shirley Graham, the widow of Dr. W. E. B. Du Bois, the great American black historian and scholar. She traveled to China often and always looked me up when she came to Beijing. I had had lunch with her earlier in the week, and had helped arrange a meeting for her with Zhou Enlai the day before.

"Please come quickly," she said. "It's important."

Shirley told me I was the only American in China she fully trusted to understand her. I rushed to the Beijing Hotel to see what she needed. And when she answered the door, I knew that she was genuinely frightened and upset. She ordered breakfast brought up to her room so that the two of us could talk. As we picked at our greasy scrambled eggs, she told me her story.

Zhou had received her in the middle of the night. She had told him that she wanted to see him before she left for Egypt, where she now made her home. Obviously, Zhou had given her the only time he had and she was very concerned about him. "I've never seen him like that before," Shirley said. "He's always been so optimistic, so charming. I've always seen him full of energy and care for other people. This time, he looked depressed. He looked exhausted.

"He was talking differently too," she went on. "He gave me a message. He told me, 'The whole Chinese Revolution may go down to defeat for a while. We may lose everything. But never mind. If we are defeated here, you in Africa will learn from our mistakes, and you will develop your own Mao Zedong, and you will learn to do it better. And so in the end, we shall succeed.'

"I asked him what he meant," she said, "but he wouldn't say. All he would say was that the situation was very complex and that the future looked uncertain. Please look after his health," she implored me. "He doesn't look well at all."

That afternoon I called Zhou's secretary. Was something bothering Premier Zhou? I asked. What had he meant when he spoke to Shirley Graham? "Pure fantasy," the secretary replied. "Premier Zhou said nothing of the sort. She's got it all mixed up."

It never occurred to me that Zhou Enlai himself might be under a grueling attack.

◆

All through the month of September I waited for my special assignment. Nothing happened. And as October approached, I waited for my annual National Day invitation. I certainly didn't expect to be on the tower with Mao again. But I did think I would be invited to join the lower reviewing stands beneath the tower, together with other foreign experts and leading Chinese cadres.

But no invitation came.

For the first time, Yulin and I sat home with the children on October 1. One by one our foreign expert friends came by. "Why aren't you ready to go?" they asked. "What, you're not going? What, you haven't been asked? Incredible!"

That's just what I thought. Incredible.

At home, alone, I had plenty of time to ponder the news I had just heard on the television set. A major editorial had been read the night before, announcing a big nationwide campaign to root out "Renegades, Special Agents, and Die-hard Capitalist Roaders." Renegades was the Cultural Revolution code word for old cadres who had worked in the party underground, and had been arrested by the KMT and released. Capitalist Roaders were leading cadres who weren't considered sufficiently revolutionary. My despair began to mount. Why such a divisive attack just as Mao was counseling calm and conciliation? Why a return to the old witch-hunting ways of controlling and coercing people?

And what of the call to smoke out "special agents"? This referred, in part, to KMT secret police agents, but far more important were "agents of foreign imperialism." Where had I heard that before? For the first time, I wondered about my sudden removal and my long wait with no new assignment. On the morning of my first arrest on spy charges, in 1949, written instructions had arrived for Liao Chengzhi that I was being sent to Beijing on a "special mission." Now, I was awaiting a "special assignment." Cold winds for early October.

Thus began the most difficult and dangerous part of the Cultural Revolution. Mao Zedong had started it. Mao Zedong now wanted it stopped. It seemed he was turning back to his time-tested ways of uniting people: throw them new enemies to fight. More and more, I began to realize that one of them was going to be me.

Most of my foreign friends stuck by me—until they saw the picture. They dropped by with political gossip, or to share a meal. The Bethune Brigade took my part and kept inviting me to meetings. Then one day a British friend arrived looking tense. He had a Chinese magazine in his hand, flipped open to expose a photograph I remembered very well. It had been taken the summer before and showed me standing with Mao, Zhou Enlai, Lin Biao, and Jiang Qing. It had been published first in the *People's Daily*. Now it was being reprinted in the English-language *Beijing Review*. But this time, there was one big difference.

I wasn't in the picture. I had been completely blacked out. "How does it feel to be a ghost?" my British friend asked.

Some innocent young friends at the Broadcast Administration said, "Old Li, it's some kind of crazy technical mistake." I knew better than that. No one would doctor a photograph with Chairman Mao without specific instructions. Friends investigated at *Beijing Review*. The doctored photo had come from above, the editors there said. No one at the magazine had anything to do with it, and no one knew what it meant.

One by one my foreign friends began to peel away. It was just too dangerous to be seen associating with me. I heard rumors about a small group of foreigners being formed to gather incriminating materials about me. Why? I didn't know.

Then the big-character posters denouncing me began to appear. At first, foreigners put them up. They were mainly in the Friendship Hotel where they lived. Some of them made great sport of me: "He has climbed up so high, and fallen so low," one poster read. "His picture is blacked out of an official publication," said another. "This symbolizes the dark nature of his insidious activities." Some attacked me, a foreigner, for having the gall to get involved in Chinese politics. Some despised my family background: "Rittenberg shows all the qualities we have long been accustomed to finding in the Jew."

There was also an unsettling piece of news from the Broadcast Administration. There had been another great upheaval and the military had been sent in to take control. My work pass was canceled and I was no longer able to go over there and talk with my friends. They told me that the military's task was to stop the factional fighting. The army men sent in to take control had begun a series of political study classes designed to pull everyone together.

The warring factions were uniting—just as I had feared—over my dead political body. The main target appeared to be Wang Li. One of his major crimes: placing me, a foreigner, in a high position of trust and authority at the party's Broadcast Administration. The two groups joined in criticizing me and creating doubts about my motives—and my background.

Now I was completely cut off.

Our family was alone. Chinese friends did not dare come to see us. Most foreign friends had already stopped coming. Only a tiny handful of the bravest paid brief visits. Once a week, I went out to Anna Louise's for lunch, but that was the only outside activity I was allowed.

Neither Yulin nor I could go to work. The schools had been closed down and the children were at home. We passed the time as best we could. Yulin knit endless sweaters in red and green. She and Mama scoured the markets for the best food they could find and cooked tasty dishes to cheer the family up.

We tried to keep our worries from the children. The three girls —Xiaoqin, Xiaodong, and Xiaoxiang—were ten, nine, and seven years old. Our baby son, little Xiaoming, was not quite two. They frolicked with the unaccustomed freedom and pleasure of having both Mummy and Daddy home with them.

We played Palace—an ironical game, I thought, in the midst of this proletarian egalitarianism. One girl dressed up as the queen and ordered her page and princesses around. We played Bones, a little game that involved casting sheep's knuckles and picking them up to the bounce of a ball.

We also sang the Cultural Revolution songs. The girls loved them and they sang Chairman Mao's quotations set to music. Little Xiaoxiang would sometimes turn around the words of songs to make them mean what she wanted them to mean. One song about a young militia woman in particular displeased her in its original form. She was said to prefer her uniform to fine clothes. Xiaoxiang, who already had a fashionable flair, couldn't believe that, and so would only sing the song backwards.

A few children tried to torment our children. One little Malaysian boy would yell, "NATO! NATO!" when they came out to play, apparently finding that reference to the North Atlantic Treaty Organization the worst foreign word he could think of. We told the children that I was being accused of something that wasn't true and not to mind the taunts.

The whole family locked arms around me. But political pressure was building on us in ways we didn't understand. One day a Red Guard group from Yulin's school came to visit us and asked for my support. Even though I was discredited at the Broadcast Administration, I could still be of help to their cause: to take power in the foreign ministry. "Chen Yi has outlived his usefulness," they said. "He's become an obstacle to the Cultural Revolution."

I would do nothing to harm our friend Chen Yi. What's more, I had further suspicions about this group. I thought they were going after Chen Yi to bring down a bigger target. "What about Premier Zhou Enlai?" I asked, probing.

"Anyone who has outlived his usefulness to the Cultural Revolution should be removed," they said with certainty. Yulin and I showed them the door.

Yulin was nervous. She wasn't sleeping well. She saw, perhaps more clearly than I, where all this was heading. But three times a day, at least, she would put her hand over mine and say, "Don't worry about a thing. Whatever happens, I'll stick with you. It will be you and me together."

She held firm under taunts and assaults. She knew the tricks that would be used against us. When a group of Red Guards barged into our house demanding my diaries and private papers, she kept them at bay. I refused to hand over anything to them, but I was wavering. The leader demanded that I simply show them the papers. "They promise not to touch anything if I show it to them. They just want proof that we haven't destroyed our notebooks," I told Yulin, in Chinese.

Yulin answered back, clearly and loudly, in English, a dangerous, defiant thing to do. By then, the Cultural Revolution had turned virulently antiforeign. "They are lying," she said. "Don't believe them. They think they have a right to lie for political reasons."

The young fanatics turned faces full of hate on her and ordered her to shut up. "It's time you remembered that you used to be Chinese," one tall young man hissed at her.

"Whoever I am or am not is my own business. It has nothing to do with you!" she said, and stood there, head proudly held high, hands on her hips, glaring right back at him.

On Christmas Day, 1967, a group from the Broadcast Administration arrived at our apartment to tell us that I was under house
arrest. I was not to leave without permission, they said, and they
confiscated Yulin's work pass so that she too was barred from the
Broadcast Administration. A young announcer did all the talking.
"We will be coming here to ask you a few questions and assigning
you to write material," she told me. We didn't say anything. We
didn't protest.

We didn't celebrate Christmas that year.

The interrogators began coming, first every day, then trickling
off to once a week. Their questions were puzzling and didn't shed
much light on my situation. How had I known the Cultural Revolution was about to begin—as evidenced by my getting rid of all
my antique furniture? Why did I contact every foreigner who
came to Beijing? Why did I talk and eat with so many foreigners?
Why was I so active in the Cultural Revolution, reaching out
everywhere, sticking my finger into all possible pies, near and far?
What was I after?

One question was particularly puzzling. I guessed that it had to
do with the interview I had given the Wuhan Red Guards, in
which I had unwisely talked about my suspicion that key pro-
Chinese Vietnamese leaders had been murdered. How did I know,
my interrogators asked, information that was only known to the
Politburo?

Yulin wanted me to do something to save myself. She asked me
to enlist Anna Louise in my fight, but I demurred. I didn't want
the old lady disturbed, and besides, I didn't think it would do any
good. At Yulin's prodding, I did write to Jiang Qing. Through a
secret conduit I still had, I arranged to have a plea for help delivered to her. I told her I was a victim in the factional struggle,
facing charges that were difficult to rebut without help from the
top.

I waited for a reply, but none came.

Then, through a few secret friends who remained, I heard the
most shocking piece of news. Jiang Qing and Security Chief Kang
Sheng were making the rounds of the major Red Guard units,
blaming the unruly leaders there for having trusted and honored
me. They were denouncing me as an American spy.

My friends reported the gist of what they were saying: "You
became so carried away with your own cleverness and importance
that you thought you could do without our leadership. And what
was the result? You put this American adventurer up on your

presidium and sat beside him and treasured his advice and built him up into a great hero. And do you know who he really is? No, of course you don't. You can't tell a longtime American imperialist agent from a revolutionary Marxist! You should all be ashamed of yourselves! We don't blame you for being basically ignorant of Marxism–Leninism–Mao Zedong Thought, but what excuse is there for forgetting your sense of national pride!"

I stayed calm, but I prepared for the worst. I read as much as I could. I read Shakespeare and memorized the works of Mao Zedong that I thought could best help keep my spirits up in prison. I read pieces on wholehearted service to the people and committed them to memory. Xiaoxiang helped me. She had learned them in school and very seriously and soberly corrected me if I was wrong. I memorized an ancient piece by a classical writer, Sima Qian: Death comes to every man, he wrote, "but it can be lighter than a feather, or heavier than Mount Tai." We each have two things to give to humanity, I thought: a life and a death.

I memorized a story about Dr. Bethune and a piece about the foolish old man who moved mountains. Day after day, he threw himself against the impossible task. "If I die, my sons will carry on. If they die, their sons will carry on," he said.

Neither Yulin nor I talked about death, what we would do, how we would carry on. Nor did we talk about what would happen if I were taken away. We spent our energies trying to keep ourselves alert and cheerful.

Yulin did try to give me some advice. "Just tell the truth and stick by it," she said. "Don't let them scare you. That's what they always try to do. And don't believe in any deals they offer you. They are most likely lying. If you tell the truth, they can't mix you up."

The night of February 21, 1968, was the coldest night I could remember in Beijing. It was hard to know exactly how cold it was because the lowest temperature the radio would report was thirteen degrees below zero Celsius. We had gone to bed early that night. Before we went to sleep, I had swapped long johns with Yulin. Mine were nice and new; hers had just been washed and she was wearing an old, tattered pair with the seat out. I wanted her to be warm that night in a nice pair without holes. The children were all asleep in their usual spots around the house. Little Xiaoming slept in a crib in our room. Xiaodong and Xiaoqin slept in the living room. Xiaoxiang slept in the other bedroom with Mama.

Around eleven P.M. we heard a knock on the back door. It was the door closest to our bedroom, so the sound was very loud. We woke up, startled.

"Something is wrong," Yulin said.

"Don't worry," I said. "I'll see what it is."

I put on my bathrobe and went to the door. There were two men I recognized from the Broadcast Administration security department. "Comrade Wang Shouren wants to talk to you about a new work assignment," one of them said, referring to one of the deputy directors at the Broadcast Administration.

"All right," I said. "I'll be right with you." I closed the door, went into the bedroom, and started to dress. I put on a plain white shirt and my dark brown corduroy Western suit.

"If it's trouble, what are we going to do?" Yulin asked. I knew what she meant. She meant, What if you don't come back?

"If it's trouble, it will be solved in the end," I said. "Don't worry about it." She was still in bed. I kissed her. "Don't get up. I am going to say goodbye to the children."

One by one, I kissed the children. "Daddy's going away for a while," I whispered to each one. They stirred but didn't awaken. Then I walked out into the cold air and as I closed the door behind me, I heard someone's radio: "The temperature in Beijing is thirteen degrees below zero Celsius."

I walked with the two guards around to the back of the Broadcast Administration building. I saw a friend of Yulin's scurry by. Then I spotted a colleague from the English section across the courtyard. We had been friends. She looked at me and then turned away.

Under the sally port of the building was a black car, Shanghai model. Two soldiers and an officer were standing beside it. "Get in the car," said the two guards accompanying me. "We will explain it to you later."

I got in the back. One soldier got in on the left, the other on the right, shoving me with his hip until I was in the center of the seat. Then the officer got into the front seat and signaled the driver to leave. Off we pulled into the black Beijing night.

Many years later I reflected on how fortunate it was that I had not paid any attention to the other black car lurking in the shadows behind mine. It was the car that had come to take Yulin and the children.

CHAPTER TWENTY-ONE

The Ice House

Our car pulled out of the compound, turned in front of the Broadcast Administration building, and headed for the Xidan crossing. "If we go straight forward at Xidan," I thought, "it may be true that they're taking me to the Great Hall of the People to discuss work. If we turn left at Xidan, it's jail."

We turned left.

The entire ride, which lasted for about two hours, was in total silence. Finally, we arrived at a large compound with identical three-story brick buildings. Lights on all three stories were ominously lit in the middle of the night. The car stopped, the soldiers on both sides of me got out, pulled me from the car, and dragged me into one of the buildings. The officer who had been in the front seat sat down behind a little desk. "Li Dunbai," he sang out in a rasping bureaucrat voice, "you have been placed under detainment."

"Yes," I said, nodding.

He looked up in surprise, as if he had expected some violent reaction. "I said you have been placed under detainment."

"I understand," I replied, nodding again.

"Search him," he ordered the two soldiers. They stripped me to my undershorts, searched me, and then handed me prison clothing. I put on a black cotton-padded jacket and trousers, and a pair of cloth socks and shoes.

A keeper appeared with a big ring of keys and walked me out of the building, through a courtyard and into one of the other buildings where lights blazed. It was only then that the shock finally hit me. Along the right side of the corridor that ran the length of the building were eleven big, red-stained wooden doors with great hasps sunk into the walls, and great iron bolts fastened with huge double padlocks.

"My God," I thought. "Each one of those ice boxes has a human being in it, shut up alone, buried alive!"

And it was only then that I fully realized what was happening to me. The impossible, the unthinkable, was about to begin. I had thought they had abandoned that inhuman practice years ago. But here I was, headed for solitary confinement again.

The keeper pushed me into a cell and slammed the door behind me. I took stock. It was much like my cell of nineteen years earlier. Six paces deep, two and a half paces wide. In front of me, a high window, closed and frosted over. Under the window a bed, made from a wooden door propped on two half-high sawhorses. Folded on the cot was a thin quilted mat to sleep on and a thin cotton quilt to sleep under. There didn't seem to be any heat. On the wall to the left was a small washbasin, and between the basin and the wall was a recess for the toilet. There was a peephole in the door for the guard, and waist-high near the toilet was another peephole.

I was completely alone. Here I was again, locked away in a kind of prison I didn't think still existed for a crime I had not committed. Had the thirteen years in between been a dream? Had I just flowed imperceptibly from one unreal world-outside-the-world into another? Had I endured six years of shock, melancholy, and mental torment, only to face the same again? How could I survive?

Yet, as I heard the clank of the metal hasp being bolted, I suddenly felt a surge of exultation: "This is going to be a fight," I thought to myself. "The truth is on my side, and I am going to win." It was not the same prison as before, and I was not the same man. I was more experienced, stronger, more committed. Back then, the worst thing was the dreadful pain of being suspected by the people I loved, of being excluded, of being misunderstood. This time, I saw my imprisonment as part of a battle. We were fighting to create a truly democratic, prosperous form of socialism through the Cultural Revolution. If we held together, we could still win.

I took up the same measured pacing I remembered from my last time in prison. Back and forth, back and forth diagonally I walked, six small paces each way, trying to pull together everything I had learned, everything I knew that would help me survive through whatever came. I would work to recover all the privileged conditions I had enjoyed after my first year in prison last time. If I could have access to a newspaper, pen and paper, books, and humane treatment I felt certain I could make it.

I would fight off the fear of madness. My worst terror was of retreating into the anguished blackness that had marked my first year in prison in 1949. I would carefully monitor myself, analyze my emotions, find what touched them off, and learn to control them. "They control the stimulus," I told myself, "but I can control the response. They can't break me as long as I use my head." I would find the way to pull back when I felt myself getting near to the brink.

With a wrenching pain, I made a firm decision. "I must not think of Yulin and the children or it will kill me." Those who had imprisoned me would try to use my thoughts of my family to break me, I knew. What was worse, my own longing for my family and terror for them would eat me from the inside like acid. Where were the children? Would they be safe? Would Yulin be struggled against? Would she face interrogations too? My biggest fear was that Yulin, in her stubbornness and honesty, would get herself killed defending me. I slammed the door of my mind. I couldn't think about it. If I did, I would die.

And I must never, never give up. I must never give up for my family, I must never give up for the cause of democratic socialism that I believed in. I must never give up for myself. I would not commit suicide, not collapse in despair, not give up for an instant the struggle to survive, and to win.

The only thing I would have to give up, I realized clearly, was the hope of any help from my high-placed friends. For the next morning, the prison officials brought a copy of my detention order for me to see. All sixteen members of the Proletarian Headquarters—including Mao Zedong, Zhou Enlai, and Jiang Qing—had signed it.

◆

I had no idea why I was in prison, or how long I would be there. For a time, I supposed that my case would be an easy one, a matter of a few weeks, a few months, or a year at most. I would rethink the Cultural Revolution and someday write a book about it. But the weeks rolled on with no word about my fate. Several times I was visited by a team of investigators. But unlike my first time in prison, they gave no clue about the charges against me. They simply admonished me to think about my guilt and left.

Then it struck me. Nothing but a major cataclysm could free me this time. The Chinese Communist Party, which called itself "Great, Glorious, and Correct," and its infallible leader, Mao Zedong, had twice wrongfully arrested the same American friend. They had publicly admitted their error the first time. But would they dare admit that they had done the same thing again, to the same person? With the importance they now attached to building Mao up as a godlike figure, it was hard to imagine they would again admit their mistake, even if they did come to realize they had made one.

After about two months, I was moved into a permanent cell from what I supposed to have been a temporary holding cell. Almost immediately, the interrogations began. On the second day in the new cell, I heard the key rattle in the lock and a woman's voice shrilly command me to come forward. I recognized the voice; it was a bad-tempered keeper I had heard shrieking at other prisoners on the floor. I walked out into the corridor and saw a skinny woman in a green People's Army uniform. She was bony-faced, with staring eyes. "Keep your head down, eyes on the ground!" she commanded me. "And don't look at the doors."

The grilling rooms ran along the sides of each prison building. The keeper led me along my own corridor, through a door and then around to another corridor running parallel to mine, but outside the cell block itself. When I entered the room, a panel of five men was waiting for me. Two of them were older and clearly in charge. One, in civilian clothes, was a lantern-jawed lean man with a strong Manchurian accent. The other, in army uniform, was a sturdy, healthy-looking man with ramrod-straight bearing. Those two men had obviously been assigned as my case officers.

The routine was always the same. The keeper motioned me in and I walked through the door, closing it carefully behind me. They shouted at me the first day when I forgot, but after that I remembered. I was ordered to bow to Chairman Mao's portrait on the wall and ask for forgiveness. That I did, for various unspecified and unknown transgressions. Then I stood behind the little round drum-stool in front of their table until they commanded me to sit down, but only after I had been told to recite various quotations from Chairman Mao that were plastered up on wall posters: "The people, and the people alone, are the motive force in the making of world history." "The masses are the real heroes, while we ourselves are often childish and laughable."

My questioners sat on the other side of a long table, formed by placing two ordinary writing tables together. There was a white cloth over the table and three or four large thermos bottles with hot drinking water. At first the sessions were mild.

"You've had a long time to think things over," said the military man, whom I secretly named "the Colonel." "Have you made up your mind what you're going to do?"

"I've been thinking very hard," I said. "I've been getting ready to give a full and clear account of all I've been doing and saying, to make it easier for the party to understand me."

One of the elder cadres wore a brown peaked cadre hat. I named him "Brown Cap." "We haven't brought you here because we need to understand you better," he said. "Maybe you need to understand your own predicament better, but that's an entirely different matter. You should know that you have no way out except to tell the truth."

"Exactly what I want to do," I said. "I have always told the truth to the party on matters of principle. I have never said things in private that I wouldn't say to the party. I am ready to explain anything, to answer any questions."

"You'd better take another look at the political situation and get a better understanding of it," Brown Cap said. "The Great Proletarian Cultural Revolution is uprooting all the freaks and monsters left behind by imperialism, feudalism, and monopoly capitalism. Do you really think you can be the one person to get by?"

"Go back," said the Colonel. "Think things over very carefully. Our patience and our time are not unlimited. We have let you keep Chairman Mao's Little Red Book. Stop using it to deceive the people. Learn from what it says and apply it to your situation. It will show you the way."

That night for the first time I heard the sound of prisoners being tortured.

I was never tortured physically. But sometimes, lying there night after night, I felt that suffering torture myself couldn't be more horrible than lying there helpless, listening to the groaning and screaming around me.

One night I heard the sound of either fists or sticks on bare flesh. I couldn't tell what the instrument was, but some of the blows went Splat! and some were heavy thuds. Then I heard a man's voice yelling. "Oh, stop . . . I beg you, I beg you, stop. I don't know anything. I'm telling you the truth. I didn't betray the party . . ."

"We're not beating you. You're punishing yourself by stubbornly refusing to talk," a young male voice said. That must be an interrogator, I thought. "All you have to do is tell the truth, and we'll leave you alone immediately. It's your fault. It's up to you." Wham! Splat! Thud! And then more pitiful cries from the victim.

Another night, from the front of the cell to the left of me, I heard a guard shouting, "That's disgusting. Don't kneel down to me. That's what the feudal landlords taught people to do. It won't do you any good to kowtow to me. It won't get you out of anything."

Then, further down the hall, I heard someone cursing and screaming at the guards. "You little hoodlums, you little bastards," he cried, then began to recite his deeds of merit for the party. "I'm a loyal follower of Chairman Mao, you scum. I have worked for the people for a long time. Who are you? You are a bunch of garbage, and they're all a bunch of garbage. You can't shut me up." I heard blows hammering down on a body and a roar of rage. "Who gave you the right to beat me? I am a citizen of the People's Republic of China. Who gave you the right to beat me?"

I felt panic begin to grip me. I reached my hand up to take my cap off because it was too tight and the pressure on my forehead was hard to bear. I touched flesh and realized I was not wearing a cap. What I felt was great tension. But in a moment the panic passed and the sounds of torment were no longer in the air.

When I was awakened the next time, it was to a different nightmare. I heard an elderly woman wailing like a mourner at a funeral. "I beg you not to torture me," she cried. "I'm a poor defenseless woman. I love our Great Leader, Chairman Mao. He is my savior. I have committed no crime. Please let me go home. My children are alone. There is no one to take care of them. I beg you, stop beating me and let me go home. I can't stand it any longer, I can't stand it, I can't stand it . . ."

And then the sounds of both a woman and a man shouting

shrilly at the woman and again the sounds of something striking against flesh and more shrieks and groans from the victim.

Worse, there were periods of utter quiet. I could hear nothing, no voices, no blows, but only silence followed by the most frantic, hoarse screams. I knew that both prisoners who were being beaten must be close to me, for me to hear them that clearly. The same people who were in charge of my fate were in charge of theirs. And there was no way out.

How could such things be happening to anyone, enemy or not, criminal or not? How dared they torture people? It was this shocking violation of party commitments, plus the agony of being forced to lie there and be helpless to do anything about it that threw me into a panic. I felt myself falling, even though I was flat in bed. The door and the walls of the little cell seemed to be closing in on me, threatening to crush me.

But I knew I could not succumb. The darkness of my last time in prison was waiting to ambush me. "It's only muscles that are tense," I thought. "There is nothing wrong with my head." I steadied my breathing, forced the muscles of my head to relax. "They are not going to be able to break me. I won't let them. I am prepared to meet again every ghost and goblin that I met last time, if I have to, and I'll still hold out until the end. They will not break me!"

◆

I soon realized that breaking me was exactly what they were trying to do, although they had apparently been ordered not to use physical force. Suddenly, without warning, the interrogations became terrifying. One day I walked into the interrogation room to confront a dozen people, including the two who had been questioning me all along. "You know the party policy," said the Manchurian chief. "Have you thought things over, and are you ready to make a clean breast of it?"

"That didn't take thinking over," I said. "I've been trying to do that ever since I came here."

He glowered at me with such focused hatred in his eyes, now stretched open to their widest, that I wondered if he was acting. "You say you have been trying to do it," he said. "What has prevented you?"

"Well, it looks like you've already made up your minds that I'm guilty of some crime and you don't want to listen to me explain—"

"Shut your mouth!" he screamed, and then banged the table with a little clacker that made a loud noise. I was amazed at how I started at the sharp sound in that small room. My heart was pounding, the blood beating in my head. "Get to your feet! Stand at attention!"

I stood up, feeling faint.

"It looks like the first thing we have to do with you is to straighten out your attitude. It is extremely bad. You have mistaken our patience for weakness. Until you change your attitude, you won't be able to speak a word of the truth."

"My attitude is that I'm ready to tell the truth, holding nothing back," I said in a little voice from somewhere up near the ceiling. "What did I say that was wrong?"

"We warned you last time," the chief went on, "that you would not be allowed to attack the People's Government. You claim that we have made up our minds that you are guilty. What you really mean is that we are trying to pin guilt on you that doesn't belong to you. You are continuing your vicious attack on the socialist system, right here in this prison, in this interrogation chamber, which is a court of law."

"A court of law?" I bleated. "You mean this is really a—"

"SILENCE!" Again a bang on the table with the clacker.

"I'm surprised at you," the Colonel said. "I knew you were slick, but I didn't think you had such guts. But you're continuing to challenge us right here in prison, even though it's all up with you. I advise you to play it a little smarter than this, or you'll find yourself paying a high price."

"Please, may I sit down," I said in a tremulous voice. They had taken me by surprise and I was still in shock. I was light-headed, wobbly in the knees, and I felt a strange tightness in my chest and shortness of breath.

"Stand where you are," yelled the chief. "Don't you dare sit down without an order. I want you to apologize to Chairman Mao for your bad attitude."

"But I really don't see what's bad about my attitude. Can you help me with this?"

"What's bad," said the chief, "is that you're still refusing to confess and you have even the gall to attack the People's Government. Isn't that bad enough? You want to be still worse, is that it?" Another big bang on the table with the clacker. "You had better apologize for your very bad attitude," he shouted, "unless you want to stand there in that spot from now on. As far as we're concerned, we have plenty of time."

"All right," I said. "In that case I apologize to Chairman Mao for my bad attitude. Please, may I sit down? I feel faint." I was afraid I was about to have a heart attack.

"Oh, you feel faint," said the chief mockingly. "You'll feel a lot fainter before long if you don't bow your head to the people and make a full confession of your crimes. Do you think the Chinese people, fully aroused by the Cultural Revolution, are going to let you slip through their fingers again?"

◆

Every morning I woke up slowly. Layer upon layer of sleep fell away until I reached the level before awakening and seeing, until I was on the verge of realizing who I was and what I was doing there. Every morning that knowledge broke through my sleep with crushing force. I heard the sounds around me, the keeper ringing the morning bell, the guards hawking and spitting in the corridor. Finally I opened my eyes and saw the thin coverlet over me, the light burning overhead, the same four gray walls, and the dull red door with the peephole.

But before sound and vision came the unbearable weight, like a boulder pressing down on my chest and head. For me, that stone had a name: solitude. "My God," I would think. "I'm still here. I'm still all alone. I'm still in this ice box, buried alive."

I had to learn to lift that stone every morning, to fight off the bitterness, self-pity, and depression that I knew could, if unchecked, make me retreat into myself, never to return. I had heard it happen to several of my neighbors. During the regular nighttime agonies, I had heard one man screaming, then sounds of beating, then screaming once more. For a week or more he had screamed his innocence, begging them to stop the beatings, begging them to check with his party committee back home who would vouch for his loyalty to Chairman Mao.

Then abruptly, the screaming stopped, and for a while I heard the guards shouting. "Don't you fool with us like that," came their voices through the wall. "We know you're faking madness. We have ways to make you get up, you know, ways that you won't like." Sounds of kicking and beating and more silence. Finally there was nothing but silence.

I couldn't let that happen to me. I had to keep pulling myself back into the world, even if it was a world of grim silence and pain. I devised a little credo for myself, learned it by heart, and began reciting it as soon as I awoke. "My name is Li Dunbai," I said to myself. "I am an American who of his own volition joined the Chinese Revolution and was accepted into the Communist Party. My aim is to turn myself into a genuine Communist, a noble, pure, and moral man, who lives to benefit the people, devoid of selfishness, devoted exclusively to the welfare of others. I vow to do what I need to do to overcome the fear of hardship and death, to listen gladly to criticism of my own shortcomings, and to constantly study to overcome my defects."

It was close to the litany I had chanted to myself during my first time in prison. I was trying to save myself by extinguishing myself, to turn my attention away from the sins visited on me as an individual to the plight of the masses. After all, what was my pain, my suffering—even my death—compared to the fate of millions?

And yet, this time it was different. There was another credo buzzing in my head, a new one, a different one. It was one that spoke out clearly on my behalf. "My name is Sidney Rittenberg," it said. "I am dedicated to seeking my happiness by contributing to the freedom and happiness of the human race. I am entitled to life, liberty, and the pursuit of happiness, and no one can deprive me of those rights as long as I refuse to give them up. I will use my philosophy to realize as many of them as possible within the circumstances in which I find myself. I will never give up. The more they try to weaken me and break me down, the stronger I will become."

The self I had killed in the first prison was coming alive in the second.

As far as it could, my credo worked. It got me up and about briskly in the morning, kept me working, fighting, and shaking off the oblivion that beckoned. I learned to live without companionship, without privacy, without love. Every comfort or diversion I had ever known was taken away from me. The conditions under which I lived were far worse than during my first imprisonment. And yet, somehow, I learned to live and survive, and even—within my misery—to be happy.

At home, I was sensitive to the cold in winter, dressing in layer after layer, thick warm sweaters over cotton padded clothing and long underwear. In prison in winter, I was always cold. The walls and floors were of stone, and there was only the faintest heat, even in the coldest weather. My shoes were cotton, thin-soled and too tight. My cotton-padded clothes were meager. When thoughts of home slipped through the barricades I built, I thought of the little kindness I had done Yulin on that last night at home. The prison authorities let me keep the long johns I had arrived in. But they were Yulin's tattered pair with no seat, not my own brand-new pair.

At night, I perfected a routine, stuffing the ends of the cotton quilt into my pants to create a makeshift sleeping bag. I never believed I could sleep in such cold, and yet sleep I did. At home I had loved sleep, cuddling up soft and warm next to Yulin under layers of blankets and quilt, with a baby or two sometimes popping into bed next to us in the morning. Here in prison, I had to sleep facing the doorway, my hands in view outside the covers of the bed between my neck and my belt. I had to sleep without a pillow or even the comfort of my crooked arm under my head. If I rolled or turned in my sleep—crack! The guards would bang on my door, rattling me with curses.

Unexpectedly, at any time, uniformed keepers burst into my cell and surrounded me, shaking their fists. "Do you know where you are?" they shouted. "Do you know what place this is?" "Yes," I answered, nodding. Ignoring my reply, they shouted, "This is the place of the dictatorship of the proletariat. Here you have no rights whatsoever, do you understand? No rights!"

At the beginning of the harsh interrogations, the guards were apparently under orders to disturb my sleep. Just dropping off I heard banging at the door, loud as a cannon cracker. The first time it happened, I leaped to my feet shouting, "Report!"

"What are you making that noise for?" an angry voice said from the other side of the door.

"Someone knocked on my door. I don't know what they wanted," I said.

"Dog-fart," said the angry voice. "What kind of rubbish are you making up? Get back in your bed and sleep or you'll be severely punished."

Then, I was just going to sleep, and bang, the noise again. I realized I was being deliberately kept awake, probably to help break me down during grilling. I decided I would steel myself to ignore the noises and try to sleep anyway. The next time the banging started, I woke up and stirred a little, but went right back to sleep. I awoke in the morning with a sense of having won a small battle.

◆

My worst enemy that first year was hunger. I lived with brutal, unrelieved hunger, tottering on the edge of serious malnutrition. Three times a day, I heard the meal cart rattling down the hall and the harsh voice of the keeper shouting curses as she delivered the food. "Hurry, you stinking bastard! Counterrevolutionary scum, be quicker than that or you won't get a scrap of food! You son of a bitch, do you want it or not!" Only at my door was she silent— no curses.

Three times a day, I pushed open the little trap at the bottom of the door and held out my earthenware bowl. Twice a day, I got thin cabbage soup—water really—with a few white stalks of cabbage floating in it. Twice a day, I got a cone or two of steamed cornbread. Or sometimes I got a bowl of coarse rice filled with debris and pebbles, or a steamed bun. At breakfast, there was a half a bowl of thin gruel with a few shreds of salted turnip. After a time, the keepers passed me an extra piece or two of cornbread or a little food left over after feeding the other prisoners. It seemed like a wondrous windfall.

On Sundays and holidays, I only got two meals, one in mid-morning and one in mid-afternoon. Those days were really hard. I sat on my bed, faint from hunger, dreaming of food. The hardest times were around National Day and the Chinese lunar New Year when, for three or four days in a row, I got only two meals. Then during the interrogations that followed, I would retreat into my own personal utopia, dreaming of an ideal world where I could have all the cornbread I wanted.

Even worse than the cravings was the physical and mental debility I felt. When I got up from sitting, I made a dizzy, wobbly stagger dance across the room. When I raised my head to look up, I felt the blood rush to the back of my head, causing dizziness and pain. I braced myself on the wall, trying to keep my head down, trying not to faint. The air was always full of floating red and blue blotches. The effect was like watching a movie full of rain.

As much as I could, I tried to use the conditions of my imprisonment as weapons in my survival plan. The peephole took away all privacy, while leaving the solitude. But it could be viewed in another light. It meant they were watching me and saw my every move and facial expression. I believed that my actions, emotions, and reactions would force them to conclude, sooner or later, that I was exactly what I said I was.

I kept my cell spotless, working it over with an eight-inch square of rag and water from the tap. At first, I was washing away caked-up grime. But after a few weeks, I had cleaned away every speck of dirt and the rag came away clean. It was one of the few honest-to-God practical things I could do.

I tried to keep myself in good physical condition. I worked out a set of calisthenics and homemade Chinese taiqi exercises that I did in the morning before breakfast, before lunch, and before supper. I started off with limbering-up exercises, stretching and twisting, went through various hoppings and skippings and bends and arm flappings, and ended up doing breathing exercises in the lotus position.

Then I jogged. The first day I started running in my cell, the guard banged on the door and yelled, "Just what do you think you're doing?"

I stood at attention and intoned in my best reciting-official-instructions voice, "It is permitted for prisoners to take physical exercise in order to keep in good enough health to tell the party their true story, provided that they strictly observe prison discipline."

Silence followed; I was never challenged again on exercising in the cell.

When I got seriously run-down and could only wobble dizzily across the room to the commode, I had to slow the fitness exercises down considerably, but I never stopped them for a single day. It was a basic part of my survival program, and it kept up my morale.

I used mealtimes as a chance to demonstrate my revolutionary fervor. I knew how sensitive these soldiers were to the way city people valued food. As country kids they knew the cost in back-breaking labor of each grain of rice. They did not like to see it wasted. So I made sure they saw me treasure my food. I held my bowl carefully so as not to lose a drop of the watery soup. I scrambled after every scrap of rice, even grains that had fallen on the floor, and ate them immediately.

I tried to turn mealtime into an event, a chance for sensory stimulation. When the guard opened the little door at the bottom of the big door, it was the only chance I had, apart from the interrogations, to see at least part of another human body. All I could see was their shoes, socks, and pants legs, but that was better than nothing. I used those clues to construct a whole picture of a human being. From their shoes and socks, I fancied I could tell who they were, where they had grown up, what they were like.

There was the old army type who wore athletic shoes with plain black or army-green socks. There was the stubborn addict to colorful displays who wore new-style Chinese cloth shoes with elastic tabs down the front for comfort and fancy colored socks with rings or dots. Then there were the unabashed modernists who wore leather shoes and socks of either good solid colors or checked and striped. Women keepers tended a little more to color and design, but only slightly so.

I tried to turn what little I had to eat into something to look forward to. Every morning at breakfast, along with the gruel, I got a thumbnail-size lump of salted vegetables. It was the only thing that had any taste, any appeal at all, and I began to look forward to that moment of the day above all others. When the weakness from hunger was intense, I comforted myself—quite effectively— with the cheerful thought that it was only ten hours, or eleven hours, or eight hours, until that wonderful moment when I could taste those salted vegetables.

◆

The interrogations continued for three years, sometimes once a day, sometimes twice a day. Sometimes there were three interrogation sessions a day, the full panel hammering away at me in the morning and the afternoon, and then either the lantern-jawed Manchurian or the Colonel returning in the evening for a quiet, more intimate session.

"Look, you've got to realize you can't get away with this," they crooned in the dark of the night grilling room. "You just confess, come clean, and tell your story." Their unctuous concern of the evening clashed with their fierce harshness in daylight.

The interrogations went in waves, three months or so at a time, followed by months of silence. While they were going on, I prayed that they would end, that the fierceness, the hatred and anger, the terror of their accusations would vanish and leave me in peace. But when the interrogations abruptly ceased, I prayed for them to return. At least they meant they still knew I was there, were still thinking about me. The worst thing I could imagine was being forgotten, buried alive.

From the questions I had been asked while I was under house

arrest, I had a pretty good idea what they wanted. They wanted to prove I was a spy, a spy connected to the leadership at the very top, with networks of influence fanning out through the foreign community.

For a time, they tiptoed around that issue, always hinting, never coming directly out with it. "We're so close to naming your real crime," they said, "that it's like it's just on the other side of a paper window in a peasant's home. All we have to do is poke it slightly with a finger and the paper will part, showing what lies on the other side. The only reason we have not named it so far is that we are giving you a chance to confess before we have to expose you. It would be much better for you that way. But we can't wait forever."

Then suddenly, they snapped. "Spy!" they shouted at me. "Foreign agent!"

This time, unlike my first imprisonment, I had no illusions. This was no test of my loyalty, no secret rectification to mold me into a trusted comrade. These were criminal charges, and there were all kinds of reasons they might want to pin them on me: connections with Wang Li, for example, who was now disgraced; the factional struggle at the Broadcast Administration and the fact that individuals like my ex-wife, Wei Lin, had repeatedly denounced me as a spy; my rash remarks to the Wuhan Red Guards about the Vietnamese Communist Party.

Day after day the interrogations dragged on. The team members changed from time to time. Sometimes there were eight people. Sometimes there were twelve. Sometimes people in civilian clothes would show up and sit silently on the sidelines. Sometimes the visitors would be wearing army uniforms. Once, for a while, a young woman appeared and assiduously took notes. But it turned out she was pregnant; her stomach grew at an alarming rate for about three months, and then she vanished.

The grilling was exhausting. When I walked into the bare room, facing the grim-looking team on the other side of the long table, I was helpless. They could smoke, sit or stand or walk around as they wished. They could drink water if they were thirsty. They could chat and joke with each other, put their feet on the table, take off or put on jackets and sweaters, or do anything they pleased.

I could not sit, stand, speak, move without a direct order. I had no water to drink, no right to don or doff clothing. Every command was given to me as a military order. "Right face!" "About face!" "Two paces forward, march!" I was not a person. I had no name, no rights, no protection, no defense. They were accuser and judge. "Talk!" they would shout. "Talk or you will soon reach the end of the road to death!"

I told them that it was not so. I was not an imperialist agent. I had always been just what I said I was. I had never lied to the party.

"How can you prove you're not a spy?" asked the Colonel, mockingly.

"I can't," I replied. "No one can prove he is not something like that. But I think I have proved it and will continue to prove it by the whole course of my life. I can't imagine anyone who could so deceive the people who are close to them for a very long period of time."

"You are not only leading a double life," the Colonel taunted, "you have a whole theory to cover up for people like you who lead double lives."

One day when I walked into the grilling room, the Manchurian announced, "We have decided to forbid you to deny that you are a secret agent. This will be good for you, because it will keep you from lying so much and adding to your guilt. From now on when we say you are a spy, you are not to deny it! Do you understand?"

I nodded. "I understand, but I have to deny it. Because you have charged me with telling the truth, and warned me that any failure to tell the truth will add to my crimes. I must answer any questions or accusations truthfully, must I not?"

"Just leave off the sophistry and do as we tell you!" the Manchurian demanded.

So over and over we repeated the same dialogue. "You are a spy and you stubbornly refuse to confess. You are a die-hard spy!"

"No, I am not a spy."

"I told you that you were not allowed to deny it!"

"But you told me first that I must always tell the truth in here. Isn't that my first obligation?"

"Shut up!"

Once, the five men behind the table rose like a swarm of bees and ran up to form a circle around me, waving their fists in my face and threatening to strike me. Several times I had heard someone being cursed and beaten in the next interrogation room, then the thud of someone falling on the floor and the continuing sound of blows on bare skin. But I was no longer afraid. I knew that one of their ploys was to bait me into expressing hatred and rage against China. This they would have seized as evidence of an imperialist attitude—just what would have been expected of an agent.

Several times they threatened to kill me. "Our patience is at an end," said the Manchurian one day. "Either you come clean right now, this afternoon, or very early tomorrow morning you will be sent with your granite head to meet your maker! It will all happen so fast that you won't even have time to cry. If you think we are bluffing, just try us."

Long-buried words from my past before China rose to my lips. "If the victory of the Cultural Revolution means the loss of my life," I said, "I will consider that a very small price to pay."

Nathan Hale. Where had that brave voice of mine come from? Little by little, I was recovering my individual will, my individual courage, my ability to think for myself. I still considered myself a devoted Communist, but more and more my mind was becoming my own.

I used my own philosophy to govern my mood. Over and over my interrogators told me I would never get out of prison; confession would buy me better conditions and that was all. One night, I lay there on my cot staring up at the light and thinking to myself, "If the rest of my life is all going to be like this, what's the point?" Depression threatened to engulf me. But a voice within me answered back: You are supposed to be dedicated to the freedom and happiness of the human race. Now that you're in trouble, how can you forget about the hundreds of millions out there, many of whom are suffering much worse than you are?

All at once, there was a remarkable swing in my mood, from gloom to tranquillity. And with that, I no longer believed their threats. I realized that this evil system of justice would never last, that the people would someday destroy it. When that day came, I would be free—as long as I could survive and not let them break my spirit. I could do it, if I could keep my thoughts focused on others and not just on myself.

Once, under grilling, I suggested they examine my record. "Let's go over my activities," I said. "Let's go over what I really did."

"*Ha!*" they laughed. "Exposures of you are flying into our office every day like snowflakes in a blizzard. Even your foreign friends are denouncing you. Do you think we need you to tell us what you were up to?"

So some foreigners were collecting information about me. I

wondered who they were. I didn't believe my real friends would speak out against me. But who were my real friends?

As for me, I denounced no one. From time to time, I was asked to report on other people. They asked me about my role in founding the Bethune Regiment. They asked about my connections with Israel Epstein and my British friend Michael Shapiro. They hinted that they wanted to talk about Anna Louise Strong. But I remembered what Yulin had said. I told the truth, no more, no less.

Once their questions stretched all the way back to before I went to Yanan. "When you rode in that Japanese truck from Kalgan, you rode with Zhou Yang. What did you talk about with him?"

Back then, Zhou Yang had been a young writer, critic, and university dean. He had risen to be vice minister of propaganda and the man in charge of controlling all writers and artists until he was overthrown in the Cultural Revolution. I didn't tell my interrogators I knew that Zhou Yang was in prison with me, and not too far away either. At night, I could hear his thick Hunanese accent as he railed against his captors, lecturing them on party history and the glorious revolutionary struggle of the past. When the guards shouted at him to be quiet, he would shout all the louder. "You little bums, what do you know about the Communist Party? Why don't you read and learn about the world?"

I told my interrogators that as Zhou and I bounced along in the back of the truck, we had talked about literature and art. "He told me that he liked to write but that he was so busy, he seldom got any time to do it."

"Is that all?" the Colonel sneered. "All you did was talk about literature and art?"

Then one day I was hauled into the interrogation room to face an entirely different group of people. There were ten of them, and they all looked as if they were from the military.

These interrogators were sober and severe, but they weren't as harsh. They had only one interest: Wang Guangmei, the wife of Liu Shaoqi, who had been president and Mao's number two man. They showed no interest in my case, except to point out that helping expose her would lighten whatever treatment I was to receive.

"When did you first meet Wang Guangmei?" they asked. "Why did you visit her in Beijing? Why did you carry messages for her?"

Everything we had done together was public knowledge, and nothing, as far as I knew, could hurt her. I told them the truth. I told them that I had met her in 1946 in Beijing at Ye Jianying's headquarters when I was trying to get to Yanan. I told them that George Hatem's wife had introduced us as possible marriage candidates, and that we had twice eaten twice-cooked pork together in Yanan.

They focused on a letter they said I had carried from Wang Guangmei to her capitalist brother, Wang Guangying. All I could remember was that once, while we were on the road fleeing from the Nationalists, she had asked me to carry a letter to the part of Hebei Province where I was headed and where someone would be able to mail it.

It seemed they were trying to prove that I ran a network of foreign spies; that I had recruited Wang Guangmei, and through her the president of the People's Republic, Liu Shaoqi. But somehow, I felt that something wasn't quite right with my interrogators. It just didn't seem that their hearts were in it. Even though they were harsh and fierce with me, jumping up, surrounding me, shaking their fists in my face and shouting, from time to time, I had an almost eerie sense that they themselves didn't believe the charges they were hurling at me.

"Be careful and speak slowly," the Colonel once charged me during an interrogation unrelated to the spy charges. "You don't want to let anything slip out that would betray your counterrevolutionary past." I heard the irony and sarcasm, but all I could see in his face was good humor.

Then, suddenly, the interrogation veered course. The spy charges vanished. Instead, they began to grill me on the Cultural Revolution. And little by little, I began to understand why I had been imprisoned. The spy charges were their attempt to bring down other people associated with me. As for me, I had brought myself down because I had fundamentally misunderstood Mao's real intention in the Cultural Revolution. I had attacked unquestioning party discipline. I had attacked the system of surveillance of the masses. I had attacked one-party dictatorship, dossiers, and snitching. I had done it with gusto and had garnered a tremendous following. I had become famous all over China for my zeal in promoting democracy.

I knew I was attacking the old party system. I just didn't realize that Mao and the other top leaders were not with me when I had done so. I thought what I was saying was the same thing that Mao, Jiang Qing, and the Cultural Revolution Group were saying. It was only under interrogation that I realized that it was almost precisely the opposite.

Mao's point in the Cultural Revolution wasn't, as I had thought, to destroy restrictions on civil rights, blind obedience to party discipline, thought control over the masses, and an arbitrary one-party dictatorship. It was to strengthen these things. Mao had two key slogans in the Cultural Revolution. One was "Great Democracy," which he used to set the masses in motion against the other leaders. The other was "Total Proletarian Dictatorship." The first slogan was the means; the second was the end.

I had taken seriously the talk by Jiang Qing and the Cultural Revolution Group about democracy. But they weren't serious about democracy. They were serious about consolidating control in their own hands. I had thought I was the mouthpiece of Mao Zedong Thought. But it was clear from my interrogation that I had been voicing my own ideas, not Mao's.

One day, during an interrogation, the Colonel handed me a copy of a speech I had made. There was a paragraph marked out. "Here," he said. "Read this."

I remembered the speech well. I had made many like it. This one had been given at the High Academy of Military Science and was about slaves and slave-masters. I had intended to denounce Liu Shaoqi and his call for unquestioning obedience to instructions of party leaders and party doctrine. But when I read the marked paragraph, I was horrified.

Wherever there are slaves, I had said, there are bound to be slave-masters. The slave only exists because he has a master. Likewise, the master is only a master because he has slaves under him. Looking downward in the party hierarchy, you see tier after tier of slaves, including slaves who have slaves under them. Looking upward from the bottom, you see tier after tier of slave-masters, including some who are also slaves. And at the pinnacle of the whole hierarchy is the biggest slave-master of all with no one standing above him. He is the supreme master of all the slaves.

And who was this supreme slave-master? I read the paragraph over and over again. The Colonel looked at me. The other interrogators looked at me. Who was the slave-master at the pinnacle?

I hadn't said. Although I had repeatedly mentioned Liu Shaoqi throughout other parts of my speech, he was conspicuously absent in this part. Why had I not said who the supreme slave-master was? The conclusion, my interrogators told me, was clear. I had not been attacking Liu Shaoqi.

I had been attacking Chairman Mao himself.

CHAPTER TWENTY-TWO

The Dynasty Collapses

The only real contact I had with the outside world was through the newspaper. I had been allowed newspapers ever since the end of the first really tough interrogation session. I nursed them, treasured them, read them slowly cover to cover. They were my only view into a world of normal people, of people who were neither caged nor keepers. Even the posed photos of farmers in the fields, miners in hard hats, soldiers in tank helmets, opera singers from Jiang Qing's model revolutionary dramas—frozen though they might be—were images of live human beings and food for a half-starved imagination.

I tried to keep myself abreast of happenings by deciphering the masked criticisms of people and current trends, to fathom what was going on in the Cultural Revolution outside. I read theoretical articles to try to guess at policy changes. Often the papers came one day late, so I even read the weather report as a kind of comic relief, to see how hot or cold I had been the day before.

There were stories about the crops, about the great accomplishments of the Cultural Revolution, about the visits of fraternal party members from Africa and Southeast Asia.

Then one day there was a different kind of story. Zhou Enlai had invited the American Ping-Pong team—in Japan on a tour—to come to China for a visit and a match. And not only did the

American table tennis team visit China, but a few months later I read that the American secretary of state, Henry Kissinger, was visiting to make plans for a visit by the American President, Richard Nixon himself.

Almost immediately my life began to change.

I had been in my cell on the second floor of the prison building for four years. One day shortly after the Kissinger visit, a keeper came in and talked to me in amazingly gentle tones. "We are moving you to another building," he said. "Your conditions are going to improve."

As soon as I got to the new cell, I knew that my life would really be different. The guards in this part of the prison talked civilly to me and didn't glare hatefully when I walked by. In the cell, I found the bed parallel to the left wall, not against the back wall under the window as it had been in my other cells. I asked the guard if I could move the bed up against the back wall, since it took up less room that way.

"You can move the bed any way you want," he said.

On the first night in my new cell, I turned my back to the door. No one pounded. I couldn't believe that I could sleep any way I wanted to for the first time in four years. But that paled before the surprise in store for me at noon. When the food cart came around, I was handed a porcelain metal set of stacking containers, the kind workmen carry for lunch. In the top container was soup—not water and cabbage, but real, thick soup. I opened the bottom container. In it were tomatoes and carrots and beans. In between were fried batter cakes and meat—real meat, not little pieces of fat. There was lots and lots of food, plenty to eat, and if it wasn't enough, the keeper said, I could get more.

I was drunk on food. For days, I could do little else than walk round and round in my cell and think about what the next meal would bring. For breakfast there were fried eggs, pork sausage, and thick sliced wheat buns. There were real pickled vegetables, not just salted turnips, and a big can full of porridge. I had real fruit to eat, and every other morning they brought me a bottle of milk. I squirreled the fruit away and ate just a half an apple at a time. There was no telling when this largesse might stop.

A few days later, I was summoned from my cell. "Another interrogation," I thought. But waiting in the interrogation room was not my case team, but two men I had never met before. They were both in uniform, one older and clearly in charge, one younger and taking notes. They were both calm and addressed me and asked me questions in a normal tone of voice.

"What do you think about the upcoming visit?" the older of the two asked me.

"I think if the President of the United States is visiting China and being received by the central government," I said, "then there is about to be a major improvement in the relations between the two countries, and I think that is a good thing."

"Do you know President Nixon?" he asked.

A brief temptation flitted through my head. Could I pretend to know him? Could I pull it off? Might it help to release me? Again, I remembered Yulin's warning and opted to tell the truth. "Just what I've read about him," I said. "I've never liked him."

The older man relaxed, almost talkative. "There has been criticism of China from some quarters"—I guessed he meant Vietnam —"for receiving Nixon. Some people are saying that this is a sign of making deals with imperialism, that we are going the same road the Soviets have taken."

I kept on watching the newspaper, and within a week or so, Nixon arrived. I saw the picture of him at the Beijing airport, arms outstretched to greet my friend Zhou Enlai. I was overjoyed that the opening between the United States and China that I had long dreamed of was finally going to take place. Maybe someday there would be a role for me, working to help build a bridge of cooperation between the two nations, just as I had planned back in those long-ago days in Fresh Flower Village, translating for the truce team.

Futile daydreams! I tossed them out of my head. They were never going to let me out of here. They would never be able to admit to the world that they had erred twice in the same way. I fought off an attack of the blues. But then the next mealtime arrived and every bad thought was swept away in a tide of pork, cabbage, and mounds and mounds of soft white rice.

◆

The newspapers were always full of quotations from Vice Chairman Lin Biao, Chairman Mao's closest comrade-in-arms and successor. They were often printed without quotation marks because all readers by then recognized their source. Every day or so there were also action photos of Lin Biao, or reception photos, or photos of him greeting foreign heads of state, or meeting with the children of heroic coal miners. His top cohorts—the ranking generals, Huang Yongsheng, Wu Faxian, Qiu Huizuo, and Li Zuopeng—also filled the press. Even the teachings of Mao himself would often be framed in Lin Biao's words: "Comrade Lin Biao reminds us that our Great Leader Chairman Mao has said . . ."

Then on September 14th it all stopped.

All mention of Lin Biao and his cohorts, all phrases and slogans associated with them completely vanished from the *People's Daily*. It was too obvious to miss. The paper seemed completely bereft. There was no news at all, and no one came out with an explanation for the silence. I didn't know what had happened to Lin Biao, but it was pretty clear he was in big trouble.

Then the usual propaganda buildup for the October 1 National Day failed to appear. On National Day, there was no parade, no fireworks, no reviewing stand. I figured that there was some national security reason for canceling the parade. But why? I had no idea. The newspapers were full of oblique suggestions, but it was only much later that they publicly reported that a few weeks before National Day, Lin Biao, his family, and several of his cohorts had been killed in a plane crash in Mongolia.

Then one rainy morning in July, I was sitting in my cell when I heard several people coming slowly down the corridor. One of them was shuffling his feet along, as though wearing big slippers. They opened the empty cell next to me and put the shuffler inside. I heard one of the keepers say, "Cold? How can you be cold? This is hot weather. If you are cold, here's your big army overcoat and fur hat. Plenty to keep you warm." Then out they all went, banged the door shut, and locked it.

That afternoon, the shuffler began to talk.

He had two ways of talking. He harangued the guards and he spun yarns. It sounded as if he had been in prison for some time and was close to losing his mind. He raved and ranted at the top of his voice about Zhou Enlai. For weeks, he kept repeating the same line over and over: "Zhou Enlai is a renegade and a traitor. He must be shot!" He used a code name for Zhou, but it was easy to figure out whom he meant.

He also talked about Mao, using the code word B-52. "Zhou has always managed to pull the wool over the eyes of B-52," he ranted. "Now the revolution is very complicated. The pressure of trying to lead the country through new problems has made B-52 sick and senile. He lets Zhou get his way about everything. And so that low-down son of a bitch does everything he can to block our great genius, Commander Lin."

Commander Lin! That must be Lin Biao, and I wondered if I would hear the story of why he had vanished.

Suddenly the shuffler broke into a yell: "He must be shot! Zhou Enlai must be shot! Until he is shot," he said, using a classical phrase, "the country will have no tranquil days."

The guard tapped on his door. "Shut your mouth," he said angrily. "You're talking reactionary rubbish."

"What do you know, you little whelp, you little bastard? You know-nothing. I grew up in a poor peasant household with no land, no money, no standing. I joined a guerrilla band with my father and we fought the Japanese and their puppet army and the KMT, all at the same time—and we beat them all. Then I went to fight the American devils in Korea and we beat them too. I was a pilot and fought in the skies against the KMT planes. Lin Liguo was a close buddy of mine, and when he got to be deputy political commissar of the air force, I became a member of the air force party committee along with him."

Lin Liguo. That was Lin Biao's son.

"We need armed struggle to assure that Commander Lin can take up the command over the entire country," the prisoner ranted on. "B-52 is old and sick, and we can't wait forever. And Zhou Enlai is a traitor who must be punished."

Was this the plot that Lin Biao had been involved in: to get rid of both Mao and Zhou by armed force and then take all power into his own hands? Was this why he had suddenly vanished? Was it possible that the plane crash that killed him was not an accident?

My neighbor's diatribes reeked of the xenophobia that had been growing since the second year of the Cultural Revolution. I was horrified as I realized what the source of it must have been, and what kind of a regime these plotters would have presided over had they been successful.

"Zhou Enlai gives away everything we need the most, giving it all to foreigners," he raved. "He gives some of our best arms to other countries, before our own People's Army can even get to see them. He gives to Guinea, to Albania, to Vietnam, to Laos, to the PLO . . . Any foreigner can get anything he wants from Zhou Enlai, but we can't get the arms and equipment we need. If that isn't betrayal, what is? Lin Liguo says we should spend our money on our own people, and use our best arms and equipment to meet our own needs. Otherwise, we help the foreigners but we don't help ourselves."

The man's xenophobia extended to China's own minority groups. "Zhou Enlai gives away everything to the minority nationalities too. If you're a Tibetan, it's easy to get into a university and you get all kinds of subsidies and special deals. Uighurs, Kazaks, Zhuangs, Mongolians—they're all little dependent nationalities, depending on the Han Chinese—they're already having it better than they ever have before. Why should we play nurse to them? No one but a traitor would follow such a policy.

"Any foreigner who comes to Beijing can convince Zhou Enlai that his advice is good for China. Zhou Enlai thinks that even a fart is fragrant when it comes from a foreigner. He must be shot, this traitor! He must be shot!" There was more talk about confederates in this plot, apparently aimed at not just Zhou Enlai, but Mao Zedong himself.

Despite the man's ravings, the prison guards treated him with kid gloves. I suspected that elsewhere in the prison he had been half killed in an attempt to make him talk, and now he was being nursed back to health. He refused to eat his prison food, shouting that it wasn't fit for pigs. And rather than beating him, they brought him special food in a set of porcelain canisters like mine, which I could see through the little trap in the bottom of my door when I opened it to get my own food.

Finally, about three weeks after he arrived, he was taken away, shuffling off as he had shuffled in. I never found out who he was or what became of him. And the true story behind Lin Biao's sudden death remained a mystery to me.

◆

My interrogations had stopped after Lin Biao's death. I should have been relieved at the end of that type of pressure, but I wasn't. They were my only chance at human contact, my only assurance that my keepers hadn't forgotten me. Now I was completely alone. How was I to live like this, perhaps for the rest of my life? The walls were gray. The floor was gray. The door was a dull reddish color. Sitting on the low-slung bed, staring at the wall, I felt the room full of aloneness. It was not just the absence of other human life, but the presence of aloneness that seemed to fill the room, to shimmer between me and the wall, to weigh down the otherwise empty air until it seemed to press in and threaten to suffocate me.

Alone alone alone alone alone. The walls beat my solitude into my head through aching eyes every hour of the day and night—great spots and bands of color floating and pulsating before my eyes, silence making my ears ring.

If this was to be my life until the day I died, why not put an end to it? But the thought of suicide revolted me. I hated the idea of giving up, of letting them win. So I had no way out.

Thoughts of my family kept pressing through the armor I had built around myself. The saddest thought I had was that I had been taken away from our four children when they were just two, seven, nine, and ten. By now our son would have no memory of me; the three girls would remember me, but they were adolescents now, not children any longer. They were becoming young women without me. Even if I ever got out, I would never be able to see them growing up.

And what if something dreadful had happened to them? I didn't think they would be harmed physically. But what if they had been turned against me as I had seen other children turned against their families in the Cultural Revolution? I knew Yulin would work hard to see that that didn't happen, but I didn't know what kinds of pressures would be put on the children.

Never a day went by that I didn't yearn for Yulin. It was like the pain of an infected tooth. Would she wait for me? If she lived she would wait. I never doubted that. She was young, strong, able, attractive, good-humored. She had a heart that was not for sale and a stubbornness that would come through to save her when all else failed. I knew she would never change.

Yet I worried for her safety. I was afraid that she might be so angry and abrasive that she could lose her life in a useless struggle against anyone who demanded that she expose me. As I walked back and forth in my cell, desperate for some sort of mental respite, for some other strength and support, I thought of Yulin, who was always like a rock, who stood stronger and taller whenever things got tough. She had told me a thousand times, "Don't worry. If we have problems, I'll stand by you. It'll be the two of us together."

I tried to pick the bright spots from the darkness. I had enough to eat. I had learned to overcome my panic and claustrophobia, a tremendous achievement. And I had my books. About six months after the Nixon visit, the officer I called the Colonel asked me if I wanted anything.

"Tell me about my wife and children," I said.

"They're fine. Fine," he replied. "They're all fine."

I realized, sadly, that such assurances were useless. Hadn't they told me that Wei Lin was fine and waiting for me, years and years after she had actually divorced me and remarried?

"Is there anything else you would like?" the Colonel asked.

"Books," I replied.

"Give us a list from your own library and we will get them for you."

In a few weeks, to my utter amazement, they delivered my own books to me: Hegel's *Logic,* Kant's *Critique of Pure Reason* and *Critique of Practical Reason,* Shakespeare, the edition illustrated by Rockwell Kent, three volumes of *Das Kapital* in English. I looked the books over inside and out in hopes of deriving from them some clue about my home, my family. But I learned nothing. The red cloth binding on the first volume of Hegel had been thoroughly chewed by rats. Other volumes had been lying in water. So I guessed that my apartment had been closed up and my belongings stored in a warehouse somewhere.

My plan to prove who I was by my behavior paid off in surprising ways. There were always one or two people who were daringly friendly to me. Once early on, I had heard an unexpected tap on my cell door. I went to the peephole and looked out. There was a young guard there.

"What are you here for?" he whispered.

"I'm not supposed to tell . . . " I said.

"I know you," he said. "You don't look like a bad egg. I've been watching you closely. You read our newspaper very seriously. You follow our rules. You don't break discipline. You eat everything, even the grains of rice you drop. You keep your cell clean." There was a long pause. "I've decided I'm going to help you. What you need more than anything else is someone to talk to. I will be on this post for another two weeks. Every time I am on duty, we can talk. But one thing is important. Every time the door to the hallway opens, I will leave suddenly. Don't tell anyone I am talking to you."

I knew better than that. I couldn't believe what he was risking for me. I knew he could have been shot if he were caught fraternizing with an accused enemy agent during the Cultural Revolution.

I never saw the young man. But for the next two weeks we talked. "Don't pay too much attention to what they are saying," he told me. "Stick to the truth. And if they threaten you, just relax. It will all pass over. Don't upset them, and do what they tell you to do."

He talked about himself, where he had served on guard duty, about his life on a peasant farm before coming to the city. He asked about me. He had seen me on television meeting Chairman Mao, and asked what it was like. He wanted to know about my life in America, and I told him about my days organizing labor and civil rights activities in the South.

He told me things I didn't know. I was in the top-rated prison, the infamous Qin Cheng prison. But while I had been here, many places in Beijing had been turned into prisons: the Qianmen Hotel, for one, and the famous Sichuan restaurant where I had entertained many foreign guests, for another. At least one of my friends was also imprisoned. Israel Epstein, the Polish-born historian, was in jail, the guard told me.

As the end of his tour of duty drew near, he tried to comfort me. "How old are you now?" he asked.

"Forty-seven," I said.

"Well, don't worry. By the time you are in your fifties you will be back serving the people again."

He meant to be kind. But a cold chill fell over me. Three more years? Was he saying it would take three more years to settle my case? As it turned out, his guess was optimistic.

◆

After the Nixon visit, I began to get medical care, the first in five years. The doctor found I had high blood pressure, which was probably the cause of the terrible, blinding headaches I suffered. I also suffered from cardiac arrhythmia, probably caused by malnutrition. The doctor gave me some medicine for tension and for my blood pressure.

Later, I even saw a dentist. One winter afternoon, a pleasant round woman's face under a People's Army cap appeared. "Are you having any problems with your teeth?" she asked. She looked around thirty to thirty-five, and her eyes were open, caring, and without hatred.

"I have a tooth on the lower left that is sensitive to heat and cold," I replied.

"I will schedule you and we'll have a look at it," she said. "Don't worry."

The doorlet shut and she was gone. I had to walk around my cell, hiding my face from the peephole as well as I could because I was crying.

One afternoon about a week later, a keeper came and took me to the dental clinic in a small stone-and-brick building off to one side of the cell buildings. He sat in a waiting room just outside the open door, and the dentist soon determined that one of my lower left teeth was very decayed and needed a root canal immediately. Even so, she was not sure she could save the tooth, she told me. She would have to build up the tooth itself, and not much healthy tooth was left to build on.

"The easiest thing in the world would be just to pull that tooth and be done with it," she said, reflectively. "But I hate to see you lose one of your natural teeth. Once it's gone it's gone and there's no calling it back. So let's do our best to save it, shall we? It will mean some discomfort for you, but if it works you'll still have your tooth. What do you think?"

What did I think? What I thought was: how long has it been since anybody talked to me like that, in that tone of voice, express-ing concern over my well-being?

Holding back tears, I said, "If the doctor thinks there's a pos-sibility of saving it, of course I'd like to try."

She tried for about two hours that afternoon. It was more pain-ful than anything that had happened to me in a dentist's chair before. In a soft voice, so that the keeper outside the door wouldn't hear, she asked me where I was from, told me that she knew Americans were good people, asked about my wife and children—any of which I knew would be enough to get her into serious trouble for fraternizing with the enemy. But to her I was a patient in need of help, not an enemy. I wondered about the hold the Cultural Revolution had on ordinary people, when even some of their most trusted People's Army officers appeared to sympa-thize with me.

When I went back to be treated two days later, I found a little transistor radio with an earphone sitting by the rinse basin on the dentist's chair. "You said you missed listening to music," she said, pointing to the radio. You can plug this in your ear and listen while I'm working."

The keeper gave her a surprised look.

"This is an advanced medical procedure," she explained to him in her professional voice. "It has been found to relax the patient and make the dentist's work easier."

The keeper nodded and went out to take his seat in the empty waiting room.

As she was working this time, she told me about her husband and her little girl, around four. Not only that, she actually showed me pictures. Her husband was in an army uniform too. When I left and thanked her, she gave me a little squeeze of the hand and said, "Let me know if your teeth bother you again." And then she looked me straight in the eye and said, "I'm sure you're going to be just fine."

◆

The days rolled by, one much like another, always in complete solitude. I never succeeded in contacting any other prisoners, although I could hear the voice of David Crook, the English teacher who had organized the foreigners' study sessions. I recognized the way he pronounced the Chinese word for "trouble" when he asked the keepers if he could trouble them for more food.

In the fifth year of my confinement, the keepers began leading prisoners out one by one to cement bins in a central, open courtyard where they could take some sun and get some exercise. For twenty minutes at a time, I stared at the sliver of sky above and occasionally saw a magpie flying overhead. I took my clothes off to catch every bit of sun that I could. Sometimes I jogged. We were required to be silent, because other prisoners were in bins just like mine. I knew David was nearby. I tried to signal him by tapping out the rhythm of British songs with my feet, but he never answered back.

I read. I studied. And I thought about my life.

I thought all the way back to my lonely, unhappy childhood, terrified of my mother's incessant quarreling with my father and her hunger for fine things and social position. I was always trying to find some meaning in a short life that ended in oblivion, always hovering on the edge of depression. I thought of the world that had opened up to me at college in Chapel Hill, when I discovered philosophy and the power of the human mind to know and to change its environment and itself. I thought of how happy my life had become when I realized that true human happiness comes from contributing to the freedom and happiness of other people, and that the greatest joy—and obligation in life—was the pursuit of truth.

How well had I done? I had stayed in China to help keep children like Wood Fairy from dying, to save her father and all those like him from starvation and oppression. I had joined with others in the Communist Party to achieve those goals. Had we succeeded?

I thought about the sad little children I had seen playing in Wuhan in the summer of 1946, their gritty red eyes testifying to the blindness that would soon claim many of them for want of treatment of trachoma. Children in Wuhan today were getting medical care, regardless of who they were. I thought of the neighborhood medical clinic where our little daughter Xiaodong was rescued when her breathing stopped. Those clinics were there for everyone now. I remembered Mama's confident cry—she who had lost eight of her twelve children to disease, hunger, and rape by Japanese soldiers. "Children don't die under socialism," she said. Her four children who survived to see the New China had all married and prospered, and not one of them or their children or grandchildren or their great-grandchildren had ever died from lack of care.

Even in political freedom, I thought, the average Chinese was better off than when I got there, when gendarmes could shoot people in the street for no reason at all. I thought about the peasants now, walking, standing straight up, not shuffling and bowing to whoever had power. Their skin was clear, their eyes were bright. I could peek into their lunch baskets and see the vegetables and grain they had, plenty to eat, in some places even meat—a far cry from the ground sorghum, chaff, and weeds I had seen peasants subsisting on when I had first arrived. If Wood Fairy had lived, she would have been well fed and cared for. She would have gone to school. She would have made a life and a future for herself and her family.

No, I thought, I had not been wrong to throw my lot in with the party that had made it all possible. It had not been wrong to suffer, even to sit in prison because of their mistake. I had no regrets. In fact, I felt a kind of triumph. For the first time in my life, I was confronting a situation from which there was no escape, no running away, no diversion—and I had learned to fight my way through it. In the process, I had overcome many of my old fears and my panic. In training myself to set aside fears of death and hardship, I had discovered a strange new freedom, and I was enjoying the tranquillity of mind it brought.

What's more, I felt I had answered the question of my youth: What difference could my life or any life make? Here in isolation, I could only make infinitesimal contributions, which would never be known to anyone. Hadn't I lost the battle for a meaningful life? My newfound freedom answered for me: No! If I could only put one drop into the long river of human progress, then my purpose would be fulfilled, even if I could no longer see or hear the results of my effort. That was the real meaning of contribution. Even one little victory, one human kindness, one small token to advance human happiness made a real difference. It lasted, it endured, it handed its influence on, from drop to drop, down through the ages. What did it matter that I wouldn't be conscious of it anymore, that I couldn't enjoy it? If I worried about not enjoying it, didn't that show that my real purpose wasn't to contribute, but to enjoy? And in that thought I found happiness.

I knew by this time that people had starved during the Great Leap Forward, although I still had no idea they had died in great numbers. I also knew that before the Cultural Revolution economic planning and controls had been greatly overcentralized, and that the working people were by no means the genuine owners and managers of the factories, mines, and railroads. The "people's" state owned the property, but the people didn't own the state, and exploitation existed under this so-called socialism.

Here in prison I realized for the first time that many in power in the party didn't think the way I was thinking. When they set out to get the party cadres in line during the rectification movements I had supported, they weren't just thinking about the future Promised Land of Communism, where all would be equal and live together in peace and abundance. Nor were they intent on finding and defending what was true. They were thinking about destroying their political opposition.

I should have seen all of this, but my mind had turned away from it. Why? I thought back over all the times in my life when I made major political mistakes, and I realized it had happened because I had followed the wrong leader, the wrong policy, or the wrong course of action. I could remember that every time my better judgment had said this is not right, this is wrong, a kind of ritualistic chant had come over me. "Don't question it," the little voice would tell me. "That's disloyal. The mere fact that you have doubts shows that you are still a prisoner of your class background, that you are weak, that you aren't fully committed to the Revolution."

I thought back about things that I considered major misjudgments in my past. My blind acceptance in my youth, overriding serious doubts, of the Soviet Union as a workers' paradise; my equally blind acceptance of the tranquil perfection of the People's Republic of China. I had felt squeamish about methods used in the land reform; I had doubts about Mao's stress on class analysis and class struggle. But in each case, my apprehensions had been overruled by my belief in Marxist theory and in some great authority. "Can I be smarter than Mao and the Central Committee? Could I understand China better than they do? Who am I to judge them?" And with that, I abandoned my own responsibility to the truth and to the people's welfare and suppressed my own viewpoint so completely that it took years for it to rise again and assert itself.

My conclusions were obvious. I had been right to help those who were working for a new China and for the betterment of all human beings, and to bring word of what was going on in China to the outside world. I had been dead wrong, however, in accepting the party as the embodiment of truth and in giving to the party uncritical and unquestioning loyalty. Only someone who thinks independently and who uses critical analysis can make the maximum individual contribution to the freedom and happiness of the people.

◆

Two more years went by and I had plenty of time to think. I looked back with regret on my own role in the Cultural Revolution. My own record on violence was clean. I had opposed it, preached against it, worked against it; we had had none of it at the Broadcast Administration during the time my group was in charge. Still, I had supported groups that advocated violence, and that had been wrong. With a start, I realized that meant the Cultural Revolution Group itself—and Jiang Qing.

I bitterly regretted having allowed myself to get involved in all the anarchism and turmoil, even for the best of reasons. I hated the fact that I had allowed myself to be drawn into the factional struggle at all. In thinking that I could unite the factions, I had fallen victim to the most basic American error about China. I had forgotten I was a foreigner.

But as for the Cultural Revolution itself, I was still blinded by my own visions for it. I read the claims about the great accomplishments of the movement and felt pleased and relieved that, for all the turmoil and chaos, it seemed to have finally come out all right. The factionalism had ended, the newspaper said, the civil war had been stopped, and all authority was in the hands of revolutionary committees, which integrated representatives of the young, the old, and the middle-aged, and which combined old revolutionary cadres with army personnel and with the heads of the old rebel organizations.

I loved the much-featured stories about a little grammar school student named Huang Shuai. A model of the politically aware Little Red Soldier, she got herself in the paper for criticizing the teacher and the teaching system for lacking class consciousness. According to the *People's Daily,* she first criticized the teacher, then helped her correct her errors. From the stories, I thought she was a good example of social consciousness—"and a little child shall lead them." I said so to one of the guards, who were now more willing to exchange a word or two with me.

His reaction startled me. "You don't know what you're talking about," he snapped angrily. "Go back and sit down and stop talking rubbish."

How could I have known that the Huang Shuai stories were part of an ultra-leftist wave of attacks on teachers that made it almost impossible for them to teach? Instead, I wondered how this guard, whose devotion to the Cultural Revolution was so low, could have possibly slipped into this high-security prison.

Still, deep underneath, I had sensed from the beginning that something was very wrong. One day, back in 1968, not long after I had been arrested, I was reading a story about the advances of the Maoist faction of Indian Communists in southern India, and I was gripped by a powerful wave of revulsion and sadness. They were leading the peasants to set up people's governments in the villages and to organize guerrilla warfare. I should have been overjoyed at this news. Instead, I felt a cold chill. A very clear voice inside me said, "What good is it for people to organize, to study, to believe, to fight, to die, finally to win and take power—when this leads to the loss of freedom, to constant harassment and cruelty among the very people who fought and won the revolution?"

Then came another thought: How strange that the leaders of Chinese Communism, who supposedly have the most advanced thinking of the whole human race, still don't know what America's colonial forefathers knew when they won their revolution: that if political rights are not guaranteed to everyone, then there is no guarantee for the rights of anyone, even the highest in the land. Wasn't Liu Shaoqi president of the People's Republic, and wasn't he laid low in a twinkling, deprived of even the most rudimentary right to defend himself?

The worst thing, I thought, would be to have gone through all this pain and suffering only to find—if and when I was ever released—that socialism had failed.

◆

I knew for a long time that Zhou Enlai was dying. His face in the paper grew thinner and more filled with tension and pain. His body became more emaciated. I never read a word about it, but I didn't have to. In the last picture of him I saw, the cancer that killed him was speaking out clearly from his face.

His death rocked the prison. Early one morning I heard funeral music playing. Coming from outside the prison, it was very loud. From the hallways I could hear the sounds of weeping. I went to my cell door to see what was happening. "What is it?" I asked a guard who was walking by.

"Premier Zhou," he said. That was all he said, but I could see through the peephole that his eyes were red. I began to cry myself. I cried off and on for the next three days. It was not only for Zhou that I wept, but for me, for our family, for Yulin and the children, for a China that seemed all at once friendless and abandoned.

For the first time in that prison, I felt I was not quite alone. The entire prison had melted into a paroxysm of grief. The guards and prisoners alike were united. I could hear weeping in adjoining cells. I could hear weeping in the hallways. Everyone was crying. From far away I could hear a prisoner's voice, an elderly man, wailing. "China has lost her last hope. What are we to do? What is to become of us?"

For some reason, the special guard cadres seemed different from the regular prison personnel. They did not weep. They belonged to a special unit that had been directly under the influence of Jiang Qing, Lin Biao, and the Cultural Revolution Group, and as such were in opposition to Zhou Enlai.

But everyone else was in mourning. The next day, I saw that the regular security people, the keepers, were wearing mourning blacks. So I tore off the cuff of a pair of my black cotton prison pants and made myself a mourning band. A little later, a ranking cadre among the special guard cadres came to the door and opened my peephole from the outside. "What do you think you are doing with that thing on?" he shouted at me.

I reacted in shock and tears began rolling down my face.

Suddenly his demeanor changed, and he looked at me in embarrassment. "Tie it on properly," he said gruffly. "It's about to fall off."

China had lost a great leader, and even though I knew that Zhou had been among those who signed the order for my imprisonment, I had lost a great friend.

◆

There is a day in late spring in China when everyone pays respects to the dead. It is called Qingming, and it is a day for sweeping and tending graves, and for remembering. That year it fell in April, and all the country's grief at the death of Zhou Enlai, and rage at those who had opposed him, broke loose. "Counterrevolutionary hoodlums create a riot in Tiananmen Square" the headline in the *People's Daily* read. The story was simple, but perplexing. Bad elements, under the guise of mourning Zhou Enlai, had gathered in the square, beaten the People's Liberation Army guards, and stormed the Great Hall of the People. A crowd of one hundred thousand had gathered, the newspaper said. That night, the Beijing Workers' Militia had entered the square and driven the bad elements out. The incident, the paper intimated, was instigated by Deng Xiaoping. Deng had been restored as vice prime minister, but after Zhou's death, he was being overthrown again.

I read the paper at about ten o'clock that morning. By two P.M. I was taken to the interrogation room for the first time in four years. There I was confronted by three older cadres who clearly looked to be members of the public security ministry.

"Have you read the papers today?" they asked me.

"Yes," I said, "I have."

"What is your reaction to what they are saying?"

"I read that bad people were making trouble in the square and that they attacked revolutionary army men. But there are several things about the story I don't understand." I felt I was about to cause myself big trouble. But my mouth just kept on talking. "I don't understand how the man behind this could be Deng Xiaoping. I know him slightly, and I think I know something about him. He may have committed all kinds of grievous errors, but I can't personally believe that Deng would incite hoodlums to attack the People's Liberation Army. He grew up in it. He led it. He lives it."

I expected to be punished. Instead, they all broke into grins.

What the hell was going on? I thought. They didn't look as if they were trying to lure me on. They looked happy. "And another thing," I continued. "This dismissive way of referring to Premier Zhou Enlai in the paper—'under the guise of mourning Premier Zhou Enlai.' What does that mean? What kind of a way is that to talk about the premier?" Tears began to run down my cheeks.

"You know Chinese politics are very complicated," one of my interrogators said. "There are all sorts of currents and all sorts of elements. We don't expect you to see everything that is going on by reading one story in the newspaper."

I went back to my cell genuinely puzzled.

♦

There is an old Chinese saying that when a ruler loses the Mandate of Heaven, the heavens, the weather, and even the earth itself will turn against him and his kingdom will fall.

The floor began to move in the middle of the night. I was sound asleep and the movement made me angry. "You shouldn't do that for so long," I thought to myself, mentally addressing the floor. "That's too long to be shaking like that." Then off in the distance I heard the other prisoners shouting, "Di zhen! Di zhen!"

Earthquake!

The floor kept on moving and here I was, trapped inside a brick building, the worst possible place to be in an earthquake. A few doors down a prisoner began to shout, "Get us out of here! Get us out of here!" And immediately the whole corridor took up the cry.

I could hear the pounding of feet on the path outside and my heart sank. "They are leaving us here to die," the prisoner next door shouted. But then I heard from the direction of the sound that guards were running into the prison, not out of it.

Doors were opened up and down the corridor and one by one we were all marched to an area where we would be safer. We were all shoved into cells that were supposed to be empty. But in their hurry, the guards put me in a cell with another prisoner, a fat, bald-headed man, the first—and last—fellow inmate I saw. We were both so startled that neither of us said a word. And the guards quickly discovered their mistake and pulled me out.

Just after dawn, when it was light enough to see, the guards formed another line to pass prisoners out into the courtyard. There, inside the perimeter of the outer wall, they had built crude earthquake shelters overnight, each one a kind of lean-to with both ends open. The area inside the outer wall was huge, and there was enough room to put all the prisoners about forty yards apart, with the openings facing in different directions so we couldn't see each other.

Each shelter had a guard whose shift changed every two hours. It was like a festival for me, the first real excitement and companionship I had had in years. I could talk to my guards, who told me the center of the quake had been in Tangshan, about a hundred miles to the north. I was worried about Yulin and the children. I didn't think that Beijing had been badly hit, but I wasn't even sure if they were still in Beijing.

Still I had a wonderful time. As long as I stayed on the inside of my shelter I could talk to the guard. I could sun myself. I could look at the whole blue sky.

◆

The earth had not been wrong.

That fall, Mao Zedong died. Once again I heard funeral music and workmen appeared to mount radio speakers in each corridor over the doors. For the next several weeks, all we could hear were the official bulletins from the radio station announcing the death of the great Chairman Mao, news about Mao, and condolences from all around the world. Then came the funeral and more announcements, more music.

I couldn't understand my reaction. In my mind, Mao was the most important man in the world, wise, gifted, philosophically sound, strategically masterful. He was the leader of the Chinese Revolution, and of the world revolution. His death was much more serious than Zhou's in its sad import for China and the world. And yet, I could not produce a single tear when news came of Mao's death. Not one.

"What will the prison personnel think?" I wondered. Where was my heart? Why were there no tears, and no deep, pervasive sadness and sense of tragic personal loss? And yet I needn't have worried. The keepers, the security personnel, my fellow prisoners —I could neither hear nor see much emotion from any of them either.

Following Mao's death, the newspapers began to bristle with a strange, unstated energy. Even from solitary confinement, I could tell that something important was happening. It started with the speeches before and during Mao's funeral. I had never seen such a sharp division revealed in the party paper between two groups of people still in power. Over and over Jiang Qing repeated what she claimed were Mao's dying words: carry on with the preset policy, which meant Cultural Revolution and class struggle. Mao's chosen successor, Hua Guofeng, on the other hand, mentioned no dying words. His speech pledged loyalty, but was all about progress and production.

Five or six days later, for the first time in more than a decade, all mention of Jiang Qing and the Cultural Revolution Group suddenly vanished from the papers. It was more effective than banner headlines. Not only did their photos vanish, along with stories and analyses of their actions, but all the key phrases associated with them disappeared as well.

The effect was striking. Since I had been imprisoned, I had heard almost no sounds from the fields around the prison as the peasants silently went about the business of tending their pigs and growing their wheat. That night, for the first time, I heard riotous music over loudspeakers from the neighboring communes. The peasants were singing, shouting, and marching around clanging gongs and cymbals. Laughter and the high wail of Chinese traditional music came from all directions. Every afternoon and evening for two or three nights, firecrackers were popping in the fields that had been so silent for so many years.

Inside the prison, the joy was more restrained—but it was there. For years, I had seen no one smile. Then one morning when a young health technician came into my cell to draw blood for a test, she was grinning from ear to ear. I asked her what was going on.

"Something good," she said.

"What is it?"

"You'll find out," she said.

And that was it until a few weeks later when I heard a voice that seemed to come from the cell directly opposite mine, across the courtyard. It was a familiar voice, high and strident, raised in a kind of shrieking wail. "Oh, Chairman Mao! Oh, Chairman Mao! I will always be loyal to you."

It was like the voice of a professional mourner at a Chinese funeral. "For your sake, I don't care what kind of suffering I will have to undergo. Oh, what true revolutionaries have to endure in the world! Comrades, never doubt we will triumph in the end." Nearly nine years had passed since I last heard that voice, but there was no mistaking it.

It was Jiang Qing.

Although as the wife of the great Chairman Mao, Jiang Qing had tried to cultivate a more refined speech, she still had that cranky nasal tone and unmistakable traces of her original Shandong accent. Now, as she called out to her late husband to save her from her captors, she affected the melodramatic pitch she always used when she made political speeches.

"We Communists aren't afraid of being cursed at," she wailed. "We were born, grew up, and have thrived among curses and blows." She was quoting Mao's own sayings from the days back in Yanan.

Her keepers weren't impressed. Across the courtyard I could hear another female voice, clearly that of a keeper. "Behave yourself," the woman snapped in a manner that I recognized only too well after all those years. This, I thought, was a tough country woman, determined, unsentimental, with a job to do. She wasn't about to take any nonsense from Jiang Qing. "You shut up!" she shouted. "Haven't you done enough harm? Look how well we are treating you. You cheated enough people, but you won't get away with that crap here. Do what you're told or else I'll fix you good."

Sometimes I heard a sound as if Jiang Qing was rushing the door, and then the sounds of shoving and pushing. The rest of her Cultural Revolution Group was in here too, I surmised. I heard one of them, Wang Hongwen, trying to call out across the exercise bins to another one. "Little brother! Little brother!" he shouted. "Big brother is thinking about you."

I grinned to myself. I had known Wang Hongwen in Shanghai in the early days of the Cultural Revolution. He was not a cotton mill worker, as he liked to brag, but an agent in the factory's security department. He had told me with relish how he played sick and checked into the hospital when the opposition planned a meeting to criticize him. In prison, I had read with wonder in the paper how this petty adventurer had climbed to the very top ranks of national leadership. Now he too had fallen.

The effect of the prisoners across the courtyard, and all that it meant, was electric. Within a few days, prison conditions improved. They put radio speakers into our rooms and we heard music and news. Milk and apples, a once-a-week event for me, suddenly appeared every day. The keepers began exchanging a word or two with me, and suddenly inside the prison everyone became, in minor ways, conspirators together, sharing the feeling that in greater or lesser ways we had all suffered at the hands of this woman.

When one of the keepers came into my cell to take me out for recreation, and the high-pitched female shouting began anew, I looked at him. "Acting up," I said, nodding in the direction of the noise.

"She'll just have to behave like everyone else here," he said with a half smile.

As soon as their names vanished from the newspaper, I realized that Jiang Qing and her cronies were out of power. And now that she was sharing my prison, I was sure the changes were real. I knew that my life was about to change too. I had long suspected that she, and her chief ally, the security chief Kang Sheng, had been the main forces behind my arrest. I knew that the process of my release would be under way soon. But how long would it take? It could be a week, or months, or even years. The bureaucracy alone could chill the process, I knew. I became tense and panicky again. The closer my release seemed to be, the harder it became to wait.

Day after day, the voice from across the courtyard continued to moan and complain. "If you keep on kicking up a fuss, it's not going to be good for you," her guard scolded. "It won't turn out well for you. You won't get anywhere making trouble like this." Apparently, the prison food wasn't to Jiang Qing's taste. Her keepers continually threatened her, trying to force her to eat.

I had plenty of opportunity to overhear such little dramas. My original fears were well founded. It would be well over a year before I was finally released.

For that last year, my life was harder to bear. The nightmares began again, and the night waking. The thoughts about my family that I had succeeded in repressing began crowding into my head. What if they were dead? What if they had been scattered to work camps and I was unable to find them? What if I got sick and died first?

In August 1977, two members of my interrogation team suddenly summoned me. "Do you have any new thoughts?" they asked.

"It was foolish of me to get involved in a factional struggle," I said. "I regret that."

"We are going to give you a chance to explain yourself again," they said. "You write up a synopsis of how you see your case. We are going to send it on up. It may be that your case can be solved."

Breakfast one morning a few months later was the same as any other morning: a bowl of rice porridge, pickled vegetables, bean curd, and fried slices of bread. That was at seven A.M. At eight, I heard the padlocks on my cell door being opened. "That's strange," I thought. "I'm not up for anything. It's Saturday. Nothing happens on Saturday."

Then in walked a keeper holding a safety razor. "Have a good shave," he said. "In two hours they are coming to take you home."

It was November 19, 1977. I had been locked up for nine years, eight months, and a day.

Then came a weird procession of bearers. I was wearing standard prison clothes: a black cotton jacket with loop closings, black trousers, cloth shoes, and homespun underwear. The first of the packages that was brought in contained a brand-new woolen suit. Then came a silk tie, a white silk shirt, shiny leather shoes, and socks.

This was the moment I had dreamed of for nearly ten years, that I had hoped for, that I had feared would never come. Now that it was here, I felt strangely calm. Still I wondered, what would I find on the other side of those prison doors? Were my wife and children there? The keeper said I was going home. Where was home?

I was taken to the interrogation room on my way out. Sitting there was the Colonel, the man from my interrogation team ten years earlier. "Have a seat, comrade," he said. It was the first time I had heard that word in a decade. He read me the conclusion to my case. The spy charges were unfounded. It was a mistake. I was a good comrade. All possible restitution would be made.

Last time I had cried when they said they were mistaken. This time there were no tears. I had been waiting for nearly ten years to hear them say that.

I was escorted from the building into a small receiving room. And there, standing amid the overstuffed chairs, was Yulin wearing a heavy overcoat. I walked up to her and we embraced. She started to cry. "Everything is going to be all right," I said. My apparent lack of emotion shocked her, but I had gone so long without expressing feelings that it was hard to start again.

We were packed into a black Shanghai sedan and whisked away to the Friendship Hotel. Just two days earlier, Yulin explained, she had been informed that I was being released. The whole family and all their belongings were moved from their tiny one-room place into three suites that took up the whole first floor of one unit in the Friendship Hotel.

The car pulled up in front of the apartment. My three girls and my boy rushed out. Laughing and shoving, they pushed and pulled me into the apartment. Suddenly, the three girls joined hands and circled around me as if I were a Maypole. "Papa, papa! Shei shi lao da? Shei shi lao da? Daddy, daddy. Guess who's the oldest?"

CHAPTER TWENTY-THREE

Coming Home

I had been away too long. I could not find the little faces of my children in the grown-up faces I now saw before me. The three girls were now twenty, nineteen, and seventeen. I hadn't seen them since the eldest was ten. They were the most beautiful people I had ever seen, three tall young women dancing and laughing about me. But I couldn't tell which was which. Who is the oldest? they sang out.

I pointed to the tallest.

Everyone laughed. It was Xiaodong, the second oldest. I looked again, and pointed again—to the girl who looked the most like the oldest had looked ten years ago. More laughter. It was Xiaoxiang, the youngest. And that left only one, Xiaoqin.

My little son, Xiaoming, was off to the side. He was two when I was hauled away; now he was twelve. "Look at him!" Yulin laughed, pointing at our son. And there he was, the son I hadn't seen since he was a baby, sitting in an armchair, one foot tucked under him—my favorite sitting position.

Chinese children customarily change their names several times over the course of their lives, going from a baby name to a school name, then to an adult name that may reflect a profession or a personal hero. In the old days, a general who had been through battle might take the name of the battleground. Scholars took on book names. During the Cultural Revolution, many took on revolutionary names.

My son came up to me.

"Daddy," my son said, "how do you say 'gaoxing' in English?"

"Happy," I said.

"That's what I want my new name to be," he announced.

Our youngest girl picked a new name for herself too. "I'll call myself 'Fly' because I feel like flying," she said. But almost immediately she changed her mind and chose another joyful-sounding name: Sunny. Yulin and I had already given English names to the two others: Jenny for the eldest and Toni for her younger sister because I thought the names fit their sweet dispositions.

It was almost too good to be true. I had returned, not just alive, but alive to a wonderful, warm family—a family that had not rejected me, but had stood by me and still loved me. I could only guess what it had cost Yulin to keep those bonds intact.

That night, she poured out a decades' old grievance. Before I had been sent to prison, she said, I had been so wrapped up in my work and my political struggles that I had sorely neglected the family. I knew she was right.

"From now on," I said, "my job is to make you happy."

It was a harder job than I expected. My emotions were still locked tight, buried in the safe place I had stored them in prison.

Over the next several days we walked quietly alone through the grounds of the Friendship Hotel and Yulin tried to tell me a bit of what they had gone through while I was in prison—her persecution at the Broadcast Administration, the beatings, her imprisonment with the children, her years of hard labor. She could not tell me these stories without dissolving in tears.

"Be calm," I said, trying to comfort her. "Don't let yourself become embittered by these things. We should forget them and move on."

My response upset her more. "You don't seem interested in hearing what happened to me," she said. "If I can't tell these things to my own husband, who can I talk to?"

It wasn't that I didn't care. I cared too much. I could have endured almost anything myself, but I couldn't bear to hear the way she and the children had suffered.

Nor could I bear the picture they painted of the world to which I had returned. In prison my worst fear was that I would come out and find that my suffering and loneliness had all been in vain, that socialism had failed. I pushed away with both hands the evidence Yulin and the children brought me that my worst fear had come true.

I had been following events with mixed feelings from my prison cell. Jiang Qing and her cohorts in the Cultural Revolution Group, now derisively called "The Gang of Four," had been jailed for plotting a coup against Mao's chosen successor, the loyal but colorless Hua Guofeng. When Hua released Deng Xiaoping from his confinement and restored him to high office, it didn't strike me that a power struggle was in the making between two very different ideas of how to salvage China and move forward.

Then, when I came home from prison and saw that Deng was making a bid for supreme power and that most people were supporting him, my feelings were even more confused. That he was reaching out for power was obvious. But what would he do when he got it?

I knew that we were living in a new world. The huge statues of Mao that had dominated Beijing's public places had begun to come down, and the process of de-deification had begun. Still, I had trouble separating myself from the power of the past.

On one of our walks, out by the swimming pool of the Friendship Hotel, Yulin told me that Jiang Qing and her security chief Kang Sheng were the two most hated people in China, and that Kang had personally played a sinister and sadistic role in having people imprisoned, tortured, and killed.

"How can you talk like that about a member of the standing committee of the party political bureau?" I asked. "When he died in 1975, the Central Committee issued a eulogy praising him highly. Have you heard anything official since then?"

"You don't understand," Yulin said. "Nobody cares anymore what the paper says, or what official Central Committee documents say."

What could she be talking about? I wondered. Frankly, I thought Yulin and the children were full of complaints and even bitterness. They told me tales of general corruption, low morale, and seedy ethics that I found hard to believe. "These must be individual cases," I said. "Everyone can't be like that. You are overemphasizing isolated cases. All you see is the negative side."

"Show us the positive side, now that you're here," they said.

"Look at how much more democratic it is," I argued, pointing at Democracy Wall. The wall, at the Xidan crossing near the leaders' compound and the main shopping district, was a place where people could post big-character posters on any subject. It was in full bloom when I came out of prison. The posters hung on the wall and on rows of ropes running along the sidewalk parallel to the wall. The sidewalk itself was crowded day and night with people craning their necks and straining their eyes to make out the squiggly writing on the posters, and to argue about the contents with other bystanders.

When I first got out of prison, Yulin got a car to drive me to see the wall. After that, I went there nearly every day. Political comment and lampoons aimed at the top leaders were a small minority of the posters, but they were by far the most important and attracted the most attention. There was a rising chorus of demands that a group of "whateverists"—those surrounding Hua Guofeng who held that whatever Chairman Mao said must be strictly adhered to—be removed from high office.

Everyone was free to express his or her own opinion. Everyone was free to post a big-character poster, criticizing anyone, praising anyone. I was enthusiastic about the wall. I thought it was a free and open democratic forum, a healthy, permanent, visible legacy of the Cultural Revolution.

What's more, Deng Xiaoping, who was now clearly in the ascendancy, seemed to be in favor of this new freedom of ideas and opinions. In an interview with an American journalist, Robert Novak, he told the world that the Chinese had a constitutional right to air their views, right or wrong.

As for my other arguments about the positive changes I saw, I cited the *People's Daily,* which had been the source of all my knowledge for nearly a decade. Weren't the revolutionary committees in charge now? I asked. Weren't people ordering their lives, plying their trades, settling their disputes through democratic consultation, as Chairman Mao had directed long ago? And weren't workers, their class consciousness raised during the Cultural Revolution, rejecting material incentives, insulted at the idea that they had to be paid higher wages in order to work to build their own socialist paradise?

Even my twelve-year-old son was exasperated. "Daddy, you're talking like the Gang of Four," he said, referring to Jiang Qing and the three other top leaders of the Cultural Revolution Group, all of them still in prison awaiting trial.

Friends came around from the foreign experts bureau. They were seasoned leading cadres, politically experienced. They had seen it all before, and they shook their heads patiently over me. "They're all like that when they first come out of the cowshed," they said. "Give him time. He has no idea how things have changed." To me, they were solicitous but firm. "Listen to Yulin and the children," they said. "They know what has been going on."

For thirty-seven years I had been a loyal Communist, both in the United States and here in China. For thirty-seven years I had listened to the party. During the Cultural Revolution when I had attacked the party, I had done so, I thought, in order to save it, to make it into the democratic body I thought it ought to be.

Now the old heads, my old friends, were telling me to look away from the party and to take my cues from my children. How could that be?

◆

I soon found out how things had changed while I was in prison. The Beijing I returned to was very different from the one I had left, and not just because the chaos of the Cultural Revolution was over. The clean orderly streets of the Chinese capital seemed strangely unkempt and unruly. Litter lay about, and gone was the old volunteer spirit that used to prompt people to scoop it up before foreign guests saw it. In front of the marketplace across from the Friendship Hotel, where most foreign visitors stayed, banana and tangerine peels and bits of paper were clearly visible.

My daughters all told me how difficult Beijing was for young girls now. Because Jenny was the daughter of a counterrevolutionary, while I was gone the best job she could find was as a lathe operator in a factory that was a two-hour bus ride from home. Riding to and from work she often ran into hoodlums on the bus who tried to take advantage of her.

Soldiers of the People's Liberation Army used to be models of courtesy and discipline in the cities; they were the favorite sons of the people. Now, rude young lads in uniform pushed their way through the long bus lines to squeeze onto the bus, and the civilians who were shoved aside eyed them angrily.

There had been construction of new housing, but the work was shoddy and the new high-rise buildings were dank. They looked old the day they were finished. Many stood dark and empty, waiting for electrical wiring, water pipes, and elevators.

But the biggest difference was in the relations between people. There was a new definition of the word "friend." A friend was someone who could get you something, who would put a few pairs of shoes under the counter and hold them until you arrived with a few choice cuts of meat. The "back door" was another term I heard redefined for the first time. Using the back door—special personal connections—was the only way to get things done.

The old slogans like "serve the people" now met with shrugs and titters. To try to alleviate the factional passions from the Cultural Revolution, Deng Xiaoping raised the slogan: "Xiang qian kan!" which meant "Look forward, don't look back!" People immediately revised it with a pun that meant: "Look toward the money."

As for the 1976 Tiananmen Square demonstrations that I had been quizzed about in prison, Jenny told me that the real driving force behind them was hatred, not just of the Gang of Four, but of Mao and the whole party. When I tried to explain to her that the party had been different in the old days, clean and free of official corruption, her reply was, "Well, my generation never saw that so we don't know about it. All we know is that the party now is the center of corruption. They protect corrupt officials, except for those who happen to be in a political faction that is opposed to them. Then they may arrest them and make a big case about them, putting out lots of propaganda to show that they are tough on corrupt officials. Actually, they're only tough on corrupt officials who are also against their particular group."

Yulin and I toured the country and I found it the same wherever I went. Corruption had seeped into the marrow of the party structure. There were statues of Mao everywhere, but the legacy of Mao was far from noble. There was so much pain, so much disillusionment, so much of a sense of betrayal. In a matter of weeks, I knew how that could have happened. I found that the party I had known was dead and gone. It had been destroyed by its creator, Mao Zedong, in the Cultural Revolution. Its prestige had vanished. No one believed in it anymore, including those who were using it to advance their own power and comfort.

Back in Beijing, a young friend of ours working as a room attendant at the Friendship Hotel asked me if I could get him a copy of Hitler's *Mein Kampf*.

"Why would you want to read that?" I asked this Communist Youth League member.

"We just want to read everything that was kept from us and labeled as bad in the past," he said. "We'll decide for ourselves what is bad."

I guessed I was pleased at this sign of self-reliance. But I couldn't help thinking back nearly thirty years ago to a young

Kuomintang soldier I had found sitting by the side of the road poring over a Maoist work. Just as it had with the Kuomintang, the rot had set in with the Communists, and even those at the very bottom of the pyramid were groping to find something to replace their lost idealism.

◆

Slowly, gradually, my family began to heal. The years of malnutrition and stress in prison had taken their toll on me. I had high blood pressure and dizzy spells. My heart would beat wildly and erratically suddenly and without warning. I began to work to recover my health.

I could see too the effects of the ordeal on the rest of the family. My daughters looked more tense than girls their age should be. Jenny had been a happy, carefree girl when I had left. Now the happiness seemed to be gone. She tired easily, got discouraged easily. Sunny was obviously elated to have me home again, but not quite able to believe the change was permanent. When we went downtown shopping together, she held my hand tight as if afraid I would slip away and disappear. When I came home after even a brief absence, she would march up to me, stand there with her hands on her hips and demand, "Now where did you go, Daddy, and who did you talk to? Did you say anything that you shouldn't say? You mustn't trust anyone. You can't believe what they say. Be careful how you talk. And don't get involved in any activity— no more political activity, you hear? I'm not going to lose my Daddy again!" Toni, for her part, said she had seen too many people suffer; she was going to be a doctor so she could help ease people's suffering.

Mama was alive, but living in Shijiazhuang with her third daughter. We went to see her and the family about a month after I returned home. She had had a stroke, was partly paralyzed, and already too ill to talk much. But she was overjoyed to see me. She hugged me and cried and cried and kept saying, "I knew this day would come, I knew it. Those turtles' eggs couldn't last forever. No way!"

Yulin's third sister was disconsolate—glad to see us, but she too couldn't stop crying. She and her brother had both been confined for years because they had refused to say anything against me. While she was in prison, their father had been beaten and harassed, made to kneel on broken glass, and finally died when he became the target of a political struggle in his neighborhood. He too had refused to denounce me. When his persecutors tried to make him tell about my spy activities, all he had said was "My son-in-law is a good man."

But in many ways it was Yulin who had suffered the most and had the most to heal. She, like her sister, would sometimes suddenly break down in tears, sobbing uncontrollably. She had held herself in all these years. Now she could afford to let go. Over the weeks and months that followed, I became more able to listen to her story. Haltingly, piece by piece, she told me just what had happened to her and the children while I was in prison.

The knock had come at the door just half an hour after I had been taken away. Six men in army uniforms crowded into the room. "Wang Yulin!" said the leader. "You can't stay here anymore. You are going to have to move." She was hustled off to the Qianmen Hotel, which, like so many of Beijing's hotels, had been turned into a prison. For eight months, Yulin and the four children were locked away in a single room, the window boarded up and papered over, the door open to a twenty-four-hour military guard.

After that, for the next ten years, Yulin was tossed back and forth. Sometimes she was returned to the Broadcast Administration, where she was the victim of daily struggle meetings and forced to sit outside the toilet with a sign above her head: "This is the unrepentant wife of the dog of an imperialist spy." Sometimes she was beaten, once badly enough to be sent to the hospital. Always she was reviled and ostracized. She was the wife of a man Jiang Qing had personally accused. No one dared speak to her. All but a few of our friends in the foreign community shunned her and cut her dead on the street.

She was forced to spend three years at labor camps in the countryside, where she worked for long hours in freezing weather, eating only a pound of rice a day, making bricks, cooking, weeding corn. For all the political prisoners there it was a bitter life. For Yulin, it was particularly bitter. The Communist Party cadre sent to supervise Yulin's group at one of the labor camps was my ex-wife, Wei Lin.

Sometimes it took all of Yulin's strength just to stay alive. "I used to think how easy it would be just to end it all," she told me, tears rolling down her cheeks. "I was filled with hatred for the Communist Party. They could order a struggle against anyone they chose. We had no way of defending ourselves. I had never labored like that before in my life. Hard labor, from early until late. They wouldn't even give me enough to fill my stomach. I would drag myself to bed at night, legs and back aching, so tired I could hardly move, and hungry at the same time. I thought of death repeatedly."

Still, she made up her mind to do a good job of whatever they gave her to do, to show them what she was made of. And she never gave up. "I knew you were no spy," she said. "I was sure your case would be cleared in the end. I wanted to see what sort of end your attackers came to. That was one thing that kept me alive."

Another thing was thoughts of the children. "If I killed myself," she told me, "the children would be saddled with the story of a mother who committed suicide for fear of punishment for her crimes. I would never have a chance to clear myself and clear their names." Even stronger was the thought of the children growing up unprotected. Yulin had seen a twelve-year-old girl, the daughter of a friend, left on her own when both her parents were imprisoned. There was no one to care for her, not even anything for her to eat, and only one brave teacher who fed the girl saved her from starving.

Even when Yulin was there to protect them the children had had a rough time. They were stoned and beaten—even little Xiaoming—by older children who taunted them, calling them "spy spawn." When they could, they lived with Yulin. But when she was sent to the country, she took only the baby with her, leaving the three girls with Mama. After the big earthquake, Yulin sent Xiaoming, by then ten years old, to safety with her elder sister. She wasn't allowed to leave herself, so the little boy went off himself on the train, a note pinned to his clothes asking everyone on the way to help him to his destination.

Through it all, Yulin never wavered, never confessed, never denounced me. And through it all, she kept the children clear and unconfused about me. "Your father is a good man," she said. "There are bad people attacking him." Mostly, she had to restrain them, to keep them from speaking out in my defense. "Never mind what they say," she told them. "Just let them say it. We say one thing inside our home, but you should just let them say what they are saying outside."

In many of the families around us, I saw wrecks of the Cultural Revolution. There were children who had denounced parents, wives who had divorced husbands, husbands who had reported on wives. Now that passions had ebbed, they were lost and adrift, their human ties severed. It was Yulin who had saved me from that tragedy, who had kept our family together for me to come home to.

◆

Over time, I learned the fate of most of my friends. Old Meng, the distinguished, erudite leader of the group that translated Mao's work, had died—the result of torture in prison. My old Yanan companion Peng Di had been struggled against and jet-planed in public meetings. He was one of the old cadres who had been a target of the most extreme rebel groups. Mei Yi was at the Academy of Social Sciences. He was gray and looked thirty years older.

I never went back to work at the Broadcast Administration. There was too much history there, too much pain, too many old factional animosities. But still many of my old friends there re-sumed their habit of dropping by our house for a meal or for a chat. Li Juan, who along with me and Kang Shuji had made up the committee that ran the Broadcast Administration just before I was arrested, told me that she had suspected something was about to happen. She had been tipped off not to side with me in any disputes. I was under investigation on spy charges, she had been told. Cui Xiaoliang, my former aide, companion, and bodyguard, believed that members of the warring factions of the Broadcast Administration had wanted me out of the way, and so had con-curred in my arrest. He also thought my connection with the deposed Wang Li had helped do me in. Wang Li himself was still in prison.

A few of my foreign friends had also been imprisoned for a time. When I first saw my British friend David Crook, I made sport of him, disingenuously speaking out loud to the air. "Could I trouble you for some more food? Could I have a bucket for a bath?" I said, using the same phrases and intonations he had used in prison. I roared at his expression; he had no idea we had been so close together for a year.

For all of us, as for the country as a whole, it was a time of reconciliation and forgiveness. There were people I didn't want to seek out. But I didn't see any reason to hold grudges. One day soon after my release, I ran into a cadre who had helped persecute me and my family just before I was taken away. We both pulled up on our bicycles at the same traffic light and I saw the color drain from his face. I jumped off my bike and held out my hand. "How's everything?" I asked.

"Old Li," he stammered. "We heard you were back."

But it wasn't always that easy. Yulin, in particular, couldn't easily forgive her foreign friends who had snubbed her and the children when they needed help. "I can understand their being afraid," she said, "but how could they just look straight through me and not even ask about the children?"

As it turned out, some of my foreign friends had a hard time forgiving me. They thought I had been mixed up in a plot to unseat Zhou Enlai. The contract workers' organization that I had briefly supported in 1966 was rumored to have been a secret conspiracy to kidnap Zhou, and it was reported that I had gone to Tianjin to take part in a national conference of writers and artists against Zhou. The Beijing press later confirmed that none of this was true. Nonetheless, some of my foreign friends claimed that Zhou himself had denounced me to one of their groups. "Li Dunbai is a bad man who has committed serious political mistakes during the Cultural Revolution," he was reported to have said. Why else would Zhou speak that way of me, unless he too believed I was part of a plot against him? my critics reasoned.

I was grateful to my old friend Zhou for those words. He was not denouncing me, but defending me. At the time he spoke, I was accused of much more serious spy charges. He was, in effect, deflecting the attack on me into less serious territory. Political mistakes committed during the Cultural Revolution were considered to be "contradictions among the people," and not crimes. My Chinese friends understood. Those who were at the meeting recalled that Jiang Qing's anger at Zhou's statement was palpable. And I knew that his wife, Deng Yingchao, didn't believe the spy charges either. Shortly after I returned, she received Yulin and me in front of a group of people. "Li Dunbai is a good man," she said pointedly. "He's an old and close friend. Premier Zhou thought highly of him during his lifetime."

◆

As a free man, I continued the painful process I had begun in prison: a deep reexamination of my belief in Communism.

I reread my old books and saw that the major problems were in Communist doctrine itself, not simply in the way it was carried out. It wasn't just Stalin, it was Lenin who had been at fault. And for all his brilliance, Marx's social and economic theories were limited like everyone else's and contained major errors. I realized I had vastly overestimated the degree of truth that any preset social ideology can hold, and the capacity of human planning to determine the development of society, whether economic, political, or intellectual.

I had been completely wrong to accept the policy decisions and interpretations of a small group of leaders as if they somehow held a monopoly over the truth. But at the core of all my political errors was accepting what Lenin held was the central point in Marxist politics: the necessity of having a tight "people's dictatorship" to prepare the ground for attaining a future perfect democracy. And I also realized that as dedicated as I was to changing the world into a better place to live, it took me such a long time to see the errors of Communist doctrine because of the stake I had acquired in the system and the life I had lived in China, a life of perks, privilege, and deluded complicity.

The final blow to my belief came when Deng Xiaoping shut down Democracy Wall and arrested some of the main poster-writers. My allegiance to the party crumbled, honeycombed from beneath by the doubts that began in prison and by everything I now saw and heard and felt around me. No longer was I willing to see the party's actions on its own terms, to put the best face on everything, to accept every repression as a necessary evil on the road to freedom. Now I was willing and able to see it for what it was. Like politicians elsewhere, China's leaders were playing a cynical game, using the democracy card to encourage attacks against their own enemies. Once those enemies had been toppled, however, they had no further need of democratic public opinion, and showed no qualms about crushing the movement they had encouraged and protected.

I did what I could to try to defend the famous Democracy Wall poster-writer Wei Jingsheng from unjust persecution, although I did not consider him one of the sounder spokesmen for democracy in China or think he had a good understanding of democratic principles. I solicited opinions from Westerners in Beijing, wrote them up, and slipped them to friends at the *People's Daily,* where they ran in a widely circulated classified publication. I got word of when and where Wei Jingsheng's trial was to be held and tipped off Fox Butterfield of *The New York Times.* Later, I got a transcript of the trial made by a Chinese human rights activist and gave it to a human rights organization in the United States.

I confronted as many high-ranking people as I could. When I cornered one of the public security heads at the theater one night, I told him that the suppression was costing China friends and support abroad. He shook his finger at me. "Anyone who denies the justice of Wei Jingsheng's sentence will end up the enemy of the Chinese people," he said.

I wrote a long letter saying that China's passion for secrecy and exclusion of foreigners from everyday life and friendships would keep it isolated in the long run. I sent the letter to Deng Xiaoping, but there was no reply.

I had followed the Democracy Wall with some hope, grasping at the possibility that something might be salvaged, that democracy and free political expression might yet rise in China. But now I knew it was too late. This generation of political leaders, like the last, would not hesitate to accomplish its aims by deception and repression. The masses, far from being the masters of the party, were still being called on to be its slaves.

Deng Xiaoping's speech on January 16, 1980, was the last straw. He ended any semblance of free speech by announcing that no paper would be allowed to print anything that didn't conform to party policy. He threatened those who continued to support free political expression and the posting of big-character posters. He warned to watch for antisocialist elements that used corruption in the party as an excuse to attack the leadership.

I recognized Deng's greatness in history. In order to preserve Communist Party rule, he was determined to reform the Chinese economy and free it of bureaucratic overcentralization and international isolation. I also knew that, no matter how appealing the calls for carrying out unlimited democracy overnight, chaos and anarchy with no leadership, no law, and no unity would overwhelm the country again and bring misery on the people. But I felt that a genuine renewal for China required a leadership that listened to public opinion, dealt conscientiously with corruption, and thus won the trust of the people. What I saw was just the opposite. Critics of the party were excluded from the People's Congress seats to which they had been legally elected. Dictatorship was back in force, although it could only be a weak and despised shadow of its former omnipotence.

The day when I was desperately needed as an English-language polisher was long gone. They could get all the professional experts they needed simply by paying for them. What's more, our home had begun to be a gathering place for dissidents—young students, cadres, and workers who wanted somewhere to come to discuss political issues freely. I was afraid that if there was another crackdown Yulin and I could be endangering them—and perhaps ourselves.

I had no complaints about my own life. Since I returned my girls had been given preference for college. I had been given an important job assisting the leadership at Xinhua, the New China News Agency. When I found the job unsupportable because of the censorship of news, I was easily able to arrange a transfer to a much more appealing and more prestigious job as adviser to institutes of the Chinese Academy of Social Sciences. The Broadcast Administration had given me ten years' back pay—nearly $15,000 —which I used to take Yulin for a visit to the United States, her first time in the country, and my first trip back in thirty years.

I returned from that trip still hoping that there was some way I could be useful in China. But when I read Deng's speech, I realized that new suppressions were on the way, corruption was being protected, and there was nothing I could do.

The time had come to leave.

When news of my decision became known, blandishments appeared almost out of nowhere: a promise of lifetime salary and housing, free medical care, the right to travel as much as I wanted each year, back to the United States or elsewhere if I wished. The crowning attraction was the offer of a seat on the Chinese People's Political Consultative Conference. I knew what that meant: fame, adulation, reverence, and special treatment everywhere I went. But I also knew the cost of the things they were offering. If I accepted I would give up my independence forever. I would live a life in thrall to a system I no longer respected.

I had come to China to serve humanity, to serve people, to change China, to change the world. I had no intention of spending the rest of my life serving those whom power had corrupted, bought by their perquisites, rendered unable to speak or act freely for what I believed in.

When I believed they were right, when I believed in their doctrine, I had gone along with them without being urged. In fact, I had always taken the initiative and wanted to be as deeply involved as possible. Now it was different: I believed they were wrong. I could not stay and serve them, nor could I accept their favors. I would have to find some other place, some other way—a new way of fighting for what I believed in.

On March 17, 1980, Yulin and I boarded a plane for America.

Epilogue

MORE THAN THIRTEEN YEARS have passed since then, and Yulin and I feel it has been the most fruitful and happiest time of our lives. We have learned more in the last decade than in the rest of our lives together. We have learned to make our own way, to rely on our own efforts to keep our house and home. And we have learned anew the value of friends, who sprang up almost from nowhere to help us when we returned to America.

I in particular have learned how to think again. I have learned how to observe and weigh events and not trust blindly in a single ideology to govern all my actions. Friends and acquaintances find it unbelievable that I am not filled with rancor or regret for the hard years of my life in China. "Why are you not bitter?" they exclaim. But far from being bitter, I am filled with gratitude for the friends, the adventure, the love, the learning, the excitement, the sheer fun of those years. If I were given the chance to rewrite my life, I would not cross out even my years in prison. I have found that my dreams of improving the world always—ironically —seemed to help me turn even the most terrible situations to my own benefit. I benefit even today from the reserves of inner strength I built for myself during those years of horror.

For some it may seem hard to accept that I believed so stoutly and for so long, that I sat patiently in prison, that I emerged even from my second imprisonment expecting a better world than the one I left. I find nothing odd or inconceivable about that. I wanted so hard to believe that I saw what I wanted to see, bent reality to fit my own notions.

Thus, it was neither a great blow nor a great tragedy to discover —late though this discovery came—that my life's vision was flawed. On the contrary, the revelation, when it came, was a great relief. Seeing the truth about the system I had followed for so many years enabled me to start again. My mind now unleashed from the rigors of dogma, I feel free in a way that I never did when the only thoughts I permitted myself were those that fit in with the world I had built in my head out of the bricks and mortar of ideology.

Of course, looking back there is much that I regret or find painful. It was only in the last ten years that I—and most of my Chinese friends—came to realize just how disastrous the Great Leap Forward was for China, and how many millions died. The Cultural Revolution, too, caused untold suffering—suffering I only fully learned of in the years after my release from prison. In retrospect, I wish mightily that I had been more detached and insightful during the various political movements of the late 1950s. I am sorry that, at least partly as a result of my zeal, innocent people were sent off to harsh times in the countryside.

Released from the hero worship of my youth, I can reassess some of the friends I idolized. I can see now that Zhou Enlai was caught up in the same ideals that I was, believing passionately that Marxism was the exact science of society, and that any means was acceptable for realizing the egalitarian dreamworld of Communism. He was a great compromiser, which enabled him to be the only one close to Mao who clung to the inner circle of power from 1926 until his death. He sometimes showed, as I had seen, a kind of unbecoming obsequiousness to Mao in private, and perhaps a too great willingness to bend with the prevailing winds, but always for the sake of maintaining a position from which to pursue his ideals.

But there were times when all his power and position couldn't help him. Sun Weishi, the hearty, talented adopted daughter he was so fond of, and whom I found so appealing in Yanan, was tortured to death in prison during the Cultural Revolution. She knew too much about Jiang Qing, who had her arrested and done away with. When Zhou demanded an autopsy, they brought him a little urn of ashes.

As for Mao Zedong, I now see him as a brilliant, talented tyrant, responsible for the misery and deaths of millions, or possibly tens of millions. Never a true friend, he twice threw me into wrongful and fearful isolation in prison when it suited some political purpose. Mao was a thinker, philosopher, analyst, general, political leader, poet, and connoisseur of great stature. He unified and led the Revolution through unbelievable hardships, overcoming unthinkable odds, to achieve victory over the established powers in China that had the support of virtually all the world's governments. If he had died before coming to power, he would probably still be remembered as a prophet and as something close to a saint. Despite the many crimes that were committed at his direction in his early years, on balance it's quite possible that he, not Sun Yat-sen, would have been looked on as the George Washington of China.

But today I believe that Mao was a tragic figure of Aeschylean proportions. Having preached and warned for years against the corruption that usually follows power, having inveighed against arrogance and exaggeration of the role, prowess, and wisdom of a single individual, he became their victim and victimized the Chinese people. He thought of China—and the world, to some extent—as an experimental laboratory in his hands. None of the ordinary human relationships of family, community, and friendship were important to him, but only the moving of people through the motions of carrying out his own grand designs.

But Mao's fatal flaw was that he was very, very wrong in a number of his key theoretical assumptions. He was wrong in his belief that terror exercised against those who opposed him was the only way to educate and govern the Chinese people. He was tragically wrong in believing that "every idea without exception bears the brand of a definite class." He was wrong in his economic ideas—a tightly controlled, centrally planned state economy secured by forced unanimity of opinion.

Still, looking back, much was accomplished during my thirty years in China. I saw the country unified and free of internal warfare for the first time in one hundred years. I saw tragically short lifespans more than double in length. I saw sick children healed and empty rice bowls filled. I also saw the beginning of some rudimentary form of justice. However much it is honored in the breach today, it is still better than the brute force of arms that once terrorized the Chinese people.

Sometimes I think we all accomplished much more than even

we expected. I went to Washington in 1989 to visit my old friend Li Xiannian. Old General Li—then president of China—was in the United States to meet President Reagan. I took him by the hand and we recalled our days with the revolutionaries in the mountains north of Wuhan. "So, old friend," I said. "Did you ever imagine that we would be meeting in Washington like this?"

He laughed. "Back in those days," he said, "I couldn't imagine anything much better than becoming mayor of Wuhan."

Despite my initial distaste for the corruption of the Deng Xiaoping era—a distaste that persists in the face of continuing repression and corruption—I must admit that he has led the Chinese people to the highest standard of living in their history. And despite the atrocious treatment of dissidents, compared to the old days the Chinese people today probably enjoy their greatest degree of individual freedom in history. It did not come as a gift from on high. The people have won it.

Still, I do not take lightly the lack of democratic freedom in China. The tragic slaughter of June 1989 in Tiananmen Square struck close to our family. Two of our daughters lay flattened on the floor of the apartment we still keep in Beijing as a storm of machine-gun bullets whizzed over their heads—bullets fired by the People's Liberation Army. The bullets chopped up the partition between the living room and dining room, destroyed the window curtains, and pitted the walls with bullet holes. Our girls weren't hurt, but we can't forget the people in and around Tiananmen Square who were. When we returned to Beijing on a trip, we cleaned up the debris, but refused to fill in the bullet holes.

June 4, 1989, the day of the suppression in and around Tiananmen Square, marked a turning point in Chinese history. For the first time since the Communists took power, armed troops were ordered to shoot down unarmed civilians, breaking a covenant with the people that Mao had announced in 1949. With that tragic move, the party swept into the dust heap whatever prestige it still retained among citizens of Beijing. I don't believe that any regime, any leader can regain it without repudiating the massacre of June 4.

The students were not, as was often portrayed here in the United States, China's last, best hope for democracy. They were both heroic and quixotic. There is no way they could have won. They keenly desired democracy, but didn't understand it well. They were idealistic, clean-cut, disciplined, nonviolent, but they were also egged on and manipulated by people in both power

factions. Still, they showed large numbers of China's new entre-
preneurs, engineers, managers, and professionals that no government can be truly stable unless it is truly representative.

I am nonetheless convinced that China will one day have democratic political freedoms, that eventually the people will secure
those rights for themselves. They will do it in their own good time,
of their own accord, in their own way. Most of them do not believe
that the answer lies merely with liberty-minded intellectuals, or
with another great upheaval, or in anarchy. I believe they will
gradually evolve a form of political democracy that, while learning
much from the West, will also draw on the best of Chinese civilization and will learn to avoid some of the mistakes that mar our
own democratic system.

◆

As for my life, today I live in a house surrounded by soaring
pine trees. The mountains behind and before me stretch up to the
sky. This is a place that feels like home to me. When I leave it, I
miss it. And it is here that I have fulfilled one promise: Yulin is
happy, happier than I have ever known her. She loves the consulting work we do together, and she loves our home. As I work, I
can see her now bending over her garden. She has a way with
plants, and her contented bustling coaxes all manner of flowers
and fruit to flourish. Our garden overflows with roses, rhododen-
drons, hollyhocks, hyacinths, columbine, lupine, and all manner
of wildflowers to draw butterflies. Our fruit trees are filled with
apples, peaches, apricots, pears, and cherries, our vines are heavy
with grapes, and big pots of jam are already settling on the sill.

We left our children behind in China when we first came back.
Gradually, one by one they joined us and today all of our children
are here in the United States with us. Like their parents, they
found opportunity still alive in America and they are all doing
well. Xiaoqin—Jenny—lives with her husband in Alaska, where
they work with Eskimo children. Xiaodong—Toni—is a doctor
doing research in Boston. Xiaoxiang—Sunny—programs com-
puters and lives with her engineer husband near enough to visit.
Xiaoming—who changed his name to Sidney as soon as he arrived
in America at age fifteen—is an advertising photographer who
works with his agent wife in Los Angeles. We hope for grandchildren soon.

Yulin and the four children are all American citizens now. I
never gave up my citizenship, never renounced it, never had it

challenged. I replaced my passport at the American embassy in Beijing in 1979, on the eve of my first trip home. When the consular officer asked when I had lost the original, I thought for a moment, going back in my mind to that long-ago ride into Yanan when my passport and all my belongings tumbled off my horse. "In 1946," I said.

"And have you made a good-faith effort since then to find it?" he asked, deadpan, then burst out laughing and clapped me on the back.

When I returned to America, I discovered that my relatives had not forgotten me while I was in China. I saw my sister, Elinor, who had read me so much of the poetry that had sustained me in prison. I found that her husband—a colonel in the marines and a man I hardly knew—had taken a great risk to try to help me. Throughout the 1950s he had written to senators and congressmen to try to find out if the government knew anything of my whereabouts. It was a particularly dangerous time for anyone—especially a man in the military—to express interest in a known Communist living in China.

My mother, too, told me that she had spent thousands of dollars —much of it on charlatans—in a vain attempt to find me. I arrived home just in time to meet with her before she died, and to introduce her to the daughter-in-law she had never known. We reconciled then, trying to reach out over nearly forty years and many hard feelings.

Making our way in America wasn't easy at first. Yulin knit sweaters to sell, taught Chinese and Chinese cooking. Sidney worked at McDonald's and the three girls as baby-sitters. I taught courses at the New School, and later Yulin and I led tours back to China. There were times when we didn't know where next week's food money would come from.

Then one day the phone rang and our lives changed again in one blink. It was Bill Millard, founder and chairman of ComputerLand. We had met once and chatted briefly about China after a talk I had given. He had a high-level delegation coming from China and no one on staff who could even speak Chinese. Would I come help him?

In the end, it was mainly Yulin who helped him, and us. It was my name, my connections, my talking, and my fame in China that got us in the door, and my ability to build relationships that positioned us to succeed. But it was my steely, pragmatic Yulin who in a few short months sold $20 million worth of computers in

China, thus securing our family's life and livelihood. In this, as in everything else, I owe her so much.

Today, we have a consulting company of our own, helping others do business in China. We do an honest business. We deal with honest people and flee from scoundrels when we encounter them. I think we help the people we work with. I think we are helping the people of China. I have come light-years from my old party days when I believed the world was divided into angels and devils, with capitalist imperialists as villains pitted against the common people as victims. I see now the decisive, constructive role of business in the present era, even as we work to limit its abuses. And I can see with my own eyes how, as our ventures flower, the lives of the common people of China improve along with them and their own efforts to make their country modern and prosperous.

So what does doing business—however honest and well-intentioned an effort—have to do with waging revolution? Nothing. In the past ten years, I have learned that whatever the world's problems—and they are grave—there is no one grand plan that will solve them. And I have learned that real change will not happen in the glorious tumult and clash of revolution, but rather in more measured and modest moves. The way to ending world poverty, gross injustice, and inequality will be longer and harder and more complex than I ever imagined it would be.

I do not know what this route will be. In my twenties, I was sure that there was only one answer, and that I knew what it was: socialist revolution. Half a century later, I find myself struggling more and more with questions and finding fewer and fewer answers. I think the way will still lie in social action, some of which will doubtless be huge mass movements like the freedom struggle led by the Reverend Martin Luther King, Jr. But an important part may be action of a smaller sort, as people of good will are stirred —not to overthrow an established order—but to change quietly the small part of the world over which they have influence.

If there is one thing my life has taught me, it is that one can change, one can learn, one can grow. And that the surest way to happiness for yourself is to fight for the happiness of others. I find myself readier than ever to pursue this same task that led me to stay in China. For even today, ten thousand miles, five decades, half a world, and a lifetime away, Wood Fairy and her brothers and sisters everywhere are much on my mind.

Acknowledgments

We would like to thank all the people in China and the United States who generously gave their time to help ensure that this story be as fair and accurate as possible. Many of the people cannot be named publicly; we are grateful to them nonetheless.

At Simon & Schuster, our thanks go to our editor Fred Hills, as well as to Daphne Bien, Laureen Connelly, and to Burton Beals. We'd also like to thank our agents Michael Cohn, and Michael Carlisle and Bob Gottlieb of the William Morris Agency.

Many China experts read the manuscript and helped provide context, and also helped verify the dates of remembered events. We are especially grateful to Professor Nicholas Lardy, Professor Jonathan Pollack, Professor Michel Oksenberg, and Professor Denis F. Simon. Professor Richard Nickson and Professor Brewster Rogerson also offered helpful comments.

Many people helped with recollections of events. These include William Hornby, Phillip G. Seal, Tracy B. Strong, and Israel Epstein. Several journalists, including Linda Mathews, John Fraser, and Daniel Southerland, generously shared their recollection of more contemporary events they observed.

Many others read the manuscript or provided other valuable help, suggestions, and comments: Stephan Batchison, Janet Bennett, Norman Bennett, Mark Berman, Gordon Castanza, Kenneth

Cloke, Adrian W. DeWind, Andrea di Tommaso, Monte and Betty Factor, Gil Fuchsberg, Joe Greene, Deborah Gobble, Joan S. Goldsmith, Jim Hyatt, Linos Jacovides, Virginia Kamsky, Susan Kinsley, Moses M. Malkin, Hannah Malkin, Katy McNamee, Michelle De Fino Rittenberg, Wendy Samberg, Jessie Samberg, Shirley Samberg, Junius Irving Scales, Elinor Rittenberg Weinberger and Florence and Richard Weiner. Jesse Salhe of Au Petit Beurre in Manhattan provided a pleasant venue for hours of interviewing and discussing.

We owe an especial debt of thanks to Ann Overton, whose interest in this book goes back many years, and to Richard Weiner for his kind interest and wise counsel.

We'd also like to thank *Newsday,* which with our permission conducted the Freedom of Information Act search of FBI and CIA files; and *Newsday* reporter Charles Zehren. The Fairbank Center Library at Harvard University helped with the task of plowing through nearly a half a century of Chinese newspapers. At *The Wall Street Journal,* managing editor Paul Steiger and bureau chief Roger Ricklefs were helpful and supportive. We are no less indebted to those who pushed, prodded and otherwise encouraged us to get the book done. These include Mike Wallace, Dr. Henry W. and Sarah Rittenberg, and Sydney Stahl.

Finally, we'd like to thank our spouses and children: Yulin Wang Rittenberg, Jenny Rittenberg, Toni Rittenberg, Sunny Rittenberg, Sidney Rittenberg, Jr.; Terence Foley and Terence Bennett Foley. We would also like to thank Terence Foley for his research assistance, and for the title of the book.

Index